STUDIES IN IMPERIALISM

general editor John M. MacKenzie

When the 'Studies in Imperialism' series was founded more than twenty-five years ago, emphasis was laid upon the conviction that 'imperialism as a cultural phenomenon had as significant an effect on the dominant as on the subordinate societies'. With more than ninety books published, this remains the prime concern of the series. Cross-disciplinary work has indeed appeared covering the full spectrum of cultural phenomena, as well as examining aspects of gender and sex, frontiers and law, science and the environment, language and literature, migration and patriotic societies, and much else. Moreover, the series has always wished to present comparative work on European and American imperialism, and particularly welcomes the submission of books in these areas. The fascination with imperialism, in all its aspects, shows no sign of abating, and this series will continue to lead the way in encouraging the widest possible range of studies in the field. 'Studies in Imperialism' is fully organic in its development, always seeking to be at the cutting edge, responding to the latest interests of scholars and the needs of this ever-expanding area of scholarship.

Welsh missionaries and British imperialism

MANCHESTER 1824

Manchester University Press

SELECTED TITLES AVAILABLE IN THE SERIES

Materials and medicine: Trade, conquest and therapeutics in the eighteenth century
Pratik Chakrabarti

Borders and conflict in South Asia: The Radcliffe boundary commission and the partition of Punjab
Lucy P. Chester

Missionaries and their medicine: A Christian modernity for tribal India
David Hardiman

Conflict, politics and proselytism: Methodist missionaries in colonial and postcolonial Upper Burma, 1887–1966
Michael D. Leigh

Servants of the empire: The Irish in Punjab, 1881–1921
Patrick O'Leary

Welsh missionaries and British imperialism

THE EMPIRE OF CLOUDS IN NORTH-EAST INDIA

Andrew J. May

MANCHESTER
UNIVERSITY PRESS

Published by Manchester University Press
Altrincham Street, Manchester M1 7JA, UK
www.manchesteruniversitypress.co.uk

British Library Cataloguing-in-Publication Data is available

Library of Congress Cataloging-in-Publication Data is available

ISBN 978 071909 9977 *paperback*

First published by Manchester University Press in hardback 2012

This edition first published 2016

Printed by Lightning Source

For Karla and Rhys

Pan aethum gyntaf ar fwrdd y 'Jamaica,' yr oeddwn yn methu peidio gofyn, 'Ai i'r farn ai ynte i India yr ei di a mi, dywed?'
When I first went on board the 'Jamaica' I could not refrain from asking, 'Will you take me to judgement or to India, I wonder?'

Thomas Jones, *Y Drysorfa*, Supplement, December 1840, p. 388

When India unvisited becomes India visited – when the ideal gives place to the real, and we see and feel, with our waking senses, clearly and palpably, what before we had only dimly dreamt, how many vain delusions are dispersed – how many idle phantoms of the brain plunged headlong into the limbo of vanity.

Calcutta Review, January–June 1845, p. 71

When once unfair influence obtains among the tribunals of any country, it is idle to enquire to what extent it may proceed; its limits will only be bounded by the limits of the power to corrupt and intimidate, the wish to screen or revenge; the influence, in short, of power or gold from the possession of a power, so irrationally gigantic, so wholly uncontrollable, so little responsible, how few human minds are capable of escaping without contamination; while therefore we blame the outrages into which it has led its possessors, the criminality should be laid less on the culprits than the system that corrupts them.

W.H.M. Sweetland to A.J.M. Mills, Commissioner of the Government of India in A.J.M. Mills, *Report on the Khasi and Jaintia Hills, 1853* (Shillong, 1901), p. 88

But there is no good unmixed with evil or no evil unmixed with good.

Babu Hiranmoy Mukerji of Muktagachha to Chief Secretary of the Government of Bengal in R.D. Oldham, *Report on the Great Earthquake of 12th June 1897* (Calcutta, 1899), p. 22

Here they are – dear dead far-away people from whom I have my being, and whose blood flows in my veins for a brief space.

T.H. Lewin in T.H. Lewin (ed.), *The Lewin Letters: A Selection from the Correspondence & Diaries of an English Family 1756–1884*, volume 1 (London, 1909), p. v

People always look most alike when we know them least.

Inga Clendinnen, *Dancing with Strangers* (Melbourne, 2003), p. 18

CONTENTS

LIST OF FIGURES

ACKNOWLEDGEMENTS

My greatest debts are to the strangers in Wales and in India who opened their doors to me when I came knocking. Nigel Jenkins in Swansea, fellow encyclopedist, forged a trail before me and opened my eyes to the delicate possibilities of history as story-telling and of the need to maintain history's emotion. Jan and Mike Harris-Edge at the mill near Welshpool were early converts and have been a family to me when I have stopped by their heavenly home by Llifior Brook. The wise and enthusiastic hand of Bill Price has many times guided my forays into Welsh regional and religious history, and from the first day I met him and went on a whirlwind tour through the hedgerows and chapels of the *bro*, he has been my intellectual companion and an endless source of material. Without him this book could not have been written. I also appreciate the generosity of Aled Jones, E. Wyn James and Bill Jones for sharing their knowledge of Welsh history with an antipodean interloper, and Sylvia Prys Jones for the translations from *Y Drysorfa*. My final Welsh debt is to the Reverend J.E. Wynne Davies. When a stranger from the other side of the world first walked into his Aberystwyth parlour over a decade ago, as then curator of the Calvinistic Methodist Archive, he put his trust in my claim to tell a difficult part of what has historically been a contested story.

In India, David Reid Syiemlieh welcomed me to the Khasi Hills and was my anchor there at the North-Eastern Hill University at Shillong. His scholarship over many years on India's north-east lies at the heart of any understanding of the British colonial period, and he has been another remarkably generous and collegiate guide. David Macadam in Edinburgh, and Anne and Anouchka Inglis in Sydney, have sagely shared their insights into networks, family economies and the reverberations of an Anglo-Indian inheritance, and commented on various drafts along the way.

At the University of Melbourne, a number of colleagues in the School of Historical and Philosophical Studies have succoured the development of what to others may have appeared as a curious change of direction in my work. The late David Philips and the late Greg Dening were particularly enthusiastic about my attempt to examine culture contact in the British colonial period. I regret that they did not see the final result, but the book is the better for the guidance and enthusiasm they gave me in the early years of its development. To Alan Mayne, my first mentor in the department in the mid-1980s, I owe my awakening not simply to the joys of urban social history, but to the practices and sensitivities of the ethnographic historian. There is in my mind a clear lineage between this book and my early work on urban street life. If micro-history privileges an intensive scale of historical research and finds grander meanings in trivial and everyday things, then in a sense my first book took micro-history literally – the original meaning of *trivium* being the crossroads, the place where three roads meet. The radical 'new history' of the 1970s and 1980s might now seem almost old fashioned, but the rewards of its careful and time-consuming methodologies can never be taken for granted in an era of government-determined 'research excellence' measures. While the old Melbourne History Department is long gone, the voices of Dening, Philips and Mayne echo resoundingly for me off the walls of the new one as a vigilant riposte to those who would encourage the next generation of historians to eschew the archive for quick fix productions. Pat Grimshaw has remained a steadfast guide and supporter of my work. Donna Merwick generously read the entire manuscript, and her encouragement to find large questions in small things, to seek further meaning in distance, and to develop intimacy with my reader, assisted me enormously in the transition to the book's completion. For others, the publication of 'that little book about your great-great-grandfather' will hopefully repay the indulgence they have shown me in its development over many years. I also thank cartographer Chandra Jayasuriya, and my research assistants Chris Bill, Joanna Cruickshank, Cate O'Neill, Liz Nelson, Keir Reeves and Tom Rogers.

Thanks are also due to Christopher Akeroyd, Margaret Allen, Clare Anderson, Pritchard Basaiawmoit, Roger Bilham, Rosa Brezac, Mark Brown, Ieuan Bryn, Barbara Caine, Peter Cattell-Jones and Catriona Campbell, Diane Carlyle, Michael Clyne, Zoe Crossland, Marianne Delroy, Rita Dkhar, Bryn Ellis, Kate Fullagar, David Garrioch, Eric Gent, Frank Hardy, Daisy Hasan, Anna Johnston, Bill Jones, Sylvanus Lamare, Iwan Llwyd, Jane Lydon, Stacey Martin, Lesley McKean, Alison Metcalfe, Toshiyuki Mise, Blatei Nongbri, Amena Passah, Hugh Perfect, David Railton, Glenys Rasmussen, D. Ben Rees, Michael Rees-Evans, Susan Reidy, Kathy Rundle, Father Sylvanus Sgni, Caitlin Stone, Helen Tassie, Ann Trindade and Stephen Welch.

I am grateful to the Australian Research Council for Discovery Project funding in 2003 and 2007–9, which facilitated research for the book. Thanks also to the staff at the British Library (especially those who have assisted me over a number of years in the Asian and African Studies Reading Room), Moray House Archive, National Library of Australia, National Library of Scotland, National Library of Wales, the School of Oriental and African Studies at the University of London,

University of Nottingham Manuscripts and Special Collections, and West Bengal State Archives. The staff at Manchester University Press have been ever patient and professional through the whole period of the book's production, and I also gained useful insights from their anonymous readers. I particularly thank Vivienne Loesch in London for allowing me access to the Shadwell letters, Stuart Band at Chatsworth and Ruth Glashan for opening the cupboards at Dr Graham's in Kalimpong. Earlier musings on the topic have appeared as 'Collision and reintegration in a missionary landscape: the view from the Khasi Hills, India' in P. Grimshaw and R. McGregor (eds), *Collisions of Cultures and Identities: Settlers and Indigenous Peoples* (Melbourne, 2007), pp. 141–61; 'Sex and salvation: modelling gender on an Indian mission station' in A. Barry, J. Cruickshank, A. Brown-May and P. Grimshaw (eds), *Evangelists of Empire? Missionaries in Colonial History* (Melbourne, 2008), pp. 33–46; 'The promise of a book: missionaries and native evangelists in north-east India' in P. Grimshaw and A. May (eds), *Missionaries, Indigenous Peoples and Cultural Exchange* (Brighton, 2010), pp. 81–95; and 'Mountain views: Welsh missionaries, diaspora and empire', *The Welsh History Review*, 25:2 (2010), 239–50.

My final thanks go to my friends and family. This book has had a very long gestation, from the moment that my late mother and grandmother first told me their family stories and inspired my personal quest to understand what on earth their ancestors thought they were doing in India in the nineteenth century. Much has happened over the decade or so that this book has been in the making, and being absent in the Hills of my mind has not always been easy on my family. I particularly thank my children Karla and Rhys, who may make some sense of what I do by reading this book one day; Mark and Carolyn Leach-Paholski for putting a roof over my head at a critical time; and Keir Reeves for his friendship and loyalty. With Christina Twomey I share an endlessly hectic and fulfilling domestic and professional life. Her belief in me has been unswerving, and a driving force in my life is her passion for history and her feeling for words. There will never be enough of them to express the love I have for her and the debt I owe her in the writing of this book.

LIST OF ABBREVIATIONS

BMS	Baptist Missionary Society
CMS	Church Missionary Society
EIC	East India Company
IMS	Indian Medical Service
LMS	London Missionary Society
SLI	Sylhet Light Infantry
WFMS	Welsh Calvinistic Methodist Foreign Missionary Society

GLOSSARY

babu	originally a title of respect, used derisively to describe an Indian who had acquired a superficial English education
banghy	shoulder yoke
burkendaz	armed office-guard of the court
chunam	lime
dâk	post
diwani	the right of receiving revenue
dobashee/ dubashee	interpreter
doloi	chief or ruler in the Jaintia Hills
doolie	covered litter
durbar	court
durkhast	application
hurkaru	messenger or courier; message
Ka	Khasi feminine article
khublei	Khasi greeting – God bless you; thank you
kwai	chewed areca nut, lime and betel leaf
maund	standard unit of weight in India, equivalent to around 82 lbs or 37 k
mawbynna	memorial stones
mofussil	country or rural station or district
moochulka	written bond
mooktear	agent or attorney
moonga	wild silk
muntree	chief official or counsellor
nabob	a European who returned from India having accrued personal wealth
naik	non-commissioned sepoy officer equivalent to corporal
parwana	a licence or pass
peon	foot soldier
pundit	learned man
ryot	farmer
sanad	treaty of engagement
sebundy	irregular native soldiery
sepoy	native soldier
sirdar	leader
sowar	native cavalry soldier

sudder station	the principal station in a district where the collector, judge, courts, and other civic officials are located
Syiem	Khasi chief (usage in original sources dates from the 1870s, and missionaries and others in the earlier period were more likely to use the word *rajah*).
Synteng	name for the Jaintia people
talook	tract of proprietary land
talookdar	landholder possessing rights to land in other villages
tonjon	portable chair
U	Khasi masculine article; sometimes rendered as the prefix 'Oo' in original sources
zemindary	land held by *zemindar* who has proprietary status through paying revenue to the government

Because of Cherrapunji's ubiquity in the colonial sources, this nomenclature is retained, even though it has in recent years been renamed Sohra: similarly (aside from in the Introduction) – Dacca (Dhaka), Calcutta (Kolkata) and Bombay (Mumbai). Idiosyncratic spellings in the primary sources of some Khasi terms are sometimes retained in the text (for example the masculine article 'Oo' rather than 'U').

The term 'Anglo-Indian' now has the meaning of a person of mixed British and Indian descent, though it originally referred to all British people in India. The original distinction will be retained, and the word 'Eurasian' used to denote persons of mixed descent.

GENERAL EDITOR'S INTRODUCTION

Empire always seems to imply size, the bigness of ambition, of expansionist intent. But imperialism, the processes by which empire is created, is also related to locality. Empire resonates in the localities of the metropole as much as in the localities of the so-called periphery. This book is about those localities, on the one hand the piety and practices, the perceptions and prejudices of people in early nineteenth-century Wales, on the other the ways in which the religious ambitions of those same people operated upon the lives and ideas of indigenous societies of the distant Khasi Hills of north-eastern India. It is thus a study which embraces forms of micro-history by means of a set of micro-narratives, as the author himself calls them, but nonetheless these are micro-studies that operate within macro-contexts, the wider global formations of ever-extending British imperial rule in the period. While the region of north Wales and this specific portion of the territory of Assam are both small areas within a much larger geo-political whole, they were brought into an intersecting orbit by empire. The study of what happened when each came into contact with the other is the central objective of this book. It is set largely in the first half of the nineteenth century before British imperialism had reached its full ambitions, before nineteenth-century industrialism and its associated transport revolution had completely matured. And it seeks to show that aspects of 'marginality' in both geographical terms in respect of the United Kingdom and of India and in respect of the peoples involved, can offer significant insights into the global 'centrality' of the imperial condition.

At the heart of this story is a group of Welsh missionaries, eager to assert their own independent Welsh agency, at least in this evangelical missionary field. They represent the tendencies of so-called dissenting Protestantism to fragment, to attempt to create separate churches in some instances or to enter the missionary field with their own organisational structures, well connected to their contributing (in a variety of senses) society. Thus the essential development for this group of Methodist missionaries was the break with the London Missionary Society, the wider British movement which had significant links to Congregationalism. They wished to transport across the world a specifically Welsh form of Christian revelation; they desired to establish a missionary 'field' which would be tied to Welsh congregations and be seen to be very much the enterprise of that 'principality'. As well as carrying with them particular biblical and devotional forms of Christian enlightenment – as they would have seen it – they also transported specific linguistic and educational perceptions, rooted in their own Welsh language, its relationship with English, and the pedagogical practices of their own villages.

But if the Welsh missionaries are central to the story, they are by no means the only plot line. The author seeks to demonstrate the manner in which the Khasi Hills were 'unveiled' and opened up to imperial influences in a whole variety of ways – through the operations of scientific endeavour (for example in botany and plant collecting), through military encroachment, through the extension of the administrative tentacles of the East India Company, through ambitions to establish 'health resorts', not least for worn-out and sick members of the military, and also the exploitative urges in the search for economic crops and valuable resources, such as lime quarrying, and their related commercial endeavours. Thus the missionaries operated within wider contexts of the imperial advance. They were soon to suffer their own internal tensions between what was seen as correct and pious practice and what actually happened 'on the ground'. But their tensions were also tied into the multiple conflicts of commercial, administrative and military operations. Though the number of Europeans was relatively tiny, their internal as well as external conflicts were multiple and highly complex. Missionary and imperial ambitions were greatly complicated, and in some ways inhibited, as a result. The author seeks to identify and explain these many points of strain and resulting shakiness of the whole religious and imperial edifice. Ultimately, much of this instability and consequent destructiveness was to be perfectly symbolised by the great earthquake that occurred in the area in 1897. The mysterious operation of geological tectonic plates thus contributed to the many mysteries of human motivations and emotional crises, not all of which can be exposed from existing documents.

The intriguing thing is that both Welsh missionaries and Scottish military and administrative figures (prominent in the area) constructed the region as somehow familiar – an environment of hills, mists and rain which reminded them of Wales and Scotland respectively. Of course this territory of north-east India was ultimately nothing like Wales or Scotland. The botanical resources were very different, as was the geology and other natural historical phenomena. Moreover, its diseases, as was soon all too apparent, were far more dangerous to European life than anything experienced at 'home'. Hills, mists and rain did not mean health-giving conditions, as was often thought. Europeans who went there died almost as readily as they did on the Indian plains or in tropical Africa. Symmetrically, this was also true in reverse. The first person from the Khasi Hills to visit Wales and Britain, U Larsing, was to find the climate equally dangerous and tragically died in the course of his visit. It was to be some time before exchanges less inimical to the parties involved were to be effected. Yet, despite all the travails and deaths, the two areas were ineluctably drawn into a process of constructing each other. Welsh identity was partially formed through its sense of participating in global endeavours, not least religious, while the people of the Khasi Hills found themselves drawn into literacy and western forms of education and economic activity that were part of their involvement in the processes of modernity and globalisation.

While this is not, as the author asserts, a family history, it contains elements of the exploration of family connections and the flow of generational aspirations. Andrew May is himself related to the early principals of the Welsh missionary endeavour and fragmentary stories of this family past were lodged in the memories of some of his maternal ancestors. This gives the whole study added piquancy. But as May himself suggests, many elements were to remain a mystery, apparently incapable of being unveiled – perhaps only to be achieved through the operations of non-evidential imaginative reconstruction. But that is very likely work for the novelist rather than for the historian.

John M. MacKenzie

PROLOGUE

At Llifior Mill in the north of mid Wales, I climbed a ladder into the loft of the old barn where the residents had been repairing some shingles. As I entered the dingy roof cavity, my eye followed a shaft of light streaming through the broken roof and which fell half way up a vertical supporting column. In the newly illuminated space I could clearly make out the initials 'T.J.' chiselled boldly into the oak.

The mill is located near the small hamlet of Garthmyl in the old Welsh county of Montgomeryshire. The nearby village of Berriew, which also gives its name to the local parish, is six miles south-west of Welshpool. An hour and a quarter's drive west will take you to Aberystwyth on the coast, and from Welshpool the English border is only three miles to the east. Retirees Jan and Mike moved to the mill in the mid-1980s. For them, each rickety joist and worn floorboard breathes the Thomas Jones story. Here is the black smudge of candle-burn on an exposed wall beam, where perhaps the soon-to-be missionary sat up reading late into the night. There are the ancient black-and-red chequered tiles on the kitchen floor, still cracked in places where logs were chopped by the fireplace. His mother stood by this window, following her son through vision distorted by tears and the ripply Flemish glass as he started his long journey up the narrow driveway lined with hawthorn hedgerows, out to the road through Welshpool and on to the port of Liverpool sixty miles away to the north. Even the blades of grass on the nearby hillside, as Jan points out, were once trampled by the crowds of faithful who had come from all over the country to hear Jones preach.

Jan and Mike are enthusiastic custodians of the Thomas Jones story, and generous hosts to Khasis who occasionally make the long trip from India to stand for a while by Llifior Brook. Pilgrims souvenir a leaf from the garden or a stone from the path, and Jan and Mike offer postcards of the mill so that visitors can have a token to take back with them to India. Sometimes belated Christmas cards find their way to the mill from India, addressed simply to the residents of Thomas Jones's Mill, near Welshpool, as if the mail needed no more specific directions to reach such a renowned place.

Imperialism is a grand concept used by historians but rarely by millers' sons or even missionaries. But the mill is as good a place as any to start my search, with small signs that might mark larger stories. It is a calm and beautiful setting, but also a hard material place where the agrarian and industrial histories of Wales can be read in the cultural landscape. I know little more about the meaning of those initials, scratched in the wood of the barn, than the fact that at some time Jones may have been here, and passed through this place.

Starting at the mill, I also asked myself, what mark did this place leave on him? My first visit to Wales was in 2000. Shadowing the pages of this book about British imperialism in north-east India is a tale about encountering ancestors and the reverberations of imperial lives. After my mother's death in 1994, perhaps to honour the stories she and my Indian-born grandmother had entrusted to me of their missionary forebears, I vowed to put pen to paper and write a book about the Welsh in India. Scouring the internet for library resources, I stumbled across a book by Welsh writer Nigel Jenkins. There on the cover, staring out at me from the screen, was my first sight of the face of my great-great-grandfather Thomas Jones, a portrait that I subsequently discovered adorns school classrooms both at Newtown in Wales, and in Cherrapunji in the Khasi Hills of Meghalaya in north-east India. In 1991, Jenkins chanced to see the BBC TV documentary *Monsoon*, based on travel writer Alexander Frater's account of the wet season in India. Frater mentioned in passing that the literary proficiency of the Khasis was due in large measure to the efforts of a nineteenth-century Welshman. Intrigued by this apparent footnote in his own national history and by the remarkable fact that the Khasi church was in a far healthier state than the dwindling 'mother church' in Wales, Jenkins subsequently published *Gwalia in Khasia*, an account of his personal visit to the site of 'the biggest overseas venture ever sustained by the Welsh'.

In 1840, the parish map of Berriew shows Jones's father Edward Jones occupying the mill buildings as well as renting around two hectares of meadows and pasture on either side of the leat up to its weir. This open water channel is now matted and choked with brambles and trodden down by cattle, and the two millponds have long since ebbed away. His tenancy also covered mixed woodlands of oak, sycamore and ash, including nearby Cefndreboeth Wood, which most likely supplied the wheelwright's raw materials for the construction of hubs, spokes and rims. The oaks of Cefndreboeth may also have been turned into looms for the factories that had in the second half of the eighteenth century superseded the smaller domestic and cottage industries and been consolidated in the larger towns of the area such as Newtown and Llanidloes.

In 1841, two months after Thomas Jones set foot in India, Llifior Mill was in the prime of its productive life. The children of a working family would have enjoyed few advantages of education, and the young

Jones, according to his own account, had been 'taken from school when young'. He had until 1836 'been employed in my father's service, mostly as a carpenter and Wheelwright, the rest attending to a corn mill-business'. By the time of his application to the London Missionary Society (LMS) in 1839, they did not 'depend upon me, in whole or in part, for their support'. In his time there, work at the mill would have required a breadth of carpentry and mechanical skills to maintain and operate the machinery and keep the leat in working order. Edward Jones and his sons had working men's hands, seasoned and strengthened by the constant touch of wood and stone. Their bodies were marked with the signs of their labours – lungs filled with dust from the mill, backs strained from lifting barrels, thumbs enlarged from constantly testing the quality of the flour by rubbing it against their forefingers.

The 1840 parish map also marks the location of limekilns and wharves by the canal at nearby Garthmyl. The canal trade peaked in the 1830s, facilitating the transportation of coal, bricks and other building materials from English factories, while timber and products from the flannel mills of Montgomeryshire were sent back the other way. The canals were also important for the transportation of lime from quarries at Llanymynech, and lime was used for agricultural fertiliser or burnt in limekilns to convert it into quicklime.

What have limekilns and corn mills to do with larger questions of Christianity and empire? For the Jones family, Llifior provided sanctuary and livelihood. But like all homes, particularly rural ones, it was also at times a place from which to escape. One of Thomas Jones's sisters went to America, and the spectre of rural poverty, the lure of travel and opportunity, and the sense of generational change, inspired many of his compatriots to emigrate. If missionaries were fundamentally instrumental in the modernising and globalising process of Western imperialism, then understanding their personal economic and social as well as spiritual worldview is key to determining their role in imperial projects. Furthermore, I soon realised that however much the Welsh may have imagined the hill area of north-east India as an utterly foreign and heathen land, the footprint of British political and mercantile control and cultural influence had already left its mark well before Thomas Jones stepped off the ship in Calcutta. Not only was this history as important as that of the missionaries; the two were irrevocably intertwined.

The Llifior mill wheel is housed in an external wheel-pit on the side of the mill. In summer it is almost completely hidden in ferny foliage and shrouded with creepers, whose denuded branches in winter snake through it in stems knotted as thick as the spokes of the great iron wheel itself. The pit is silted up over the bottom of the rusting wheel, and the launder or iron box that once fed the overshot wheel from above is now crumbling with age. Likewise, the clamour and rattle from the engine of empire is long silent; in the archive as much as in the field, I have strained my ears to notice its refrain.

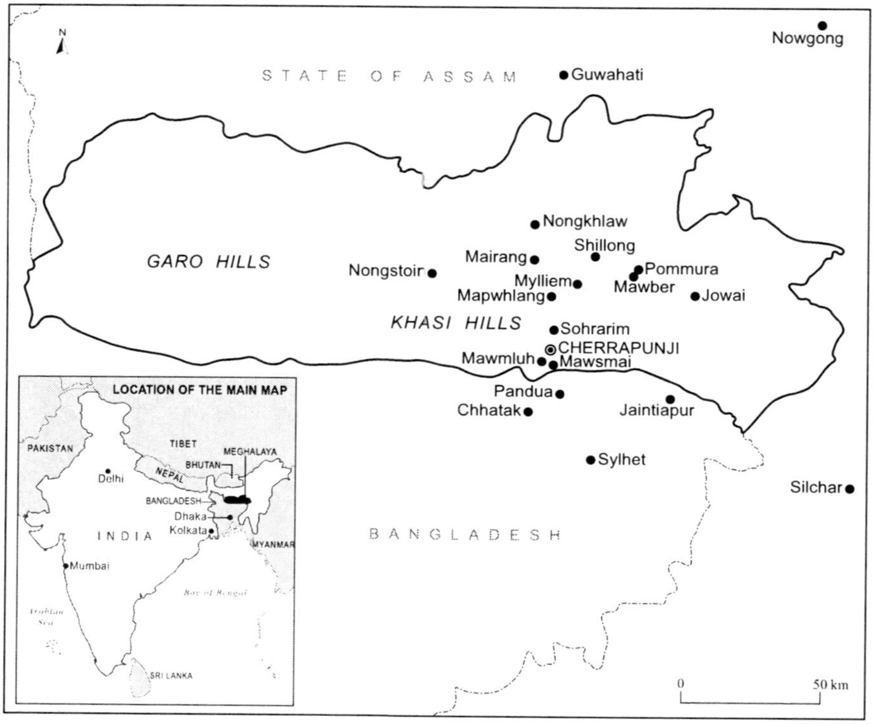

1 Map of the Khasi Hills.

Introduction

High up in the Khasi Hills of north-east India, a surreal flotilla of coloured balloons suspended with letters of the alphabet hung briefly on the dry April air. Had the prevailing breezes caught them, they might have floated up past the nearby eminence of Lum Sohpetbneng (the navel of heaven), out beyond the northern extremities of the east-west running Shillong Plateau and over Guwahati in Assam. There the Brahmaputra coils around the edge of Meghalaya, further to Bhutan, or north-west onwards towards Everest itself. From high in the clouds their sightline to the eastern horizon would extend over Manipur and Nagaland. South over the sharp escarpment at the edge of the Khasi Hills their view would hover above the plains of Sylhet towards Dhaka in Bangladesh, and beyond to the south-west, over the heated plains of Bengal and another six hundred miles on to Kolkata.

In barely a month, the skies would be of a different hue. While the baking plains sweltered below, rain would soon be the currency again as the monsoon made its annual pilgrimage up the Bay of Bengal, alternately dispensing its favours and despairs. Up here in the milder clime of the land known to the people of the Khasi-Jaintia Hills as *Ri Hynniewtrep* (the land of the seven huts), at a mean elevation of nearly 5000 feet, the onset of the monsoon will herald a summer season of almost continuous rainfall for six months. Mawsynram and the former British station of Cherrapunji (now known as Sohra) on the southern edge of the escarpment will experience the highest rainfall readings of any place on earth.

As chance would have it, the letters were too heavy and the balloons did not ascend to any great height. But this did not dampen the spirits of the assembled company, who had gathered there on 14 April 2007 to inaugurate a programme of celebratory events leading up to the bicentenary in 2010 of the birth of an esteemed figure. Plans were afoot to set up a museum in his name and release a postage stamp bearing his portrait. The President of the Khasi Authors' Society, S.S. Majaw, gave a long speech on his contribution to Khasi literature and education. D.D. Lapang, Chief Minister of the state of Meghalaya, hoisted a flag and launched a small booklet on his life written in Khasi and English, and an international dignitary unveiled a commemorative plaque.[1]

So who was this man who attracted such devotion, at home and abroad? In a year when India commemorated the sixtieth anniversary of independence, and 150 years had elapsed since the Indian Uprising of 1857, one might expect that such veneration was being accorded a local freedom fighter or cultural icon. But the flags and balloons were in honour of Thomas Jones, who came to India in 1841 under the auspices of the newly formed Welsh Calvinistic Methodists' Foreign Missionary Society (hereafter WFMS). At the function held at the Pynthorumkhrah church, Moderator of the Presbyterian Church of Wales, the Reverend Dr John Tudno Williams, spoke with pride of the man who forever linked the Welsh and the Khasis, who not only brought Christianity to the hills, but who in transposing an oral culture to written form has also been revered as the founding father of Khasi literature.

The 'empire of clouds' of this book's subtitle is both literal and metaphorical. 'Meghalaya' means the 'abode of clouds', and the monsoon clouds that fly north across the plains of Bangladesh continuously assault the Shillong plateau from April to September. But clouds are also symbols of religion and of belief. In general terms, they reference an indeterminate and liminal space between solid and void, earth and heaven. In Christian doctrine, the pillar of cloud is more specifically the visible symbol of God's presence in Exodus 13:21. In one version of a traditional Khasi belief, sixteen families originally lived with God in heaven and could move freely between heaven and earth via a ladder in the form of a tree that grew through the clouds on Lum Sohpetbneng. Seven families were eventually stranded on earth after sinning against God, and became the originating clans of the Khasi people. Whether Welsh Nonconformity or Khasi animism, I don't believe what they believed, but as a cultural historian I trust in their entitlement to beliefs, however foreign they are to me. 'To avoid anachronisms', Edward Muir reminds us, we must 'begin with the assumption that the past is utterly alien to the present'.[2]

It is surprising that the nineteenth- and twentieth-century evangelical encounter has been claimed for at least a decade as 'a relatively neglected area of study'.[3] As part of continuing reappraisals of the 'unfinished business'[4] of mission history in which new approaches address the role of the missionary as more than just a 'faceless imperial agent',[5] this book seeks to inflect the history of one particular mission station in the under-studied north-east region of India with alternative readings of the interactions between missionary, indigenous peoples and other British imperial agents. Both the hagiographies of the insider chroniclers and the stern critiques of the missionary as colonialism's Trojan horse have together had a marked tendency to undervalue an appreciation of intercultural exchanges. Missionaries meddled with the local cultural practices of indigenous peoples; more than that, at times they were brutal in their ideological and practical techniques of persuasion. Yet a totalising image of the missionary as cultural terrorist going in with Bible strapped under hair shirt is somewhat outmoded, and belies the complexities of lived experiences on the imperial frontier. If the first instinct of this book is to disrupt the monolithic category of missionary, it has a further and wilful purpose to penetrate other essentialising labels – British, Indian, soldier, scientist, merchant, administrator – that can become easy shorthand for broad processes of the expansion of European hegemony, but which blur the complex interactions and negotiations of imperialists and indigenous peoples.

The presumed inevitability of the association between missions and cultural imperialism remains to be tested. Indeed some scholars have gone so far as to assert that effective though they were in promoting cultural change, missions were in fact among the least effective agents of cultural imperialism.[6] What therefore were the degrees of missionary presence, influence or imperialism, or of indigenous reaction, resistance or oppression? To what extent, for example, did Christianity furnish an anti-colonial medium?[7] Such broad interrogations set an agenda for a very specific study centred on the British station at Cherrapunji around the middle decades of the nineteenth century.

In a predominantly Hindu country, Christians are a tiny minority of the population (2.3 per cent), but in the present-day state of Meghalaya, which now encompasses the Khasi Hills, they form a majority. Meghalaya had a population of 2,318,822 at the 2001 census, and encompasses three main indigenous groups: Garos (who self-identify as Achiks) in the western region, Khasis in the central district and Jaintias in the eastern districts of the state. Shillong ('the Scotland of the east') in the East Khasi Hills is the state capital, and Khasis are the largest group of the state's tribal[8] population, which is around 85 per cent of the total.

As an Indian state that is overwhelmingly Christian (70 per cent), Meghalaya forms part of the north-eastern region of India so often overlooked in surveys of the nation and its history. A leading international travel guidebook omits any detailed reference to India's north-east.[9] India itself is sometimes mildly confused in its orientation to its part-Christian tribal populations with their distinctive cultural and linguistic identities. To some Indians, the inhabitants of the north-east are still characterised as uncivilised tribals in an India that promotes itself as a modernising economy. Non-Khasi Indian scholars and writers are routinely condescending, and representations of Khasi society can draw on outmoded anthropological discourses[10] to depict an insular, even degenerate society, where primitive skill levels and 'centuries of stagnation' left it ripe and right for the picking by external influences, including Welsh missionaries.[11] The views of social anthropologist B.B. Kumar represent a growing critique of the dominant isolationist narrative of the north-east that belies its history of geographical, cultural and political interconnectedness. Many Indian historians themselves, argues Kumar, inculcated with racist and colonialist paradigms, have 'failed to incorporate regional histories in the broader frame-work of Indian history. They are so ignorant that a paper on the North-East was categorised as "non-Indian" in a volume of the Indian History Congress'.[12]

While general and regional studies of north-east India abound, including studies of British administration in Assam and Meghalaya, there is no history of the state of Meghalaya as a whole.[13] The history of Christianity in north-east India is also fragmented, and is variously and unevenly addressed by Natarajan's dated study which included aspects of the history of resistance movements to the spread of Christianity,[14] Piggin's brief elaboration of the social and educational backgrounds of some of the early Welsh missionaries,[15] an official history of the Mission published in Welsh by the Welsh church in 1988,[16] reprints and more recent histories written by missionaries or theological students,[17] a biographical register of Welsh missionaries in India compiled by a minister in the Presbyterian Church of Wales,[18] and scattered studies of Catholic, Baptist and other denominational missionary enterprises.[19] The Reverend John Hughes Morris wrote an official history of the mission in Welsh, published in 1907.[20] Welsh historian Aled Jones, noting the remarkable historiographical silence when it comes to the activities of Welsh evangelists, and concentrating on a period from the latter decades of the nineteenth century, has more recently and astutely addressed the ways in which the Welsh missionary presence in India re-entered mainstream post-colonial history in Wales through the medium of missionary writings.[21]

Aside from popular accounts of Khasi folklore, there are a number of accessible survey histories of Khasi society and culture.[22] Scholarly interest in Khasi culture has often taken a linguistic turn, a path signposted by the seminal role played by Thomas Jones, but which has almost exclusively been pursued in terms of Khasi as a Mon-Khmer language, its morphology, lexicology, phonology and the oral-written continuum.[23] The role of Jones in fostering Khasi language and literature is often cited in passing, but the opportunity has not been taken to analyse how the indigenous language in the Khasi context may have been reshaped to facilitate British colonialism.[24]

In his history of missionaries in Punjab, Jeff Cox writes of the 'daunting intellectual difficulties, not merely of documentary and textual interpretation but also of defining a point of view from which to tell the story'.[25] If my perspective is particularly concerned with the Welsh as missionaries, and set unusually in a traditionally non-Hindu and non-Muslim tribal area of India, what other vantage points do I establish? This study is less a macro-history of missions and imperialism in the vein of Porter or Cox,[26] and more a local-level study of the ways in which macro-processes play out for individual people 'as they lived their lives, engaged hopes and fears, experienced successes and failures, and dealt with intractable problems'.[27] In this sense I am concerned with acts in the field and with the varieties of empire that transcend theory or prescription. Colonialism, as Thomas reminds us, is a fractured project, 'riddled with contradictions and exhausted as much by its own internal debates as by the resistance of the colonised'.[28]

If my study is inflected by any particular historical approach, perhaps it is the concern of micro-history for an 'ethnographic history of everyday life' that resists the 'gigantification of historical scale'.[29] When the history of empires is at stake, the role and experience of individuals can be all too easily condemned to irrelevance, so I have been determined to see the sweep of human endeavour in trivial and minute actions, and in real people making real choices. Part of my methodology has been to gather as far as I can from the archive those who may have been at the small British station at Cherrapunji from the 1820s to the 1860s, and to construct the kind of 'prosopography from below' that micro-history requires.[30] Cherrapunji, with a population of just 10,086 in 2001, may seem an odd choice as empire's ground zero. In one way this book is something of a biography of Thomas Jones, and I have deliberately chosen the most marginal and far-flung place to set my study; yet through the historical circumstances of my family's history, the place has also chosen me. Standing metaphorically at the side of the road leading from the plains to the hills provides an uncommon vantage point for a reconsideration of nineteenth-century British imperialism in north-east India. Yet the hills are as much 'in here' as 'over there' when it comes to empire's geography. The tactics of micro-history also involve an intensive struggle with documentary sources, a tussle that at times throughout the narrative needs to be made explicit.[31] The book has been shaped by what I have found as well as what I have been unable to find. As a history that is intimately shaped by the nature and inscrutability of my sources – many in the form of correspondence and other texts translated or retranslated between Welsh and English – my work has also been influenced by that of Liz Stanley, whose insights into the epistolary practice have made me more comfortable about being less certain when it comes to the elisions and inconsistencies of such sources.[32]

How the Welsh missionaries happened to arrive in India in 1841 is the subject of the first section of the book, from the origins of their Calvinistic Methodist denomination in the eighteenth century, their split from the LMS as an assertion of Welsh identity, the voyage to India and their arrival in the hills at a time when earlier missionaries from Serampore had already wielded some influence. The second section foregrounds broader political, scientific, racial and military ideologies that mobilised the hills into an interconnected vision of imperial control. Once arrived, the work of the first generation of missionaries is explored in the third section of the book in relation to language translation, education, proselytism and negotiation with native polity. It is here too that crises of authority in the mission are explored in the context of geographical isolation, interpersonal rivalry and competing ideologies of mission. These scandals erupt in the final section of the book, an appraisal of the complex and divergent ways in which ideologies of mission and the rule of law were interpreted on the frontier.

In putting the geographically and archivally inaccessible Cherrapunji at the centre of an imperial history, I am also inserting distance as a fundamental structuring device. Space is a useful metaphor; my book is at one level an overview of the mental topography of imperialism. Distance is an irrefutable consequence of empire – officer to officer, village to village, continent to continent. In each chapter of the book I take different perspectives on this sense of distance in order to come to diverse conclusions about the nature of the British empire. Importantly, while following the prescription of Catherine Hall and many others to analytically link colony and metropole,[33] I have also tried to make intimacy out of distance by telling stories of individual relationships. In analysing the individual lives that flash in and out of this history, this book is a performance within the effort to break down the many dimensions of distance that the imperial scene prescribes.

The bookends of prologue and epilogue frame this study as a personal as well as a professional journey. A further and principal axis along which this book can be understood is that of the voyage. Literally, Thomas Jones the missionary sails to India in Chapter 2. Along with him I take the opportunity to transport a further cast of personnel and associated objects and ideas (missionary, scientist, administrator, merchant and soldier) that will be operationalised in India in the subsequent five chapters that conclude the first two sections of the book. This cast is closely interlocked; we will not understand Jones or what he does in India until we understand these pre-existing networks of imperial operation and influence; in Alan Lester's terms, we need to pay attention to a 'networked conception of imperial interconnection'.[34]

In the scene changes and flashbacks, sideshows and recapitulations, I might run the danger of disorienting my reader. Yet I trust that such disruption, which is often the traveller's most constant accessory, can be endured in order to appreciate the view after the final mountain ascent with Thomas Jones is made in June 1841. In a structure that does not deliver Jones to Cherrapunji until Chapter 8, there is also deliberate simulation. From the moment the Joneses wave goodbye at Liverpool in November 1840, spatial and temporal slippage begins. Once departed, the missionary is as much imagined as real, and news of his arrival and subsequent activities becomes keenly anticipated. 'The missionary is not dead when he leaves his native land, as some seem to suppose', assured the *Calcutta Christian Observer* in 1837. 'He lives, and is awake to the landscape, the bright sun, the mild breeze, the animated world around him'.[35] Yet in practice, family and brethren at home feared the worst, their anxieties exaggerated by absence and imagination and barely soothed by irregular correspondence. The missionary was gone. And what if he were never to return? Once delivered to the Khasi Hills, however, Jones's evangelising among the Khasis as well as his conflicts with church and state authority are observed in Chapters 8 to 11, through to his eventual demise. Here again my obligation to micro-history is to determine the relative freedom of the missionary's actions in the context of 'the constraints of prescriptive and oppressive normative systems'.[36] The final two chapters of the book reprise some aspects of the micro-politics of mission and state in the two decades immediately following Thomas Jones's death.

Nigel Jenkins might be credited not just for admitting the destruction wrought to Khasi culture by the Welsh missionaries, and the broader dishonourable implication of Wales in 'her neighbour's "absent minded" frenzy to paint the planet pink', but also for starting the conversation that has been entered into by historians like Aled Jones about what imperialism meant for the Welsh themselves.[37] Professor David Syiemlieh of the North-Eastern Hill University at Shillong, who had contributed some of his own historical findings to Jenkins's project, continued to research the Thomas Jones story.[38] While Linda Colley reminds us of Joseph Conrad's remark that empire is 'not a pretty thing when you look into it too much', she also mindfully counsels that a concentration on the bald question of whether empire is/was a Good Thing or a Bad Thing does not allow for the development of 'a more complex and realistic appreciation of what imperial ambitions and interventions in the past have entailed for *all* of those involved'.[39] Both Jenkins and Syiemlieh had assumed that the mission history was little known outside of India, and I hope that my own contribution to other people's histories connects divergent perspectives on imperialism across time and space, and at an individual as well as transnational scale.

Notes

1 'KJP Assembly remembers Thomas Jones I'', *Shillong Times*, 16 April 2007; Pers. comm., Professor David Reid Syiemlieh.
2 Edward Muir, 'Introduction: observing trifles' in Edward Muir and Guido Ruggiero (eds), *Microhistory and the Lost Peoples of Europe* (Baltimore and London, 1991), p. x.
3 Saurabh Dube, 'Paternalism and freedom: the evangelical encounter in colonial Chattisgarh, central India', *Modern Asian Studies*, 29:1 (1995), 173.
4 Norman Etherington (ed.), *Missions and Empire* (Oxford, 2005).
5 Dana Robert, 'Introduction' in Dana Robert (ed.), *Converting Colonialism: Visions and Realities in Mission History, 1706–1914* (Grand Rapids, Michigan, 2008), p. 3.
6 Geoffrey A. Oddie, '"Orientalism" and British Protestant missionary constructions of India in the nineteenth century', *South Asia*, 17:2 (1994), 27–42; Andrew Porter, '"Cultural imperialism" and Protestant missionary enterprise, 1780–1914', *The Journal of Imperial and Commonwealth History*, 25:3 (1994), 367–91.
7 Grzegorz Kaczynski, 'Ambiguity of the mission Christianity in the colonial Africa: historical and anthropological essay', *Africana Bulletin*, 44 (1997), 39–62.
8 While the terms 'tribe' or 'tribal' are generally contested in terms of their denoting outmoded racialised hierarchies, they have ubiquitous currency in India's north-east as self-identifiers of distinctive regional identities in opposition to Bengali hegemony.
9 P. de Bruyn, K. Bain, D. Allardice and S. Joshi, *Frommer's India* (Hoboken, NJ, 2010), 4th edition.
10 See for example J.H. Hutton's 'Primitive tribes' in L.S.S. O'Malley (ed.), *Modern India and the West: A Study of the Interaction of their Civilizations* (Oxford, 1941), pp. 415–44.
11 N. Natarajan, *The Missionary among the Khasis* (New Delhi, 1977), p. 58.
12 B.B. Kumar, 'North East India: crisis of perception & credible action', *Dialogue*, 1:2 (1999), www.nenanews.com/ne.htm (accessed 14 July 2011).
13 David Reid Syiemlieh, *Survey of Research in History on North-east India 1970–1990* (New Delhi, 2000); M.S. Barkataki, *British Administration in North East India 1826–1874: A Study of their Social Policy* (New Delhi, 1985); David Reid Syiemlieh, *British Administration in Meghalaya: Policy and Pattern* (New Delhi, 1989); Helen Giri, *The Khasis under British Rule (1824–1947)* (New Delhi, 1990).
14 Natarajan, *The Missionary among the Khasis*.
15 Stuart Piggin, *Making Evangelical Missionaries 1789–1858. The Social Background, Motives and Training of British Protestant Missionaries to India* (Appleford, 1984), p. 228.
16 Ednyfed Thomas, *Bryiau'r Glaw* (Caernarfon, 1988).
17 Riewah Robert Cunville, 'A study of the growth of the Presbyterian Church in the Khasi and Jaintia Hills', MA in Missiology, Fuller Theological Seminary, 1974; B.L. Nongbri, 'Thomas Jones: a "scandal" to the church – a "hero" to the people', Seminar Paper, John Roberts Theological Seminary, 22 September 1998.
18 D. Ben Rees (ed.), *Vehicle of Grace & Hope: Welsh Missionaries in India 1800–1970* (Pasadena, 2002).

19 Such as Frederick Sheldon Downs, *History of Christianity in India: North East India in the Nineteenth and Twentieth Centuries*, volume 5 (Bangalore, 1992).

20 John Hughes Morris, *Hanes Cenhadaeth Dramor y Methodistiaid Calfinaidd Cymreig, Hyd Ddiwedd y Flwyddyn 1904* (Caernarfon, 1907); John Hughes Morris, *The History of the Welsh Calvinistic Methodists' Foreign Mission to the End of the Year 1904* (New Delhi, 1996, first published 1910).

21 Aled Jones, 'Welsh missionary journalism in India, 1880–1947' in Julie F. Codell (ed.), *Imperial Co-histories: National Identities and the British and Colonial Press* (Madison, NJ, 2003), pp. 242–72. See also Aled Jones, 'Gardens of Eden: Welsh missionaries in British India' in R.R. Davies and Geraint H. Jenkins (eds), *From Medieval to Modern Wales: Historical Essays in Honour of Kenneth O. Morgan and Ralph A. Griffiths* (Cardiff, 2004), pp. 264–80; Aled Jones and Bill Jones, 'The Welsh world and the British empire, *c.*1851–1939: an exploration', *The Journal of Imperial & Commonwealth History*, 31:2 (2003), 57–81.

22 Mrs Rafy, *Folk-tales of the Khasis* (London, 1920); P.R.T. Gurdon, *The Khasis* (Delhi, 1975, first published 1907); J.N. Chowdhury, *The Khasi Canvas: A Cultural and Political History* (Shillong, 1978); Promatha Nath Dutta, *Impact of the West on the Khasis and Jaintias: A Survey of Politics and Social Changes* (New Delhi, 1982); Hamlet Bareh, *The History and Culture of the Khasi People* (Guwahati, 1985); Soumen Sen, *Social and State Formation in Khasi-Jaintia Hills: A Study of Folklore* (Delhi, 1985).

23 K.S. Nagaraja, 'Khasi dialects: a typological consideration', *Mon-Khmer Studies*, 23 (1993), 1–10; I.M. Simon, 'On first looking into Paul K. Benedict's Sino-Tibetan linguistics', *Mon-Khmer Studies*, 27 (1997), 155–9; Hanjabam Surmangol Sharma, 'A comparison between Khasi and Manipuri word order', *Linguistics of the Tibeto-Burman Area*, 22:1 (1999), 139–48.

24 Cf Derek Peterson, 'Colonizing language? Missionaries and Gikuyu dictionaries, 1904 and 1914', *History in Africa*, 24 (1997), 257–72.

25 Jeffrey Cox, *Imperial Fault Lines: Christianity and Colonial Power in India, 1818–1940* (Stanford, 2002), p. 7.

26 Andrew Porter, *Religion Versus Empire? British Protestant Missionaries and Overseas Expansion, 1700–1914* (Manchester, 2004); Jeffrey Cox, *The British Missionary Enterprise since 1700* (New York, 2008).

27 Marilyn Silverman and P.H. Gulliver, 'Historical anthropology through local-level research' in Don Kalb and Herman Tak (eds), *Critical Junctions: Anthropology and History beyond the Cultural Turn* (New York, 2005), p. 155.

28 Nicholas Thomas, *Colonialism's Culture: Anthropology, Travel and Government* (Cambridge, 1994), p. 51.

29 Muir, 'Introduction', pp. ix, xxi.

30 *Ibid.*, p. ix.

31 Giovanni Levi, 'On microhistory' in Peter Burke (ed.), *New Perspectives on Historical Writing* (Cambridge, 2001), p. 110.

32 Liz Stanley, 'The epistolarium: on theorizing letters and correspondences', *Auto/Biography*, 12 (2004), 201–35.

33 Catherine Hall, *Civilising Subjects: Metropole and Colony in the English Imagination, 1830–1867* (Cambridge, 2002), p. 9.

34 Alan Lester, 'Imperial circuits and networks: geographies of the British empire', *History Compass*, 4:1 (2006), 133.

35 *Calcutta Christian Observer*, 61 (1837), 316.

36 Levi, 'On microhistory', p. 98.

37 Jones, 'Welsh missionary journalism'.

38 David Reid Syiemlieh, 'Thomas Jones' "Injudicious Marriage?"', *Proceedings, North East India History Association, XIV Session* (1995), 240–4.

39 Linda Colley, 'Introduction: some difficulties of empire – past, present, and future', *Common Knowledge*, 11:2 (2005), 207, 212.

PART I

Preparations

CHAPTER ONE

Some kind of preacher

Of the early life of Thomas Jones there is sparse documentary evidence, and nothing written in his own hand until August 1839 when he applied to the LMS to be sent overseas as a missionary. The question of what knowledge and practices Jones carried with him, both in terms of religious belief and practical know-how, is important in determining both the force and character of the Welsh mission, as well as the 'slippages of meaning',[1] the ways in which such processes were contested, co-opted or reworked by indigenous agency and resistance. As Ryan Dunch suggests, despite the monolithic paternalism of the Christian mission, the experience of particular missionaries and their ability to negotiate cultural difference was very much determined by their individual character, adherence to particular religious doctrine, social and economic circumstances, adaptability and education.[2] The categories of 'Christian' and 'British' need to be nuanced by closer attention to 'Calvinistic Methodist' and 'Welsh'.

A further reason to focus on the social and religious world that spawned the WFMS in 1841 is to acknowledge that a subtle but nevertheless cogent effect of missionary endeavour overseas was cultural change in the country of origin as well as in indigenous cultures. The desire of the Welsh to send their own missionaries to India was representative of far more than just generalised evangelical religious ideologies. It betrayed as much about their own self-fashioning and identity as it did about their construction of a racialised and heathen other. Intertwined with the transformation of Khasi culture was a parallel process in which imperialism entailed 'the cultural representation of Wales to the Welsh'.[3] The process by which the Welsh diverged from their long-established tradition of support for the LMS – in financial terms as well as by providing candidates – was the result of a combination of factors including individual motivation and generational change, as well as to an assertion of collective ethnic identity.

The rise of Welsh Nonconformity

As well as comprising beliefs about the existence of the soul, the supernatural and the afterlife, the religion of the Welsh Calvinistic Methodists was a negotiated set of religious doctrines – codified in the forty-four articles of their *Confessions of Faith* (1823).[4] The Puritan movement from which Nonconformity emerged grew from a concern among some radical Protestants that the reformed English church had not gone far enough in breaking with Catholic modes of ecclesiastical structure. Puritan belief asserted the supremacy of God over human affairs (that neither pope nor monarch could be head of the church on earth, though they were accountable to God); the regulative principle of scripture (that biblical example should strictly dictate forms of worship); the sanctity of the Sabbath; and the importance of education in spreading the word of the Bible.

It was not until the reign of William and Mary and the passing of the *Toleration Act* (1689) that religious freedom prospered and dissenters were able to build their own chapels. The increased circulation of religious texts and the fillip given to education by the *Toleration Act* led to a rise in literacy in Wales. With the support of the Society for the Promotion of Christian Knowledge, established in London in 1699, a growing number of religious tracts were distributed in English and Welsh. The Circulating Welsh Charity Schools (1738–61) also played a crucial role in bringing education to a Welsh-speaking constituency and indeed laid the foundation for the religious revival that was to sweep the country over the ensuing century.

The Church of St Tysilio and St Mary occupies centre stage in the village of Meifod, seven miles north-west of Welshpool. This was the home parish of wheelwright Edward Jones, who married Mary Owen at Llanfihangel on 11 February 1807. Their second son Thomas was born in the parish of Llangyniew at Tan-y-ffridd, a farm between Llanfair and Meifod, on 24 January 1810. That year, a meeting of the South Wales Calvinistic Methodist Association at Swansea ratified the motion of their north Wales confreres to split from the Anglican Church. On 20 June 1811, the first eight preachers from north Wales were ordained at Bala, a flannel manufacturing town in Merionethshire at the foot of the Berwyn mountains.

The eighteenth-century Methodist Revival in Wales that had produced this Calvinistic version of Methodism is associated with three key figures: Howell Harris of Trefeca, Daniel Rowland of Llangeitho and William Williams of Pantycelyn. Harris had developed an interest in the teachings of the Moravians when he met their brethren during his visits to London, and in particular their model of communal religious life at religious settlements such as Herrnhut. At Trefeca in 1752, Harris established a community of his followers known as *Teulu Trefeca* (the Trefeca family). The self-sufficient community comprised blacksmiths, farmers, carpenters, millers and other necessary trades, all instructed in the faith by Harris, and both the Trefeca family and the Moravian model that inspired it would later influence Thomas Jones's methods in India.

Harris had first visited Berriew in 1738, and local tradition records that he also preached at Pied House, on the hillside above Llifior Mill.[5] Edward and Mary Jones, and Edward's brother John Jones, represented a more theologically literate Methodism when the movement revived in the early nineteenth century. The societies in this area of Montgomeryshire were among the oldest and strongest in Wales, having survived periods of significant persecution, and were in the vanguard of Welsh Calvinistic Methodism at the time of the split in 1811.

Christians in Wales entered the nineteenth century in an establishment church riven with entrenched resentment against a mostly Anglo-centric and often absentee clergy disconnected from their church's grassroots. Methodism owed its origins to the evangelical teachings of John Wesley, though of course Wesley knew little Welsh and spoke through interpreters when he visited local societies. Despite Wesley, Harris and George Whitefield's early co-operation, divisions emerged within Methodism on key issues of doctrine. Just as Whitefield's Calvinist proclivities had led to a rift with the Wesleyans, so too Welsh Methodism was more Calvinist in temper, despite its links with the English movement.

The central sticking point was the issue of predestination. For the Welsh Calvinistic Methodists (following the sixteenth-century theologian John Calvin), only those God had already elected would ultimately experience his salvation. For the Wesleyans, on the other hand, who subscribed to an Arminian view (after the Dutch theologian Jacob Arminius), free-will allowed any believer to attain the salvation of a God who died for all sinners.[6] Though they saw themselves as part of the Established church, Calvinistic Methodists in Wales in the early nineteenth century were increasingly at odds with a church structure in which their exhorters could not be ordained, and where communion could only be given by ordained ministers. While secession was anathema to many, the situation whereby ordained clergymen and unordained exhorters preached to the same congregation by turns, the first inside the church and the second outside, had become a source of great tension and instability.[7]

It has been argued that the three decades after 1785 were 'the most successful period ever for religion in Wales'.[8] Thomas Jones's parents were members of a Methodist society that was in the vanguard of the formation of the breakaway church in 1811. The Calvinistic Methodist cause first took root in the neighbourhood of Pontrobert at Penllys, Llanfihangel-yng-Ngwynfa, when in the early 1770s a licensed *seiat* (private society) had formed at the house of Thomas Jones's grandfather, Morris Owen.[9] This area is most well known as the home of the Welsh Christian mystic poet Ann Griffiths, whose family lived at Dolwar Fach, a farm just south of Llanfihangel-yng-Ngwynfa.

The parish of Llanfihangel-yng-Ngwynfa was the subject of sociologist Alwyn D. Rees's *Life in a Welsh countryside*, based on fieldwork undertaken between 1939 and 1946. The farms of Dolwar Fach and Penllys appear, but the society of the old Wales of Thomas Jones's parents is depicted as having been unable to stand the test of time. Rees characterised a modern Wales where the emergent religious experience of the eighteenth and nineteenth centuries could not be sustained into the twentieth; the motors of decline were Anglicisation, industrialisation and the fading of a religion formed around inner experience rather than outward show and which could only be sustained through revivalism. An ethnography of Llanfihangel recorded the remnant ways of thought and practices that were at their apogee a century and a half earlier in the days of Thomas Jones's parents: Sunday school, prayer and preaching-meetings on the Sabbath and through the week, the 'Welsh Sunday' (or 'Puritan Sunday'), *gweddi o'r frest* (prayers from the heart) rather than set prayers, scriptural knowledge, the 'close correlation between prosperity and virtue', pictures of well-known preachers on the walls of family homes. But to Rees the legacy of Nonconformity was clear: political radicalism, a passion for education, and 'versatility, the "culture" of the common people, what makes the connotation of the term *gwerin gwlad* qualitatively different from that of its English equivalent, *country folk*'.[10]

If Thomas Jones did stand and preach on the hillside below Pied Farm, then his resolute stance, his spirited gestures and his artful words would have been coded with powerful meanings for those who gathered to listen. As a man of humble rural origins, he embodied the local involvement of ordinary people in the everyday labour of his faith, the egalitarianism of Nonconformity that had taken root in the late eighteenth century as a key cultural and social movement in Wales: 'Grounded in religious and cultural dissent and subject to constant schisms . . . a hegemonic cultural institution based on notions of community, respectability and resistance to the perceived threat of English cultural and linguistic domination'.[11] Jones sermonised within a rigorous tradition and as an inheritor of the ardent founders of his faith; he was a shining acolyte of the matured movement. The fervent eloquence of his address exemplified the *hwyl* of his forefathers and compatriots, that emotional and inspired quality of impassioned and sustaining speech, like the wind that fills the sails of a boat.

In the Wales of 1801, with a population of less than 600,000 (around a fifth of what it is today), the lives of many rural people were circumscribed within a small radius around their home farms, villages and market towns. At a neighbourhood level, as would have been understood by his contemporaries and as later church biographies of Thomas Jones make explicit, the strength of his family's links to the local flowering of Calvinistic Methodism assured his lineage to the progenitors of the creed and valorised his position as its anointed scion. The centrality of biblical immersion to the Calvinistic Methodists – the Bible read privately and aloud, studied, discussed, committed to memory – was the dominant influence on the daily lives of its readers. As literacy and education unlocked the Bible's treasure trove of images and exemplars, infusing the language to potent and heady effect, a religious revival morphed into a cultural one.

The Liverpool Welsh

By the time of the birth of their fifth child, Anna, in August 1816, the Jones family had removed from Meifod to Gascoyne Street, Liverpool. In the previous half century, the emerging position of Liverpool as a significant European seaport had been reflected in the ever-growing volumes of shipping using its docks, and the increased export of goods to colonial markets greedy for the industrial productions of Lancashire and Cheshire.[12] This magnet of industry and opportunity attracted many Welsh emigres in search of work and escaping the poverty of their smallholdings. The city became a popular refuge, and as the century progressed, a stepping-stone in a more general exodus to America or to empire destinations in Canada, South Africa, Australia or New Zealand. Most famously, in 1865 a group of idealistic Welsh left to found a new colony in Patagonia.[13]

At mid-century, the Irish-born population was around four times that of the 20,262 Welsh-born, but Liverpool would be characterised by the 1880s as 'a kind of auxiliary capital for north Wales'.[14] William Llwyd from Flintshire is celebrated as holding the first religious service of the Welsh Calvinistic Methodists in Liverpool in 1782, and by the time the Jones family arrived just over three decades later, the chapel played a significant role not just in a spiritual sense, but as an employment bureau and information exchange for the newly arrived, often non-English speaking immigrant from Wales. The Reverend John Elias, the first Welsh Calvinistic Methodist minister ordained in 1811, was soon baptising Elijahs, Joshuas, Eunices and Nathaniels at Pall Mall Chapel and Rose Place Chapel in Mulberry Street.[15]

While the local economy was centred on the port, the Welsh had a particular monopoly in the building trades. In an often casualised and unpredictable labour market, their ethnic and religious cohesion provided ballast against economic instability, as Welsh property developers and contractors favoured the employment of their compatriots and co-religionists as workers.[16] The rural wheelwright Edward Jones from Meifod was now the urban joiner from Merseyside, and the registers of chapels such as Rose Place record the occupations of his fellow countrymen, the labourers, brick-makers, bricklayers, marble masons, tanners and coopers on whose skill and toil the city was built. Some of the Liverpool Welsh grew fat on the riches of urban expansion; the city that they played a major role in constructing buttressed their own fortunes. Owen Elias from Anglesey (1806–80) famously left his mark in Walton where the initials of thirty consecutive streets spelt the name of his eldest son. Workers like Edward Jones may not have prospered so readily, and he returned to Wales around 1819, according to some accounts, due to his failing health.[17]

The Jones family stayed first at Brithdir just to the north of Berriew, where for a time Edward fostered preaching and ran the Sunday school, before he took up the tenancy at Llifior Mill. The farm at next door Pied House was run by John Jones, who conducted religious meetings as well as a Sunday school there, and was treasurer of the Home Mission for the Montgomeryshire border area. The Home Missionary Societies had been formed as a means of evangelising in the non-Welsh-speaking areas closer to the English border. The Calvinistic Methodist cause in the Berriew district was assisted in 1830 by the arrival of Thomas Francis, who had been commissioned by the Home Mission Board to evangelise in the district. Forty-five chapels were built in Montgomeryshire by 1840, in a church that a decade later accounted for around 80 per cent of churchgoing attendance in Wales, but there were still many localities where prior to the further construction of chapels in the 1850s and 1860s, preaching and Sunday schools were still conducted in farmhouses. Pied House was the centre of worship in the local area before the opening of the stone-built Refail Chapel at Berriew in 1852.[18] The Refail had been established by Edward Jones and his brother John, and was the first chapel in Montgomeryshire self-financed by the local community and built without having to borrow funds from the denomination.

Spiritual awakening and evangelical religiosity

Although he had been 'brought up in a religious family and in the society', and had 'felt strong religious impressions since I was about 8 or 9 years old', Thomas Jones dated his own religious awakening to around the time that his family returned to Wales in 1819. He considered that he had 'been very careless about religion' prior to this period, 'but in the Spring of 1834 I felt stronger religious impressions than before; which have continued ever since'.[19] The individual call to belief could be personalised and localised, but might also be set against the general rhythms of revivalism that swept through Wales in the first half of the nineteenth century, with a fourth noted crescendo in 1839–43.

The novel characteristics of worship that saw mass ritual trembling and convulsions among crowds of believers were easily pilloried by the Methodists' antagonists, who saw the Welsh as fanatics.[20] Historically, the Welsh 'jumpers' joined the ranks of the rollers, ranters, quakers and shakers, whose extroverted and impulsive physicality was partly feared as threatening radical political action, and easily mocked, such as in a pejorative depiction by the Congregationalist Charles Buck: 'Several of the more zealous itinerant preachers encouraged the people to cry out *gogoniant* (the Welsh word for glory,) amen, &c. &c. to put themselves in violent agitations: and, finally, to jump until they were quite exhausted, so as often to be obliged to fall down on the floor or the field, where this kind of worship was held'.[21] Protesting the gross caricature of the revivalists, Thomas Rees noted in his 1861 history of Welsh Nonconformity that such effects were at least heartfelt rather than feigned, and he defended the Welsh as a 'naturally excitable people'.[22] The powerful and dramatic oratory skills of the first wave of great preachers set a standard for those preachers who captivated their audiences in the first four decades of the nineteenth century, such as Ebenezer Morris, Christmas Evans, John Elias and David Davies. At the annual Associations, an Elias or a Morris could captivate crowds of many thousands. When Morris spoke, 'A single word from his mouth would often roll over the people like a mighty wave', and Elias would have thousands under the spell of his voice: 'As the preacher waves his hand, the crowd is swayed backwards and forwards as a field of corn is swayed by a gentle breeze; copious tears are falling, there are not a few sobs and cries'.[23]

Aside from the public performance of revivalist zeal, the private local fellowship or 'experience' meetings were a further key to a newly developing sense of spiritual life in the everyday worlds of the Welsh Calvinistic Methodists, and would have shaped Thomas Jones's early experiences of religious belief and fortified the core of his theological insight.[24] The persuasiveness of the public preacher and the warmth of the communal experience meeting nurtured the spiritual experiences of the Calvinistic Methodists, but it was conversionism that underscored evangelical religiosity. The moment of conversion or reawakening could be the culmination of a process of emotional self-examination that led the believer through a sequence of anguish and guilt, before reaching an uplifting and relieving moment of religious faith and a conviction in the idea of the spiritual grace of the Christian God as infinitely loving and merciful. In the case of Methodism, conversion was often experienced as a sudden and startling revelation rather than as a gradual stirring of dedication.[25] The moment of decisive commitment for Thomas Jones (which along with his early nineteenth-century brethren he typically experienced as a young adult in his twenties) is said to have occurred at the Reverend Humphrey Gwalchmai's Bethel Street Chapel in Llanidloes.

In Wales, as much as they later did in India, Christianity's proponents set their belief in its enlightening effects against the gloom of primitivism, as Thomas Rees proclaimed when opening his 1861 history of Welsh Nonconformity:

> A movement, commenced by a few persecuted clergymen of the Established Church, which in the course of two centuries resulted in the elevation of the Welsh from the depths of moral degradation, ignorance, and superstition, to the highest rank amongst the enlightened Protestant nations of the world, not only without the aid and countenance of the State and the upper class, but under their frowns and against their most bitter and hostile opposition.[26]

Alwyn Rees's characterisation of the message derived by the pastoral and patriarchal Welsh rural worker from the Hebrew literature of the Christian Bible could easily be applied to Thomas Jones, as he sat reading by the light of a candle at Llifior Mill: 'a picture of tribal society in many ways reminiscent of his own . . . a people devoid of urban culture could fully share the contempt of Old Testament prophets for the extravagances of the cities of the plain'.[27] Perhaps too in their missionary impulse the bullied Nonconformists of the eighteenth century became the bullies of empire in the nineteenth. But if we determine that their conviction was instinctive and innate, that men like Thomas Jones who became evangelical missionaries could act in good faith and in concert with their true beliefs, are they therefore absolved of any guilt in their destruction of indigenous cultures? Perhaps this again is not the question; the historian may be charged instead to find the everyday conformities as well as contradictions of the individual exercise of mission and imperialism. In his actions, Jones could concur with and at times disrupt such goals, adapting daily practices to the circumstances of his belief, and in so doing tinkering with the machine of empire.

The call to mission

Soon after his spiritual conversion in 1834, Thomas Jones expressed his desire to become a missionary. This desire was fuelled by a number of factors: the general missionary inclination of the evangelical revival; and the particular knowledge he had at a local level of the endeavours of missionaries before him, and in particular of the work of John Davies, Tahiti. Perhaps too the 1839 revival in the churches in north Wales and Liverpool's Welsh chapels – influenced by the 1835 American publication of Charles Finney's *Lectures on Revivals of Religion* – was some spur to Jones's impulse for conversions.[28] A key characteristic that distinguished the eighteenth-century evangelical revival was the significance it gave to both local and foreign missionary activism, and there were few more dedicated exponents than the Methodists. Through the late eighteenth and early nineteenth centuries many Welsh Christian evangelicals were very much attentive to the need for the word of the gospel to be spread to the heathen. The Wesleyan Thomas Coke from Brecon in south Wales played a leading role in the establishment of local Methodist missions to north Wales and also foreign missions in the United States, the West Indies and Sierra Leone.

The missionary impulse was powerfully expressed in Welsh hymnology. The hymnody of Methodism as expounded by Charles Wesley in England and William Williams, Pantycelyn, in Wales, was central to its forms of worship, even more so for the Welsh for whom hymns formed the core of the liturgy.[29] From his first published collection of hymns in 1744 (*Aleluia I*), Williams regularly imbued his writings with a zeal for mission. One of his popular hymns, *Trysorau'r groes* ('Treasures of the cross'), was evocative of the lure of India ('There is more treasure in your name / Than all the treasures of India'). But most well known of his missionary hymns was *Dros y briniau'r tywyll niwlog* ('O'er those gloomy hills of darkness'), composed for the Methodist patron Selina, Countess of Huntingdon in the 1770s:[30] 'Let the Indian, let the negro / Let the rude barbarian see / That divine and glorious conquest / Once obtain'd on Calvary'.[31]

The Northamptonshire-born Baptist William Carey was inspired to mission by reading in the mid-1780s the accounts of the voyages of Captain James Cook to the South Seas, and publication of his *An Enquiry into the Obligations of Christians, to Use Means for the Conversion of the Heathens* (1792) inspired the foundation in Kettering in that year of the first evangelical missionary society – the Particular Baptist Society for Propagating the Gospel among the Heathen (later known as the BMS).[32] Carey exhorted his fellow Christians to take up Christ's commission to his apostles to 'go and teach all nations'. The practicability of such a mission was confronted by a range of impediments: 'either their distance from us, their barbarous and savage manner of living, the danger of being killed by them, the difficulty of procuring the necessaries of life, or the unintelligibleness of their languages'.[33] Carey inspired others to action, including Baptist minister John Ryland, and a broadly denominational Missionary Society was formed in 1795, and renamed the LMS in 1818. Its board of directors focused efforts first on the South Seas of the Pacific, where the first group of missionaries arrived at Tahiti on the *Duff* in March 1797.

Missionary zeal had been inspired in the Welsh Nonconformists of the late eighteenth century by leading ministers such as Thomas Charles, Bala and David Jones, Llangan. Jones had been present at the inaugural meetings of the LMS, and financial contributions from the Welsh were recorded from the first report of the society. Both Charles and Jones were elected to the board of directors in 1797, and the Welsh connection with the new movement was firmly established when John Davies was accepted as an LMS missionary in 1799. Welsh audiences were regularly informed of missionary activities across the globe, through the Missionary Society's *Transactions* as well as other publications.

John Davies had been born at Llanfihangel-yng-Ngwynfa in 1772, and was a contemporary of Thomas Jones's mother, Mary Owen. Indeed his first experiences of the Calvinistic Methodist cause were at the *seiat* at her home at Penllys, and he was intimately associated with the circle of Ann Griffiths and the Reverend John Hughes, Pontrobert. Davies and Hughes had for a time conducted an itinerant school established by Thomas Charles, and prior to his missionary career Davies had been teaching at Llanwyddelan.[34] Thomas Jones's family roots were therefore not only embedded in the heartland of Calvinistic Methodism, but were intimately linked with the first Welsh missionary activities under the auspices of the newly formed LMS.

The East India Company (EIC) had long restricted the admission of missionaries to India on the grounds that it was in direct conflict with their commercial operations. Evangelical Charles Grant was appointed a director of the EIC in 1794, and his *Observations on the State of Society among the Asiatic Subjects of Great Britain* set the scene for the shift in EIC policy towards missionaries, which eventually came to fruition in the *Charter Act 1813*. This act abolished the trade monopoly in India of the EIC, and also allowed missionaries to enter. The Welsh provided three further missionaries under the auspices of the LMS. Evan Evans, Llanrwst, sailed for South Africa with Scottish Congregationalist missionary Robert Moffatt, and died in 1828 soon after ill-health forced his return to Wales. Manchester-born Isaac Hughes was sent out as a missionary artisan to Africa in 1823, and worked there until his death in 1870. Liverpool-born Josiah Hughes had initially hoped to be sent to India, but the directors sent him to Malacca. Hughes fell out with the London directors and his co-workers, and split from the LMS in 1836.[35]

The rejection of Welsh missionary candidates by the LMS

Despite the involvement of their countrymen in some of the formative operations of the British missionary movement, the Welsh Calvinistic Methodists were to become increasingly disaffected when the LMS began to reject their candidates. It was an emblem of pride to many in the Welsh church that despite the poverty of many of their supporters, they were ardent contributors to the missionary cause. 'Missionary sheep' and 'missionary chickens' were donated by poor rural workers to raise money for the society (over £36,000 during a forty-four-year period to 1840).[36]

The rejection of the Reverend David Morgan of Welshpool, a strongly recommended and eminently qualified candidate, was seen as more than just a simple oversight. For the Reverend David Charles, Carmarthen (brother of Thomas Charles, Bala), it reeked of 'Egotism, Bigotry & Malevolence' and a deep-seated prejudice against the Welsh. In highlighting their financial contributions, Charles was also articulating a particular sense of Welsh identity, locating its proud, self-sufficient, hard-working and God-fearing people in a rural heartland:

> whatever the sums might have been, they were obtained by much gratuitous ministerial exertion, – not in rich populous cities – but from a population covering many hundred miles. They were not the excressencies [*sic*] of excessive capitals, nor the surplus of the superabundance of lucrative commerce, but they were the collective droppings from brows seldom dry from the sweat of extreme labour, and were augmented by many a last mite of pious poverty . . . Not a stone of the many hundred chapels they have erected has been laid with English money. No cases from them have been cringing at the doors of the rich citizens on the banks of the Thames. No sums have crossed the Severn to their assistance.[37]

William Alers Hankey, Scottish-born ex-banker and treasurer of the LMS, sought to assure the Welsh that Morgan's rejection did not proceed from any lack of respect on the part of the LMS for the

Calvinistic Methodist body, but rather was on account of Morgan's deficiencies of language, being a native Welsh speaker, as if this in itself were reason enough.[38]

One of the firmest supporters of the LMS was the Reverend John Elias, the 'Anglesey Pope'. As 'the most popular preacher of his generation', one of the original group of ministers ordained in 1811 and the principal architect of the 1823 *Cyffes Ffydd y Methodistiaid Calfinaidd* (Confession of Faith of the Calvinistic Methodists), he was a strict adherent of religious orthodoxy and had become by the 1830s the doyen of the Welsh Calvinistic Methodist Church. In 1835, Elias wrote to the Reverend John Arundel, Home Secretary of the LMS, asking that an explanation be sent to the upcoming Bala Association as to why another Welsh candidate, Owen J. Rowlands from Anglesey, had been turned away. Elias noted that when Morgan had been rejected as a missionary candidate in 1822, 'I had much to do, to prevent our connexion to turn their collections to another chanel [*sic*]'.[39] Arundel's response demanded that the Welsh be obedient to the decision of the directors, and explained Rowlands's rejection on the grounds of his ill health, depressed spirits and poor communication skills. The latter deficiency, according to the directors, might arise from his poor English-language skills: 'surely your Christian friends will never withdraw from a Society because in *one* instance the Directors have had different views from them'.[40]

Others were more nervous about calling the Welshmen's bluff. Independent Minister William Griffiths wrote from Anglesey to the LMS, reporting the undertow of unrest among the Calvinistic Methodists: 'They have gone so far as to talk of entirely withdrawing from the Society . . . They are already prone to be a little jealous of us Independents, and on the present occasion think they have been unjustly despised'.[41] John Foulkes wrote to Arundel on behalf of the Welsh connection, reporting on the deliberations of the Quarterly Association at Bala. The Welsh were seriously aggrieved: unhappy with the reasons given for the rejection of Rowlands, who the Association concurred was a fit, pious and competent candidate; perturbed that even those of their number who sat as directors of the LMS had unaccountably not been informed of the decision; affronted that in accordance with their Rules, Disciplines and Confessions of Faith, an insult to one of their brethren was a slur on their body as a whole. The LMS was also seen to have reneged on a promise given to the late Reverend David Charles when Morgan had been rejected in 1822, 'that if in case any individual should *afterwards* be submitted to their notice by our connexion he would be *accepted*'. Foulkes demanded that if a satisfactory explanation were not received by the time of the Quarterly Association at Bangor the following month, the Welsh would sever their links with the LMS.[42]

The mood of the Bangor meeting was split, some supporting the withdrawal of missionary funding to the LMS, others favouring its continuance.[43] 'I feel dear Sir', wrote Elias, 'more sorrow than I can express that things have come to this crisis . . . I truly fear that our connexion with your Society is at an end!'[44] The Welsh had not officially given up on their goal of having a candidate accepted, and were taking active steps to ensure that the next candidate they offered would be irresistible. The 1837–38 LMS accounts noted contributions from the Montgomeryshire churches 'Paid for the Education of Mr. T. Jones, the intended missionary'.[45] Late in 1838, letters in support of the Welsh 'acting independently in our foreign missionary efforts' were tabled at both the Bangor and Ruthin Associations. The missionary candidate Thomas Jones was to be the final test case as to the sincerity of the LMS towards its Welsh supporters. Aside from any ethnic dimension to the rejection of the Welsh, as Piggin notes there is evidence that the 'rather respectable directors' of the LMS were exercising their discretion along sectarian lines, deliberately shunning applicants tainted with Arminian views and the 'imputation of methodism'. The fundamental principle of non-denominationalism that had been enshrined in the LMS constitution was effectively being disregarded. Of those missionaries it sent to India prior to 1859, over 85 per cent were Congregationalist.[46]

The Thomas Jones case

Around August 1839, the LMS had received an intimation from Jones of his wish to become a missionary, and soon considered Jones's formal answers to its standard questionnaire for intending missionary candidates. The answers reveal that from the time of confirming his devotion to the cause and the stirrings of his missionary instincts in 1834, he began his activities as 'some kind of a preacher', although prior to this watershed moment he 'had been a teacher in the Sabbath School for many years before, and had also been much engaged in the distribution of tracts &c'. He joined the first intake of students at a newly formed theological college at Bala, where he studied theology, mathematics and the classics. The college had been opened in 1837 as a private institution for ministerial education under the direction of Lewis Edwards and David Charles, who had completed a BA at Oxford in 1835. Edwards had an MA from Edinburgh University, and in 1836 had married Charles's sister Jane, the granddaughter of Thomas Charles. Her illustrious forebear had once made Bala 'the Jerusalem for the Methodists of north Wales',[47] and had been a great proponent not just of education, but education in *Welsh*, the lingua franca. 'As to the *expediency* of teaching young people, in the first place', Charles had written in 1816, 'to read the language they generally speak and best understand, if imparting religious knowledge is our primary object . . . it needs no proof, for it is self-evident'.[48]

His tutors from Bala concurred that Jones 'possesses in an eminent degree all the essential qualifications of a Missionary'.[49] The LMS medical adviser Dr Conquest, however, reported unfavourably on Jones's health for a posting to the West Indies, but on 25 November resolved that he be appointed as a missionary to South Africa.[50] The longstanding fears of the Welsh constituency may well have been assuaged, but Jones now had other ideas. At a board meeting on 23 December, a letter from Jones was read in which he claimed that the question of his health had been misunderstood, that he believed he could tolerate the climate of India, and that India was the place he had set his mind on since he had first felt the call to mission. The board resolved to inform Jones that this was simply not possible, and 'that in India a higher state of education is required than is desirable from him, at his period of life, to remain at home to attain'.[51] Again the issue of physical and mental capability intertwined in a complex and ambiguous helix.

On 23 January 1840, Thomas Jones sought advice from John Roberts, an elder at Liverpool's Bedford Street Chapel and an avid supporter of missionary work. LMS members John Arundel and Arthur Tidman had advised Jones that should he secure new and more favourable medical opinions, then the board might 'accede to your wishes, & send you to the East Indies'. But Roberts was perturbed:

> I cannot see how you can get off your engagement with the Society in an honourable manner, & although I should rejoice heartily if you were free from them altogether, without occasioning any reproach to yourself or our connexion, I am inclined to think that, under all the circumstances, it would be better for you to go out under their direction. I should however let them know (was I in your place) that I hoped they did not intend to treat me as 'an enemy in the camp', but expected to be allowed the same liberties as are enjoyed by their other missionaries.[52]

At the next meeting, Jones tabled medical reports favourable to an Indian posting, but to no avail.[53] The board was resolute: 'That as Mr Thomas Jones, Missionary Student from Bala appointed to South Africa has refused to accept the appointment, and the Committee with the medical opinions before them do not feel at liberty to select any other Station, and regarding his decision as equivalent to declining the service of the Society, his connexion with the Society be considered as dissolved'.[54]

Jones returned to Liverpool, and delivered an account of his rejection to a meeting held at Rose Place Chapel on 31 January, convened by John Roberts, who tabled a motion 'that we incorporate as a Foreign Missionary Society, and that Rules be drawn out to be presented to the Quarterly Association at Llanfaircaereinion [*sic*]'.[55] While some leading figures in the church saw the move as precipitous, the proposal was carried.[56] For John Roberts, it seemed, the time was ripe: 'I have been long anxious that we should establish a Society of our own, & rejoice not a little that there is now some prospect of this being done'.[57]

A letter detailing the resolution of the Liverpool meeting was tabled at the Llanfair Caereinion Association on 28 April. Well aware 'that we are undertaking a great responsibility', the renegades also appealed to a higher authority 'of Him who said, "Go ye into all the world and preach the gospel to every creature"'.[58] To the supporters of an independent Welsh mission, it was a strategic move to put their resolution to the floor in Montgomeryshire, where the depth of feeling was resolute for mission generally and for Thomas Jones in particular. Important too was the absence from the meeting of John Elias, one of the main opponents of the split, due to ill health. The decision to form the WFMS was taken unilaterally by the North Wales Association, and it was not until after an Incorporated Assembly of representatives from the churches of both north and south Wales in August 1841 that the action was finally settled on with unanimity.[59]

Thomas Jones's desire for India had clearly been influenced by the Reverend Humphrey Gwalchmai and rejected missionary candidate David Morgan.[60] Well before the formal decision to split, the inclination demonstrated by the Montgomeryshire brethren in late 1838 to separate from the LMS was revealed in correspondence between the Reverend Jacob Tomlin and Morgan, whose desire to put himself forward as a missionary had evidently been rekindled. Tomlin had joined the LMS in 1826 and was appointed to work in Malacca. In 1844 he published his *Missionary Letters and Journals*, an account of eleven years' work in the Far East. Tomlin had refused a recall issued by his directors, and his connection with the LMS was terminated in 1834. In Malacca, he had befriended the Welsh missionary Josiah Hughes. Tomlin ran a school in Malacca for a short time before deciding to return to England, but after finding himself in Calcutta after his ship caught fire, he ended up spending nine months in the Khasi Hills in 1837. On his return to England in May 1838, Tomlin lived for a time in Liverpool where he was a friend of the Welsh community. There was no love lost between the Baptist missionary and the body that had spurned him, and he actively advised the Welsh Calvinistic Methodists in their own squabble with the LMS.[61]

The June 1839 issue of the Calvinistic Methodist monthly denominational magazine *Y Drysorfa* (The Treasury)[62] included one of Tomlin's replies to Morgan, in full support of the Welsh desire to form a breakaway missionary society.[63] Tomlin advised the Welsh to consider Malacca and Manipur as fields of labour for their missionary activities. But it was the 'ignorant and superstitious' natives of the Khasi Hills that seemed to most take his fancy. Like 'sheep without a shepherd' but having no idols or temples, they would also in Tomlin's view be more amenable to Christian conversion than the lowland Hindus.

John Roberts had also been quick to glean intelligence. Prior to the Llanfair Caereinion Association, he had written to the Church of Scotland missionary, the Reverend Dr John Wilson, in Bombay informing him of the recent decisive action to form a missionary society.[64] Roberts was appointed Foreign Secretary to the WFMS, and as he flicked through all the books about India on his shelves, he could find no reference at all to the Khasi Hills. Acutely aware of the responsibility now facing the new society, his joy and enthusiasm at having finally 'obtained my long-wished for object' was tempered by an intense anxiety 'lest we should fail in our enterprize'. Roberts wrote to Tomlin in early May soliciting further information on the practicalities of establishing a mission in the Khasi Hills.[65] The Welsh Missionary Society reported the progress of their research to the Dolgellau Quarterly Association in October 1840, having finally decided to send Thomas Jones to the Khasi Hills on account of its favourable climate and relatively cheaper cost of living.[66]

'The hills of Kassiah' beckon

As a clerk of the shipping company J.B. Yates & Co., Roberts's connections proved useful to the infant society. A cargo ship, the *Jamaica*, was being loaded, and was due to sail to Calcutta on 6 November, and the ship's commander, Captain Gibson, had agreed to carry Thomas Jones and his new wife Ann – whom he had recently married in Liverpool – for £50 less than the usual fare. A message was sent out to the chapels for prayers, financial support and blankets to distribute among the natives.

The letter addressed to the Dolgellau Association had caused something of a stir. The berth secured had been presented by Roberts as a providential intervention, but as he would have been well aware was more likely to have been an important strategic initiative to snuff out once and for all the opposition that would have been voiced at the meeting by those still not convinced of the probity of the split. Roberts's support for the missionary cause was bearing fruit; indeed, a suggestion that a special prayer should be offered up for Thomas Jones at the monthly prayer meetings was seconded by none other than the Reverend John Elias, who 'after making several attempts to throw discredit on our proceedings, appeared prior to the close of the meetings to have come round very much'.[67]

A full and extensive account by John Roberts of the farewell meeting for Thomas Jones at an overflowing Rose Place Chapel on 4 November was published as a supplement to the December issue of *Y Drysorfa*.[68] John Roberts carefully constructed his narrative version of the three and a half hour ceremony to underscore his Christian belief in the providential favours wrought through small signs of his God's presence. As a prelude, the congregation sang a hymn to the tune of 'Calcutta', a melody composed by Reginald Heber, writer of the most popular nineteenth-century missionary hymn, *From Greenland's Icy Mountains to India's Coral Strand* (1819), and later Bishop of Calcutta. As Catherine Hall has noted, in the hymn's imperialist language, there was no greater emblem of colonialism's 'contradictory and ambivalent legacy'.[69]

Further lengthy preliminaries included scriptural readings and the anointing of the society officials. Prayers for mission were now being replaced by actions: 'will you be willing', the Reverend Ellis Phillips asked the mothers and fathers in the crowd, 'to release the boys whom you intend to raise up as heirs to your possessions, to go as missionaries for him to a far off country'? Finally, Thomas Jones was introduced to the meeting. 'Many (especially amongst the women) were weeping copiously', recorded John Roberts, 'and my emotions were so agitated, that in vain I tried to write down what my friend said with any consistency'. In an extensive narrative, Jones recounted his call to mission, the inner torment he felt at leaving his family, and conquering his own self-doubt as to his spiritual steadfastness. Jones fashioned himself as a jack-of-all-trades, well suited to the role: 'I will not have a house to live in, if I do not build it myself; nor meat to eat if I don't become a butcher'. As the spellbound congregation visualised, he pledged his willingness to sacrifice himself to their cause: 'I have never been able to think of this, without being willing to die – drowning at sea, starving in the desert, being torn to pieces by tigers in India, or killed by barbarians; and I cannot consider going now without being willing for this if the Lord wills it'. After his address, Thomas Jones signed a pledge of assent to Rule IX of the Confessions of Faith, vouching his obedience to the disciplinary rules of the denomination and vowing to teach only doctrine consistent with the Calvinistic Methodist faith.

The Reverend John Hughes, Pontrobert, then pointed to the examples of Morrison and Carey, who rose from humble beginnings to become two of the most famous missionaries of their era and who translated the Bible into Chinese and Indian dialects respectively. When the time for departure finally came, hundreds were at the Pier Head to see the ship sail, 'and many were the tears shed by men and women, as they bade farewell to our brother and sister, whose faces will very probably never be seen again by many of us, if not all'. An especially composed Welsh *awdl* (heroic poem) was dedicated to the Reverend Thomas Jones and his wife Ann. 'The sons of the Lord God are coming', chanted the Christian faithful across the water, 'You will pull all the Khassians from the ravine of ungodliness'.

Notes

1 Sanjay Seth, 'Which good book? Missionary education and conversion in colonial India', *Semeia* (2001), 113–28.

2 Ryan Dunch, 'Beyond cultural imperialism: cultural theory, Christian missions, and global modernity', *History and Theory*, 41:3 (2002), 301–25.

3 Jane Aaron, 'Slaughter and salvation: Welsh missionary activity and British imperialism' in Charlotte Williams, Neil Evans and Paul O'Leary (eds), *A Tolerant Nation? Exploring Ethnic Diversity in Wales* (Cardiff, 2003), p. 38.

4 See William Williams, *Welsh Calvinistic Methodism: A Historical Sketch of the Presbyterian Church of Wales* (Bridgend, 1998, first published London, 1872), pp. 224–6.

5 From *Methodistiaeth Trefaldwyn Uchaf*, p. 125 in D.W. Smith, 'Berriew in the eighteenth century', *The Montgomeryshire Collections*, 70 (1982), 124.

6 Donald G. Knighton, 'English-speaking Methodism' in Lionel Madden (ed.), *Methodism in Wales: A Short History of the Wesley Tradition* (Llandudno, 2003), p. 2.

7 Williams, *Welsh Calvinistic Methodism*, p. 209.

8 E. Wyn James, 'Bala and the Bible. Thomas Charles, Ann Griffiths and Mary Jones', www.anngriffiths.cardiff.ac.uk/bible.html (accessed 14 October 2007), citing Henry Hughes, Bryncir, *Hanes Diwygiadau Crefyddol Cymru* (Caernarfon, [1906]).

9 Rees (ed.), *Vehicles of Grace & Hope*, pp. 100–3.

10 Alwyn D. Rees, *Life in a Welsh Countryside: A Social Study of Llanfihangel yng Ngwynfa* (Cardiff, 1961, first published 1950), particularly pp. 109–30, from where the short quotations are drawn.

11 Paul Chambers, 'Religious diversity in Wales' in Neil Evans, Charlotte Williams and Paul O'Leary (eds), *A Tolerant Nation? Exploring Ethnic Diversity in Wales* (Cardiff, 2003), p. 125.

12 Richard Foster (ed.), *Liverpool's South Docks. An Archaeological and Historical Survey. Part I Mann Island – Wapping Basin* (Liverpool, n.d.).

13 Glyn Williams, *The Desert and the Dream: A Study of Welsh Colonization in Chubut, 1865–1915* (Cardiff, 1975).

14 K.O. Morgan, *Rebirth of a Nation: Wales 1880–1980* (Cardiff and Oxford, 1981), pp. 6–7, cited in R. Merfyn Jones, 'The Liverpool Welsh' in D. Ben Rees (ed.), *The Liverpool Welsh and their Religion: Two Centuries of Welsh Calvinistic Methodism* (Liverpool, 1984), p. 37.

15 John Hughes Morris, *Hanes Methodistiaeth Liverpool* (Liverpool, 1929).

16 Jones, 'The Liverpool Welsh', p. 23.

17 Richard Williams, 'Montgomeryshire worthies', *Collections Historical & Archæological Relating to Montgomeryshire and its Borders*, 16 (1883), 223; biographical sketch of Thomas Jones by Katie Pritchard of Berriew, *Monthly Tidings*, 1891, quoted in David Pryce, 'History of the Calvinistic Methodist (Presbyterian) churches in the Montgomeryshire and Salop borders', n.d., typescript, p. 54.

18 Smith, 'Berriew in the eighteenth century', 128.

19 LMS, Candidates Papers.

20 Christopher Hill, *The World Turned Upside Down: Radical Ideas during the English Revolution* (Harmondsworth, 1975), esp. chs 9 and 10.

21 Charles Buck, *A Theological Dictionary* (Philadelphia and Pittsburgh, 1830, first published 1802), p. 219.

22 Thomas Rees, *History of Protestant Nonconformity in Wales* (London, 1861), pp. 416–17.

23 Williams, *Welsh Calvinistic Methodism*, pp. 248, 245.

24 William Williams, *The Experience Meeting: An Introduction to the Welsh Societies of the Evangelical Awakening, tr. Mrs Lloyd-Williams* (London, 1973), p. 52.

25 D.W. Bebbington, *Evangelicalism in Modern Britain: A History from the 1730s to the 1980s* (London, 1989), pp. 5–8.

26 Rees, *History of Protestant Nonconformity in Wales*, p. 1.

27 Rees, *Life in a Welsh Countryside*, p. 129.

28 Rees, *History of Protestant Nonconformity in Wales*, p. 460; Bebbington, *Evangelicalism*, p. 116.

29 'William Williams, Pantycelyn; 1717–91' in John Davies, Nigel Jenkins, Menna Baines and Peredur I. Lynch (eds), *The Welsh Academy Encyclopedia of Wales* (Cardiff, 2008), p. 963.

30 E. Wyn James, 'Welsh ballads and American slavery', *The Welsh Journal of Religious History*, 2 (2007), 59–86.

31 Rev. J. Aldrich, *The Sacred Lyre: A New Collection of Hymns and Tunes, for Social and Family Worship* (Boston, New York and Cincinnati, 1859), p. 169.

32 William Carey, *An Enquiry into the Obligations of Christians* (Leicester, 1792).

33 S. Pearce Carey, *William Carey D.D.: Fellow of the Linnaean Society* (London, 1924), p. 67.

34 Morris, *The History*, pp. 310–11.

35 Rees, 'Hughes, Josiah (1804–1840)' in Rees (ed.), *Vehicles of Grace & Hope*, pp. 65–6; Morris, *The History*, pp. 310–12.

36 Morris, *The History*, pp. 27–9.

37 Charles to Directors of LMS, August 1822, Copy in CMA 27159

38 Hankey to Charles, 4 September 1822, Copy in CMA 27159.

39 Elias to Arundel, 7 April 1835, FBN LON 4.

40 LMS to Elias, 2 June 1835, FBN LON 4.

41 Griffiths to LMS, 8 June 1835, FBN LON 4.

42 Foulkes to Arundel, 27 August 1835, FBN LON 4.

43 Davies to Arundel, 12 September 1835, FBN LON 4.

44 Elias to LMS, 12 September 1835, FBN LON 4.

45 *Report of the Directors to the Forty-fourth General Meeting of the Mission Society, Usually Called the London Missionary Society, on Thursday, May 10th, 1838* (London, 1838), p. lix.

46 Piggin, *Making Evangelical Missionaries*, p. 110.

47 James, 'Bala and the Bible'.

48 Williams, *Welsh Calvinistic Methodism*, p. 194.

49 Quoted in letter from Roberts to Wilson, February 1840, CMA 28720.

50 LMS Board Minutes Box 26, pp. 443–4, Item 45, 25 November 1839.

51 CMA 27159; notes relevant to the London Missionary Society, 23 December 1839.

52 Roberts to Jones, Liverpool, 25 January 1840, CMA 28720.

53 Copies of the Rev. Thomas Jones's Health Certificates, NLW.

54 LMS Board Minutes Box 26, p. 498, Item 15, 27 January 1840.

55 Morris, *The History*, p. 38.

56 *Ibid.*

57 Roberts, [4] March 1840, CMA 28720.

58 Morris, *The History*, p. 40.
59 The name 'The Welsh Calvinistic Methodists' Foreign Missionary Society' was finally adopted by mid-1843. See Morris, *The History*, p. 47.
60 Biographical sketch of Thomas Jones by Katie Pritchard of Berriew, *Monthly Tidings*, 1891.
61 R. Arthur Hughes, 'The romance of Rose Place', 1981, pamphlet in National Library of Wales, CMA E43/7; Rees (ed.), *Vehicles of Grace & Hope*, pp. 65–6, 225–6. As Rees notes, Tomlin's *Missionary Journals and Letters Written During Eleven Years' Residence and Travels amongst the Chinese, Siamese, Javanese, Khassias, and Other Eastern Nations* (London, 1844) was printed in Chester by Thomas Thomas, a Calvinistic Methodist elder who also printed *Y Drysorfa*. John Roberts is listed as a subscriber.
62 The monthly newsletter of the Calvinistic Methodists, published 1831–1968. Huw Walters notes in *Llyfryddiaeth Cylchgronau Cymreig* (A Bibliography of Welsh Periodicals 1735–1850) NLW, 1993, that 'the Welsh denominational monthlies were the main sources for both local and national news before the tax on advertisements and the stamp duty on newspaper copies were abolished in 1853 and 1855'. Cited at www.genuki.org.uk/big/wal/WelshPeriodicals.html (accessed 1 December 2010).
63 *Y Drysorfa*, June 1839, 185–6.
64 Roberts to Wilson, February 1840 (signed by 19 of the directors and board members), CMA 28720.
65 Roberts to Tomlin, 9 May 1840, CMA 28720.
66 Roberts to the Editor, 19 October 1840, *Y Drysorfa*, November 1840, 349–50.
67 John Roberts to Joseph Roberts, 28 October 1840, CMA 28720.
68 Roberts to the Editor of *Y Drysorfa*, 15 December 1840, *Y Drysorfa*, Supplement, December 1840, 385–92.
69 Hall, *Civilising Subjects*, p. 441.

CHAPTER TWO

Voyaging: two places at once

'Poor Jones', as John Roberts called him, had now been farewelled.[1] The fledgling mission organisation had drawn on all its resources to outfit Thomas and Ann for the voyage, and had seized the opportunity through Roberts's shipping connections to secure a cheap passage, for which sympathetic friends paid half. Jones's 'poverty' was no measure of his material circumstances, but rather the stark acknowledgement that there was a fair chance he would never return to his native shore. As a free agent under the banner of the rebel missionary society, Jones cleansed the bitterness from the mouths of old men who had seen the failure of candidate after candidate, and personified the impatience, initiative and idealism of the young. But in the midst of the eagerness and excitement of their leave-taking, there was still time for the Welsh congregation to heed that Thomas and Ann Jones were their sacrifice, a sister and a brother, a son and a daughter, surrendered for the sake of something their beliefs had them truly value more highly. 'Poor Jones' was their offering.

The *Jamaica* departed the Pier Head on 25 November 1840. After losing sight of the Welsh mountains and Ireland, Thomas and Ann headed for the Cape of Good Hope and on across the Indian Ocean to the Bay of Bengal. They were quite consciously the inheritors of those Welsh missionaries who had gone out under the auspices of the LMS – John Davies, Evan Evans, Isaac Hughes and Josiah Hughes. They left in Liverpool their family and the weight of expectation; ahead of them was only an idea. As for all first-time voyagers to India, this space between leaving and arriving was also a space of initiation into the practical ways of empire. As the human cargo of imperialism, the missionary now rubbed shoulders with the merchant, the sailor, the soldier and the civil servant. The real dangers of the sea voyage mingled with imagined fears and emotions, and for many agents of empire the personal motivations and meanings of their passage were challenged, fortified and sometimes changed. Dreaming about future prospects was also a metamorphosis into new roles; heading towards an idea of India was also heading away from Britain. Plotting the passage of the *Jamaica* as a metonym of the broader British imperial project in India also introduces key institutional frameworks, racialised ideologies and individual personnel – David Scott, Robert Lindsay, Henry Yule and William Lewin – important to an understanding of the practice of empire in the north-east.

Faith tested

As days became weeks, John Roberts plotted the *Jamaica* in its imaginary course to Calcutta. As month after month went by he could only suppose that the vessel had arrived at its destination, and he could only wait again until a return ship brought word of the mission's progress. The job of the home secretary would keep him only and forever at arm's length from his envoys. The intimacy of his personal connection with Jones would slowly but ineluctably be replaced with that of the correspondent, whose words and letters were second hand, set solid and immovable on the page, and which could never again be checked against direct speech, inflected with gesture or modulated by face-to-face expression.

Yet as mission secretary, Roberts's business had only just begun. He wasted no time in spreading the word of the mission's purpose and strengthening its supporters. On the day of Jones's departure he wrote to Alexander Duff, Free Church of Scotland missionary in Calcutta, with news that the Welsh were establishing a mission, and requesting information on the Khasi Hills for Jones. Roberts was acutely aware that the advancement of the Welsh mission would be materially advantaged by any intelligence that could be derived from experienced missionaries on the ground. Jones may have been crossing the Indian Ocean for the first time, but his vessel sailed in the wake of many previous missionary voyages, and both Wilson and Duff were key contacts.

Wilson had been ordained in June 1828, had married a minister's daughter Margaret Bayne in August, and within a month the newlyweds had sailed from Portsmouth on board the *Sesostris*, en route to their missionary field in Bombay. No diary exists of the Jones's crossing, but the shipboard experiences of the Wilsons just over a decade before might suggest some of the similar religious and emotional territory they traversed. For Margaret, the landscape of their departure was veiled in sadness as her beloved city of Edinburgh slipped from sight, Arthur's Seat 'like a dark cloud on the horizon'.[2] The 'deathlike stillness'[3] she felt at the prospect of leaving her loved ones was almost too oppressive to bear: 'I can, at such times', she wrote, 'see nothing before me but interminable wilderness, where all is barrenness, and where death, in his most appalling aspects, seems ready to seize upon me'.[4]

For all the missionary's training, preparation and idealism, it was on the sea voyage that a transmutation took place from aim to enactment, where the pious individual crossed the threshold of intention into the world of accomplishment. Having been dispatched, Jones became an emissary. Carrying a religious message in his head and heart, he now needed to acquire ways of performing his new identity as a missionary, and the ship's rhythms and spaces provided a multivalent setting for contemplation, struggle and transformation. The ship was laden with emotion, the yearnings of departure from loved ones carried up the gangplank with the material provisions. Like the Wilsons, the Joneses were only recently married, and this was also the first time the missionary couple had spent extended time in each other's company as man and wife. The ship was a site where periods of fear and self-doubt needed to be overcome with recommitment to the cause. Jones's nerve and his faith were continually tested, and answers found in Christian scripture from *'yr Hwn sydd yn dal y moroedd ar gledr ei law, ac yn casglu y gwynt ynei ddyrnau'* ('the One who holds the seas in the palm of his hand, and gathers the wind in his fists').[5]

Britain's was a maritime empire, but imperialising across the waves was certainly not without its risks. It was natural for the new hand to catastrophise, and fears of seasickness, foundering, shipwreck, pirates, or disease were never far from mind. The burial registers at St John's Church in Calcutta had numerous entries for passengers and crew who had sickened and died by the end of their voyage. An 1836 House of Commons Select Committee inquiry into the causes of shipwrecks estimated the annual loss of life at around a thousand people a year, and the cost to the British nation at £3m sterling per annum. Between 1807 and 1809, fourteen heavily laden trading ships had been lost to the EIC, their cargo valued at over a million pounds. A fleet of over a dozen ships, which had sailed from Madras via present-day Galle in Sri Lanka, ran into a great whirlwind in mid-March 1809 in the Indian Ocean, and suffered perhaps the greatest calamity of the EIC fleet.[6] Unable to navigate a course that gave a sufficiently wide berth to the hurricane region in the vicinity of Mauritius, the scudding convoy was taken by surprise, with the loss of the *Jane Duchess of Gordon*, the *Lady Jane Dundas*, the *Bengal* and the *Calcutta*.[7]

Lieutenant-General Hay Macdowall, who had gone down with the *Lady Jane Dundas*, had been returning to England in the aftermath of rebellion and disaffection in the Madras Presidency. *Sepoys* and *sowars* in the Indian Army mutinied at the garrison of Vellore near Madras in

July 1806, after they had been ordered by Lieutenant-General Sir John Craddock to be 'clean-shaved on the chin', to desist from wearing customary caste marks or earrings and to adopt hat-shaped turbans and leather belts, thus offending the religious sensibilities of Muslim and Hindu alike.[8] In the uprising, and the reprisals that followed, around 650 *sepoys* and 130 Europeans were killed. While a range of factors may have led to the uprising, a 'pamphlet war' erupted back in Britain on the subject of whether or not missionary activity had fuelled a fear of forced conversion among the native troops. Charles Grant had been pressing against Company policy for some years to foster Christian missions in India with government backing. Whatever the manifest reasons of the Vellore revolt, Grant played down religious conflict as a cause, and performed a skilful role in politicking for the eventual insertion of a clause in the 1813 *Charter Act* permitting the licensing of missionaries in India.[9]

Baptists such as William Carey had in the 1790s circumvented the ban by establishing a mission station in Danish territory at Serampore near Calcutta, and the 1813 charter renewal included a clause that permitted missionary ingress to India under licence from the Board of Control. William Wilberforce and his allies had won a decisive victory in their attempts to ameliorate 'fearful penances, licentious rites, female degradation, human sacrifices, and horrible infanticide'.[10] Others like MP Charles Marsh were not so sure about the benefits of Christianity, the contradictory doctrines of Calvinist, Unitarian, Methodist, Independent, Presbyterian, Swedenborgian and Moravian (perhaps themselves 'the dream of mysticism and folly'), or 'whether predestination and gin will be a compensation to the natives of India, for the changes, which will overwhelm their habits, and morals, and religion?'[11]

Religion, loyalty and service

Out of sight of land, the ocean over which the *Jamaica* sailed in late 1840 and early 1841 was a novelty for the Joneses. In the mind's eyes of those waiting back in Liverpool and Wales, the missionaries were flying across an indeterminate void ('*Cenhadon cu'n ehedeg – a fyddoch / O feddwl diatreg*'; 'Dear missionaries, flying – may you be / of a swift mind'), travelling to what was in their imagination a dark and sinister zone ('*Mewn ardaloedd tywyll iawn, / Bryniau Kassia*'; 'In the very dark areas / The hills of Kassia').[12] This India was vague and unfixed – and therefore their emissaries were cast as pioneers and adventurers on a voyage of discovery as well as an epic quest. In a sense, the India they had constructed was unspecific, not anchored to the detail of this particular time or that particular place. At another level, however, the Jones's voyage of discovery became an expedition that confirmed and validated the real India. In finding India, they also remade it. For Thomas Jones, the voyage was at once a metamorphosis (of becoming a missionary), and a process of imperial corroboration, in which all those who had preceded him – the military and mercantile men, missionaries like William Carey, Jacob Tomlin, the Wilsons and the Duffs – became fixed nodes in an interconnected cartography.

Alexander Duff had been twice shipwrecked before reaching Calcutta in 1830, but the enemy of the venturer could also be the torpid calm of the doldrums, or the light winds that beset the *Jamaica* after being a month or so at sea. But the religiously minded saw the hand and presence of God in all things, and biblical analogy was again used as the balm for exasperation or despair. Furnished with a sofa bed, some chairs, a small chest of drawers, and perhaps a water-stand that doubled as a writing desk, the cabin could be sanctuary from storm, seasickness or the constant company of the crew or other passengers. The candle that burned in a suspended glass lamp was an incessant cue to the motion of the ship. There was time and place for contemplation and meditation. There was also preparatory and productive space, where reading and study could profitably fill in the weeks and months at sea. Here Margaret Wilson commenced her study of Hebrew, and while it is unclear what books Thomas Jones had with him on the voyage, John Roberts had regarded as a boon the fact that 'a native of Hindustan' approached the Captain a few days before the *Jamaica* left, asking for a passage back to Calcutta. The Captain agreed, and he was seen as both a potential first convert for Thomas Jones, as well as a help in teaching him the Bengali language 'in which the few books published in the language of the dwellers of Kassiah have been printed'.[13] Day after day the *Jamaica* edged forward to its destination, and on each of these days Roberts worried about details. He was anxious about the fate of this 'colored youth' who he hoped was teaching Bengali to Thomas Jones. Friends in Liverpool and Bala had donated sundry items for the missionary and his wife, and John Roberts was annoyed too for forgetting in the haste of departure to supply the Joneses with soap.

Most importantly for the missionaries was keeping up Sabbath observance through family devotions and public worship. While the *Jamaica* was not an EIC ship, after 1773 the Company usually had a chaplain on board their vessels to keep up at least irregular services. By the 1820s a fine could be levied on ships' captains for neglecting to hold Sabbath observance without good reason.[14] A sympathetic Christian captain could be a source of comfort and support, turning the secular spaces of the vessel for a time into sacred ones. With the decks of the ship washed clean, the crew were rested from unnecessary work and tidied up their appearance to come to worship. The Captain might read the Sunday order of service or parts of a sermon, the missionary preaching to those assembled in a cabin or on the quarterdeck, or leading prayers to a group gathered on the forecastle in the evening. At other times, the missionaries might retreat below deck to the seclusion of their cabin: for example, during the 'folly and absurdity'[15] of the Neptune ceremonies on crossing the equatorial line, when there had been a tradition of newcomers paying for the crew's liquor. Among passengers and crew, the missionary could find the first objects of conversion, his wife teaching sailors to sing hymns, he counselling the grog-filled hands or the giddy young writers and idle cadets who lounged on the quarter deck and played cards in the cuddy.

It was on the voyage out to India that the spiritual chains binding soldiers to Christian virtue could start to loosen without the 'salutary and consoling' presence of a clergyman. The potential disaffection of European troops domiciled in India was also traced to an absence of the restraints of Christianity. Again in Madras, European officers in charge of a rebel force who marched from Chittledroog to Seringapatam in 1809 were court martialled for 'unofficerlike and highly disrespectful conduct, such as is subversive of military discipline'.[16] To some observers, the connection between rebellion and the absence of religious instruction was clear:

> Of the individuals engaged in the late disturbances at Madras, there were perhaps some, who have not witnessed the service of Christian worship for twenty years; whose minds were impressed by the daily view of the rites of the Hindoo religion, and had lost almost all memory of their own. It is morally impossible to live long in such circumstances, without being in some degree affected by them. That loyalty is but little to be depended on, whether abroad or at home, which has lost the basis of religion.[17]

But the duration of the voyage sometimes allowed for profound transformations. The nature of the connection between the flag and the cross – between missionary evangelism and colonial policy – is still much debated, and in particular the extent to which missionaries promoted or rode the coat-tails of imperial expansion.[18] Here on the ship, in the context of the post-1813 re-evaluation of missionary activity on the part of the government, the strands of religion and imperialism were being untwisted and spliced together in more unexpected ways. In his reminiscences, William Charles James Lewin – who was to greet the Joneses at Cherrapunji – characterised his eighteen-year-old self as excessively proud, obstinate, self-sufficient, licentious and superior. Newly qualified from the EIC's Military Academy in May 1822, for the novice artilleryman 'the desire of practising wickedness had been long rendered familiar to me by the example of my fellow students'.[19] Lewin left Portsmouth the following month, bound for India on the *David Scott*, and over the course of the voyage was drawn into contemplation of spiritual matters under the influence of the Reverend W.C., a chaplain proceeding to Bengal. A sudden hard gale was his road to Damascus; the violence of the storm 'suggested to my mind the idea of foundering, dissolution, eternity! How stood my soul? Had I repented of my past life? In this painful state of doubt and fear I sought the company of my friend, and was much surprised to find him reclining on his berth in calm and placid frame of mind . . . he assured me that if I was sincere in my repentance I should be accepted of God without reference to works. Thus I did receive comfort'.[20]

The following year, in 1823, Henry Havelock of HM's 13th Light Infantry sailed for Calcutta on board the *General Kydd*, and experienced a similar epiphany, as 'the Spirit of God came to him with its offer of peace and mandate of love, which, though for some time resisted, at length prevailed'.[21] The Christian could thus become, like the mariner, a 'humane navigator . . . as useful in directing sinners to avoid the shoals and rocks, &c. of life's treacherous ocean'.[22] If the soldier could become Christ's servant (while remaining a warrior), was there any danger that the solo missionary could be sullied with more worldly concerns? There perhaps, symbolically, lies an explanation as to why John Roberts was so unduly concerned about having forgotten in his haste to supply the Joneses with soap.[23] Out of sight of land, there were different points of reference, different lines of influence. The authority of the mission board could now only be sent in the mail, watered down. As the shoreline of Britain had been left behind, would Wales itself become for the Welsh missionary an abstraction?

Constructing centre and periphery

John Roberts was in limbo. Where the old East Indiamen of the eighteenth century might have struggled against currents and storms to complete the London–Calcutta trip in under six months, Roberts would have been confident that the passage of the *Jamaica* should take just a couple of months, though ships reaching Calcutta could still be delayed by some weeks navigating up the Hooghly River (a distributary of the Ganges).[24] Of course even if the Joneses had arrived in Calcutta in late January, he would not get return word of the fact much before April. Roberts was itchy but not idle. In a letter to John Wilson on 2 December 1840, he was more particular about why the Welsh had chosen to send missionaries to the Khasi Hills specifically, and encapsulated their intuitive rationale with disarming ingenuousness: 'many of our friends had felt, – I was nearly saying *instinctively* (for you know the Welsh are very fond of hilly countries) – a strong inclination to establish our first settlement there'.[25] The imperial instinct is here grounded literally as well as figuratively. Moreover, by invoking notions of homeland, belonging, and more particularly of Welshness, Roberts's reasoning ties the missionary enterprise with identity, and invests it with emotional as well as nationalist commitment. Such equivalence might work multidirectionally: as a motive for choice (the Welsh are fond of hilly countries), and as a strategy of cultural imperialism (hegemonic beliefs might be more easily laid over existing patterns that are familiar).

By January 1841, *Y Drysorfa* published the already dated news that as the weather had been fair and favourable, Thomas Jones was probably now past the Bay of Biscay and a quarter of the way through the voyage.[26] Roberts's eager thoughts and his anticipatory letters jumped ahead of the mission's physical progress. More subtly, as Jones's correspondence was always addressed through the office of the mission secretary, Roberts took on the job as reporter, translator, sometimes censor, a gatekeeper between the missionary in the field and the mission board in Liverpool.

On 28 January 1841 Roberts wrote to Jones by the overland mail, expecting his letter to reach Calcutta before Jones did, and to be in readiness to say 'Welcome to Calcutta, – How are you, & how is dear Mrs Jones, & how have you been? and all the other *Hows* which it may be customary or natural for one friend to ask another on shaking hands with him in a strange country'.[27] The laboriously slow East Indiamen laden with Company freight could take anywhere from four to eight months or even more to deliver mail from England to India in the late eighteenth and early nineteenth centuries. It could be a year before intelligence could be sent and a reply received. By the mid-1830s a quicker overland route, pioneered by Lieutenant Thomas Waghorn, had been authorised by the Post Office. Mail now by-passed the Cape of Good Hope and could reach India in less than two months.[28]

In the decades prior to the eventual opening of the Suez Canal in 1869, the distance from empire's edge was contracting, and the British were 'pulling the periphery of empire closer to the centre'.[29] Empire was negotiated in this in-between space. Like the peripatetic and ubiquitous Waghorn, who according to English novelist William Makepeace Thackeray 'can be at two places at once',[30] Britain and India could appear to be coterminous, their interchangeable boundaries enclosing routes of trade and exchange. Thomas Jones was being sent from rural Wales to the ends of the earth, to the darkest extremities of India, but both wittingly and unknowingly he was being stitched into the canvas of empire. Thackeray and Jones were born a year apart, one in Calcutta the son of an EIC secretary, the other to a wheelwright in Montgomery. It was an insignificant but telling measure of the possibility and the strength of the empire as a 'vast interconnected world' that Thackeray's wife would later be related to Thomas Jones by marriage.[31]

A few months before Roberts's letter had passed through, Scottish-born Lieutenant Henry Yule had also travelled to Aden via the overland route. The nineteen year old had been appointed to the Bengal Engineers in 1840. While Yule and Jones would cross paths in the Khasi Hills, his first assignment was to supervise the transport of meteorological instruments from England for the Aden observatory, to provide British ships with time-keeping for the rating of their chronometers. But on his arrival it was discovered that seawater had corroded essential parts of the equipment. New magnets were requested from England and later installed at the Colaba Island observatory at Bombay, where the cockroaches and white ants gnawed away at the documents in the chart office. With his assignment thwarted, at the end of September Yule was permitted to join his regiment in Calcutta.[32]

Yule's father Major William Yule had retired from the service of the EIC in 1806, and had donated an important collection of Persian and Arabic manuscripts to the British Museum. In 1840, the year after his father's death, young recruit Henry on his first voyage to India must have looked in wonder at the places he had long known from his father's reminiscences. Henry's notebooks soon filled up with notes and observations, some no doubt laying the foundation for what was nearly half a century later to become *Hobson-Jobson*, that remarkable compendium of Anglo-Indian words which for so many years was for Yule 'the companion of my *horae subsicivae*, a thread running through the joys and sorrows of so many years'.[33]

Where accounts of direct experiences were handed down family lines to the scions of the Indian service, essentialised views of Eastern customs and practices abounded more popularly in the stock motifs of British culture. Travel narratives as well as fiction provided a template for perception, and each new traveller was subservient to the shared lineages of imagery and the conventional motifs of culture and place that had gone before. Thackeray's pen portraits of the places he visited on his 1844 cruise to Cairo, derogatory through the European leg (Lisbon was a 'failure', Athens 'shabbier than Ireland', Malta 'not worth the trouble and sea-sickness'),[34] were more romanticised when it came to Turkey:

> Some men may read this who are in want of a sensation. If they love the odd and picturesque, if they loved the *Arabian Nights* in their youth, let them book themselves on board one of the Peninsula and Oriental vessels, and try one *dip* into Constantinople or Smyrna. Walk into the Bazaar, and the east is unveiled to you; how often and often have you tried to fancy this, lying out on a summer holiday at school! It is wonderful, too, how *like* it is; you may imagine that you have been in the place before, you seem to know it so well![35]

In a sense, travellers had already made the journey before they ever left England, and relationships of colonialism and racial superiority were implicit in the persistent literary *topoi* they created.[36] Antoine Galland's French rendition of *Les Mille et Une Nuits* (Paris, 1704–17) soon proliferated in English translation, and visitors to the East such as Thackeray enthusiastically checked the reality of what they saw with the literary version in their mind.[37] By the time Thackeray reached the pyramids, the dissonance between the authentic and the imagined world left him strangely unmoved: 'Several of us tried to be impressed', he admitted, 'but breakfast supervening, a rush was made at the coffee and cold pies, and the sentiment of awe was lost in the scramble for victuals . . . My sensation with regard to the Pyramids was, that I had seen them before: then came a feeling of shame that the view of them should awaken no respect'.[38]

If a negative and superficial depiction of the Orient formed as a counterbalance to the presumed superiority of the West, then the translations by William Yule or Sir William Jones of Eastern classics would seem to contradict imperial intentions. Any monolithic and reductive view of British hegemony would also make cultural contraband of the hundreds of volumes of ancient texts that Alexander Johnston had stowed on the ill-fated *Lady Jane Dundas*. 'What imperial purpose', queries Bernard Lewis, 'was served by deciphering the ancient Egyptian language, for example, and then restoring to the Egyptians knowledge of and pride in their forgotten, ancient past?'[39]

Finally, by April 1841, the *Jamaica* made her way up the Bay of Bengal towards the great mouth of the River Hooghly. Near Sagar Island to the east of the channel's opening, a pilot was taken on board to chart the vessel's course the eighty or so miles up to Calcutta. Snow-rigged pilot vessels criss-crossed Ballasore Road in search of ships, waiting their turn to mount the small red flag that signalled their place at the head of the queue. With its massive tidal range of twenty-two feet, the Hooghly had long been susceptible to silting up, and the notoriously shifting reefs, sandbars and islands at its entrance – whose names seemed as nonsensical and Learesque as their shape-shifting form (Codjee Deep, Peply Sand, the Eastern Brace, the Barabulla and the

Swatch of No Ground) – required skill, patience and high water to be navigated.[40]

The attraction of India to Thomas Jones's generation was tantalising; like the Scots, service in the Company or its army offered prospects for young Welshmen of fortune and adventure. Each time he had travelled the road from Garthmyl to the market town of Welshpool, Thomas Jones would likely have been reminded of the power, the possibilities and the reach of empire. A mile south of Welshpool, the commanding red walls and terraced baroque gardens of Powis Castle sit high on a narrow ridge overlooking the Severn Valley. Originally a medieval fortress of the Welsh princes of Powys, it was purchased by the Herbert family in 1587 and subsequently passed through marriage into the hands of Edward Clive, son of Robert Clive. Edward had taken up the position as Governor of Madras in 1798, playing a part in the successful final campaign against Tipu Sultan and the subsequent expansion of British supremacy in south India. But it was his father Robert ('Clive of India'), created first Baron Clive of Plassey, who was regarded by many as the founder of British rule in India. Having gone out as a writer in 1744, he later joined the EIC army and was involved in various campaigns against French interests in India, at the same time accumulating a large personal fortune. In early 1757 he led a campaign against Siraj-ud-daulah, the Nawab of Bengal, who had seized Calcutta and besieged the Company's defence post at Fort William. It was in a small dungeon there, known for generations as the Black Hole of Calcutta, that a number of captured British prisoners suffocated to death on the night of 20 June 1756. Whether or not there were the 123 casualties recorded in the contemporary account by John Zephaniah Holwell, the incident effectively licensed British retaliation and marked a watershed between commercial exploitation and more expansive imperial design. For Lord Curzon, Viceroy of India (1895–1905), the victims were 'men whose life-blood cemented the foundations of the British Empire in India'.[41] Robert Clive subsequently led an operation that overthrew the Nawab at the Battle of Plassey, replacing him with the more sympathetic Mir Jafar. As Governor of Bengal, Clive ushered in a period in which the EIC's stranglehold on trade and power was systematically assured. It was the battles at Plassey (1757), at Buxar (1764), and the Anglo-Mysore (1766–99) and Anglo-Maratha wars (1755–1818), that established and consolidated British supremacy in India. By the end of the eighteenth century, the rooms of Powis Castle were embellished with the dazzling booty of ivories, skins, textiles, weapons and jewels, the accumulated loot of Clive's depredations in Bengal after the victory at Plassey, and his son's spoils from Seringapatam, which included the jewelled tiger head finial from the throne of Tipu Sultan, and the golden hilt of his sword. While Thomas Jones may not have been privy to the plunder of artefacts that lay inside the castle walls, its outward splendour signified imperial power and control abroad as well as at home.

The south-east side of the mangrove covered and tiger infested Sagar Island boasted an ancient Hindu temple where pilgrims gathered annually in great numbers. Gangasagar (*Ganga Sagara*, Ocean Ganges) had long been a pre-eminent place of pilgrimage during Poush Sakranti in the Bengali calendar, when adherents converged at the holy confluence of the Ganges and the sea. In 1833, an EIC pilot had excavated from the mud of the island at the low water mark a marble sculpture nearly six feet high, representing the son god Surya, the visible and everyday manifestation of God. The sculpture once stood in the island's Temple of the Sun, in an ancient city long since ransomed to the sea, one of the most significant sacred places in eastern India whose last remnants were being washed away in the year the *Jamaica* sailed past.[42] For Serampore Baptist missionary William Ward, Sagar Island featured as a backdrop for the cruelties of Hindu superstition:

> At Saugar island, formerly, mothers were seen casting their living offspring amongst a number of alligators, and standing to gaze at these monsters quarrelling for their prey, beholding the writhing infant in the jaws of the successful animal, and standing motionless while it was breaking the bones and sucking the blood of the poor innocent! What must be that superstition, which can thus transform a being, whose distinguishing quality is tenderness, into a monster more unnatural than the tiger prowling through the forest for its prey![43]

Criticisms of the practice of sati and infanticide were bound up with broader Christian missionary depiction of Hinduism as a morally inferior and conflicted religion.[44]

While Charles Marsh had noted in 1813, in his argument to the House of Commons against the need or desirability for missionaries in India, that it was Lord Wellesley rather than any missionary who had extirpated the evil practices of infanticide on Sagar Island, the trickle of missionaries under licence after 1813 had become a stream by the 1830s.[45] As the river pilot pointed out these features of the delta to the new arrivals, the Joneses would have caught on the breeze the memory of a refrain from the hymn composed on their departure in November, which had made perfectly explicit the purifying purpose on a degenerate religion of spreading the word of the Christian gospel:[46]

> It will teach the wife* to gaze tenderly,
> Upon the face of her beloved baby,
> Saying 'The babe of Bethlehem
> Suffered for you'.

† This will teach the Hindu son joyfully,
Smiling purely,
To pour the oil of peace on the sad, sad
Breast of his widowed mother . . .

* In reference to the custom of the women of this place of throwing their babies to the Crocodile, as a sacrifice to their religion.
† A reference to the religion of the country, which forces the son to watch his widowed mother being buried alive with the body of her husband.

The missionaries made their way up the Hooghly, past the Company factories, gentlemen's residences and native villages, and finally arrived at Calcutta late on the Friday night of 23 April 1841, having travelled more than 11,000 miles in the two days short of five months since they had left Britain.

Notes

1 John Roberts to Joseph Roberts, 28 October 1840, CMA 28720.
2 John Wilson, *A Memoir of Mrs Margaret Wilson, of the Scottish Mission, Bombay: Including Extracts from her Letters and Journals* (Edinburgh, 1840), p. 119.
3 *Ibid.*, p. 117.
4 *Ibid.*, p. 111.
5 D.J., 26 November 1840, *Y Drysorfa*, January 1841, 20. A rendering of Proverbs 30:4: 'who hath gathered the wind in his fists? who hath bound the waters in a garment?'.
6 Evan Cotton, *East Indiamen: The East India Company's Maritime Service*, ed. Charles Fawcett (London, 1949), p. 136.
7 Edward Pelham Brenton, *The Naval History of Great Britain, from the Year MDCCLXXXIII to MDCCCXXXVI*, volume 2 (London, 1837), pp. 363, 691–4.
8 Devadas Moodley, 'Velore 1806: the meanings of mutiny' in Jane Hathaway (ed.), *Rebellion, Repression, Reinvention: Mutiny in Comparative Perspective* (Westport, CT, 2001), pp. 87–102.
9 C.H. Philips, *The East India Company 1784–1834* (London and New York, 2000, first published Manchester, 1940), pp. 163, 169.
10 'Resolutions of the committee of the Protestant society for the protection of religious liberty, 2 March 1813', from *Papers Respecting the Negociation for a Renewal of the East India Company's Exclusive Privileges*, 1813, pp. 276–8, in P.J. Marshall, *Problems of Empire: Britain and India, 1757–1813*, volume 2 (London and New York, 2000, first published 1968), p. 185.
11 Charles Marsh, 'Substance of the speech of Charles Marsh, Esq. in a committee of the House of Commons, July the 1st, 1813. In support of the amendment, moved by Sir Thomas Sutton, Bart. on the clause in the East-India Bill, "Enacting further facilities to persons to go out to India for religious purposes"', 1813, in *The Pamphleteer: Respectfully Dedicated to Both Houses of Parliament*, 4:2 (London, 1813), pp. 525, 527. See also Marshall, *Problems of Empire*, pp. 70–2.
12 *Y Drysorfa*, Supplement, December 1840, 392, 390.
13 John Roberts, 15 December 1840, *Y Drysorfa*, Supplement, December 1840, 391.
14 Cotton, *East Indiamen*, p. 77n.
15 Mary Lewis, 25 August 1842, Diary of her voyage from Liverpool to Calcutta, CMA 27223.
16 See summary of events in 'Madras occurrences', August–October, in E. Samuel, *The Asiatic Annual Register* (London, 1811), pp. 118–34.

17 Claudius Buchanan, 'Ecclesiastical establishment for British India' in *Two Discourses Preached before the University of Cambridge, on Commencement Sunday, July 1, 1810. And a Sermon Preached before the Society for Missions to Africa and the East; at their Tenth Anniversary. June 12, 1810. To which Are Added Christian Researches in Asia* (London, 1811), pp. 261–2.
18 Ian Copland, 'Christianity as an arm of empire: the ambiguous case of India under the Company, c.1813–1858', *The Historical Journal*, 49:4 (2006), 1025–54.
19 Lewin, T.H. (ed.), *The Lewin Letters: A Selection from the Correspondence & Diaries of an English Family 1756–1884*, volume 1 (London, 1909), p. 250.
20 *Ibid.*, p. 253.
21 John Clark Marshman, *Memoirs of Major-General Sir Henry Havelock, K.C.B.* (London, 1867), pp. 11–12.
22 *Calcutta Christian Observer*, June 1837, 326.
23 Roberts to Jones, 28 January 1841, CMA 28720.
24 Daniel R. Headrick, *The Tentacles of Progress: Technology Transfer in the Age of Imperialism, 1850–1940* (New York and Oxford, 1988), p. 20.
25 Roberts to Wilson, 2 December 1840, CMA 28720.
26 *Y Drysorfa*, January 1841, 20.
27 Roberts to Jones, 28 January 1841, CMA 28720.
28 John K. Sidebottom, *The Overland Mail* (London, 1948).
29 Edward Ziter, *The Orient on the Victorian Stage* (Cambridge, 2003), p. 44.
30 M.A. Titmarsh, N*otes of a Journey from Cornhill to Grand Cairo, by Way of Lisbon, Athens, Constantinople, and Jerusalem, Performed in the Steamers of the Peninsular and Oriental Company* (London, 1846), reprinted in William Makepeace Thackeray, *Burlesques; From Cornhill to Grand Cairo; and Juvenilia* (London, 1911), p. 366.
31 William Makepeace Thackeray married Isabella Shawe in 1836. Shawe's brother Merric married Ellen Cattell (the sister of Emma Cattell) in 1853.
32 Felix Driver, 'Yule, Sir Henry (1820–1889)', *Oxford Dictionary of National Biography* (Oxford, 2004), www.oxforddnb.com/view/article/30291 (accessed 4 February 2010); Robert MacLagan, 'Obituary: Colonel Sir Henry Yule, K.C.S.I., C.B., LL.D., R.E.', *Proceedings of the Royal Geographical Society and Monthly Record of Geography*, 12:2 (1890), 108–13; Lieutenant H. Yule to Captain Hobson, 24 September 1840, IOR F/4/1852, 78314; Clements R. Markham, *A Memoir on the Indian Surveys* (London, 1878); Gordon Waterfield, *Sultans of Aden* (London, 1968).
33 Henry Yule and A.C. Burnell, *Hobson-Jobson: The Anglo-Indian Dictionary* (Ware, Hertfordshire, 1996, first published 1886), p. viii; IOR L/MIL/10/32, 347.
34 Titmarsh, *Notes of a Journey*, pp. 274, 280.
35 *Ibid.*, p. 280.
36 Rana Kabbani, *Europe's Myths of Orient: Devise and Rule* (London, 1986), p. 10.
37 Fatma Moussa-Mahmoud, 'English travellers and the *Arabian Nights*' in Peter L. Caracciolo (ed.), *The* Arabian Nights *in English Literature: Studies in the Reception of* The Thousand and One Nights *into British Culture* (London, 1988), p. 95.
38 Titmarsh, *Notes of a Journey*, p. 363.
39 Bernard Lewis, *Islam and the West* (Oxford, 1993), p. 126.
40 Rhoads Murphey, 'The city in the swamp: aspects of the site and early growth of Calcutta', *The Geographical Journal*, 130:2 (1964), 248; James Horsburgh, *The Indian Directory*, volume 1, 5th edition (London, 1841), pp. 613–36.
41 Jan Dalley, *The Black Hole: Money, Myth and Empire* (London, 2006), p. xiii.
42 'An ancient Hindu sculpture', *Bulletin of the Pennsylvania Museum*, 5:20 (1907), 68; Yule and Burnell, *Hobson-Jobson*, p. 798; Dineschandra Sircar, *Studies in the Geography of Ancient and Medieval India* (Delhi, 1971), pp. 223–4.
43 William Ward, '*The Hercules*, at sea, April 2 1821', to the Rev. Dr Steadman of Bradford, in William Ward, *Farewell Letters to a Few Friends in Britain and America, on Returning to Bengal in 1821* (Lexington, 1822), pp. 78–9.

44 Brian K. Pennington, *Was Hinduism Invented? Britons, Indians, and the Colonial Construction of Religion* (Oxford, 2005), pp. 82–3.
45 Marsh, 'Substance of the speech of Charles Marsh', p. 525.
46 *Y Drysorfa*, Supplement, December 1840, 392.

CHAPTER THREE

Networks and precursors

William Carey, whose voyage to Calcutta in 1793 had also taken five months less two days, had arrived in India with no intention of ever returning to England, though he could not have dreamt that his work in India would last forty unbroken years until his death at Serampore in 1834.[1] As Thomas Jones arrived in Calcutta in April 1841, he had a similar resolve in mind. His strength of purpose had been hinted at in his application to the LMS in 1839, in which he expressed his missionary calling not simply as the professed duty of any young Christian man, but as a determination 'to go whether any Society would send me or not, and trust to providence for my support and protection'. He was proud to be the standard bearer of the novel Welsh enterprise, but at a deeper level his sense of mission transcended such affiliation. In doctrinal terms, he was clearly committed to the Welsh Calvinists. But his instructions – such as they were – also gave him licence to make what he wished of the role. After all the preparation and anticipation and the long sea voyage, as the missionary finally stood on solid ground the enormity of the task would have dawned on him, and the question of what on earth to do next suddenly became more urgent. Jones's ability to prosper in the Christian community in Calcutta must firstly be understood in relation to pre-existing networks that had been carefully tended by John Roberts, as well as the ecumenical temper particularly of his Church of Scotland colleagues. Jones's literary and evangelising ambitions also need to be grounded in the context of previous missionary excursions in the north-east. In both spheres, the missionary relied on a network of elaborate symbioses that had developed among a range of colonial agents.

The Calcutta Christian alliance

Five days before the *Jamaica* had left port, Roberts had informed Jones that the committee found it unnecessary to hand him any formal instructions as to how he might proceed with his work in the Khasi Hills, trusting their missionary to take 'the most prudent, & at the same time the most active measures towards accomplishing the important object for which you are sent out'. With little information on the country to which they were sending him, they could only advise that his 'first business must necessarily be the attainment of the language spoken by the natives', and that Cherrapunji should be the most suitable station for his residence. More than that, Roberts advised, the committee would be able to form a better opinion when reports were received. Jones was advised that such correspondence should be 'as frequent & as full as possible'.[2]

The lack of detailed instructions reflected the inexperience as much as the novelty of the undertaking by the Welsh Society. The *Calcutta Christian Observer* in June 1837, for example, reported most favourably on the detailed written instructions delivered to four missionaries from the American Board of Commissioners for Foreign Missions, who were about to embark for Java and Sumatra. Key proscriptions included avoiding interference with other existing protestant missions, not requiring or expecting much from the local government, establishing a safe residence for their families, learning the native languages, raising an indigenous priesthood, and ensuring they garnered sufficient local subjects to keep themselves occupied and to encourage home patronage. 'Your appropriate sphere of action', it was advised, 'is not to be the external and material, but the intellectual and moral world. Your chief concern is to be with thoughts and feelings'.[3]

Newly landed in Calcutta, therefore, Jones's first tasks were to seek patronage, glean intelligence, gather stores and find out how to get to the Khasi Hills. In the years since the British had first established a trading post up the River Hooghly in the late seventeenth century, Calcutta had become not only the commercial powerhouse of British India, but also its civil headquarters. Fort William, damaged during the 1756 siege and rebuilt by 1773 to house a garrison of up to 10,000 soldiers, gave the Company's troops a regional base in Bengal, while the neoclassical architecture of the 'White Town' reflected its status as the imperial capital of the Empire's richest province. White Town's *nabob* was an Anglo-Indian who would take his fortune back to Britain; in Calcutta's north, Black Town's *babu* was disparagingly so-called by the British, a 'superficially cultivated'[4] Bengali 'attempting unsuccessfully to imitate his western superiors – rather as nabobs like Clive had attempted to imitate their social superiors in Britain'.[5] Such a presumed simplistic spatial division of the *nabobs* and the *babus* masked the realities of a hybrid urban fabric where the geographies of Calcutta's indigenous and foreign denizens were much more fluid and interpenetrating.[6]

To the newcomer, Calcutta's alluring spectacle of empire was a riot of cultural difference, in which a new sense of order required fashioning out of chaos. Baptist missionary W.H. Denham had described his arrival in Calcutta in 1844:

> In the city are splendid edifices and mud hovels, naked children and half naked adults, various and discordant sounds, mechanics at their employ, vendors sitting by their goods. Innumerable sledges drawn by oxen, fashionable European carriages, buggies, garees, palankins, grooms running to clear the way, in fact, a ceaseless din. Reflection, however, soon dissipated the wonder the scene excited. Degradation and idolatry were around us; 'destruction and misery' walked hand in hand by our side. We may have read – but the reality![7]

Thackeray had deployed scenes from the *Arabian Nights* in negotiating his lived encounter with the East. To Fanny Eden, sister of the new Governor-General Lord Auckland who had arrived in Calcutta in 1836, the scene of a dinner at Government House exemplified the slippage between imagination and reality: turbaned attendants, native guards, and 'this enormous building looking more like a palace, a palace in the "Arabian Nights," than anything I have been able to dream upon the subject. It is something like what I expected, and yet not the least, at present, as far as externals go: it seems to me that we are acting a long opera'.[8] India took its foreign recruits by surprise, caught them off guard, challenged them to re-establish order amidst disorientation.

Britain's mercantile supremacy was manifest in the incessant maritime traffic that plied the Hooghly. British civil and political authority was expressed in the imposing architecture of Calcutta's administrative district on the river's east bank, between the Old Fort and Esplanade Row, which contained the Writers' Building, Supreme Court, Government House and Town Hall. For the evangelical missionary, the distancing space between the envisioned heathen horde, so long imagined, and the real Indian subjects that thronged the streets, collapsed in the first encounter. The monolithic category of 'savage' could now begin to be renegotiated at an individual level, with room for evangelising and humanising, or as Jane Sampson has observed, for 'othering' and 'brothering'.[9] In the midst of this disequilibrium, knowing whom to trust was not just a matter of being wary of the natives; it was also a matter of learning how to negotiate with those Europeans who were the missionary's moral or political enemies, as well as those who had already been subtly transformed by India, perhaps without their own knowledge. Who could you trust in the confusion of a city of a quarter of a million souls? Jones would later write that 'every day convinces me that the further a missionary lives from these wicked Europeans, the better'.[10]

The coming weeks that Thomas Jones would spend in Calcutta were an abrupt acclimatisation, and connections from home were essential in stabilising a sense of self and of mission amidst the confusion of arrival. Jones was armed with letters of introduction from Tomlin to various gentlemen in the city,[11] and from Henry Grey of Edinburgh to Alexander Duff. Jones was not personally known to Grey, but had been recommended by his friend the Reverend Lewis Edwards, Thomas Jones's teacher at Bala. Edwards's wife Jane was the granddaughter of Grey's 'beloved & revered friend the late Revd Thos Charles of Bala'. Thomas Charles had died in 1814, but Grey's affection both for the man and his denomination was still evident in his glowing appraisal of their 'fine & practical Christianity'. In their decision to break away from the LMS, and 'quiet & unostentatiously' to send their own ministers to India, the Welsh missionaries found a willing supporter in Grey, who underscored the desire that 'every section of the Xtian church should be ambitious of a direct & personal share in the honor of occupying that field even *the world*, which they have it in trust to sow with the good seed'.[12]

On his arrival in 1844, Denham was greeted by his fellow Baptists George Pearce and a deacon of the church, Mr Gray, and it was the latter and his wife who had welcomed Thomas and Ann Jones into their house in April 1841 with 'the greatest kindness, tenderness, and care imaginable'. An ecumenical spirit had already been evident back in Britain, through the correspondence and connections between the Welsh Calvinistic Methodists and their Church of Scotland and Baptist brethren; here in Calcutta, there were mutual benefits and economies of scale when the denominational groups banded together. 'The Revd Dr Duff is extremely brotherly & friendly', noted Jones, 'and offers to do all in his power for me, and that is certainly not very limited. Besides, he has introduced me to other persons, who perhaps, have it in their power to do more directly for me than himself, and are equally willing'.[13]

Jones kept up a busy round of visiting, garnering the support and approval of many of the missionaries of Calcutta. On 4 May, Thomas Jones was 'warmly received' at the Monthly Missionary Conference. 'I might add', he gloated to Roberts, 'what may perhaps be of some consolation to you, that one of their number observed afterwards, though not to me personally, that he never saw any newly arrived missionary, [receive] so general & warm a reception!'[14] Calcutta's missionaries had convened Monthly Missionary Prayer Meetings from 1816, and the Baptists Geoffrey and William Hopkins Pearce inaugurated the

Calcutta Missionary Conference when they had asked their fellow Protestant missionaries to breakfast in 1829.[15] The Conference became an alliance between missionaries of the various Protestant denominations (Independents, Baptists and Scottish Presbyterians, 'together with any others whom they consider as legitimate & worthy missionaries of Christ'). From 1832 their journal – the *Calcutta Christian Observer* – published a range of material, from observations and essays on temperance, native customs, education and conversion, to book reviews, essays on the duty of private Christians, and debates around the substitution of Romanisation for native orthography. It was here, too, that a monthly digest of missionary and religious intelligence was disseminated, promoting the activities of missionary societies across the Indian Presidencies and beyond. Alexander Duff had spearheaded the Church of Scotland's work in Calcutta from 1830, and was for a time editor of the journal.

Thomas Jones also carried in his pocket a letter of credit on a Calcutta mercantile house for £100 sterling or 10,000 rupees, with which he was to purchase supplies as needed. The WFMS had agreed to cover his travelling expenses to Cherrapunji, and then to pay him an annual salary of £150.[16] The society as yet had no corresponding secretary or treasurer in Calcutta, and with the minimal funds at its discretion was loath to pay any commission to local banks or agency houses to manage its financial affairs. Duff referred Jones to John Wallis Alexander, an official assignee of insolvent estates, who agreed to act as his agent, pay his bills and disburse the finances as required, and invest any remaining assets with his own, and at a higher rates of interest than available back in Britain.[17] Though Alexander was a member of the Church of England – and regarded suspiciously by some in Calcutta because of his pious association with missionary causes – Jones recognised that he had found a trustworthy sympathiser and advocate. Jones's warm reception at the Missionary Conference also alerted him to the reality that '*good men* are more wanted in India than money'.[18] While the choice of the Khasi Hills was generally applauded, there were many more areas 'ripe and ready for the harvest', and Jones had received a number of offers to cover the expenses of mission salaries, printing and building, if only the Welsh could send out more men.

No sooner had he regained his land legs, than the journey to the Khasi Hills beckoned. But before Jones finally set out, he gleaned further vital information. In his first report to Roberts from Calcutta, Jones noted that the Reverend John Mack of Serampore, who had previously been at Cherrapunji, had paid him a visit, 'and kindly promised to furnish me with all the manuscripts, Books, &c relating to the Cossias & their language, which they at Serampore have in their power to find for me; and (as you are aware) they are able to do more in this way than any body else in Calcutta'.[19]

The Serampore mission: Krishna Chandra Pal, James Rae and Alexander Lish

The original intent of the EIC to prevent missionary work throughout India was clearly eroded by the amendment to the Charter in 1813. Prior to this, however, missionary activity in Bengal, inaugurated by the Serampore Baptists, had slowly but surely permeated informally throughout the province, by means of a network of converts and emissaries, and leaving a paper trail in the tracts and scriptures that continued to roll off the Mission Press. By default, and despite the EIC's 'own selfish ignorance', the appointment of Carey as language professor at Wellesley's new Fort William College was seen by mission supporters as confirmation that 'the company became a principal partner in the Christianisation of India and China'.[20]

The Serampore missionaries were the benchmark of all Indian missions. In November 1793 Carey had arrived in Bengal on a Danish ship, with Surgeon John Thomas, to commence missionary work. After managing an indigo factory, in 1800 Carey set up a mission base at the Danish trading settlement of Serampore, about fifteen miles north of Calcutta. Together with Joshua Marshman and William Ward (the three became known as the Serampore trio), Carey established a Mission Press (1800), and later Serampore College (1818). Aside from a number of Indian grammars and dictionaries, with assistance from Indian *pundits* the whole Bible was translated into six Indian languages, while parts of it were translated into a further twenty-nine. Carey was appointed professor of Sanskrit, Bengali and Marathi at the EIC's Fort William College in 1801.

In 1804 Carey wrote to John Ryland, one of the founding members of the BMS, detailing the *modus operandi* of the Baptist mission. Here the nexus was explicit between Bible translation, education and conversion, as well as the model (influenced by Moravian ideals) of the communal and financially independent mission station supported by native preachers.[21] On 28 December 1800, after seven years in India, Carey's mission had borne its first fruit with the conversion of a Hindu carpenter named Krishna Chandra Pal.[22] News of the first Hindu convert was a milestone in the history of the mission, and reports of Pal's rejection of his past ways were widely circulated to home audiences in what was to become a familiar narrative style and an important fillip for fundraising efforts. 'Ye Gods of stone and clay!', reported Joseph Belcher's tract: 'Did ye not tremble when, in the name of the

Father, Son and Holy Spirit, one of your votaries shook you as the dust from his feet?'[23]

In early 1813, Pal and Gorachund, another native Christian, set off for the eastern region of British Bengal. Carey had given Pal a letter of introduction to his friend Mathew Smith, an English magistrate at Sylhet, who gave him a further letter of introduction to the judge of Sylhet. There is no evidence that Krishna Chandra Pal travelled to the Khasi Hills proper, but rather itinerated in the foothills for eight months, visiting the market town of Pandua, an important centre where Khasis from nearby villages came down to trade with Bengalis from the plains.[24] It was in this district that Pal claimed to have converted seven individuals, including two Khasis named Dewankhasee (U Duwan) and Ooana-khasee (U Anna). Pal's evangelising – which had particularly excited the Baptist brethren, as it had pushed the mission's reach to within a week's journey of China – certainly had the effect of adding Khasi to the growing list of Bible translations running off the Serampore Mission Press.

In December 1813, after Pal's return to Serampore, Carey secured the services of a *pundit* to undertake the Khasi translation of the gospels, believing him to be 'the only one in that nation who could read and write'.[25] According to some sources, a translation of the Gospel of St Matthew was circulated in 1817, and 500 copies of a New Testament translation were printed in Khasi in 1824. One of Carey's Sylhet contacts had suggested in 1816 that Khasi boys could be procured from the local Rajahs to help in Bible translation,[26] while another account claims it was in fact the widow of a local Rajah who had helped Carey in the translation work.[27] Serampore College, which had opened in 1818, also admitted two Khasis among its first intake.[28] Some Khasis may also have been studying at Fort William College in Calcutta in order to gain the necessary educational skills to conduct more advanced trade negotiations with the plains people.[29] While Krishna Chandra Pal died of malaria in 1822, there is also a suggestion in some sources that he wrote two introductory primers for elementary education among the Khasis.[30] After Pal's departure, and despite the first missionary attempts to circulate Christian scriptures in the Khasi language, the process of active evangelisation the Khasi Hills went into abeyance through the 1820s. Even the texts that were circulated had little local impact as they were not only printed in Bengali characters, but used the Shella dialect which was not comprehensible to Khasis in Cherrapunji or those further upland.[31]

Pal's work had been undertaken thirty years before Thomas Jones arrived in Calcutta. John Mack provided Jones with whatever copies of those early documents and publications that were still at hand, and he would certainly have given a verbal account of the more recent developments in the hills through the 1830s. David Scott, the British Political Agent in Assam, encouraged the establishment of a mission and school on the northern side of the Khasi Hills at Guwahati, the principal *sudder* station in the region (the location of the collector, judge, courts and other civic officials). In 1829, the Serampore Baptists opened a mission station there, while Adam White, Assistant to the Commissioner in Lower Assam, opened a mission school with assistance from Scottish-born James Rae of Serampore. In 1830, Rae reported that the twelve students at the school included three Khasis and nine Garos, who had been committed to his care by David Scott.[32]

In 1831, Rae again reported on three Khasi princes under instruction at the Guwahati school. One Khasi was the brother of U Tirot Sing, *Syiem* of Nonghklaw, while the other two were from Cherrapunji 'where Mr Fenwick has his school'.[33] Charles Fenwick had been adopted as a missionary in 1825, moving from Chinsurah to Sylhet in 1827.[34] Rae had resigned by the end of 1831, and the Reverend John Mack informed some friends in England in June 1832 that the missionaries were 'strongly inclined to form a Station at Cherrapoonjee, where the British Government had recently established a Sanatorium'.[35] Alexander Burgh Lish, a young Eurasian student at Serampore, was accepted for missionary work and left for the Khasi Hills in March 1832.

Lish worked among the station's European residents, as well as teaching and preaching to the Khasis at schools he established at Cherrapunji, Sohra, Mawsmai and Mawmluh. He gave up on teaching English, establishing instead a class for teaching the Bengali characters in which the Khasi New Testament had been printed.[36] Lish had revised the translation of the St Matthew's Gospel, and according to varying accounts translated the Sermon on the Mount, some of the Parables, the Acts of the Apostles, as well as setting down a Khasi vocabulary and grammar.[37] He was assisted in the schools by U Duwan Rai (one of Krishna Pal's converts), U Jungkha and U Laithat, but the thirty-six enrolments recorded in the early years ultimately fell away as little progress was made teaching in Bengali script.[38]

Lish lived and worked at Cherrapunji from 1832 until 1837, aided by Joshua Rowe, who taught at the mission school. The mission at Cherrapunji was regarded by Serampore as one if its 'advanced posts', a base for extending its activities into Bhutan, Manipur, Cachar, and even China.[39] There was a continued close association with the Serampore Baptists, not only through the visits to the recuperative climate of the hills by the Macks and the Marshmans, but also through the more extended residence there of B.W. Marshman, the son of Joshua Marshman.

Tomlin observed that the work of the Serampore missionaries over their four or so years of their time in the hills, 'sowing the precious seeds of God's word', was already achieving results among young Khasis in the mission schools. In September 1837, Tomlin wrote to Mr Marshman from Cherrapunji, noting the fertile agricultural tracts and the industry of the Khasis.

> There is, however, room enough for other settlers, if they can be contented to eat their bread in the sweat of their brow; and to bring their wants within a narrow compass; and be more anxious to benefit the people, than to fill their pockets. Small Christian settlements or colonies, on the plan of the United Brethren, would, I think, do well in the neighbourhood of Moflong and Myrung. Thence, the gospel might be spread over the hills, east and west, and be preached in every village of the Khassias in a few years; and the joyful tidings of the gospel would doubtless soon reach the Jynteah Khassias to the east, and the Garrows on the west.[40]

In Tomlin's eyes the Khasi Hills were ripe for mission work, free from the influences of Islam and Hinduism, and just as importantly from Catholicism. Tomlin stayed in the Khasi Hills for about nine months. His wife was very ill during the rainy months through to September, after their son was born on 15 June 1837 at the Mission House at Cherrapunji (and named Joshua Cherra, commemorating both the place and the last of the original Serampore trio).[41] Tomlin and Lish had both left the hills and were in Calcutta by the start of 1838.[42] In March 1838 an extended account of the Khasis by Alexander Lish was published in the *Calcutta Christian Observer*.[43] It appears that by that time he had abandoned the Khasi mission, and in October 1838 he was appointed to Dacca.[44]

Heading for the hills

Direct missionary intervention in the Khasi Hills, sustained primarily by the Serampore Baptists, could therefore draw a straight line from the work of Lish, Rowe and Tomlin, and Rae's Guwahati mission school in the 1830s, back to Pal's 1813 preaching tour and ensuing period of scriptural translation, and finding its source in the originating work of William Carey himself. As Mack briefed Thomas Jones in Calcutta in May 1841, Jones would have realised both the opportunities and the impediments to the establishment of a successful mission in the region. The reasons for the failure of the Baptists to gain a foothold in the hills over the preceding three decades were various, and the Welsh inheritance from Serampore, though it had laid the groundwork, was at best erratic and at worst perhaps unreliable. The inaccessibility of the terrain, the vagaries of the severe rainy season, the absence of appropriate printed language materials, and the palpable lack of progress were a stark legacy of three decades of spasmodic effort. The lack of conversions and the inevitable stresses of isolation, deprivation and ill health on the young missionary families in the Khasi Hills, saw their efforts relinquished by the end of the decade.[45]

If Thomas Jones had been buoyed by the welcome and support he had received at the Monthly Missionary Conference on Tuesday 4 May, he had not long to wait for a test of his resolve. Ann Jones had been in ill health for much of the voyage, and Thomas often expected his pregnant wife 'to fall a victim to the king of terrors'. On the evening of Wednesday 5 May, Ann went into a labour that lasted three days, ended only on the Saturday night when 'a fine baby boy' was delivered by means of instruments, 'which however by being dragged into the world with irons, was strangled on its way into this world of sorrows, and its spirit returned to God who gave it, before it knew any thing of the toils & troubles of time'.[46] On the following morning, the Sabbath, the child was buried in the Scotch Burial Ground, and became in Thomas Jones's eyes the first 'hostage' of the Welsh Calvinistic Methodist mission in India.[47]

Had he looked about him, Jones would have seen enough freshly dug ground to know that mortality here was tenuous. It was just over a year since the Reverend William Pearce was laid to rest in the same cemetery. It was barely a year more since the same plot of graves had in 1839 claimed both the Baptist missionaries the Reverend George Barton Parsons, at the youthful age of twenty-six, and the Reverend James Penney. English Anglicans and Scotch dissenters had been buried together in Calcutta until purchase of the Scotch and Dissenters Burial Ground in 1820.[48] The Scotch Burial Ground also held the remains of Scottish missionary the Reverend John Adam, who had come to Calcutta for the LMS in 1828, but was dead by April 1831 at the age of twenty-seven. A year before, in April 1830, Adam had followed the road past the Scotch Burial Ground, conversing with Hindu and Muslim alike, and 'gave away all my books, and exhausted myself with talking'.[49] The following month he welcomed Alexander Duff to Calcutta, in whom he had encouraged the missionary impulse at the university at St Andrews in the mid-1820s.[50] In 1826, prior to his departure for India, Adam had articulated the usefulness of the missionary as resting in a range of actions and effects including scriptural translation, the conversion of the heathen and the positive reaction produced at home. In Adam's mind particularly, the missionary 'gives a greater proof of sincerity than the Minister at home. His testimony approaches nearer to that of martyrdom'.[51] This spirit of sacrifice, in which Thomas Jones had been farewelled by his Liverpool brethren, was now indelibly underscored by the death of his first-born son, and further emphasised by the mortal remains of his religious brethren, many of whom had gone to an early grave.

Ann Jones slowly recovered her health in the days that followed. The committee of the WFMS had determined that in the event of Thomas Jones's own death, they would bear the costs of returning his wife and any children to England, and 'provide for their future support in the best way they can'.[52] The trials and sorrows of the original delay to their voyage and subsequent departure for the hills, and the illness of his wife and death of their baby, were seen by Jones as a test of his patience and a balance to the 'pleasure, comfort, & consolation' he derived in other ways. Thomas Jones read his experience against the invocations of prayer and the actions of 'wise providence'. In this world-view, he sought signs of divine favour or disapprobation at every turn. Each event was portentous, each ominous experience ('Although the Lord seems to frown upon my domestic aide') reconciled with a positive one ('he certainly smiles thus far upon the missionary enterprize').[53] If the end in which he believed was a sacred one, then events and phenomena encountered along the way were simply part of the planned guardianship exercised by his deity, and could only be explained and justified in terms of the mission's success.

While in Calcutta Jones had also fortuitously received correspondence from Lieutenant William Lewin, with an offer of temporary accommodation at his house at Cherrapunji, just as he had done for Tomlin four years earlier. Lewin had also put Mr Harley, his agent in Calcutta, at Jones's disposal.[54] Before he had even left Calcutta, Thomas Jones had almost arrived in the Khasi Hills. 'I think from the omens I have already had', he informed Roberts, 'that when you receive this you can venture to tell all our friends at home that we have arrived safely at Cherrapoonjee . . . My address will be *Revd T.J. Missionary, Cherrapoonjee, Cassia Hills, Bengal*'.

Notes

1 Carey, *William Carey*, p. 139.
2 Roberts to Jones, 20 November 1840, CMA 28720.
3 *Calcutta Christian Observer*, June 1837, 314.
4 Yule and Burnell, *Hobson-Jobson*, p. 44.
5 Krishna Dutta, *Calcutta: A Cultural and Literary History* (Oxford, 2003), p. 35.
6 Swato Chattopadhyay, 'Blurring boundaries: the limits of "White Town" in colonial Calcutta', *The Journal of the Society of Architectural Historians*, 59:2 (2000), 154–79.
7 Denham to Bowes, 8 August 1844, in *The Baptist Magazine for 1844*, p. 588.

8 Emily Eden, *Letters from India* (London, 1872), p. 91, cited in Chattopadhyay, 'Blurring boundaries', 175.
9 Jane Samson, 'Translation teams: missionaries, islanders and the reduction of language in the Pacific' in Patricia Grimshaw and Andrew May (eds), *Missionaries, Indigenous Peoples and Cultural Exchange* (Brighton, 2010), p. 99.
10 Jones to Roberts, 28 July 1841, *Y Drysorfa*, November 1841, 347.
11 Roberts to Wilson, 2 December 1840, CMA 28720.
12 Grey to Duff, 28 October 1840, CMA (5): 27066, copy. Probably the Reverend Henry Grey (1778–1859) of St Mary's Church, Edinburgh.
13 Jones to Roberts, 11 May 1841, CMA 1(F): 5898 (copy).
14 *Ibid.*
15 Eleanor Jackson, 'From Krishna Pal to Lal Behari Dey: Indian builders of the church in Bengal, 1800–1894' in Dana L. Robert (ed.), *Converting Colonialism: Visions and Realities in Mission History, 1706–1914* (Grand Rapids, Michigan and Cambridge, 2007), p. 194, f. 83.
16 Roberts to Jones, 20 November 1840, CMA 28720.
17 Roberts to Alexander, 27 October 1841, CMA 28720.
18 Jones to Roberts, 11 May 1841, CMA 1(F): 5898 (copy).
19 *Ibid.*
20 George Smith, *The Life of William Carey, D.D. Shoemaker and Missionary. Professor of Sanskrit, Bengali and Marathi in the College of Fort William, Calcutta* (London, 1885), p. 158.
21 Carey to Ryland, 14 December 1803, in Smith, *The Life of William Carey*, p. 162.
22 *Ibid.*, pp. 132–56. See also *American Baptist Magazine and Missionary Intelligencer*, 1:2 (1817), 65–7, 'Short account of the conversion and baptism of Kristno Paul'.
23 Joseph Belcher, *The First Hindoo Convert: A Memoir of Krishna Pal, a Preacher of the Gospel to his Countrymen more than Twenty Years* (Philadelphia, 1852), p. 15.
24 Philomena Kharakor, *Biblical Influence on Pre-Independence Khasi Literature* (New Delhi, 1998), p. 12.
25 Carey letter 11 December 1813, cited in Carey, *William Carey*, p. 408.
26 Jayanta Bhusan Bhattacharjee, 'Social and religious reform movements in Meghalaya in nineteenth and twentieth centuries: Khasi and Jaintia Hills' in S.P. Sen (ed.), *Social and Religious Reform Movements in the Nineteenth and Twentieth Centuries* (Calcutta, 1979), p. 451.
27 Samuel Bagster, *The Bible of Every Land* (London, 1851), Class I, p. 15.
28 Carey, *William Carey*, p. 332.
29 Bareh, *The History and Culture of the Khasi People*, p. 392.
30 Bhattacharjee, 'Social and religious reform movements in Meghalaya', p. 452; Sharmila Das Talukdar, *Khasi Cultural Resistance to Colonialism* (Guwahati and Delhi, 2004), p. 32.
31 O.L. Snaitang, *Christianity and Social Change in Northeast India: A Study of the Role of Christianity in Social Change among the Khasi-Jaintia Hill Tribes of Meghalaya* (Shillong and Calcutta, 1993), p. 66.
32 Barkataki, *British Administration in North East India*, p. 87. See also Morris, *The History*, p. 83.
33 Notes from Periodical Accounts of the Serampore Mission, New Series, volume 1, from January 1827 to December 1833, in CMA 27159.
34 *Ibid.*
35 Cited in Morris, *The History*, p. 83. See also Notes from Periodical Accounts of the Serampore Mission, New Series, volume 1, from January 1827 to December 1833, CMA 27159.
36 Notes from Periodical Accounts of the Serampore Mission, New Series, volume 1, from January 1827 to December 1833 in CMA 27159.
37 Morris, *The History*, p. 83; Dutta, *Impact of the West on the Khasis and Jaintias*, p. 195, cites Periodical Accounts March 1834 No. 81.
38 Snaitang, *Christianity and Social Change*, p. 67, cites Periodical Accounts of the Serampore Mission, 3D Series, No. 67 (January 1833), p. 2; Kharakor, *Biblical*

Influence, p. 13; Dutta, *Impact of the West on the Khasis and Jaintias*, p. 184, cites Periodical Accounts, July 1834 No. 85, September 1836, No. 140; and June 1837 No. 115.

39 'Serampore Mission', *Friend of India*, 19 March 1835, p. 92.

40 J. Tomlin, *Missionary Journals and Letters Written during Eleven Years' Residence and Travels amongst the Chinese, Siamese, Javanese, Khassias, and other Eastern Nations* (London, 1844), p. 379.

41 East India Register and Directory, 1838; Tomlin, *Missionary Journals*, p. 383.

42 *Calcutta Christian Observer*, February 1838, 116.

43 A.B. Lish, 'A brief account of the Khasees', *Calcutta Christian Observer* (March 1838), 129–43.

44 *Calcutta Christian Observer*, October 1838, 587.

45 Bareh, *The History and Culture of the Khasi People*, p. 392; D. Ropmay, *Ka Centenary History Ka Balang Presbyterian* (1940) in H.W. Sten, *Khasi Poetry (Origin and Development)* (New Delhi, 1990), p. 45; P.R.G. Mathur, *The Khasi of Meghalaya (Study in Tribalism and Religion)* (New Delhi, 1979), p. 14; Bhattacharjee, 'Social and religious reform movements', p. 452.

46 Jones to Roberts, 11 May 1841, CMA 1(F): 5898 (copy).

47 The Scotch Burial Ground is at 3 Keraya Road, Kolkata.

48 Robert Travers, 'Death and the Nabob: imperialism and commemoration in eighteenth-century India', *Past & Present*, 196:1 (2007), 96–7, n. 41.

49 John Adam, *Memoir of John Adam, Late Missionary at Calcutta* (London, 1833), p. 269.

50 Piggin, *Making Evangelical Missionaries*, p. 232.

51 John Adam to John Urquhart, July 1826 in Adam, *Memoir*, p. 131.

52 Roberts to Jones, 20 November 1840, CMA 28720.

53 Jones to Roberts, 11 May 1841, CMA 1(F): 5898 (copy).

54 Roberts to Tomlin, 5 July 1841, CMA 28720.

PART II

The flag on the mountain

CHAPTER FOUR

Drawing the frontier

The first sighting of the Khasi Hills from the plains of Sylhet in June 1841 was a long anticipated moment for the missionary. At last the mountains that had risen before his imagination now towered ahead in meridian splendour, rising over 6000 feet above the plain like a great island out of an ocean.[1] He had set out with Ann from Calcutta sometime in late May to make the 350-mile trip to Cherrapunji, with the wet season coming on. Travelling mainly by water, shadowed here and there by porpoises on the watery expanses of the Surma River, they took a week or so to reach Chhatak in the district of Sylhet, to be within twenty miles of the southern face of the Khasi Hills. From Chhatak the Joneses would have proceeded by boat a few miles up the river to Companiganj, and thence to Pandua. In the dry season the river networks were reduced to beds of sand and stone, and travellers walking through the forest to Pandua carried burning torches to ward off the tigers that roamed the *nullahs*. But with the arrival of the monsoon, boats plied the expansive network of stagnant marshy water, ten or twelve feet deep, known as the *jheels*. They sailed over huge trees submerged under the water, and in places the waterlogged jungle was so dense that the boats became stuck in the branches. From Pandua, the travellers pushed on the three miles to Therriaghat, right at the base of the mountains, and from there ascended the hills.

The *jheels* gave way north of Pandua to the limestone lowlands of the great elevated plateau. The bare face of the precipitous sandstone escarpment high above could be seen to run like a band along the whole length of the mountain range. Strips of orange groves fingered up the sides of the foothills, and as the climb became steeper, the tropical vegetation grew more luxuriant. The gradual ascent gave way after a few thousand feet to a steeper and rockier path set with red sandstone blocks like giant flagstones, at times the gradient at almost a forty-five degree angle.

Thomas Jones travelled up to Cherrapunji on the back of a mule, and his possessions were carried up the mountainside by a hundred 'coolies'. Ann Jones was transported up the steep mountain path in the traditional Khasi mode, borne on a *Khoh-Kit-Briew* (basket for carrying persons), a kind of semi-enclosed cane chair with a seat and footrest, strapped to a man's back and partly supported by a cane band looped around his head.[2] As the higher reaches of the Mawsmai Valley escarpment came into view, silvery waterfalls jumped from the flat summit and down its perpendicular sides, cascading thousands of feet to the emerald forest below. After around eight hours of travel from Pandua, the Joneses reached the high stony plateau that led them up to their journey's end at the station of Cherrapunji, nearly 5000 feet above the level of the sea.

From the 1770s to the early 1840s, a succession of imperial agents confronted the mountains of the north-east from the plain at Pandua. Whether making their ascent in the wet or the dry, they all climbed to the top along the same winding route, resting where others had rested by the great rock at the pass of Mahadek at around two and a half thousand feet, before making the final hike to the mountain's hazy tableland. Under the hills, Pandua was a frontier village and a borderland. To some it was a gateway between two different zones, to others the limit of their knowledge. For the Khasis, Pandua was a border constructed out of habit, a trading post that had served as a permeable threshold for goods and for people. For the British, it came to be a line constructed out of imagination and increasingly drawn by force. As each British soldier, administrator, scientist or missionary scrambled up the mountain, they mapped different appraisals onto the landscape of the space beyond. Broader contours of empire can be determined in their observations and impressions of this very particular route. A road constructed onwards through the hills to Assam in the 1820s made the British more able to travel and therefore to control, but no more able to see beyond their confining gaze of power and privilege.

In order to understand where precisely Thomas Jones arrived when he crested the mountain in 1841 – and what he did when he got there – it is instructive to see the hills through the eyes of those who had gone before him, which is the work of this and the following three chapters. British soldiers and civil servants – Scottish-born revenue collector Robert Lindsay (arrived 1772) and administrator David Scott (1802), and English soldier William Lewin (1822) – also climbed that steep mountain pass in the name of empire, each with a particular task or purpose. Their letters and journals describing their time in the north-east constructed certain versions and visions of the kind of place it was and might become – military cantonment, health retreat or even

European colony. At different times their presence can be explicitly read as being in the service of particular imperial purposes: surveying the land for a road; observing the suitability of the climate; assessing natural resources; securing commercial or political agreements with the Khasis; prosecuting military actions; converting the natives to Christianity. Their expectations and intentions mark transitions in scientific, commercial, geo-political, gendered and religious ideologies. Most of all, they complicate a version of British imperialism that pits state against church, science against industry, pragmatism against idealism. The purposes of the magistrate, the artilleryman, the geologist or the evangelist are rarely mutually exclusive; they are more often than not overlapping and reciprocally constitutive of empire. At times, indeed, they do each others' work.

In the written sources from the period, the non-literate Khasi people never appear first hand; nothing is rendered in their own words or written by their own pens. As British India extended its networks of influence and control over the hills of the north-east, British presence and intervention (through travel, treaty and military force) irrevocably regulated the autonomy of tribal political alliances, and intervened in well-articulated district economies. Spatial histories suggest ideological ones, as micro-geographies of empire were fashioned out of hill and plain. From the British point of view, the Khasi Hills were coming into clearer focus as destination, refuge, lived domestic space, defence and resource. As British presence was established at Cherrapunji, just down the plateau from the native village, we can still attempt to read the deeper cultural entanglements of action and reaction, of influence and agency.

Circumscribing British territory: Robert Lindsay

Over sixty years before Thomas and Ann Jones ascended to Cherrapunji, Robert Lindsay stood in the foothills at Pandua – 'one of the most stupendous amphitheatres in the world' – and marvelled at the romantic mountains that rose abruptly from the pestilential plains. He felt 'transplanted into one of the regions of Paradise', but the 'wild-looking demons then dancing on the banks before me' were a rude and uncharacteristic imposition on his reverie of the garden of Eden.[3] Lindsay, son of Scottish peer James, fifth earl of Balcarres, was appointed resident collector of Sylhet in 1778. Lindsay's Indian career was no doubt facilitated by his family connections; his seven brothers also had diverse military, political and naval careers, including Alexander (Governor of Jamaica) and Hugh (an EIC marine commander, one time captain of the *Lady Jane Dundas*, later a company director).[4] Lindsay's view of the hills drew explicitly on the picturesque tropes of eighteenth-century landscape ideology. He also saw a profoundly moral landscape – pure and paradisiacal – in which heathen tribesmen were devils rather than innocents, as yet undeserving of its bounty and its benefits.

For Lindsay, this *mise en scène* of British imperialism in the north-east also had a particularly Scottish hue: in observing his 'Cusseah friends' descending the mountain, 'the scene had much of stage effect, the tribes descending from rock to rock as represented in Oscar and Malvina'.[5] *Oscar and Malvina, or the Hall of Fingal* was a long-running opera first staged at Covent Garden in 1791, and was most likely inspired by Scottish poet James Macpherson's *The Works of Ossian* (1765), which purported to represent translations of ancient Celtic epic verse. By drawing on such specific cultural allusions, Lindsay referenced key concepts of the burgeoning Romantic nationalism of the late eighteenth century. In lowland eyes, the image of the tartan-clad highland warrior was transmuting from untrustworthy and barbaric insurgent to heroic patriot.[6] Yet the correlation is deceiving. Partly a literary device in Lindsay's narrative, the linking of the Scottish and Khasi highlander performs ideological work in racialising martial stereotypes, and anticipates later nineteenth-century discourses linking Scottish highlanders and Nepalese Gurkhas.[7] Nascent Celtic revivalism sought connections with and origins in a heroic folk past; the tribal Indian was racially inferior, a remnant rather than a progenitor. The temperament of the mountain-type was also unstable and unpredictable. For Lindsay, the Khasi warriors were 'by no means unlike our native Highlanders when dressed in the Gaelic costume . . . still it was evident, from their complexion and the war-yell that occasionally escaped their lips, as well as the mode in which they handled their weapons, that their temperament was not dissimilar to that of other mountaineers'.[8]

For the mobile tribal societies of the north-east, two centuries of Mughal and then British incursion had by the 1820s seen a transition from a region characterised by dynamic and permeable relationships, subject to little overall state authority, to much more hardened economic and political geographies. The circumscription of Khasi territory in the mountainous regions was partly a result of Mughal expansion that forced Khasis, Garos and others from lowland reaches and brought the markets, land uses and cultural practices of the Sylhet region under more centralised government control.[9] As collector of Sylhet, Lindsay was responsible for revenue collection and other general aspects of local administration. In 1765, Robert Clive on behalf of the EIC acquired the *Diwani* of Bengal (or the right to collect revenue) from Mughal Emperor Shah Alam II, in return for a specified annual tribute. The Mughal emperors had now lost much of their effective power, but since the Khasis and Jaintias had never been subject to Mughal control, they could continue to remain aloof from British authority.[10]

In a letter to Scottish soldier and diplomat Sir Robert Murray Keith in 1782, Robert Lindsay was frank about the remoteness of his borderland posting in Sylhet, 'at the bottom of a high chain of mountains, which separates it from the kingdom of Assam and the countries bordering upon China, with which we have no communication, the intermediate space being inhabited by a savage race of people'.[11] But the career of Lindsay came to exemplify the business opportunities that civil service employment offered the man who had 'a shrewd commercial mind and was not hampered by scruples'.[12] He was able to amass a great personal fortune through monopoly trade and speculation in salt, oranges, elephants, *chunum* (lime) and other resources of the region.[13] During Lindsay's meeting with the Khasis at Pandua, he had secured leases on limestone quarries in the hills above, and his brief excursion upriver to survey his claims is the first recorded British foray into Khasi territory.

Prior to the imposition of British authority in the region, Sylhet had functioned independently as a coherent and self-sufficient regional economy of interconnected plains and mountain territories. Lindsay was able to exploit the local practice of paying land tax in cowries – which made up Sylhet's payable land revenue – by holding back cowries to fund his own commercial interests, and remitting to Calcutta the equivalent value in goods over which he held trading monopolies. As a private arm of state power, Lindsay was thus personally able to broker to his own considerable advantage the economic relationship between the enclosed market of Sylhet and the Bengal Presidency.[14]

Lindsay's professed ambition was 'to retire and enjoy "otium cum dignitate" at home',[15] the dignity of his leisure guaranteed and justified in his eyes by the fact that at a time when Company officials were allowed to engage in private trade, his fortune was acquired through his own hard labour rather than taking unfair advantage of the system or manipulating wealthy *nabobs*. A later biographer concurred: '*Ornatur propriis industria donis* would have been a suitable motto for this shrewd merchant-administrator' – the British empire offered its canny servant the moral certainty of industry having its due reward.[16] Later Bangladeshi critiques of his incumbency have been less equivocal: 'When the ruler is also a businessman, oppression on people becomes inevitable. Lindsay was no exception to the rule'.[17] New regulations announced in July 1787 put an end to the lucrative practice of collectors indulging in private trade. 'An abuse of this power', warned Secretary Jonathan Duncan, 'either factual or by connivance, on your part, will be productive of consequences highly prejudicial to the Company and to the country. Reward has now been annexed to responsibility'.[18] Lindsay resigned by the end of the year.

The establishment of British political authority in Sylhet from the 1770s inaugurated a process of disentangling the traditional relationships between hill and plains people. Where once Khasis had conducted more intimate economic and personal relationships with plains societies – through proprietary interests in land as well as through intermarriage – British military aggression, as well as Khasi defence, drew more visible lines on the map of the frontier. To dissuade Khasi 'raiding parties' who plundered lowland territories and inhibited the lucrative trade interests of the British by preventing the river passage of quarried limestone, collector Thackeray (grandfather of the novelist) initiated military action to 'chastise' the Rajah of Jaintia. A battalion of *sepoys* led the first concerted punitive military action against the hill people, taking Jaintiapur in 1774. With his territory now annexed to the British, the Rajah was forced to agree terms with the Company, which included the payment of financial compensation, a promise to allow unhindered navigation of the Surma River, and never again to interfere with the Company's business.[19] Khasi raids in 1783 were met with severe force; Lindsay's Pandua limestone works were destroyed, and there were numerous losses on both sides.[20] J. Willes, a collector of Sylhet after Lindsay, was unequivocal about the need for coercive measures against the Khasis. 'Civilized man', he reasoned to Governor-General Cornwallis in 1789, 'is not restrained from encroaching on his neighbours by morality or by treaties, but by opposition. Can we expect, therefore, that savages, who are always armed, when successful, will of themselves relinquish the prospect of further advantage? In this district defensive measures solely should be adopted'.[21] Pandua, once a commercial and cultural entrepot, had by the 1790s become a more formalised frontier post between Sylhet and the highlands, and the Khasis had experienced their first encounters with British military force. Corralled in the mountains, the Khasi (capricious, primitive, alien) could now be more easily distanced in cultural, economic and racial terms from Hindu or Muslim Bengali (settled, cultivated, authorised).[22]

Control and colonisation: David Scott

By the mid-1820s there were new reasons for a British foothold in the frontier. In 1825 surveyor G. Lamb, accompanied by Charles Tucker, ventured out from the plain north of Pandua to report on the suitability of the climate of the Khasi Hills for a government sanctioned invalid station. Lamb's party followed the age-old trade route between the mountains and the plains. Passing through the orange orchard of

Bengal, they met Khasi men and women laden with baskets on their backs, which were strapped to their foreheads with a belt, and filled with loads of over a *maund* (around 82lbs). In this way the iron and cotton from villages to the north were traded through the marketplace at Cherrapunji for rice, betel-nut and dried fish. Lamb reported that state revenue was derived from minor taxes on imports and exports, and profits from the monopoly of the trade in ivory, *moonga* (wild silk) and beeswax. The *Syiem* also derived income from *talooks* in Sylhet on the plains and at Khyrim.[23]

The desirability of establishing a medical station for invalids in the hills had first been suggested to the government by David Scott, Political Agent to the Governor-General on the north-east frontier of Bengal.[24] Scott suggested in 1824 that the road to Cherrapunji could be improved, and that land there be procured from the *Syiem* in return for a small *zemindary* estate he wanted near Pandua, which the government could procure for a 'trifling sum'.[25] Scott's interest in the hills was borne out of his personal involvement in mitigating the Burmese threat to the eastern frontier of India. Under the 1826 Treaty of Yandabo, the King of Ava had renounced any claims on the principality of Assam, which lay to the north of the Khasi Hills and which Burma had invaded in 1817. In 1828 and 1833, first the lower part and then the remainder of Assam were ceded to the British and incorporated into the province of Bengal. The annexation of Assam by the British thus ended the ascendancy of the Ahom dynasty, which had been established in the thirteenth century and reached the height of its territorial power in the seventeenth century when it successfully resisted Mughal expansionism into the Brahmaputra valley.

David Scott was appointed Political Agent in 1823, and in 1829 became the first Commissioner of Revenue and Circuit of Assam. Headquartered at Guwahati, as ambassador to the *Syiems*, he acted for the Governor in representing British colonial power in the region. The effective role of the agent was as political advisor and diplomatic mediator, and he could also undertake the duties of a local magistrate. To his superiors, Scott was well qualified for the new role. Scott had arrived in India in October 1802, and after some years' service as assistant collector and magistrate, saw service as judge and magistrate at Goruckpore, Rungpore and Agra.[26] He was also a close friend of George Swinton from Fort William College days, Swinton having now risen to the position of Chief Secretary to the Governor.

Prior to the cessation of hostilities marked by the 1826 Treaty, the British were eager to muster the support of local princely states against the Burmese threat. As Patrick Wolfe has articulated, the type of franchise-colonialism of the British Raj, like that in the Dutch East

Indies, was predicated on the exploitation of indigenous land and labour, rather than on the practices of elimination or relocation which marked settler-colonial or slave societies.[27] The political alliances forged through a variety of legal instruments – treaties, agreements, covenants or *sanads* (treaties of engagement) – constituted a mechanism for paramountcy, whereby local rulers conceded certain obligations to the British, but mostly retained control over issues of internal governance, and in some respects could carry on their rule in accordance with ancient customary practices. In the north-east as elsewhere, this strategy of indirect rule had the intention of ceding to the British local rights and practices of negotiation in respect to the external affairs of petty states, as well as limiting any territorial ambitions they may have harboured of their own.[28]

After his appointment, Scott wasted little time in bolstering various alliances in the Assamese buffer zone between British India and its Burmese foe, as part of the 'determination thus shown by the British authorities to maintain the integrity of their frontier'.[29] Burma had invaded Cachar and made advances to the Jyntea Rajah demanding support for its military actions, so it was imperative from the British perspective that Scott place Cachar and the Jaintia Hills under its protection. Escorted by a detachment of the 2nd Battalion 23rd Native Infantry under the command of Captain Horsburgh, Scott's party set out from Sylhet in the south, skirted the eastern edge of the Khasi Hills, travelling through the Jaintia Hills to Bishnath on the Brahmaputra in the northern part of Assam. This 130-mile trip, accomplished in thirteen marches, is credited as the first European crossing of the hill territory.[30]

On 6 March 1824 at Badarpur, Scott concluded a treaty with Rajah Govind Chunder, in which the ruler of Cachar acknowledged allegiance to the EIC, accepted British protection against his enemies, surrendered any communication with foreign powers to British arbitration, while maintaining authority for the internal government of his country.[31] Four days later, Scott signed a second treaty, with Rajah Ram Sing of Sutnga in the Jaintia Hills, who similarly placed his country under British protection, agreed to co-operate in a spirit of 'mutual friendship and amity', and importantly promised to lend military assistance to the British in the war against the Burmese to the east of the Brahmaputra in Assam. Any land thus conquered by Rajah Ram Sing to the east of Guwahati would be granted to the Rajah 'proportionate to the extent of his exertions in the common cause'.[32] Scott's observations during his 1824 trip form some of the earliest recorded European accounts of the topography, agriculture, political and social organisation of the Khasis and Jaintias.[33]

After the treaty with the Burmese in early 1826, the British realised the necessity of imposing more strategic lines of communication between Sylhet in the south and Assam in the north. A lack of proper access through the Khasi Hills was inimical to the quick carriage of troops, the rapid interchange of intelligence, as well as the potential exploitation of trade and commerce across the region. On 30 November 1826, Scott finalised further agreements with the rulers of Nongkhlaw and Khyrim in the Khasi Hills. U Tirot Sing, the *Syiem* of Nongkhlaw, in return for British protection from foreign enemies, committed his people to giving military assistance to the British. More significantly, he agreed to British terms for putting a road through the Khasi Hills to connect Sylhet and Guwahati in Assam, via Cherrapunji, Mawphlang and Nongkhlaw. Now British troops would have free and unencumbered passage through his territory.[34]

According to his own account, Scott had in 1826 been invited to Nongkhlaw, the capital of the chief's territory, to attend an assembly of the tribe and to mediate a dispute that had arisen between U Tirot Sing and other family members over an issue of succession. Using the promise of land grants on the plains, Scott was able to undermine the claims of the five-year-old brother of the late *Syiem* Chattar Singh, in favour of U Tirot Sing. Scott then took this opportunity to press home a request he had previously made to allow troop passage and the building of a road through the territory. The assembly made clear that its wish was to secure a similar agreement as had been accorded the Rajah of Jaintia, and the chiefs of villages including Mawphlang and Cherrapunji all desired the protection of government. While non-intervention into the internal administration of affairs was a caveat of British indirect rule, Scott seemed at pains to reiterate that there was no need to interfere with Khasi customary law, impressed as he was by the manner in which the assembly was conducted 'with a degree of independence coolness and propriety which could not have been exceeded under similar circumstances by the inhabitants of the most civilized countries'.[35]

Captain Adam White, Scott's assistant, had also travelled from Guwahati to attend the Khasi assembly in late 1826, an account of which he recorded in a hagiographical memoir published in 1832 after Scott's death.[36] At work in the narratives of Scott and White is a general characterisation of the Khasi tribesman as the personification of the noble savage: physically and morally robust, courageous, truthful, in harmony with nature and innately intelligent. Astonished when around 600 warriors armed with swords, bows and arrows gathered for the event, White described them 'arrayed in the picturesque garb of the Cassyas, resembling the Roman Toga'.[37] There was a self-serving logic in personifying the Khasis in such a way, as a kind of moral surety for the treaty. Frustrated with the lack of progress late on the first day of the assembly, Scott had procured a supply of rum to hasten the debate; the Khasis declined the offer. It was very much in their interest for the British to characterise the Khasis as complicit: univocal (representatives of all the petty states were assembled), hospitable (Scott had been invited to attend), willing and sober participants in a process that could only mean erosion of their customary rights and practices.

The Khasis were further and quite distinctly characterised as *hill* people, not plainsmen. From his first encounter with the Khasis on his 1824 crossing, Scott's vision for the hills was broader than that justified by pure strategic military interest. The process of domesticating the hills for possible British settlement meant pacifying the tribal threat through particular racialised constructions. This was part of a process which Dane Kennedy has argued was 'shaped by the special significance these highland sites held for the British'; as was the case with a number of Indigenous peoples elsewhere (the Todas of Ootacamund in the Nilgiri Hills in south India, the Lepcha people of Darjeeling, and the Paharis of Simla), hill tribes were favourably represented in contrast with their plains neighbours.[38]

Control and resistance: the Nongkhlaw massacre

On the southern flank of the hills, Sylhet had been drawn within the pale of British authority after the acquisition of the *Diwani* of Bengal in 1765. On the northern margin of the hills, the Brahmaputra valley was annexed under the Treaty of Yandabo six decades later. Lindsay's view of that southern precipice from Pandua in the 1770s, where a frontier became increasingly fixed, was flavoured by his personal as well as broader British commercial interests. In Lindsay's eyes, the mountainous regions were a source of capital, their inhabitants aliens: 'you might as well attack the inhabitants of the moon as those of the mountain above'.[39] By the mid-1820s, by contrast, what Scott saw was a quite different place – now strategically more important after the Burmese war, and while not completely subjugated, certainly ready at an experimental level to be exploited in the broader interests of empire.

In 1827, revenue surveyor Lieutenant Thomas Fisher had been instructed to review the line of road from Pandua to Cherrapunji, and took another view of the southern approach to the hills. The treaty with U Tirot Sing had given the British the imprimatur to proceed with construction of the road connecting their territories north and south of Khasi territory. Fisher set out through the low jungle plain and started the gradual ascent through the foothills and on to the higher ranges.

Three hours walk from Pandua, he passed through Bairong ('a miserable Cossya village') with its commanding view over precipitous slopes, then proceeded northwards for five hours through a narrow valley to the pass of Mahedek and onward to Cherrapunji. Fisher reported favourably to Charles Tucker, Commissioner of Sylhet, on the fertile and well-watered open country on the Cherra plateau. Cattle, goats and bullocks were already pastured and 'in much better state than they are usually seen in the plains of India'.[40]

Fisher's report also gives an insight into the real effects of British annexation, the invigilation on the border and an effective economic blockade. The British had imposed trade sanctions on the Khasis by closing the bazaars at the foot of the hills, in order to have miscreants given up by those who might be protecting them. As their produce rotted on the ground, it was apparent that the individual hill states were independent enough, under the rule of different chiefs, that the British could not expect some unanimity of action. If anything else, it just had the opposite effect of encouraging internecine conflict, as battles for power, resources and influence became more acute. Dewan Sing, the *Syiem* of Cherrapunji, held sway over an increasingly circumscribed territory. In putting his case against trade sanctions most urgently to Fisher, he revealed his effective dependence on British patronage and protection, his pliability being noted in Fisher's report in terms of his 'good conduct' at a period of 'great distress'. Mokum Rajah, a relative of the Cherra chief who also claimed interests in surrounding villages, was initially more equivocal. Annoyed that he had not been consulted on the matter of allowing Fisher's ingress into the territory, he and his followers threatened the surveyor's party at the pass of Mahadek. Mokum Rajah visited Fisher at Cherrapunji 'and after professing the most unqualified submission to the British Government . . . he expressed great anxiety to obtain an estate in the plain, on terms similar to those by which that of Dewan Sing is held in consideration of which he would probably be very ready to assign any ground on the heights of which he may have possession'.[41] While vulnerability of the Khasi *Syiems* to British manipulation of their internal affairs was now endemic and inescapable, they would also adjust this relationship to their own ends and purposes.

Sometime around the start of March 1829, two young English-born lieutenants from the Bengal Artillery – Richard Gurdon Bedingfield and Philip Bowles Burlton – both in their mid-twenties, went to Nongkhlaw where David Scott had established a temporary sanatarium for recuperating soldiers. On 4 April, after an invitation from U Tirot Sing through a *dubashee*, Bedingfield took off his coat, came out of the bungalow and was taken to sit in the courtyard of the house of Boree Ranee, U Tirot

Sing's maternal grand aunt. After a short conversation between the two, U Tirot Sing went off a short distance and spoke in Khasi to some of his compatriots, including Mun Sing, who then went to Bedingfield, tied his hands and slashed the tendons of his legs with their *kuttras* or long knives. As others fired arrows at his body, Bedingfield pleaded with his attackers to be put out of his misery. He was then decapitated and his scalp exposed on a stick outside the bungalow.[42]

As hundreds of Khasi warriors massed, Burlton remained holed up in the bungalow with Bowman, an apprentice from the revenue survey, and some *sepoys* with muskets. They held off their attackers by firing through holes in the walls. Before the next morning they made their escape and headed for Guwahati, with Mun Sing and his supporters in pursuit. Hounded, exhausted, their ammunition ruined by the rain, the party split up, and Burlton and Bowman were set upon and killed near Nowgong, the former in the act of extracting an arrow from his wrist. Their heads were brought back to Nongkhlaw. The death toll on either side is impossible to determine, but both at Nongkhlaw and in the pursuit of Burlton, at least fifty people were killed.

The British response was swift; Scott declared martial law.[43] Scott had escaped death himself, having left Bedingfield and Burlton at Nongkhlaw on 1 April after a tip off. Scott avoided the passes blockaded by seven or eight thousand of U Tirot Sing's men, and made his way to Cherrapunji, where he found refuge with his ally Dewan Sing, *Syiem* of Sohra. The Nongkhlaw killings ushered in half a decade of instability across the Khasi Hills, as the confederated Khasi *Syiems* mounted a determined guerrilla insurrection against the British. Ringleader U Tirot Sing was a wanted man.

What had happened between the 1826 treaty and the 1829 outrage? A week after the killings, Scott seemed genuinely puzzled. 'The conduct of the Rajah', he wrote to Lamb, 'is quite inexplicable'.[44] There appeared to have been some complaints about the treatment of Khasi women by members of the road survey party. But to the British, the murder of their young officers was treacherous, inhumane and seemingly unprovoked. For his part, when U Tirot Sing spoke with Bedingfield in the courtyard at Nongkhlaw, minutes before the ailing soldier's murder, he accused Scott of having gone back on his word by not supporting him in a dispute with the Rajah of Rani, who he also accused of trying to kill his parents by witchcraft. Under the terms of the 1826 treaty, U Tirot Sing understood that Scott was under an obligation to 'protect the Rajah's country from foreign enemies, and if any other Chief injure him, to enquire into the facts, and if it appears that he has been unjustly attacked, to afford him due support'.[45] In reply, Bedingfield said that he was a sick man, but that he would write to Scott on these issues.[46] U

Tirot Sing also had the support of the *Syiems* of Mylliem, Mawsmai and Jowai, who had sent their seals to Nongkhlaw before the attack. As time went on the British pushed their superior military advantage, and stopped the Khasi supply lines from the markets on the plains. From 1830, when Bor Manick of Khyrim was captured, a succession of outlaw chiefs were forced into capitulation, acknowledging British suzerainty, signing agreements that ceded their lands and judicial powers, paying monetary reparations and vowing to give the outlaw U Tirot Sing up to the British.[47] Governor General William Bentinck casually dismissed the 'slight insurrections' in the region. 'The insurgents', he reported to Lord Ellenborough, President of the EIC's Board of Control, 'are only armed with bows and arrows'.[48] But across the hills the rebel Khasis ambushed supply parties, blockaded roads or planted them with bamboo stakes. British military reinforcements scoured the mountains and ravines, setting stink pots off in caves to flush out opponents. Mounted on a mule, David Scott scoured the jungle fastness dressed in a tartan shooting-jacket with a double-barrelled gun in his hand.[49] But the *Syiem* of Nongkhlaw remained elusive.

Notes

1 As described by J.D. Hooker, *Himalayan Journals or, Notes of a Naturalist in Bengal, the Sikkim and Nepal Himalayas, the Khasia Mountains, &c* (Dehra Dun, 1999, first published 1854), volume 2, p. 262. Descriptions of travel to the hills are also found in Tomlin, *Missionary Journals*; H. Yule, 'Notes on the Kasia Hills, and people', *Journal of the Asiatic Society of Bengal*, 13:152 (1844), 612–31; H. Walters, 'Journey across the Pandua Hills, near Sylhet, in Bengal', *Asiatic Researches*, 17 (1832), 499–513; Lamb to Shakespear, 30 April 1828, IOR F/4/1448/56964.

2 Chowdhury, *The Khasi Canvas*, pp. 32–3, citing an account of a journey by Ethel St Clair Grimwood in her *My Three Years in Manipur* (1891). The term 'coolie' has derogatory overtones, but consistent with nineteenth-century convention, subsequent uses will not be in quotations marks.

3 Lord Alexander William Crawford Lindsay (ed.), *Lives of the Lindsays*, volume 4 (London, 1849), p. 177.

4 Cotton, *East Indiamen*, p. 183.

5 *Ibid.*, p. 179.

6 Robert Clyde, *From Rebel to Hero: The Image of the Highlander, 1745–1830* (East Linton, 1995).

7 Heather Streets, *Martial Races: The Military, Race, and Masculinity in British Imperial Culture, 1857–1914* (Manchester, 2004); Kenneth McNeil, *Scotland, Britain, Empire: Writing the Highlands, 1760–1860* (Columbus, 2007).

8 Lindsay, *Lives of the Lindsays*, p. 177.

9 D. Ludden, 'The first boundary of Bangladesh on Sylhet's northern frontiers', *Journal of the Asiatic Society of Bangladesh*, 48:1 (2003), 2–5.

10 W.W. Hunter, *A Statistical Account of Assam in Two Volumes* (Delhi, 1975, first published London, 1879), volume 2, p. 205.

11 Robert Lindsay to Sir Robert Murray Keith, 29 June 1782 in Lindsay, *Lives of the Lindsays*, p. 199.

12 L.S.S. O'Malley, *The Indian Civil Service, 1601–1930* (London, 1965, first published 1931), p. 33.

13 Jacques Weber, 'The British conquest of Bengal (1757–84)' in Claude Markovits (ed.), *A History of Modern India 1480–1950* (London, 2002), p. 245.
14 O'Malley, *The Indian Civil Service*, p. 34; William Wilson Hunter, *The Thackerays in India and some Calcutta Graves* (London, 1897), pp. 86–93; Ludden, 'The first boundary of Bangladesh', 13–16.
15 Lindsay, *Lives of the Lindsays*, p. 200.
16 O'Malley, *The Indian Civil Service*, p. 34.
17 Dewan Nurul Anwar Hussain Chowdhury, 'Lindsay, Robert (1754–1836)', Banglapedia: National Encyclopedia of Bangladesh, 2006, www.banglapedia.org/httpdocs/HT/L_0146.htm (accessed 26 May 2009).
18 Duncan to Lindsay, 18 July 1787, in Walter K. Firminger (ed.), *The Sylhet District Records* (Shillong, 1913–19), volume 2, p. 146.
19 F.B. Bradley-Birt, *'Sylhet' Thackeray* (London, 1911), Chapter 7, 'The Jaintia expedition'.
20 Lindsay to Edward Wheler, [March 1784], in Firminger (ed.), *The Sylhet District Records*, volume 1, p. 150.
21 Willes to Cornwallis, 15 September 1789, in Firminger (ed.), *The Sylhet District Records*, volume 3, p. 164.
22 Ludden, 'The first boundary of Bangladesh', p. 5 and passim.
23 Lamb to Shakespear, 'Report on climate of Cossya mountains with view to establishment of sanatarium', 30 April 1828, IOR F/4/1448/56964.
24 On Scott, see N.K. Barooah, *David Scott in North-east India 1802–1831: A Study in British Paternalism* (New Delhi, 1970).
25 Scott to Swinton, 24 March 1824, IOR F/4/1448/56964.
26 H.T. Prinsep, *A General Register of the Hon'ble East India Company's Civil Servants of the Bengal Establishment from 1790 to 1842* (Calcutta, 1844), p. 332.
27 Patrick Wolfe, 'Land, labor, and difference: elementary structures of race', *The American Historical Review*, 106:3 (2001), 868.
28 Maya Unnithan-Kumar, *Identity, Gender and Poverty: New Perspectives on Caste and Tribalism in Rajasthan* (Providence RI, 1997), pp. 51–2.
29 Horace Hayman Wilson, *Narrative of the Burmese War, in 1824–26, as Originally Compiled from Official Documents* (London, 1852), p. 26.
30 Gurdon, *The Khasis*, pp. xvii–xviii; R.B. Pemberton, *The Eastern Frontier of India* (New Delhi, 2005, first published 1835), pp. 75, 218–20. Scott's travelogue was extracted in Pemberton, and apparently first published in Horace Hayman Wilson, *Documents Illustrative of the Burmese War; With an Introductory Sketch of the Events of the War, and an Appendix* (Calcutta, 1827).
31 C.U.I Aitchison, *A Collection of Treatises, Engagements and Sanads Relating to India and Neighbouring Countries (Revised and Continued up to 1929). Vol. XII: Jammu & Kashmir, Sikkim, Assam & Burma* (Delhi, 1983), p. 117.
32 Aitchison, *A Collection of Treatises*, pp. 118–19.
33 Pemberton, *The Eastern Frontier of India*, p. 219.
34 Aitchison, *A Collection of Treatises*, pp. 122–3. Scott forwarded to government for ratification in January 1827 a copy and translation of the treaty with U Tirot Sing, which Swinton's reply of 2 March 1827 confirmed (IOR F/4/1448/56964).
35 Scott to Swinton, 13 January 1827, IOR F/4/1448/56964.
36 A. White, 'A memoir of the late David Scott, Esq.' in Archibald Watson (ed.), *Memoir of the Late David Scott, Esq. Agent to the Governor General, on the North-east Frontier of Bengal, and Commissioner of Revenue and Circuit in Assam, &c. &c. &c.* (Calcutta, 1832), pp. 15–67.
37 White, 'A memoir', p. 34.
38 Dane Kennedy, *The Magic Mountains: Hill Stations and the British Raj* (Berkeley, 1996), p. 84.
39 Lindsay, *Lives of the Lindsays*, p. 186.
40 Thomas Fisher to Charles Tucker, Political Agent at Sylhet, 28 April 1827, IOR F/4/1448/56964.
41 *Ibid.*

42 For various accounts of the Nongkhlaw killings see White to Swinton, 8 April 1829; 14 April 1829, IOR F/4/1448/56963; eyewitness accounts in IOR F/4/1506/59035; Holmes & Co., *The Bengal Obituary* (Calcutta, 1848), pp. 375–6.

43 See IOR/F/4/1448/56963.

44 Scott to Lamb, 10 April 1829 in Watson (ed.), *Memoir*, p. 110

45 Articles of agreement between David Scott and U Tirot Sing, 30 November 1826, F/4/1448/56963.

46 Giri, *The Khasis*, pp. 63–7.

47 Hargovind Joshi, *Meghalaya Past and Present* (New Delhi, 2004), p. 69; Giri, *The Khasis*, pp. 68–81.

48 Bentinck to Ellenborough, 2 August 1829, C.H. Philips (ed.), *The Correspondence of Lord William Cavendish Bentinck, Governor-General of India, 1828–1835* (Oxford and New York, 1977), volume 1, p. 266.

49 Watson (ed.), *Memoir*, p. 79.

CHAPTER FIVE

The tranquillity of the borders

A party of thirty-eight invalid soldiers from the British artillery base at Dum Dum outside Calcutta arrived at Pandua on 29 September 1830, under the care of Assistant Surgeon William Rhodes.[1] As the sick men pushed on to the base of the hills, many suffering from dysentery and high temperatures, wet weather prevented their advance. For the invalids marooned in the malarial jungles of Therriaghat, the mountains loomed ahead like a mirage. Some who stood up were overcome with nausea or abdominal pain and slumped to the ground. Others who lay prone and febrile in clothes soiled with frequent passing of mucous and bloody diarrhoea, struggled out of their lassitude to gain their feet. Weakened by travel, their fevers made monsters out of the shapes of jungle, cascade and precipice. They spent a whole night bivouacked in the open air, and several more days in tents before ascending the mountain, those too ill to walk being carried in *doolies* by hill porters. Where Lindsay had calculated the worth of the hills in cowries, and Scott by way of political advantage, each man of this straggling bunch of feverish sojourners clung for his very life to its indeterminate outlines.[2]

In the geo-politics of empire from the 1770s to the 1830s, the north-east was undergoing a period of transition, in which a zone of indeterminacy became an edge, and a barrier became incorporated into a known region. Cherrapunji thus became a distinctive landmark, a node in the imperial network. At an intimate and personal level, the Khasi Hills were becoming a domesticated destination and end point as much as a staging post and site of transience. The first recorded birth of a European child at Cherrapunji occurred on 31 December 1829, when a son, Frederick, was born to Margaret Ford, wife of John Ford, Quarter Master Sergeant of the Sylhet Light Infantry (SLI) Battalion. Almost exactly a year later, one of Rhodes's invalid charges shot himself 'in a fit of insanity'. The cycles of birth and death inescapably tied people to place, and from the early 1830s some British officials commenced what turned out to be long professional and personal associations with the region. Rhodes's invalids headed for Cherrapunji as the first residents of a newly established British sanatarium, and for a time the hills became a laboratory for testing and transforming imperial ideas of health and disease, military ascendancy or vulnerability, the permanence or impermanence of settlement, and the racial categories of Indian, Eurasian and British.

In analysing the role of medical theories in constructions of racial difference in British India, Mark Harrison has noted that when it came to the issue of the susceptibility of Europeans to local diseases, 'feelings of superiority and vulnerability were two sides of the same imperial coin'.[3] By the early decades of the nineteenth century, a knowledge of the deleterious effects of India's pathogenic climate on Europeans stationed there had begun to replace earlier medical opinion that had anticipated the adaptability of Europeans to acclimatise and over time build up immunity to local diseases. The kind of colonisation that had taken place in settler societies such as Australia and North America would be presumed to be fatally flawed in India; overexposure to India's climate came to be viewed as having deleterious physical as well as moral consequences. It was in such a context that the hill stations became important places of refuge.[4] Towns such as Simla, Darjeeling and Ootacamund would become synonymous as the seasonal highland headquarters of social and political power in India, and at the height of the colonial era around seventy hill stations dotted the country.

The regional subtleties of climate in India may not have been fully understood either by the LMS or the WFMS. India was generally thought to be a hot, unhealthy and insalubrious station for Europeans. The Khasi Hills were something altogether different and unexpected. From the sultry plains the Joneses would arrive in 1841 at a much more temperate climate, moderated by cool mountain breezes, where the average temperature was approximately 10° C lower than that of the plains. In winter (December to February) the temperature could be as low as 0° C – the sanatarium would need stoves from England to heat the barracks in winter – and in the height of summer in June it would very rarely exceed 30° C. But the major effect on life in the region was the summer monsoon from May to September. Neither the Joneses nor their mission masters were really prepared for the impact of this singular fact on the morbidity and mortality of its men, women and children in its early years.

The sanatarium at Cherrapunji

David Scott had been laying the groundwork for the hills as a place of European refuge since his first visit in 1824. He had initially been authorised to erect bungalows at Nongkhlaw 'for the reception of invalids', and through the wet season in the middle of 1827 'had some reason latterly to doubt the salubrity of Nunkhlow' and to favour Cherrapunji instead.[5] Scott was well aware that the success of the concept would very much depend on the ability of those in charge to mediate between the needs of the invalids (as well as British visitors 'and their followers'), and the 'fiery mountaineers', with whom careful negotiations would be required 'for lands, and privileges, and whatever else may be required to give efficacy to the plan'.[6]

After events at Nongkhlaw in 1829, Scott switched his focus to Cherrapunji as the site for the sanatarium. Land had been purchased for the purpose from the *Syiem* of Cherrapunji, in exchange for land lower down the mountain at Bhola-haut where he established a market. The *Syiem* had been an early ally of the British, and his negotiations were reputedly the source of some friction among his own people, who complained that he was simply benefiting financially from such dealings.[7] Scott fixed a site for a house at Cherrapunji, and from mid-1829 Charles Fenwick assisted with the accounts and superintended building works. With U Tirot Sing on the run, the troop presence at Cherrapunji became an important beachhead against the Khasi insurrection.

In June 1830 the official imprimatur was finally given for the establishment of the sanatarium.[8] The building works continued, and by October included accommodation for artillery and other European officers, as well as a hospital, public stables and twenty-one other small houses, which were rented from the government. Aside from his duties as Superintendent of Buildings, Fenwick had been appointed Commissariat Agent and interpreter, 'being well acquainted', according to Swinton, 'with the language and the people of Churra Poonjee'. In Scott's opinion, Fenwick had had substantial experience among the Khasis – clearly enough to have a working knowledge of their language – and was 'a person on whose good temper and discretion perfect reliance may be put'.[9]

The station at Cherrapunji comprised the Commissariat, Building and Survey, and Clothing Departments, each with their European sergeant or overseer, and staff including *mohurrir* (native writer), *peon* or Khasi *hurkaru* (messenger), or *godown sircar* (native accountant in charge of stores). To all intents and purposes the sanatarium was a trial establishment, yet it was clearly an extensive enterprise, and represented in spatial as well as symbolic terms a significant base in the north-eastern hill territory. Even in its nascent form at Cherrapunji, the hill station was one of the paradoxical sites of empire; as Dane Kennedy notes, these were sites of surveillance as well as resort, places that were integral rather than ephemeral to the imperial project.[10] Cherrapunji was a key material element from the kitbag of colonialism. The expanding network of barracks and ancillary buildings reified imperial authority. Over the previous decade British troops and officials had passed through the hills on military, commercial or survey business; now they stopped and put down roots of sorts. British presence was now more permanently interpolated into the north-eastern frontier zone, inserted into existing indigenous landscapes to tamper with their forms and meanings.

Communication technology was central to imperialism, and the road was a crucial tactic in making subject peoples 'politically submissive and economically profitable'.[11] The Grand Trunk Road from Calcutta in Bengal – through Agra, Delhi and Lahore to Peshawar in Pakistan – was an extension of ancient trade routes, but for the British was 'the backbone of their dominion in northern India'.[12] On a smaller but nonetheless strategically important scale, Scott's road was a key component of making British authority permanently visible, particularly at a time of guerrilla war when despite their inferior weaponry, the Khasi mountaineers had the advantage of the terrain. The road made British imperial power overt, transportable and extensible, linking stockades and supply depots across the region. Just as in north-western India, road-building was as much about tribal control as access.[13] A grander discourse on the infrastructure of imperialism was not lost on contemporary commentators. 'The wisdom of the British Government', trumpeted the *Friend of India* in 1835, 'if they wish to ensure peace and safety of the inhabitants of this fine, beautiful territory, is to imitate the example of the Romans'.[14] Four decades later, William Thornton was even more triumphalist: the British had found India 'as trackless as Britain was before the Roman invasion', but had made it 'in most directions as permeable as England was in the early part of the Georgian era'.[15]

Building public works was also a means of disciplining the natives, and Lieutenant R. Boileau Pemberton and Captain Jenkins recommended that Khasis work alongside Assamese prisoners on the heavy parts of the work in order to harness their intractability to 'habits of labour and industry'.[16] In December 1830, Scott urged to government the necessity of improving road construction in the hills, both on the lower road from Pandua and the upper part connecting with Assam, as well as constructing bunds (embankments against flooding) to improve navigation on the river from Pandua.[17] Prisoners from Assam were stationed at the sanatarium and employed in construction of the road to Cherrapunji. Under Fenwick's superintendence, the Assamese prisoners were instructed in bricklaying, blacksmithing, carpentry and lime-burning, and were engaged on a range of other public works projects. The existing route had seen the passage of lightly laden cattle, mules, horses and *doolies*, but a key to the consolidation of British strategic military presence in the north-east was to upgrade roads to bear the weight of guns and wheeled carriages. Coolies were an expensive mode of transporting camp equipment and supplies, and while elephants could be used to carry stores from boats to the foot of the hills, it was difficult to source their food on the plateau. Aside from the invalid depot, the stationing in the hills of military corps to be within easy march of Assam or Sylhet was of strategic necessity for the British. A system of telegraphs would further complete the intelligence network and connect the hill region within hours to Dacca to the south, and Manipur on the western borders of Burma.[18] The 400-mile route between Assam and Sylhet via the Brahmaputra could now be reduced to 125 miles over the mountains.

With British authority established more permanently at the station, its salubrious possibilities were also attracting other war-worn soldiers. Such was the growing demand for land that Scott was authorised by the middle of 1831 to grant perpetual leases on blocks of land at Cherrapunji on behalf of the government for individuals to erect houses. To this end, Fenwick was appointed surveyor of the sanatarium lands, allotting sites for people who wished to build their own houses, and collecting the rents that were owed to government. Major Thomas Colclough Watson was one such military man who came up to the hills for his health, and in March 1831 he was granted land on which to build a house.

The frontier tracts were still troubled with hostilities between Khasi and British. 'I wish much that I had the arms', Scott confided in Swinton in March 1831, 'the Cossyas and Garrows having attained a degree of confidence that it will require some beating to take out of them'.[19] As champion of the invalid station, Scott himself had long been feeling the effects of heart disease. At times the symptoms were so extreme he was obliged to sleep in a seated position, and by early June 1831 Scott could neither 'breathe, sleep, nor eat'. Contemplating a sea voyage to Van Diemen's Land for his health, in early July Scott came up to the hills hoping for respite, but with his legs terribly swollen he could barely walk at all and was reduced to getting about on the back of a mule.[20] Surgeon Rhodes had himself at this time been confined to bed for three weeks in extreme pain, not able even to turn himself over in bed. On 20 August 1831, Watson, Rhodes and Lieutenant Day stood at Scott's deathbed and heard his last sensible comments: 'I wish you, gentlemen, to bear witness to Government, that I am no longer able to conduct the affairs of the country'.[21] Rhodes immediately performed an autopsy, and Scott was buried that same evening next to Ensign Brodie on a hillock at Cherrapunji.[22]

Aside from his support for the sanatarium, Scott had promulgated the hills as a potential site for more substantial European colonisation.[23] With Scott's death, an alternative vision for the hills lost its most ardent proponent. William Cracroft, judge of the Provincial Courts of Appeal at Dacca for Civil Cases and an old friend of Scott's from college days in Calcutta,[24] was appointed Acting Agent to the Governor-General on the north-east frontier for a few months until the post was assumed on 28 October 1831 by Thomas Campbell Robertson, who had been present in the capacity of Civil Commissioner at the Treaty of Yandabo.[25] Lieutenant Townshend remained in civil charge of the Khasi Hills until Captain Frederick George Lister's appointment as Political Agent in early 1835.

In the Khasi Hills of the early 1830s, the British were only really in possession of a strategic road threaded between Sylhet and Assam, and a military establishment cum retreat where invalids and worn out military men came to idle or to die. The military presence in 1831 comprised detachments of the Sylhet and Assam Light Infantry, Sebundy *sepoys*, and Miri and Khasi irregulars. A survey in late 1831 shows the nascent British station in the vicinity of present-day Nongsawlia, laid out across a wedge-shaped section of tableland at the mountain's edge, on a strip of land just over five hundred yards wide and one and a half miles long.[26]

In what was a relatively small resident population, birth and death happened in equal but excess share. At the sanatarium, there were by early 1832 thirty-six men, with three women and some children, at a time when marriage rates among soldiers was still very low.[27] But many of those civil and military officials who had taken up private allotments elsewhere on the station were living in family groups. Major Watson's wife Sara bore a son and a daughter at Cherrapunji in April 1832 and November 1833, and their large family enjoyed a 'residence of considerable duration' in the Khasi Hills, although Watson himself was dead and buried in Dacca by 1834.[28] While the sanatarium's first Assistant Surgeon William Rhodes was to die at Bareilly at the age of thirty-two in 1836, Assistant Surgeon Dr Frederick Furnell and his wife Elizabeth had two children at Cherrapunji, returning to England in 1834, and Assistant Surgeon Henry Chapman and his wife Mary had a son in January 1834. One of Major Watson's allotments had previously been occupied by William James Turquand, chief magistrate and collector of Sylhet, who had only recently died in April 1831 aged thirty-three. Major Irwin Maling had been invalided from the service and repaired to the hills for his health at his own request in April 1829, but the ink had barely dried on the survey map when the Bengal Presidency Paymaster died in Calcutta on 17 November 1831. Maling's son Lieutenant Charles Ricketts Maling was later to become interpreter and quartermaster of the 28th Bengal Native Infantry. Just three months after his baby son died in March 1845, Charles himself succumbed at the age of just twenty-five, and was buried at Cherrapunji.

Race and authority: subordination and the limits of identity

The British officer elites may have had precious little control over mortality, but their social connections were rock solid. The paths of men such as Captain Adam White, Major Irwin Maling, Charles Trower and Captain Francis Jenkins may have crossed at Cherrapunji, but periodically they also interacted in the coffee or reading room at the Bengal Club in Calcutta, of which they and Sir Charles Theophilus Metcalfe had been founding members in 1827.[29] Between Calcutta and Cherrapunji, the racialised meanings of Britishness would be tested.

Charles Augustus Fenwick had served the station well in a variety of capacities since its inception, as interpreter, surveyor, commissariat agent, rent collector, as well as superintendent of gardens and building works and of convict workers. Prior to his association with David Scott, Fenwick had worked for some years as a registrar for the mofussil record committees, and been adopted as a Baptist missionary in 1825, moving from Chinsurah to Sylhet in 1827. Scott had previously recommended Fenwick's assistance in establishing schools among the Garos, a plan that had originated from the Church of England Bishop Heber, but the idea was dropped because he was a Baptist.[30]

On Scott's death in August 1831, Fenwick's position at the British station suddenly became precarious. Deprived of Scott's patronage, he was also stripped of the means of support for his wife and seven children. Swinton had accepted Scott's advice on the appointment of Fenwick, noting him as 'an European established at Churrapoonjee'.[31] Fenwick was in fact Eurasian, born in 1792 the illegitimate son of Captain Fenwick, at the end of a period where around half of children baptised in Calcutta at St John's Cathedral were illegitimate Eurasians.[32] Major Watson's growing influence at Cherrapunji put him in conflict with Fenwick, whose official roles Watson wished to countermand, and a war of words ensued. Fenwick was accused of selecting the best land for himself, of using his public position for personal financial gain, and of penning increasingly disrespectful letters to government officials. Fenwick resigned (or was removed) in 1832, and was frustrated that his complaints found a deaf ear first with Scott's officiating successor William Cracroft, and then his replacement Robertson, both of whom, according to Fenwick, were 'particular friends' of Major Watson.

On 1 January 1833 Charles Fenwick sent a letter of extortion to Cracroft, demanding that unless the judge paid him 2000 rupees he would reveal an alleged 'crime of S – – '. Fenwick was arrested and tried at Cherrapunji on 24 April 1833 before Robertson, aided by Francis Goldsburg, late officiating judge of the district of Sylhet. Fenwick was convicted and sentenced to four years' jail at Bhaugulpore.[33] Whatever the merits of the case, while Fenwick's intemperate outbursts opposed the clout of the old boys of the Bengal Club, his skin colour was a more direct affront to imperial ideology. The Eurasian population of India had now surpassed that of the British, but mixed race unions were far less common than they had been half a decade earlier. At the very time in the late 1820s and early 1830s when the Eurasian community was vocally advocating its interests as a class, attitudes to its social and political manifesto were hardening. Fenwick was typical of many Eurasians in being literate and educated (he claimed qualifications in the oriental languages). His employment at Cherrapunji was also characteristic of the kinds of subordinate roles assigned to a mixed-race class, jobs that were nevertheless critical in undergirding the mechanisms of British rule. Despite their growing protestations, Eurasians were to be ruled rather than rulers in their own right, in-between rather than ever fully British. This harsh lesson was sheeted home after the failure of an East Indians' Petition – presented to the British parliament in 1830 – to influence government policy in determining who was British and who was Indian.[34] Hawes notes that when restrictions on land regulations were relaxed in 1831, the rights of Eurasians were discouraged at the local level, as they were being increasingly defined as '"troublesome" to the constituted authorities'. Local officials could dispose of such 'troublesome' Eurasians by means of trumped-up charges.[35]

Sitting on Fenwick's jury was another Eurasian, the Serampore missionary Alexander Lish. Both he and Fenwick were paradoxically the product of Baptist missionary policy that saw the enrolment of Eurasian missionaries as a cheaper alternative to paying British missionaries higher salaries. The Serampore Baptists were, however, noted as champions of the Eurasian cause, and had printed at their press an account of the 1830 petition.[36] Charles Fenwick was not just emblematic of the multitude of Eurasians in India who challenged British social and political policy; he was one of its most vocal advocates. His views were published by the Baptist Mission Press in 1828 as an

Essay on the Colonization of Hindostan by East Indians, in which he mounted an argued case for the Eurasian colonisation of India.[37] Where others had argued for improved employment opportunities for Eurasians through trade and apprenticeships, Fenwick saw the future for those of mixed-race descent in farming colonies.[38] If Fenwick's view of the advancement of the status of the Eurasian was primarily based on a 'permanency of footing in the country',[39] then what happened at Cherrapunji in the aftermath of the failed 1830 petition dashed these ideals. Like David Scott and Adam White, he had believed in the mutual benefits to British and Indian as well as Eurasian, who would all be influenced by 'intelligent Christians living among them engaged in similar occupations and leading them by example and precept'.[40]

Fenwick was an insider/outsider, and his incarceration marked a further end to the Scott era. He had escaped from Nongkhlaw with Scott in the days before the massacre in 1829; he was instrumental in establishing Cherrapunji as a British beachhead in the ensuing three years, and as translator he assisted as an interlocutor between the Khasis and the British. Fenwick was a loyal servant of British control in the hills, a two-faced interlocutor who mediated the 'friendly disposition' of the people of Cherrapunji and its vicinity, 'at a time when the link of the Khasis national confederation was broken, and an [*sic*] universal suspicion, that we had entered their hills for the purpose of conquering and subjugating them to our Government began to prevail among the Khasias'. When Khasi resistance saw in the nature of the rugged country its strength and elusiveness to British control, Fenwick counselled Robertson that 'the way of thinking among the Khasias is very different from ours. They are extremely slow in comprehending the nature of our policy and the modes by which it is conducted'. On this score, Fenwick argued that the rebel *Syiem* Muken Sing 'only requires to be palavered a little more on the subject', and he claimed the credit for successfully enticing him to submit to Cracroft and eventually to move to the sanatarium where he lived 'as a pensioner of Government'.[41]

Permanent impermanence and the subjugation of the hill tribes

Well might Fenwick have wondered if there was 'something in the climate of this place which has a tendency to depreciate the value of my services, while at the same time it magnifies those of others'.[42] Whatever its metaphorical qualities, others were also questioning the atmosphere of the hills. In early 1832 Superintending Surgeon George Skipton reported to the Medical Board that after the fifteen-month trial of the Cherrapunji site, a more eligible situation should be considered for the sanatarium, one with milder weather in the rainy season, fewer mists and fogs, more room for exercise, more commodious barracks accommodation, and 'attended with a better feeling on the part of the Cossyas in that neighbourhood'.[43]

Cherrapunji continued to expand as camp followers and workers from the plains sought employment in the service of gentlemen domiciled on the station. With the road from Pandua to Cherrapunji still vulnerable from Khasi attack, the increased population needed a more regular police establishment. While Watson claimed in 1834 that cholera was unknown in the hills and that no children had died at Cherrapunji in three years,[44] the 'English' cemetery at Cherrapunji continued to harvest the dead: in 1832, two-year-old Mary McCarton and Calcutta judge Gilbert Coventry Master; in 1833, Lieutenant John Asprey Wood and Captain J.S. Pitts (three months after he had sat on Fenwick's jury); and 1834, Ettrick Havelock, the infant son of Captain Henry Havelock.

By 1834, the tide was turning against the Cherrapunji sanatarium; departing Political Agent T.C. Robertson recommended Mairang as a more suitable locality. Although some like Thomas Watson still argued the merits of the site 'as highly congenial to the European constitution' (and may have been the anonymous correspondent writing as *homo in nubibus* – man in the clouds – to the *Hurkaru* in support of the sanitarium), by mid-1834 the sanatarium was officially abolished.[45] The case for establishing a hill station at Darjeeling was still not confirmed at this point, with its unhealthy approach through the Terai jungle. But shrouded in cloud for too many months of the year, the progression of Cherrapunji from sanatarium to high refuge, then from hill station to town that was to characterise the development of many of India's hill stations, did not materialise.[46]

Although the sanatarium was closed down and its buildings decommissioned, Cherrapunji still retained the British military presence in the region and became the headquarters of the 11th SLI, raised in 1824. By the mid-1830s, the region was considered to be under the influence if not the rule of the British government. The Khasi Hills were a critical buffer zone for British Bengal, situated about a hundred leagues from its metropolis to the south, and a hundred leagues north 'between the mountains of Cherra and the heart of the Chinese province of *Yun-nan*'.[47]

Those occupying bungalows and paying rent to the government saw themselves as constituting a distinct community with a sense of belonging to this tenuous place, a feeling that was now threatened by the withdrawal of government interest and investment. In October

1834, the 'residents of Churra Poonjee' petitioned Francis Jenkins, incoming Agent to the Governor-General on the north-east frontier, on the matter of the removal of the medical officer from the station. Cherrapunji was now 'a very common place of refuge for invalids of all classes', and the lack of medical expertise would jeopardise the viability of such a remote community of European residents. The petitioners noted that schools had been established both for European children and 'for the instruction of the natives themselves, and the population generally have been both civilized and improved in circumstances by their communication with the European residents'. The dozen petitioners included the missionaries Lish and Rowe, Lieutenant Lewin and Harry Inglis.[48]

Francis Jenkins considered that the salary of an assistant surgeon was a small price to pay for maintaining British influence in the region. Advising the government against abandoning its general influence in the hills, Jenkins believed that aside from its ongoing potential as a European resort, the region would prove 'of increasing value to all the European population of Bengal', with its natural resources of lime, sandstone, timber, coal and iron. To withdraw from the hills would be to encourage civil unrest and the scourge of barbarism. 'The tranquillity of the borders', asserted Jenkins, 'can only be effectually and economically provided for, by maintaining our ascendancy in the Hills'.[49]

The *Friend of India* (printed at the Mission Press at Serampore) continued to champion Cherrapunji, encouraging the government – in the name of Scott's legacy – not to give up its strategic, commercial and health-giving advantages.[50] Having succumbed to British authority, the paper argued paternalistically, the Khasis ('these sons of nature') were due the protection of their benevolent conquerors: 'what can afford higher satisfaction than their answering the design of providence in confiding such tribes to their care?' The boosterism of Cherrapunji, formerly a desultory outpost where barely twenty families eked out a living, now boasted 'an appearance of English comfort seldom seen in India'. The effective re-establishment of Cherrapunji, with the appointment of Frederick Lister as Political Agent on 11 February 1835, and its consolidation as the headquarters of the SLI, gave some comfort to such hopes.[51] At the end of 1832, Harry Inglis, who had been 'in all the fights with the Cossya insurgents & is a capable shot', had been rewarded for his services by newly appointed Agent T.C. Robertson, with a paid commission in the SLI, and was put in command of the post at Nongkhlaw. In February 1835 he was appointed Lister's assistant.[52] By the end of 1837, the station residents – including Major and Mrs Lister, Lieutenant Lewin, and George and Harry Inglis, together with supporters in Sylhet such as judge Stainforth – had pledged nearly

500 rupees to build a church.[53] The increased numbers of pilgrims and traders now crossing between Sylhet and Guwahati – 126 miles or fourteen marches – were evidence 'that the spirit of improvement is abroad'.[54] Up the zig-zag mountain path they came, people and goods, carried in baskets or on foot; *sepoys* and ladies alike, soldiers from Sylhet, merchants from Manipur, even a square piano forte borne on the back of a Khasi porter.[55]

The British station in the Khasi Hills occupied the high ground, as it were; as Kennedy notes, British imperialists were alert to 'the symbolic significance of altitude'.[56] The British station was, however, at a distance from the huts of the native village, on a ridge to the north of the plain, with a population estimated in 1837 at around 3000. The independent village of Mawmluh to the west had a population of around 2000, while the smaller village of Mawsmai lay to the south. In the further vicinity of a mile or so around, there were other villages with around 15,000 inhabitants. Those in charge of the sanatarium had been alert to keeping a distance: 'The most strict injunctions should be given to keep the men within the limits of the Sanatarium, which are distinctly marked and contain ample space for exercise'.[57] Despite such caution, and while it is difficult to find references of specific interactions between Khasi and British, there was constant exchange and interaction, economic, linguistic and intimate. When supplies were short, the soldiers procured goats, pork and poultry from the Khasis, 'fine turnips' were brought down from the village of 'Churra', and potatoes were procurable from the Khasis at Mairang.[58] Surgeon Rhodes had been instructed to introduce vaccination in the hills, and noted that many Khasis were scarred with small pox, but was frustrated in his attempts to garner vaccine supplies from Calcutta.[59] Over the early months he spent at Cherrapunji, he developed the trust of at least some of the locals, Khasis coming to him from villages to have treatment for wounds and bites, and he felt 'perfectly convinced that Chirra people would readily submit their children to be vaccinated'.[60]

Rhodes wanted Khasis to come to him. But the parameters of spatial distancing and interpersonal proximity were deployed by the British to enforce particular definitions of culture, civility and otherness. There is a sense in the archive that David Scott was just a little too friendly with the natives; White, in his admiration of Scott, took this as a sign of Scott's remarkable personal qualities and his respect for the Khasis: 'they were treated on a footing of equality; indeed, took greater liberties than are allowed in that state; penetrated at all times, without ceremony, into your most private apartment'.[61] From the Khasi perspective, what 'liberties' were these, set against British penetration into their public and private affairs? For the government in Calcutta, the

Nongkhlaw massacre and subsequent insurrection of the 'rude tribes' were partly attributable to Scott's lack of perspective, his *misreading* of distance. Scott, it appeared, was misinformed about the general undercurrent of disaffection precisely because he had been overly indulgent and liberal in his relationships with the Khasis. In the eyes of government, Scott had 'viewed these mountains generally with too sanguine an expectation of their capabilities'.[62] 'On a review of these events', chastised the EIC Court of Directors from London, 'we see in the conduct of the officers of your Government much to be regretted, and something to be blamed'.[63] Scott's liberality of views could now be mobilised to justify a more forceful and coercive military response.

Once established in the mid-1820s, British presence in the hills could swing from aggression to apparent conciliation, and their motives and actions could be unpredictable from the Khasi perspective. Rhodes and his party arrived barely a year and a half after the events at Nongkhlaw, so it was no wonder that the Khasis 'for some time kept back from the intercourse now established'.[64] Alexander Lish also considered the play of social distance when he wrote of the Khasis in 1838, and clearly articulated the ideology that to be civilised did not mean to be an equal. The 'savage incivility' that he observed on first arriving in the hills in 1832 was paradoxically manifest in his 'being often greeted with a hearty shake of the hand; which, however significant of goodwill, I would much rather have dispensed with, knowing my friends were not very remarkable for cleanliness'. By the time of his departure six years later, the Khasis wore 'more the appearance of human beings than before'; handshakes had now been replaced by 'a polite nod' and a *khublei*, the Khasi welcome meaning 'may God [the Khasi God] be with you'.

By early 1833 Inglis and Lister had reduced U Tirot Sing into a state of desperation by blockading the bazaars and destroying his provisions. According to his own account, sometime in the afternoon of Tuesday 9 January 1833, Harry Inglis went to a place half a mile east of Oomchilong, where he had arranged to meet Jeet Roy, U Tirot Sing's *muntree*. Jeet Roy had understood from Inglis's *dobashees* (interpreters) that Inglis had been authorised by government to treat for the surrender of the *Syiem*. The pair agreed on terms – principally, that U Tirot Sing's life was to be spared should he surrender. Harry Inglis licked salt from the blade of a sabre to seal the pact, according to Khasi custom. It was agreed that U Tirot Sing would meet Harry Inglis on the following Saturday, at a spot to be agreed on two hours beforehand, and that both Inglis and U Tirot Sing would be unarmed and each attended by only two servants. U Tirot Sing met Inglis at the agreed time at Nursingare, a mile east of the post at Oomchilong. Soon after U Tirot Sing was seated, a band of thirty archers and swordsmen and eleven men with muskets

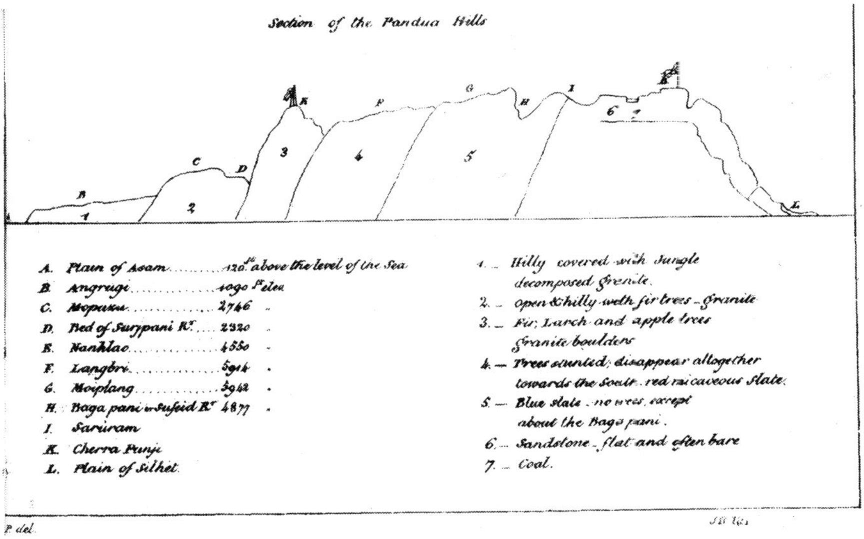

2 Plate from H. Walters, 'Journey across the Pandua Hills, near Sylhet, in Bengal', 1832.

surrounded the party. Jeet Roy justified the breach of promise on the basis that it would 'not be respectful for his master to come without a smaller retinue, and that this was to show the people, he was not made captive but surrendered'. U Tirot Sing questioned Inglis for a time, before again demanding that he lick salt from a sabre as proof of his word. U Tirot Sing was taken by Inglis to Lister at Mairang, and on 15 January handed over to Lieutenant Vetch of the Assam Light Infantry.[65]

When interrogated by magistrate Matthie at Guwahati following his surrender, U Tirot Sing claimed that Harry Sahib had actually promised 'that all circumstances connected with his past proceedings should be forgiven and forgotten, and that his life and respectability should be preserved'.[66] Inglis denied ever having offered such a pardon to U Tirot Sing,[67] but the differing version of events was the basis of a lasting mythology that U Tirot Sing was lured into captivity by the treachery of Harry Inglis.

Robertson recommended that U Tirot Sing be jailed in Dacca rather than the penal settlement on the Tenasserim Coast, in order that he might be 'seen occasionally by some of his countrymen who cannot otherwise be convinced of our having adhered to our promise in sparing his life'.[68] U Tirot Sing was eventually moved into an individual apartment in the prison compound at Dacca, with a cook and general servant.[69] At one o'clock in the afternoon of 17 July 1835, U Tirot Singh died in jail.[70] The Khasi uprising was all but vanquished. Resistance from Sngap Sing of Maram in 1838 – during which time a number of *sepoys* and servants of the SLI were murdered, and the ten-year-old son of an SLI *naik* was beheaded – was soon crushed by the British. Lister's request to 'enforce tranquillity' through 'distress and starvation' was approved,[71] and by 1839 Sngap Sing's surrender marked the end of a decade of Khasi military resistance to British rule.[72]

To illustrate H. Walters's account of his 1828 'Journey across the Pandua Hills', published in *Asiatic Researches* in 1832, a cross section of the Khasi Hills showed the British ensign planted on the mountain-top at Nongkhlaw and at Cherrapunji. By the end of the 1830s, Walter's symbol of intention had indeed become an emblem of fact. With the job done, according to Pemberton in 1835, 'there now scarcely remains a single line of any political or geographical interest to be explored, in this portion of our frontier'.[73]

Notes

1 Rhodes to secretary of the Medical Board, 4 August 1831, IOR F/4/1449/56965.
2 Rhodes to Skipton, 1 January 1831, IOR F/4/1449/56965.
3 Mark Harrison, '"The tender frame of man": disease, climate, and racial difference in India and the West Indies, 1760–1860', *Bulletin of the History of Medicine*, 70:1 (1996), 70.
4 *Ibid.*, 79–81.
5 Scott to Lamb, 18 July 1827 in Watson (ed.), *Memoir*, p. 102.
6 Scott to Lamb, Singamaree, 20 May [1827], in Watson (ed.), *Memoir*, p. 91.
7 'Observations on the British Territories to the east of Bengal', *Friend of India*, 5 February 1835, 42.
8 IOR F/4/1279.
9 Scott to Swinton, 1 July 1830, IOR F/4/1449/56965.
10 Kennedy, *The Magic Mountains*, pp. 1, 4.
11 Daniel R. Headrick, *The Tools of Empire: Technology and European Imperialism in the Nineteenth Century* (New York and Oxford, 1981), p. 11.
12 Jan Morris and Simon Winchester, *The Stones of Empire: The Buildings of the Raj* (Oxford, 1983), p. 123.
13 J.R. Spencer and W.L. Thomas, 'The hill stations and summer resorts of the Orient', *Geographical Review*, 38:4 (1948), 647.
14 'Observations on the British Territories to the east of Bengal', *Friend of India*, 5 February 1835, 42.
15 William Thomas Thornton, *Indian Public Works* (London, 1875), p. 24 in David Arnold, *The New Cambridge History of India: Science, Technology and Medicine in Colonial India* (Cambridge, 2000), p. 107.
16 Jenkins and Pemberton to Chief Secretary, 4 October 1831, IOR, P/126/56, No. 112, 15 October 1832.
17 Scott to Swinton, 6 December 1830, IOR F/4/1449/56965.
18 Fisher to Scott, 16 October 1830, IOR F/4/1449/56965.
19 Scott to Swinton, received 11 March 1831, PWJF 2781/5.
20 Swinton to Benson, 1 September 1831, PWJF 2811/13.
21 Watson (ed.), *Memoir*, pp. 136–7.
22 Rhodes, 21 August 1831, PWJF 2811/13; Scott to Swinton, 24 July 1831, PWJF 2811/19a.

23 See for example Scott to Swinton, 1 July 1830, IOR F/4/1449/56965.
24 Cracroft to Swinton, 3 September 1831, PWJF 2811/9.
25 Robertson was relieved by Francis Jenkins, who held the post 1834–61.
26 Cracroft to Swinton, 11 November 1831, IOR F/4/1449/56965.
27 C.J. Hawes, *Poor Relations: The Making of a Eurasian Community in British India 1773–1833* (Richmond, Surrey, 1996), p. 4, citing S.C. Ghosh, *The Social Condition of the British Community in Bengal, 1757–1800* (Leiden, 1970), pp. 58–61.
28 Lieut.-Col. Thomas C. Watson, 'Chirra Punji, and a detail of some of the favourable circumstances which render it an advantageous site for the erection of an iron and steel manufactory on an extensive scale', *Journal of the Asiatic Society of Bengal*, 3:25 (1834), 25–33.
29 H.R. Panckridge, *A Short History of the Bengal Club* (Calcutta, 1927).
30 Much of Fenwick's involvement is his own testimony in a long letter to Governor Bentick, written from prison on 16 January 1834, IOR F/4/1506/59037.
31 George Swinton, 2 July 1830, F/4/1279, No. 137.
32 Hawes, *Poor Relations*, pp. 4, 162.
33 On 16 January 1834 Fenwick wrote an extensive memorial to Governor-General of India William Bentinck, appealing his case, to no avail. For details of the case see IOR/F/4/1506/59037.
34 Hawes, *Poor Relations*, pp. vi–x.
35 *Ibid.*, p. 38.
36 *Ibid.*, pp. 51, 87.
37 C.A. Fenwick, *Essay on the Colonization of Hindostan by East Indians* (Calcutta, 1828).
38 Hawes, *Poor Relations*, pp. 115–21.
39 Cited in *Ibid.*, p. 118.
40 *Ibid.*, citing Fenwick, *Essay*, p. vi, and editorial, *Bengal Hurkaru*, 4 September 1828.
41 Fenwick to Robertson, 3 May 1832, F/4/1506/59037.
42 Fenwick to Robertson, 4 September 1832, F/4/1506/59037.
43 Skipton to J. Hutchinson, January 1832, F/4/1449/56965.
44 Watson, 'Chirra Punji', 26.
45 *Ibid.* The *Hurkaru* correspondent mentioned in 'The sanatarium at Cherrapoonjee', *Friend of India*, 1 January 1835, 2.
46 Kennedy, *The Magic Mountains*, pp. 11–12. See also *Friend of India*, 24 August 1837, 266; 16 November 1837, 364: 23 November 1837, 372.
47 'Observations on the British Territories to the east of Bengal', *Friend of India*, 5 February 1835, 42.
48 Petition from the residents at Churra Poonjee to the Agent to the Governor-General north-east frontier, 27 October 1834, IOR F/4/1583/64359.
49 Jenkins to Deputy Secretary to Government, 3 November 1834, F/4/1583/64359.
50 'Observations upon the territory on our eastern frontier continued', *Friend of India*, 12 February 1835, 50.
51 'Re-establishment of Cherra-poonjee', *Friend of India*, 26 February 1835, 65.
52 Swinton to Benson, 2 August 1832, PWJF 2851/27.
53 *Friend of India*, 9 November 1837, 355.
54 *Friend of India*, 16 November 1837, 364.
55 Watson, 'Chirra Punji', 27.
56 Kennedy, *The Magic Mountains*, p. 196.
57 George Swinton, 24 June 1830, IOR F/4/1448/56964.
58 Watson, 'Chirra Punji', 27.
59 Rhodes to Skipton, 1 January 1831, IOR F/4/1449/56965.
60 Rhodes to Scott, 1 May 1831, IOR F/4/1449/56965.
61 White, 'A memoir', p. 39.
62 Extract Political Letter from Bengal, 16 January 1834, IOR F/4/1448/56963.
63 Extract Political Letter to India from Court of Directors to Government, 3 December 1834 (No. 14), IOR F/4/1549/61881.
64 Rhodes to Swinton, 23 February 1831, PWJF 2781/50/2.

65 Inglis to Lister, 14 January 1833, IOR F/4/1506, 59035.
66 Matthie to Robertson, 26 January 1833, IOR F/4/1506/59035.
67 Inglis to T. Brodie, 7 March 1833, IOR F/4/1506/59035.
68 Robertson to Macnaghten, 1 May 1833, IOR F/4/1506/59035.
69 Richardson to Middleton, 11 April 1833; Middleton to Macnaghten, 16 April 1833, IOR F/4/1506/59035.
70 Scott to J. Lowis, 28 July 1835, IOR F/4/1583/64359.
71 Lister, 16 July 1838, IOR F/4/1787/73605; see also IOR F/4/1832/75909.
72 Giri, *The Khasis*, p. 80.
73 Pemberton, *The Eastern Frontier of India*, p. 76.

CHAPTER SIX

The richest collections

Half way up the ascent from Pandua to Cherrapunji in 1835, with the odd feeling that he was being shadowed by a native boy, Scottish surgeon John McLelland found himself on a precipitous part of the mountain route, over 2000 feet above the height of the plain. Here on a narrow ridge, 'several hundred miles from the sea, as well as several thousand feet above it', he made the extraordinary discovery of a fossil beach. McLelland was able in a few hours to gather a thousand specimens, and over the course of the next few days established that an organic belt of fossilised shells ran at a comparable elevation on other adjacent slopes of the mountain, and that tertiary fossils could also be found about Cherrapunji itself. The surgeon easily excavated a new genus of *Echinida* (sand dollar) from the friable sandstone, and later tabled a collection including cockles, sea snails and marine worms. Here was material evidence from the third great period of geological time in which the earth's climate had cooled ahead of the ice age, dinosaurs had become extinct, and mammals including the first hominids had emerged as dominant life forms.[1]

An account of the discovery opened the second volume of the *Calcutta Journal of Natural History* in 1840, which McLelland was to edit until its demise in 1847.[2] McLelland was just one of many members of the Indian Medical Service (IMS) who spent their time in the country in the service of science – exploration, natural science, philology, ethnology – as well as in harness to their official careers.[3] This interest in science can be tracked through the careers of soldiers, civil servants and missionaries themselves. The Asiatic Society of Bengal, which counted many of them as its members, had been established in 1784. In south India, Johann Gerhard König, a surgeon and botanist at the Danish medical mission at Tranquebar in the 1770s and 1780s, had studied in Sweden under Linnaeus, and Moravian missionaries at Travencore were sending specimens to Joseph Banks in the 1770s.[4]

William Carey was perhaps one of the best known botanists in India. A friend and ally of Nathaniel Wallich of the Calcutta Botanic Gardens,[5] Carey also edited botanist William Roxburgh's *Hortus Bengalensis* (1814) and *Flora Indica* (1832).

The former work included a number of collections made by magistrate Mathew Richard Smith on the eastern frontier of Bengal, in Sylhet and the Garo Hills, between 1810 and 1812.[6] It was Carey's friend Smith who in 1813 had welcomed the Serampore missionary Krishna Chandra Pal to Sylhet. Smith, like many other semi-professional residents of British India, was an indefatigable cog in the wheel of imperial science. In 1810 he had first drawn Roxburgh's attention to rubber growing in the Khasi Hills and elsewhere in the region, in the form of a sample of two gallons of Khasi honey in a cane container called a *turong*, which had been lined with caoutchouc as a sealant.[7]

The north-east was an important node in shaping ideologies of colonial science. Scientific explorations between Sylhet, the Khasi Hills and Assam constructed knowledge of the economic potential of natural resources (lime, coal, oranges, tea), which in their turn helped to build, power and feed the British empire in India and beyond. Landscape as a social construction could be harnessed in the ideological as well as practical service of empire. Just as interesting are the ways in which such scientific knowledge and discourse elided questions of indigenous science or agency, and constructed particular connections between moral and environmental improvement. At arm's length from the metropole and often operating as enthusiastic amateurs rather than officially endorsed imperial agents, the extra-professional endeavours of subscribers to scientific journals such as McLelland's played a nonetheless important role in determining the practices and ideologies of colonial science as well as supplying Europe's scientific community with specimens and data.[8] The nexus between imperialism and botany (both plant hunting and experimental agriculture) is a pivotal one.[9] 'Gardens of science', Axelby reminds us, 'were also the nurseries of Empire'.[10]

Gleanings in Science (1829), edited by Major James Herbert and James Prinsep (1831) and printed at the Serampore Mission Press, was incorporated in 1832 into the *Journal of the Asiatic Society of Bengal*.[11] The Governor-General Lord Bentinck and the Court of Directors were listed as subscribers of *Gleanings of Science* in 1829, and military surveyors and civil administrators of the north-east were well represented in its subscriber list: David Scott (Assam), George Lamb (Dacca), surveyor Lieutenant Thomas Fisher (Sylhet) and Charles Tucker at Dacca, and Political Agent Captain Francis Jenkins.[12] The third and last volume of *Gleanings in Science* in 1831, to which Dr Rhodes of Cherrapunji was also a subscriber, was dedicated to Bengal Chief Secretary George Swinton, 'in testimony of his well known exertions for the extension of science generally'. Natural science and colonial strategy were intimate bedfellows. While Desmond suggests that the EIC was not completely dictated by economic interests – as evidenced in their role as scholarly patrons and in their museum and library at Leadenhall Street – he also notes that there 'were comparatively few professionals until well into the nineteenth century.[13] The Court of Directors, despaired the *Friend of India*, might more properly encourage the cause of science as exercised through the 'talent of their own officers'.[14]

The observation of the natural environment of the north-east, as a key resource of British imperialism, melded the needs of science and strategy, and was an important institutional form for the EIC in its transition from an empire of trade to one of territorial administration and control.[15] Botany, geology and geography served multiple purposes; being scientifically minded, as Arnold notes, could be 'politically advantageous'.[16] As Lieutenant Richard Wilcox of the Great Trigonometric Survey recovered his health at the invalid bungalow at Nongkhlaw in October and November 1827, he could also take the opportunity to keep a record of diurnal temperature and barometric pressure.[17] Climate and acclimatisation had been key elements in strategic decision-making regarding the viability and placement of the sanatarium. The surveys of the Khasi Hills that informed road engineering or military movements also elicited a range of narratives in which ideals of science, race and empire were further coded.

Geography as an appropriating gaze

An account of a trip to the Khasi Hills by 'F' (possibly Fisher), published in *Gleanings of Science* in 1829, self-consciously viewed the region as a resource, with an economic eye for its botanical and geological productions, as well as for the exigencies and prospects of imperial control over the native population. The author again felt the power of nature, of the 'stupendous and magnificent' waterfalls, 'calculated to excite mingled sensations of pleasure and awe in the beholder'. In such a natural pleasure-ground, a keen and pragmatic eye was still cast over nature's bounty: fossil-bearing limestone, exported for making *chunam*; slate, iron (smelted by the Khasis) and coal, which appeared in a three-foot wide surface seam between Sohrarim and Cherrapunji; oranges, areca nut, pineapples and limes, all grown in the lower portion of the Khasi Hills and traded to lower Bengal. The terrain was also seen through the lens of its agricultural potential for supporting European crops of wheat, barley and oats. If the fir trees and the moderate climate could make the locality seem more European ('cloth dresses' were required to be worn in May, usually the warmest month of the year in India), F's account more overtly constructed particular paternalistic and racialised narratives about Khasi primitivism and ineptitude, reinforcing their potential as docile and productive subjects of the British empire. In the aftermath of the 1826 treaty, and in the presumed certainty that the area was now 'under the sway of the British Government', part of the practical purpose of the visit had been to determine the best line of road through the hills. As a road map of annexation and pacification, the narrative reinforced stereotypes of native peoples as uncivilised ('There are not throughout the hills any places deserving the names of towns'), cowardly ('the reputation for bravery which had been assigned to them by some observers has suffered a considerable abatement'), and idle and unmanly ('throwing all labour upon the women'). The correspondent concluded that little more had been learned about the Khasis than Scott had gleaned in his 1824 visit, and that increased contact with Europeans – perhaps under a scheme of European settlement – could only raise their moral and physical conditions. 'The power and equity of the British Government', asserted the writer, 'will ensure them the possession of their rights, while its moderation will encourage them (under the guidance of qualified settlers) to develope [*sic*] the resources of their country, in the quiet enjoyment of which, it may be expected, these people will speedily become an orderly, happy, and contented race'.[18]

Henry Walters, a judge of the City Court at Dacca, toured the Khasi Hills in late October and early November 1828.[19] His account rehearsed many of the standard observer stereotypes of the hill people: the bold, independent and athletic Khasis with their 'beautiful muscular limbs', both physically and morally superior to the people of the plains. At Cherrapunji, he was transported back to his youth in Somerset: 'I can almost fancy myself on the top of *Bannerdown*!' Walters's Indian tenure was now in its sixteenth year – the mountains were a liminal territory rising out of the familiar reality of his current circumstances but also penetrating the memory of his homeland. Each *aide memoire* on this tour transported him to fondly remembered times and places ('the landscape assumed more of an English character'; 'saw the first hoar frost since leaving England'), but at the same time exacerbated his separation from them. In these associations Walters echoed a common correlation of British visitors in the hills. The exposed country between Cherrapunji and Mairang reminded botanist William Griffith in 1835 'somewhat of the woods of Buckinghamshire',[20] and according to an 1837 account, 'is not without its charms to those whose memory recurs to the bleaker spots of the Downs of England, or who greet, as an old friend, the sight of a fir tree'.[21]

Walters's descriptive narrative frequently frames the landscape in terms of the picturesque, the grand and the sublime. Physical ascent matches elevation of spirit, its apotheosis at Prospect Rock at Nongkhlaw, from where he could see stretched out before him the Garo Hills, the Brahmaputra River snaking through the plains of Assam, and the snow-capped mountains of Tibet and Bhutan. This totalising gaze is generally revealed throughout Walters's narrative, his observations of the Khasis themselves recorded in terms that are at once distancing, objectifying, claiming scientific accuracy: 'They are devoted to chewing *paun* and betel, very fond of spirituous liquor, and eat and drink whatever comes their way. In religion they follow some of the Hindu customs. They have no written character'.[22] The stone monuments of the Khasis, reminiscent for Walters of Stonehenge and the cromlechs of Wales, served to consign the Khasis to a primitive stage of civilised development: 'how singular it is that the customs of nations, in the same stage of society indeed, but situated at such an immeasurable distance from each other, should be found so exactly to coincide!'[23] If in 'moral character' the Khasis 'tower, like their mountains, over the natives of the plains', Khasi women were characterised as unusually workmanlike (working the iron-smelter bellows, acting as 'the best porters'), and Khasi men by implication less manly. It is in Walters's description of the cremation ceremony of a young child at Sohbar that he reveals most starkly a racialised conception of both Khasi men and women as sub-human:

> a dead child was brought out of the stockade by its mother and female relations, who made a dreadful howling. They placed it in a sort of wooden cradle prepared in the place of concremation, and after the fire was placed under it, retired to the village. A priest then mumbled some prayers, while the dogs and pigs fought for the plantains, oranges, and green betelnut, which had been offered on the occasion, and would doubtless have fought for the roasted child also, were he not too hot for them. The people looked on with perfect indifference – the father, a stupid looking brute, stood chewing his *paun*.[24]

During their treaty negotiations with U Tirot Sing in 1826, Scott and White had been impressed by the democracy of Khasi law. For Walters in his whistle-stop survey of 1828, political control was seen to be ineffectual rather than democratic. Under the governance of 'numerous petty Rajas' the Khasis were forced to defer all matters of importance to a council of elders as well as to the 'Queen Mother'. Perhaps after the capture of rebel leader U Tirot Sing, it was again easier by the mid-1830s for the Khasis to be characterised by the British as a 'free, bold, robust race', whose independent villages governed by a Rajah and his councillors could be contrasted favourably to the total rule of the Bengal Rajahs.[25]

A further account of a four-day excursion to Cherrapunji by an anonymous visitor from Dacca was published in *Gleanings in Science* in 1831, and repeated the traveller conventions used for figurative effect to denote panoptic command, racial difference and superiority: observation of stone monuments, collection of rock and insect specimens, a visit to the native village at Cherrapunji and the breathtaking view of the plain.[26] As in Walters's account, while the generic Khasi could be ascribed potential moral qualities and capabilities (when set against the inhabitants of the plains), individuals encountered were still ranked dismissively. Pleased to buy oranges from the smiling locals, any possibility of equilibrium was marked by 'the offence offered to our olfactory nerves; the scent emitted by the persons and dress, more closely resembling that of a dirty dog kennel, full of dried fish'. Particular cultural thresholds of tolerance again marked the Khasi as inferior. That the crowds of women at the Cherrapunji bazaar comported themselves with 'no noise, or scolding' made them less barbaric rather than more civilised, and certainly never fit to be equals: 'If these people were not so dirty, their good tempers, and freedom from prejudice of castes; their strict adherence to truth, and their honesty, would render them really valuable servants'.[27]

In its cognisance of native industries such as iron smelting and silk production, and its description of natural resources like coal, limestone and native fruits, Walters's vision of the hills encompassed at least an amateur appreciation of its scientific and economic potential. While he himself made collections of plants and rocks, the hills were 'an ample unexplored field for a Botanist – also for a Mineralogist'.[28] The lime trade had long been carried on at places such as Chhatak and Chuna Ganj at the foot of the hills. In the early 1830s the Khasis continued to supply stone from quarries rented from them by Inglis & Co. and Terraneau, which they broke and rolled to the boats that would transport it to the wood-fuelled lime kilns that lined the Surma river banks, where fires would burn for four days and nights until the stone glowed white hot.[29]

Botany and the harvest of empire

During his time at Cherrapunji in the early 1830s, Acting Agent and Dacca judge William Cracroft had published a series of papers on iron smelting and rainfall,[30] and had donated specimens of coal and limestone to the museum of the Asiatic Society's physical class lecture series. In 1834, while journeying from Cherrapunji to Assam using captain Fisher's sketch as a guide, Cracroft not only made strategic observations on the best line of road and on possible sites for stockades, but made detailed notes on geology and natural history. To the hooting echoes of the gibbon and in the company of wild elephants and leopards, Cracroft collected more samples of granite, felspar and gneiss for the cupboards of the Asiatic Society in Calcutta.[31]

Cracroft's expertise stretched to more than just geology. In June 1829 he had read a paper before the Agricultural and Horticultural Society of India on the Cape Fig,[32] and he reported from the sanatarium at the end of 1831 on the progress of horticulture at Cherrapunji.[33] The society's transactions were partly printed at the Serampore Mission Press. William Carey had been a co-founder of the society in 1820, and was one-time president, and its aims consciously linked moral, industrial and economic improvement.[34] At Cherrapunji, Cracroft distributed seeds sent by the society to the European residents, and distributed horticultural products to the *Syiem* of Mawphlang, and Dewan Sing (the Agent's interpreter), both of whom were already producing excellent crops of turnips at Mawphlang and at the native village at Cherrapunji. He reported that the Khasis were very keen to receive seeds and plants: 'the old women of Mowflong refuse to sell any more potatoes on the grounds of requiring all that remain as seed for the next crop'.[35] The society's president, Sir Edward Ryan, also visited Cherrapunji in 1831. London-born Ryan – lawyer, judge and patron of science – had arrived in India in 1827, and was regarded by Bentinck as 'the sergeant major of the march of the intellect' and 'one of the most *useful* men in India'.[36] At Cherrapunji, Ryan distributed seeds and plants, and had some fruit trees planted out at Nongkhlaw and Mairang. David Scott's imperial mark was still indelible: 'Every place on these hills bears testimony to the liberal and philanthropic spirit of the late Mr. Scott, which led him to leave no experiment untried which might lead to useful and beneficial results'.[37] Ryan was the first to record Khasi domestic crops including the *sooplong* root, *kookorroo dhan*, Indian corn and a species of cucumber.[38]

If tobacco and wheat were being trialled as crops in the Khasi Hills, tea was also in the government's mind, to compete with the China trade that had been opened up after the *Charter Act* in 1833. Before tea was discovered as being native to Assam in 1834, the government had established a Tea Committee to investigate where the tea plant might be best grown in India. Though the discovery of indigenous tea was recorded from at least 1815 – and David Scott himself had planted tea in one of his gardens in 1826 – no official identification was made until the 1830s.[39] Specimens of Assamese tea had been sent in late 1834 via Political Agent Francis Jenkins, himself an amateur botanist, to Nathaniel Wallich at the Calcutta Botanic Garden, and a deputation was sent to Assam in August 1835 to explore the 'tea forests' and research the natural history of the region.[40] The Assam Tea Deputation, comprising Wallich and William Griffith as botanists, and Dr John McLelland as geologist and soil expert, came in sight of the Khasi Hills on 14 September 1835. It was on this trip that McLelland discovered his fossil beach. Griffith's journals, arranged for publication after his death by McLelland in 1847, record in some detail the varied flora, fauna and geology of the Khasi Hills observed on this and a later trip in September/October 1837.[41] The findings of the Tea Deputation anticipated the immanent commercialisation of the Assam tea crop, which by the early 1840s was becoming a viable contender with the China tea trade.[42]

After twenty days based at Cherrapunji, Griffith recorded on 30 October 1835 that 'Our stay here has proved a source of great delight, and accumulation of botanical and geological treasures'. On his 1837 visit he confirmed his view that the flora around Cherrapunji, located as it was at the juncture of sub-tropical and temperate vegetation zones, was the richest of any locality in the Khasi Hills: 'I have no doubt, that within a circle of three miles of Churra, 3,000 species might be found in one year'. For the members of the Assam Tea Deputation, each step through the hills revealed yet another botanical wonder, as they waded through swathes of orchids, ferns, rhododendrons and magnolias. The route of their botanical enumeration was determined by the line of the military road through the hills, and Captain Jenkins and Major Lister also advised them on further routes to follow to the Garos and Cacharees. They also gained intelligence from other officers stationed in the hills. Lieutenants Townshend and Vetch passed on their views on a particular species of snipe, and having spent more time in the hills (rather than passing through) were able to comment on the seasonal variation in bird numbers, or Khasi views on the wood-cock. The Khasis themselves appear as shadowy figures in Griffith's account, never acknowledged as direct informants. The Tea Deputation passed through Khasi villages en route, and noted areas where cultivation occurred: sugarcane and capsicum near Syniasya; *Digitaria* (Khasi *Raishan* or crabgrass), *Glycine tuberosa* (ground nut), *Coix lacryma* (Khasi *Sa riew syiar*, Job's tears, used as a cereal substitute) and rice on the slopes about Mawphlang; cotton and a species of *Eleasine* at Cherrapunji.[43] Eloquent on matters of sublime landscape or exquisite ferns, Griffith was more circumspect on the question of the Khasis. These he regarded as a people degraded by contact with Europeans, 'the women in regard to shape being exactly like their mates; and as these are decidedly ugly – somewhat tartarish-looking people, very dirty, and chew pawn to profusion – they can scarcely be said to form a worthy portion of the gentler sex'. Griffith noted the Khasi practice of erecting stone memorials, but in his calculation, nothing was to be learned from them that could be useful to the purposes of the Tea Deputation. Their utility was only to be measured as a source of labour as porters, though 'Their hire is, considering the cheapness of their food, very expensive'.

At a village of blacksmiths near Kullung Rock, 'the sound of their anvils when beaten is very soft and musical, not unlike that of a sheep bell'. The Khasis were in a sense just background noise for the more important task of scientific discovery, although McLelland's beach and Griffith's tree ferns – like Watson's coal field – were of course already known to the Khasis, and invested with other practical and symbolic meanings. Griffith observed an absence of caste among the Khasis, but had no understanding of the spiritual importance of many of the sacred forests (the Khasi *Ki Law Kyntang*) in which he sought specimens, forests that were the dwelling places of tutelary spirits. Each seed, flower and plant had explicit material or symbolic uses, for food, as items of taboo, for use in hunting or building, or in religious rites and ceremonies. The serpentine stems of *Bauhinia* found by Griffith near Nartiang would be carried by Khasis on trips through the jungle to ward off snakes. *Rhododendron arboreum* found on the slopes of Chillong Hill was the *Tiew saw* of the Khasis, which they believed attracted evil spirits if planted near dwellings. A story attached to the *Hedychium* seen growing near Syniasya was that it was a young girl who had turned into a flowering plant – the *Tiew Iap Kmie* – after committing suicide in grief at her mother's death. The *Bucklandia populnea* observed by the Assam Tea Deputation growing along the watercourses at Cherrapunji was known to the Khasis as the *Dieng doh* tree, and gave its name to a local clan.[44]

The herbarium of the Calcutta Botanic Garden, dating from the time of Wallich's return to India in 1832, included part of the collection made by the Assam Tea Deputation. Missionary Alexander Lish had other ways of bringing the mountain to the metropolis. As the Assam Tea Deputation botanised across the hills in 1835, Lish visited Calcutta with a group of Khasi youths, including two young princes, nephews of the *Syiem* of Cherrapunji, one reportedly proficient in English. While there is no record of what the Khasi boys thought of the trip, the *Friend of India* constructed the excursion as a disciplinary exercise in which science and military power coalesced with salutary effect. A tour of Calcutta's principal public, educational, military and commercial buildings was calculated 'to enlarge their conceptions of the triumphs of science, and the power which it imparts to those who possess it'. While exemplary, such power was perhaps never intended to be placed in their hands, but rather to reinforce their distance from it. What was selected by the paper to have made the most impression, however, was a military review and mock battle: 'The Khasias are independent-spirited highlanders, and are loath to admit the idea of supremacy or superiority in any other people whatever. But the array of the review at once filled them with admiration, and struck them with awe'. After a private audience with Governor-General Bentinck, Lish and his charges returned to the hills with a large number of books, but with little more access to the powerful spoils of science than when they left.[45] A year later, when Emily Eden, sister of incoming Governor-General Lord Auckland, wrote of the students of Calcutta's Hindu College, she crystallised this view that government patronage in providing a liberal education to Indian students using the medium of English was as much about maintaining racialised categories as encouraging their permeability:

> they are 'British subjects,' inasmuch as Britain has taken India, and in many respects they may be called well-educated young men; but still I cannot tell you what the wide difference is between a European and a Native. An elephant and Chance [her dog], St. Paul's and a Baby-Home, the Jerseys and Pembrokes, a diamond and a bad flint, Queen Adelaide and O'Connell, London and Calcutta, are not further apart, and more antipathetic than those two classes. I do not see how the prejudices ever can wear out, nor do I see that it is very desirable.[46]

If the landscape and climate of the Khasi Hills could remind the sentimental European of home, for the princely Khasi youths strolling Strand Road in Bengal's capital, what sights would have made them homesick? The operation of imperialism in the north-east could be observed in the conquering mechanisms of geographical knowledge, as maps turned the unknown into the known, and by the specimens of natural history that made their way to the museums and laboratories of Calcutta, London and Edinburgh. If the Khasi Hills may have reminded the homesick European visitor of his native land, back in Britain the quest for the exotic precipitated other forms of authority and appropriation of India's north-east.

Orchid fever as an imperial sickness

At his family seat at Chatsworth in Derbyshire, the Sixth Duke of Devonshire, William George Spencer Cavendish, stared out across the Derwent valley where his family had been in residence since the mid-sixteenth century. Among other collectibles, the 'bachelor duke' had developed an obsession with orchids after seeing the *Psychopsis papilio* at an exhibition in London in 1833. The flower motif of this butterfly orchid is carved into the trellis pattern of the golden picture frames in the Gold Drawing Room at Chatsworth.

In 1826 he employed the services of Joseph Paxton as head gardener of his estate. Cavendish had been one time president of the Royal Horticultural Society, which in the early 1820s had leased a portion of his land at Chiswick for the purposes of establishing an experimental garden. If the search for exotic specimens was spurred on by the cause of botanical science and horticulture, it was also to become a favoured pastime of the rich as a sign of conspicuous wealth and a symbol of status. A specimen of the orchid *Cattleya labiata*, inadvertently brought to England in some packing material from Brazil in 1818, inspired determined competition among upper-class collectors to procure the rarest and most beautiful specimens. 'Orchidelirium' mirrored the seventeenth-century Dutch tulip mania, and anticipated 'pteridomania', the Victorian craze for ferns that was to reach its height in coming decades.

Competition was far from hypothetical. When Devonshire acquired Huntley's large orchid collection in 1835, Paxton informed the Duke that his collection 'has now mounted completely to the top of the tree. I am fearful some of our neighbours will be a little jealous of our progress. The race now will lay betwixt ourselves, Lord Fitzwilliam, and Mr Bateman'.[47] In 1836, Paxton began construction of a great iron and glass 'stove' or conservatory at Chatsworth. At around 277 feet long, 123 feet wide and 67 feet high, it was claimed to be the largest greenhouse in the world. Heated by eight underground coal-fire boilers that used more fuel to heat than the house, the greenhouse was the model for the Crystal Palace which Paxton went on to design for the Great Exhibition of 1851. Three smaller greenhouses were built to receive the Indian plants, and Paxton's innovative methods of temperature, ventilation, humidity and drainage control were foundational in orchid culture.[48] Exotic jungles in faraway places could now be tamed in 'jungles on the doorstep'.[49]

To fill his great stove, Cavendish sent twenty-year-old John Gibson, a junior gardener who had been apprenticed to Paxton three years earlier, on an orchid hunting expedition to India.[50] The Duke's personal Indian network dated at least from 1828 when his cousin Lord William Cavendish Bentinck became Governor-General at Fort William, and soon after their arrival Lady William had sent flower seeds from their Barrackpore garden to the Duke.[51] Gibson left Chatsworth with a letter of introduction to Nathaniel Wallich, and on 3 October 1835 set sail for India on the *Jupiter* in the retinue of George Eden, Lord Auckland, who was replacing Bentinck as Governor-General. Gibson's primary instruction was to procure from southern Burma a specimen of *Amherstia nobilis* (the Pride of Burma or Orchid Tree), whose bright crimson flowers hanging from a pendulous inflorescence made it one of the most beautiful flowers in the world.[52]

Gibson arrived in India in March 1836. The obsessive Duke had picked the right man for the job; 'when he sees the Amherstia nobilis or a new orchidia', reported Masters to Paxton from Calcutta, 'he runs round it clapping his hands like a boy who has got three runs in a cricket match'.[53] Wallich assisted Gibson in preparing an itinerary for a two-month collecting trip in the north-east. Having recently returned from the Assam Tea Deputation, Wallich had no hesitation in recommending Cherrapunji as Gibson's base, and informed the Duke 'that imagination cannot depict to itself a richer country in Botanical rarities – above all in *Orchideous plants*'.[54] The vast majority of the plants in the Linnean Society's East India Herbarium catalogued as having come from Sylhet, Pandua, Cachar and Khasi Hills were sourced in Cherrapunji.

Gibson set off from the Garden Reach pier on the Hooghly on 6 July 1836, accompanied by two Indian gardeners. On his arrival, he was overwhelmed by the mass of tropical vegetation that covered the plains and the jungles, the air filled with innumerable butterflies. 'I am in my glory', Gibson later wrote to one of Miss Eden's maids.[55] On his arrival at Cherrapunji on 31 July 1836, Gibson rented a bungalow for 30 rupees a month and located half way between Harry Inglis and Captain Lister. Inglis had sent down a mule to convey Gibson up the mountain and also provided him with a *chuprasee* (messenger) and a Khasi attendant. While Gibson was in situ, Wallich sent up plants and seeds for Gibson to plant in Inglis's garden, including *Pinus deodara* (Himalayan cedar).[56] In the moist air of the hills, Gibson tried to dry his specimens by the fire. Live plants were trussed up with moss around their roots and packed in shallow cane baskets ready for the homeward trip. The baskets were carried down the hills by a man using a *banghy* or shoulder yoke, and sent on boats to Calcutta on the first of each month, courtesy of Harry Inglis.

Like Griffith, Gibson could only revel in the botanical bounty of the hills: 'I am delighted beyond every-thing to see such a grand display of the vegitable [*sic*] kingdom. I find something new every day, which not only affords me pleasure and encouragement now, but to look forward to the time when the great satisfaction of having these Rarities in England, to arrive which will give my Employer so much pleasure and satisfaction'. He was dazzled by the fecundity of the forests: 'a person may go to one of the woods and reap a most splendid harvest, yet leave behind some of the most lovely of Plants. Another person shall go the

3 'Cane suspension bridge over the Témshang River, in the Khássia Hills', original aquarelle by Hermann de Schlagintweit, November 1855.

next day to the same wood, and bring with him also valuable treasures, which the former person could not find, nor believe that they come from the same wood'.[57]

A decade and a half later, J.D. Hooker was to doubt 'whether in any other part of the globe the species of orchids outnumber those of any other natural order, or form so large a proportion of the flora'.[58] Gibson's expedition was dramatised by Kenneth Lemmon in his 1968 account of the lives of the great plant hunters as a 'journey into completely unknown country'.[59] Such hyperbole exaggerated both the bravery of these botanical agents, and licensed their exploitation of the human and natural resources they found. 'There was neither road nor track', reprised the Duchess of Devonshire in 1999, 'to the far-away garden of Eden'.[60] As the Duke's operative, entrusted with delivering the jungle to the Chatsworth doorstep, the dangers of Gibson's adventurous trek were augmented in both contemporary and later narratives; the botanical prizes were all the more glorious if wrested from the demesne of savage natives. Gibson was apparently apprehensive of the Khasis on his hit-and-run raid of their hilltops, although in all his letters to Wallich, Paxton or the Duke, he very rarely mentions any observations about the 'far from being civilized' Khasis, aside from them climbing trees to collect his specimens.[61]

Lord Auckland's sister Emily Eden was similarly circumspect on Gibson's behalf in an account sent to the expectant Duke:

> Scene, a tent at Cherra Poonjee with a foreground of palanquins & bearers, and Gibson in the midst crowned with an orchideous wreath, and holding a large purple Emperor by one wing. George [Lord Auckland] gave him a travelling case containing a silver bottle, goblet, knife, fork & with an inscription on the goblet mentioning that it was the gift of the Governor-General as a mark of his regard for Mr Gibson's character – or words to that effect and it charmed the aforesaid Mr G. But as he felt sure the Indian savages would kill him for the sake of his goblet and then eat him with his own knife and fork he left the casket in my care, & I feel my responsibility deeply.[62]

The original idea had been for Gibson to proceed to Martaban in southern Burma to collect an Amherstia, 'one single plant of which alone would no doubt be considered at Chatsworth as fully compensating the cost of sending Gibson to this country',[63] but so rich were the pickings in the Khasi Hills that Gibson had more than enough bounty to return to the Duke. On 8 November 1836, Gibson informed Paxton from Cherrapunji that his hoard would be 'one of the richest collections that has ever crossed the *Atlantic*'.[64] On 9 January 1837, having descended the hills as far as Pandua, he stressed again the wilds from which his spoils had been won. 'I am almost lost', he wrote to Paxton, 'with being [so long] in the Woods & Jungle . . . nothing but the Blacks from day to day. But all this adds to my expected satisfaction when I arrive on the little spot where little else but my Native tongue is universally spoken'.[65] Gibson's exaggeration is again at odds with the presence of the well-established European station at Cherrapunji, and the clear help he had received from people like Harry Inglis.

At a quarter past eight on Saturday 4 March 1837, Nathaniel Wallich watched from his verandah in Calcutta as the *Zenobia* sailed past the Botanic Garden en route for England, its precious cargo of a dozen Wardian cases filled with botanical specimens clearly discernible and snugly secured on the poop deck. Gibson had been allocated a light and roomy berth, in which he surrounded himself with bottles and baskets of plants, a collection of seeds, dried specimens and insects, and living orchids still attached to tree branches suspended in his cabin.[66] Gibson returned to England in triumph, in his charge a thousand exotic specimens for the Duke's stove, including over a hundred orchid species new to the country, as well as insects and other natural history collections. While Gibson had been labouring in India, the Duke had been on a visit to the Continent where over the course of around nine weeks he dined out forty-seven times and attended thirty-seven soirees and twenty-three balls.[67] The hypochondrial and chronically deaf Devonshire – a 'Victim of plants & lumbago'[68] – waited nervously for his bounty of 'beloved plants'; his diary records his fever of expectation about the arrival of the *Amherstia* in a britzka from the docks.[69] If Gibson's expedition was facilitated by Devonshire's patronage and colonial connections (many specimens were to be named after the Duke), Wallich saw it as an opportunity of firming up his own career and authority. Running the Duke's agent, Wallich was alert to the benefits of a powerful sponsor. In his correspondence with the Duke, he bolstered the success of the mission, the indefatigable zeal of Gibson and the magnitude of the collection: 'there never was anything equal to this seen in India – I had almost said anywhere else'.[70]

After three weeks in India, Barrackpore for Emily Eden was like a reverie: 'It is more like a constant theatrical representation going on; everything is so picturesque and so utterly un-English'.[71] When Wallich enclosed a letter from Gibson to the Duke in August 1836 from 'Chirra Punjee on the Khasseea range – the grand scene of his present operations', he too presented India as merely a backdrop to the imperial show. The botanist, like the geographer, was *in* the landscape but not *of* it.[72] Terminology betrayed ideology; on his arrival in the Khasi Hills, Gibson increasingly referred to the expedition as 'My Mission' and his collections as his 'harvest'. If the language of capitalism was clearly invoked by scientists to signal the commodification of India,[73] so too was the language of evangelicalism. The Duke of Devonshire, a liberal-minded politician who favoured Catholic emancipation, the abolition of slavery and ameliorating the condition of children working in factories, also 'suffered a lengthy attack of religious mania in middle age'.[74] Botanical collector and missionary could do similar work.

The Reverend John Williams, the LMS missionary who had first gone to the Society Islands in the south Pacific in 1817, returned to England in 1834. Williams published *A Narrative of Missionary Enterprises in the South Sea Islands* in 1837. The Society Islands – which included Tahiti – had been named by Captain James Cook, and Williams's own book became the bestselling work on the Pacific since Cook's *Voyages* in 1790. Fifty copies of the work were distributed to various members of the nobility with a view to bringing the work of Christian missions under their notice, and more particularly for raising funds for his next voyage. The Duke of Devonshire was the first nobleman to lend his patronage to the cause. 'That so few of the nobility identify themselves with this work of mercy', Williams wrote to the Duke in June 1837, 'is a matter of deep regret'. But Williams also cannily recognised that Duke was 'ardently attached to Botanical science', and promised to forward specimens for the great stove from the islands of the south Pacific, at no expense.[75] In November 1839, the Duke's collector suffered a fate similar to Cook in Hawaii in 1779, when he was clubbed to death on the beach at Eromanga in the New Hebrides.

While Gibson sailed for England, Queen Victoria ascended the throne in June 1837. As a thirteen year old in 1832, she had visited the Duke at Chatsworth with her mother, the Duchess of Kent. On that occasion she had seen a fly-catcher plant in Paxton's garden. Eleven years later, she was to visit again, this time as queen and with her consort Prince Albert. Queen Victoria was driven down the central carriageway of the great conservatory, with the empire's jungle spoils on either side, under the light of twelve thousand lamps.[76] Charles Darwin too visited in 1845, thrilled with nature's simulacrum. 'I was, like a child, transported with delight', he reported; 'Really the great Hot house, & especially the water part, is more wonderfully like tropical nature, than I could have conceived possible. – Art beats nature altogether there'.[77] According to Wallich, Gibson would have been glad to send his harvest of orchids 'forests and all if he could'.[78] But even so, here the Duke had reconstructed perfect tropical jungle, without the natives. The replica, moreover, was not in any way deficient, and in its imperialising synthesis improved rather than simply mimicked nature: 'all the most striking vegetable forms of India, Africa, and America', reported the *Gardener's Magazine*, 'will be seen in, perhaps, more than their native luxuriance with its ample boundaries; and thus, amidst the wildest scenery of Derbyshire, there will be found an example of tropical vegetation, richer, and more varied than could be met with in any of those baleful latitudes themselves'.[79]

Through travel, science and survey, the Khasi Hills were centrally appropriated into networks of colonial knowledge and the exercise of power.[80] Standing by the pathway from Pandua up to Cherrapunji – watching the successive trips of Walters, McLennan, Griffith and Gibson – is in David Arnold's critical framework to take up a central ocular vantage point, to be 'culturally attentive' to the ways in which imperial rule was legitimated.[81] The Indian north-east that was constructed through this period was a novel place, part of what Matthew Edney has called the 'geographical rhetoric of British India', which overlaid previous diverse geographies, polities and cultures with a more unitary entity.[82]

On the evening of 22 June 1897, sixty years after Gibson's return from Cherrapunji with his harvest of flowers, at a dinner party at Buckingham Palace to mark the occasion of her diamond jubilee, a nine-foot-high crown graced the Queen's table, made from 60,000 orchids from every one of her dominions.[83] In the grand regal bouquet, the Khasi's sweet-scented *Tiew lyngksiar iong*, which they metaphorically compared to a sweet natured and virtuous person,[84] had been plucked from its roots and transposed into the *Cymbidium traceyanum*, to take its place in a heady arrangement symbolising the might and reach of the British empire.

Notes

1 Dr McLelland, 'Fossil shells found in the Kasya Hills', *Journal of the Asiatic Society of Bengal*, 4:45 (1835), 520.
2 *Calcutta Journal of Natural History* as reported in *Friend of India*, 23 July 1840, 467.
3 Lt.-Colonel D.G. Crawford, *A History of the Indian Medical Service 1600–1913* (London, 1914), chapter 29; R. Desmond, *The European Discovery of the Indian Flora* (Oxford, 1992), p. vi.
4 Ralph R. Stewart, 'Missionaries and clergymen as botanists in India and Pakistan', *Taxon*, 31:1 (1982), 57–64; Desmond, *The European Discovery of the Indian Flora*, pp. 39–40.
5 David Arnold, 'Plant capitalism and Company science: the Indian career of Nathaniel Wallich', *Modern Asian Studies*, 42:5 (2008), 906–7.
6 Ray Desmond, *Dictionary of British & Irish Botanists and Horticulturists* (London, 1994), p. 638.
7 William Roxburgh, *Flora Indica*, volume 3, p. 543 cited in William Griffith, 'Report on the caoutchouc tree of Assam made at the request of Captain Jenkins, Agent to the Governor General', *Journal of the Asiatic Society of Bengal*, 7 (1838), 133–4. Griffith renders the Khasi word for rubber as *Ka-gi-ri*. See also Desmond, *The European Discovery of the Indian Flora*, p. 247.
8 Arnold, *The New Cambridge History of India*, pp. 20–31; Deepak Kumar, 'The evolution of colonial science in India: natural history and the East India Company' in John M. MacKenzie (ed.), *Imperialism and the Natural World* (Manchester, 1990), pp. 51–66.
9 L.H. Brockway, *Science and Colonial Expansion: The Role of the British Royal Botanic Gardens* (New York, 1979); Donal P. McCracken, *Gardens of Empire: Botanical Institutions of the Victorian British Empire* (London and Washington, 1997).
10 R. Axelby, 'Calcutta Botanic Garden and the colonial re-ordering of the Indian environment', *Archives of Natural History*, 35:1 (2008), 150.
11 Desmond, *The European Discovery of the Indian Flora*, pp. 185–8.
12 *Gleanings in Science*, 1 (1829), Subscribers 1829, xi–xii.
13 Desmond, *The European Discovery of the Indian Flora*, pp. v, vii
14 *Friend of India*, 23 July 1840, 467.
15 Axelby, 'Calcutta Botanic Garden', 152.
16 Arnold, *The New Cambridge History of India*, p. 21. See also Kumar, 'The evolution of colonial science in India', p. 61.
17 Richard Wilcox, 'Register of the thermometer kept at Nungkhlow, during parts of the months of October and November, 1827', *The Quarterly Oriental Magazine, Review, and Register*, 8:15 (July–December 1827), Calcutta, 1828, 15.
18 F., 'Some account of the Cásiah Hills', *Gleanings in Science*, 1:9 (1829), 252–5.
19 *Asiatic Journal and Monthly Register for British India and its Dependencies*, 28: 165 (1829), 321–3; Walters, 'Journey across the Pandua Hills'. For an extended interpretation of Walters's account, see M.H. Edney, *Mapping an Empire: The Geographical Construction of British India, 1765–1843* (Chicago, 1997), pp. 64–76.
20 William Griffith, *Journals of Travels in Assam, Burma, Bhootan, Afghanistan and the Neighbouring Countries, 1847, Arranged by John M'Clelland* (Calcutta, 1847).
21 'Kassiya Hills', *Friend of India*, 16 November 1837, 362.

22 Walters, 'Journey across the Pandua Hills', 501.
23 *Ibid.*, 509.
24 *Ibid.*, 502–3.
25 *Friend of India*, 5 February 1835, 42.
26 C., 'Excursion to the Chirra Púnjí Hills', *Gleanings in Science*, 30 (1831), 172–4.
27 *Ibid.*, 174.
28 Walters, 'Journey across the Pandua Hills', 509.
29 T.R. 'On the manufacture of the Sylhet lime', *Gleanings in Science* (1830), 61–3.
30 W.C., 'Smelting of iron in the Kasya Hills', *Journal of the Asiatic Society of Bengal*, 1:4 (1832), 150–1; W. Cracroft, 'Rain at Chirra Púnjí, registered by W. Cracroft, Esq.', *Journal of the Asiatic Society of Bengal*, 1:9 (1832), 420, 1:10 (1832), 477.
31 W. Cracroft, 'Notes relative to the collection of some geological specimens in the Kásia Hills between Assam and Nunklow', *Journal of the Asiatic Society of Bengal*, 3:30 (1834), 293–6.
32 W. Cracroft, 'On the Cape Fig by Mr Cracroft', read 10 June 1829, *Transactions of the Agricultural and Horticultural Society of India*, 2 (1836), 4–5.
33 Cracroft, 'Remarks on the progress of *Horticulture* at Cherra-Poonjee, and on a method of grafting the apple on the Khasiyah Crab tree, by W. Cracroft', read 14 January 1832, *Transactions of the Agricultural and Horticultural Society of India*, 2 (1836), 81–2.
34 William Carey, 'Address respecting an agricultural society in India', *Friend of India*, September 1820, 50–9; Arnold, *The Tropics and the Traveling Gaze: India, Landscape, and Science, 1800–1856* (Seattle, 2006), p. 106.
35 Cracroft, 'Remarks on the progress of *Horticulture*', 81.
36 Bentinck to Grant, 18 December 1832, cited in Katherine Prior, 'Ryan, Sir Edward (1793–1875)', *Oxford Dictionary of National Biography*, Oxford University Press, 2004; online edn, May 2006, www.oxforddnb.com/view/article/24385 (accessed 3 Dec 2010).
37 Extract from the proceedings of the Agricultural and Horticultural Society, at a meeting held on 3 November 1831, *Transactions of the Agricultural and Horticultural Society of India*, volume 2, 1836, 35–7.
38 Possibly *U Soh phlang* or *Flemingia procumbens*, and *Dieng kha-riu* or *Uraria crinita*, whose roots are used in traditional medicine. See A.A. Ahmed and S.K. Borthakur, *Ethnobotanical Wisdom of Khasis (Hynñiew Treps) of Meghalaya* (Dehra Dun, 2005), pp. 47, 187.
39 Desmond, *The European Discovery of the Indian Flora*, pp. 236–7.
40 Arnold, 'Plant capitalism and Company science', 925–7; Dr Wallich to Pakenham, 7 December 1834 in Philips (ed.), *The Correspondence*, volume 2, pp. 1385–6.
41 Griffith, *Journals of Travels in Assam*.
42 Desmond, *The European Discovery of the Indian Flora*, p. 238.
43 See Ahmed and Borthakur, *Ethnobotanical Wisdom*, p. 99.
44 *Ibid.*, pp. 205, 208–9, 216, 218.
45 *Friend of India*, 14 January 1836, 11.
46 Miss Eden to Mrs Lister, 25 January 1837, in Violet Dickinson (ed.), *Miss Eden's Letters* (London, 1919), pp. 281–2.
47 Paxton to Duke, 19 March 1835 (No. 3287), 6th Duke's Correspondence, Devonshire Mss.
48 Merle A. Reinikka, *A History of the Orchid* (Portland, 1995), p. 166.
49 Keith Lemmon, *The Golden Age of Plant Hunters* (London, 1968), p. 182. See also Susan Orlean, *The Orchid Thief* (New York, 1998), pp. 69–74; Nicholas Barker, *The Devonshire Collection: Five Centuries of Collecting at Chatsworth* (Alexandria, Virginia, 2003), pp. 282–3.
50 Tyler Whittle, *The Plant Hunters* (London, 1970), pp. 129–32. See also Reinikka, *A History of the Orchid*, pp. 193–5.
51 Lady William Bentinck to the Duke of Devonshire, 19 August 1828 in Philips (ed.), *The Correspondence*, volume 1, p. 67.

52 Benedict Lyte, '*Amherstia nobilis*: plants in peril 28', *Curtis s Botanical Magazine*, 20:3 (2003), 172–6; Desmond, *The European Discovery of the Indian Flora*, pp. 86–7.
53 Masters to Paxton, 15 March 1836, Indian Correspondence 1835–37 (No. 8), Devonshire Mss.
54 Wallich to Duke, 15 May 1836, Indian Correspondence 1835–37 (No. 13), Devonshire Mss.
55 Mentioned in an extract from a letter of Miss Eden, Calcutta, 27 September 1836 (No. 25), Indian Correspondence 1835–37, Devonshire Mss.
56 Gibson to Wallich, 2 August 1836 (No. 19) and 15 August 1836 (Nos. 20–1), Indian Correspondence 1835–37, Devonshire Mss.
57 Gibson to Wallich, 11 October 1836 (No. 29), Indian Correspondence 1835–37, Devonshire Mss.
58 Hooker, *Himalayan Journals*, volume 2, p. 281.
59 Lemmon, *The Golden Age of Plant Hunters*, p. 196.
60 Deborah Vivien Freeman-Mitford Cavendish Devonshire, *The Garden at Chatsworth* (Sydney, 1999), p. 59.
61 Gibson to Paxton, 9 January 1837 (No. 36), Indian Correspondence 1835–37, Devonshire Mss.
62 Extract from a letter of Miss Eden, Calcutta, 27 September 1835 (No. 25), Indian Correspondence 1835–37, Devonshire Mss.
63 Wallich to Paxton, 9 May 1836 (No. 11), Indian Correspondence 1835–37, Devonshire Mss.
64 Gibson to Paxton, 8 November 1836 (No. 32), Indian Correspondence 1835–37, Devonshire Mss.
65 Gibson to Paxton, 9 January 1837 (No. 36), Indian Correspondence 1835–37, Devonshire Mss.
66 Wallich to Duke, 4 March 1837 (No. 47–8); Gibson to Duke, 14 July 1837 (No. 49), Indian Correspondence 1835–37, Devonshire Mss.
67 6th Duke of Devonshire, Diaries, 1836–37, Devonshire Mss.
68 22 July 1837, 6th Duke of Devonshire, Diaries, 1836–37, Devonshire Mss.
69 Two specimens of *Amherstia* had been sent from Wallich, one for the Duke and one for the Court of Directors. The Duke's one died, but the Court of Directors gave him theirs.
70 Wallich to Duke, 2 November 1836 (Nos. 30–1), Indian Correspondence 1835–37, Devonshire Mss.
71 Miss Eden to Lady Campbell [3 March 1836], in Dickinson (ed.), *Miss Eden's Letters*, p. 264.
72 Edney, *Mapping an Empire*, p. 74.
73 Arnold, 'Plant capitalism and Company science', 916.
74 Devonshire, *The Garden at Chatsworth*, p. 38.
75 Williams to Duke, 14 June 1837 (No. 3668), 8 April 1838 (No. 3878), 6th Duke's Correspondence, Devonshire Mss.
76 Orlean, *The Orchid Thief*, p. 73.
77 Darwin to J.S. Henslow, Darwin Correspondence Project Database, Letter No. 921, www.darwinproject.ac.uk/entry-921/ (accessed 13 July 2010); see also Darwin to Charles Lyell, Letter No. 919.
78 Wallich to Duke, 2 November 1835 (Nos. 30–1), Indian Correspondence 1835–37, Devonshire Mss.
79 'Floricultural and botanical notices, Cavendishianum Batem', *Gardener's Magazine*, volume 13 (November 1837), 505.
80 Arnold, *The Tropics and the Traveling Gaze*, pp. 3–6.
81 *Ibid.*, pp. 6, 24.
82 Edney, *Mapping an Empire*, p. 15.
83 Jeffrey Richards, *Imperialism and Music: Britain, 1876–1953* (Manchester, 2001), p. 138.
84 Ahmed and Borthakur, *Ethnobotanical Wisdom*, p. 223.

CHAPTER SEVEN

Creatures of a day: Christian soldiers

The EIC's ongoing reticence to officially sponsor botanical research in India in some respects matched their antipathy and later ambivalence in allowing the spread of missionary activity. That the practice of science and of religion may at times have been unofficial or *ad hoc*, belies the extraordinary and adaptive network of individual operatives who under the guise of the civil servant, surgeon or soldier were able to make personalised, speculative and opportunistic decisions about the character of their own imperialism. Being attuned to the cultural kitbag of each British traveller up to the hills does not, of course, mitigate imperialism's effect: hubristic superiority towards native populations, fundamental ignorance of their culture, inimicality to their spirituality and destruction of their traditions. But we are more able to see how processes of imperial control actually worked if we place the more complex and less obvious motivations of individuals ahead of the colour of their banners or the official sanction of their position. For David Scott, science and experimental horticulture could serve the local needs of the army on the ground, as well as feed into broader ideologies of pacification, colonisation and moral improvement. If the ideology of the British empire 'made subtle use of reason, and recruited science and history to serve its ends',[1] then in what other more nuanced ways was it practised? Douglas Peers added the category of 'gentleman-officer-scholar' to the cast of 'hyphenated characters' in the landscape of imperialism, who produced particular varieties of colonial knowledge.[2] If the missionary could labour in the cause of science, what might a soldier do for evangelism?

Empire as family service

Through August 1841, the rains were incessant; 264 inches of rain fell at Cherrapunji, or a staggering twenty-two feet.[3] Lieutenant William

Charles James Lewin sought refuge from the rains in a small, damp house, crowded already with five children and his wife expecting a sixth. Lewin would not have been in Cherrapunji had it not been for his ill health, and it was there that his father hoped he would recover, away from the 'destructive influence' of the plains of Bengal.[4] As was the case for many of the British, his connection with India was a family affair. William Lewin's grandfather Richard had been an EIC ship's commander and director of the East India Dock Company. Richard secured an EIC writership for his son Thomas, who went to India as an eighteen year old and worked first in the military department at Fort St. George, and then as private secretary to the Governor. One family story recounts that Thomas Lewin was a lover of Catherine Noele Grand (née Worlée), the daughter of an official at the French colony at Pondicherry. On a return trip from India in 1780, Thomas and Catherine found themselves in Paris. The social connections Lewin had made among the residents at Pondicherry gave him entrée into high society: he is reputed to have seen Marie Antoinette dance a minuet at Versailles. Thomas Lewin married Mary Hale in 1784. Hale's father, General John Hale, had as a colonel been in command of the 47th Regiment at the Siege of Quebec in 1759, when British forces under the ill-fated General James Wolfe overcame the French and thus precipitated the end of French rule in Canada.

William Lewin was thus representative of the typical socio-economic background of the army officer corps, the well-connected landed gentry, motivated by ideals of honour, respectability and service – the 'fighting class, duty-bound and historically conditioned to protect civil society from invasion and disruption'.[5] Born in 1806, he had a classical education in his early years, and had been recommended for Company service by his father, who was by then a magistrate in Kent.[6] One of twelve children, at least two of William's brothers also saw service in India.[7] William graduated as an artilleryman from the EIC Academy in May 1822, and the following month sailed for India on the *David Scott*.

Lewin was promoted to Lieutenant in May 1825, and in that year saw service during the First Anglo-Burmese war. His tour of duty with the Bengal artillery in Arracan in 1825 saw him active in one of the more unhealthy regions of the subcontinent. After the onset of the rainy season, the British army was struck down by fever and disease, and Lewin himself had reported sick by the end of the year. While 150 soldiers were killed in action, around 3000 of the 3500-strong force died of disease.[8] Nearly 60 per cent of H.M.'s 44th and 54th Regiments perished over an eight-month period, and when the survivors landed at Calcutta and Madras there were barely enough men alive to escort the regimental colours.[9] Lewin's ensuing military record was marked by frequent periods of extended furlough. In August 1832 he was granted a year's leave to proceed to Cherrapunji.

The cutting edge of empire

On his 1822 voyage to India, Lewin was shocked at the brutal slave economy around the Dutch settlement at Paarl at the Cape Colony: female slaves were 'prostituted to the sensual gratification of their masters' passions'; others served him at meals, and their 'naked feet, the badge of slavery, quite offended my freeborn British feelings, and I inwardly thought – "What right has man to tyrannize thus over his fellow creatures?" . . . It is scarcely to be wondered at under such a system, that the great ends of religion and morality are entirely lost sight of'.[10] After his arrival in India as a fresh cadet, he read the Bible every day, a practice that isolated him from his comrades: 'suspicions began to be entertained that I was somewhat "methodistical," and thenceforth I stood alone'.[11] Then 'God raised up a helpmeet for me' in the form of Jane Elizabeth Laprimandaye, daughter of a Calcutta merchant, whom he married in 1827. The notion of a 'helpmeet' provided by God, drawing on biblical precept (Genesis 2:18: 'I will make him an help meet for him'), reinforced the dual role of wife as domestic help and moral guardian that by the early decades of the nineteenth century lay at the heart of respectable Christian culture. Their first child was born the following year at Mathura in the United Provinces, and when Lewin transferred to the Invalid Establishment in the Khasi Hills on a permanent basis in December 1833, he already had two children and a third on the way.

In its filial and religious dimensions, the figure of the soldier-Christian – as father, son and husband – can be profitably read against the grain of the archetypal British Army soldier-imperialist. William Lewin was literally at the violent, savage and oppressive cutting edge of empire, however much colonial wars were 'shorn of guilt by Social Darwinism and racial ideas'.[12] But to look more closely at the contours of his moral world is to upend the ubiquitous question in studies of religion and empire (did missions succour or subvert imperialism?),[13] interrogating instead the extent to which imperial forces abetted religious proselytism. While India had been opened to missionaries under the *Charter Act* of 1813, it was the 1833 act that brought missionaries into the field in more significant numbers. While the principle of non-interference in Indian religious practice was still paramount at this time, there was a groundswell among EIC operatives 'of moving from an earlier attitude of mild disapproval of missionary work to one of enthusiastic personal support'.[14] Invalided to the Khasi Hills in the 1830s – at this particular time and in this particular place – Lieutenant

4 Henry Yule, 'Portrait of unidentified civilian seated on a chair', 1841, possibly William Lewin or one of his fellow invalids.

Lewin was both transformed by and transformative of this aspect of the imperial project.

The British empire was a religious as well as a cultural, economic and political web, constructed in real places as well as in the virtual space of correspondence. Its filaments spanned the physical distance between being at home and abroad, and in Lewin's case were threaded across continents by his parents and siblings. Christianity was a base ingredient of empire's essential glue. While his shipboard experiences may have been a fillip to his religious outlook, it is clear that his parents played a formative role in modelling his Christian outlook. Writing to William in March 1825, care of his brother Thomas in Calcutta, his mother Mary showed keen interest in his health amid the privations of active duty, and in his prospects, on hearing of his promotion to the horse artillery. Her maternal role was manifest in the affectionate address ('My dear Billy Boy') and her reminiscences of a time long past 'when a sword stick was so often resisted by your anxious and fearful Mother', both of which served to assert her role as senior, experienced, protective. William's accounts of his army life had moved his mother to tears, 'for there was a corresponding feeling of the soldier in your old Mother, and had I been a man the Army would have been my choice'. While covertly critiquing the constraints of nineteenth-century Victorian sex-role stereotypes, Mary Lewin also saw herself in other ways as a manly equal, marshalling the lives of her dozen children, collecting and analysing intelligence, and enduring physical pain and emotional trauma.[15] Her moral dominion was the domestic sphere, but she had a keen interest in the enlightening powers of education, for girls as well as boys. Writing to the Lewins in the Khasi Hills in 1833, she was eager to learn whether first daughter Jane Elizabeth could read and write, anxious 'that she will treat me with a letter, and tell me all she has acquired'. In terms of gender roles, her son William's martial aggression as a child was naturalised as manly, in the same way that her granddaughter's behaviour was observed within the appropriate strictures of ladylike behaviour: 'I trust, my dear Jane, with a little more strict attention to her Temper as she gets older, she will turn out what we all wish'.[16]

William's sister Mary H. Lewin, who had married another Indian military man, Hippisley Marsh, died aged thirty in 1825, and other correspondence from Mary Lewin to her son negotiated the emotion felt on the death of a sister and a daughter: 'the big tear drops on the paper even now at recalling the sad idea'.[17] Another sister Frances had married a Swedish noble Nils von Koch (later the reformist Attorney-General of Sweden) and moved to Stockholm, from where she wrote to William's wife – her 'dear friend and sister' Jane – in February 1833: 'I cherish a hope', she wrote, 'that I may be allowed to embrace my old folks in 1835 . . . I want you more than anybody of my family as a person to apply to, in children's affairs and housekeeping, as well as fun'.[18] Three years later, Frances could commiserate on the death of William and Jane's sixteen-month-old daughter Emma, who had died in August 1835: 'how my heart ached for you both in your distress, with which I could the more intimately sympathize from having been myself bereft of my own baby . . . I never think of you without longing that we lived near one another'.[19]

William's condition was clearly of concern to his parents and siblings, who felt deeply for the effect that his poor health would have on his material circumstances. His mother had expressed some disquiet when he had mentioned in 1826 that perhaps he might remain in India ('Now I can't think you serious in saying you shall be content to end your days in India – I'm sure I shan't').[20] By 1833, his mother was distressed to hear how unwell he had been, and was much concerned that his invalid status would not enable him to retire to England with comfortable means. His sister Frances too had been anxious on the matter. 'I suppose that even if you weather out four years in India by dint of frequent recourse to the Cossyah Hills', she wrote to Jane, 'you will possess but £100 a year, so that the great thing is to find out a habitable place possessing pleasurable essentials, but where you could hope, at any rate, to keep even with the world'.[21]

Empire in extremis: *exiled in Cherrapunji*

Mary, matriarch of the Lewins, had memories and keepsakes, the toys still in her cupboard that William and Jane's baby daughter had played with when they visited England in 1829, and a much admired lock of their son Edward's hair, which she carried round in her pocket to show her friends.[22] But as each year passed, the contentment that she had hoped for in her son's advancement was elusive, and up to the time of her death in 1837 she must have realised the fragility and vulnerability of her sickly soldier son with his wife and by then four children, invalided out in a small damp house in the far-off Khasi Hills. A letter to Frances from Harriet – another of Lewin's sisters, who had married British historian, radical politician and reformer George Grote and went on to lead a distinguished life in literary and political circles – could refer to their brother as 'poor Billyrag, as father used to call him. I hail the recovered light of reason and sense in his mind, and pray Heaven it may never more cloud over'.[23] William was a grown man, an army officer responsible for a wife and large family, but in another sense the family could still infantilise him. Through circumstance and character, he found himself bogged down on the family's well-worn imperial route of geographical, generational and class mobility. Cherrapunji should not have been a final destination, but rather a transitional place and a stepping-stone to career advancement, domestic maturity, financial security and mature manhood. Lewin's family was increasingly concerned that William was mired *in extremis* at empire's end.

In some respects, the nature of William and Jane Lewin's presence in Cherrapunji from the early 1830s was unusual. William's long-term invalid status enabled him, Jane and the children to be domiciled there as a family group. For the active soldier, family life in India would have meant much more disruption and certainly more extended and frequent periods of separation. The army wife in India has been described most baldly as a piece of 'camp equipment'.[24] While Jane Lewin would have shared with her fellow army wives some of the risks and privations of Indian life – and certainly the physical demands of repeated pregnancies and the emotional impact of having one of her young children die – her family were able to maintain proximity and cohesion at the invalid station. Where familial separation enforced by colonial service could often be a challenge to desired models of domesticity, the Lewins were able to maintain a greater degree of intimate family unity. William's depressed financial circumstances also meant that he was self-schooling the children at Cherrapunji, rather than sending them home to Britain for education, which was more the norm for those officers who could afford it.

William Lewin's brothers, father and grandfather had all been in Indian service. India for the Lewin tribe was clearly a 'family concern'; exile was its corollary. Here they were familiar with a state of 'permanent impermanence – repeated comings and goings – between metropole and colony, between "home" and "away"'.[25] The family correspondence criss-crossing from England, Switzerland, Sweden and India exemplifies the process of a widely dispersed family maintaining and negotiating the meanings of identity, intimacy and allegiance across an intermediate and transnational space. Letters written under such circumstances of separation also meant that they could 'articulate so much that they normally took for granted'.[26] While letters themselves were important physical objects and a vicarious means of sustaining relationships,[27] the exchange of gifts also mediated family relationships. Jane Lewin sent her mother-in-law an 'elegant shawl . . . universally admired when I go out',[28] and some tortoise-shell combs and a collar and cuffs to Frances in Stockholm.[29] These were tokens that could stand in the place of the absent family members, testifying to the gendered propriety of a daughter-in-law's domestic accomplishments, reifying both the exotic and the familial, certifying to the meanings of home and away.

A further exchange between Cherrapunji and England – this time by way of opinions – also cemented and sustained the paternal authority of William Lewin's father. Like Mary Lewin, her husband Thomas had been much concerned about the ill-health of his son, and in particular the deleterious effects of invalidity on his prospects. A spell at Cherrapunji, he hoped, would restore William's health and enable him 'to pursue the Vocation in which your Lot has been cast, thereby laying a secure Foundation for your future Fame and Fortune'.[30] While it was Mary Lewin who primarily conducted the letter-writing exchange, Thomas occasionally intervened to assert his expectations of the meanings and experience of fatherhood. 'Your continuing to furnish me from time to time', he advised his son, 'with your Opinions upon the Political or other Occurrences of the present Day will be ranked among the most welcome proofs you can give me of filial affection, trusting as I do that they will also contain evidence of your intellectual acquirement and of a well-grounded knowledge of "Men and Things"'.[31]

Christianity and paternalism

The Lewin children owed their careers and connections to the labours of their father and grandfather, and for William the protection and education of his own children was of paramount concern. His ideas of fatherhood were also very much bound up in a Christian model, and his paternal role was a metaphor of God's own authority. In terms of his Christian responsibilities, this was a role he extended not only to his children, but to his brothers and to anyone else he considered in need of reform.[32] William's own missionary project was born out of parental influence, a youthful shipboard epiphany and the comfort a suffering invalid could find in religion. In an 1829 letter to his brother George, William zealously expounded his belief on the 'practical doctrines of truth' in the Bible, which could expiate the guilt of the sinner.[33] Writing again to George in 1842, William was horrified at the ten-year hiatus in their correspondence. George had married in 1837 and had children of his own, and William could now empathise at the dual level of brother and father, as he reminisced about their boyhood, and then sketched in the pieces of his own family history:

> I have got five children, including a baby of 8 months old; 3 have been removed by death in the course of our history . . . When the poor dead old man departs, the family history will then assume its last phase I presume. If I ever have money enough, and it be the Lord's will that I should retire to Europe, I think at present of settling in Switzerland . . . I should choose to settle my sons as agriculturalists if I could, getting them a University finish abroad somewhere, and so lay my bones among them: but of course we mortals cannot talk about the future, for we are creatures of a day.[34]

The categories of 'soldier' and 'Christian' might seem contradictory, or perhaps too easily assume the more fixed categorisation of later versions of Christian militarism or of the soldier as popular hero.[35] In the early decades of the nineteenth century, the army was a fringe institution less central to British society.[36] The British public's heroic adulation and idealisation of its troops by the end of the nineteenth century had replaced those more cynical earlier civilian attitudes towards the nation's brutal army, characterised by Edmund Burke as a 'rapacious and licentious soldiery'.[37] The watershed may have been the Crimean War, and more particularly the hagiographical literature that ensued, such as Catherine Marsh's *Memorials of Captain Hedley Vicars, 97th Regiment* (1855). The novelty of the mid-Victorian rehabilitation of the moral image of the soldier was that he could be Christian without compromising his soldierly qualities; that there were more Christian soldiers in its company than hitherto recognised; that the remainder could be a target of missionary action; and that Christians in fact could make the best soldiers.[38] In Lewin's time, all of these contentions were much more presumptuous. His self-conscious Christian avowals – subject as they were to the suspicion and denigration of his fellow soldiers as well as the commentary of his family, bemused at its unusual tenor – may indicate that he was the exception that proved the general rule.

Furthermore, over the course of the nineteenth century the British military was refocusing its attention from its own lower-class disorders and radical civil disturbances such as Chartism, towards a newer foe that was racially differentiated and in its view ethically inferior and morally suspect. As John MacKenzie has argued, part of the self-justification of colonial wars (as opposed to a moral abhorrence of European war) lay in the view that they 'fitted the religious and moral thrust of imperialism'.[39] It was in the figure of Henry Havelock that Britons found the apotheosis of heroic Christian militarism, and his statue (erected 1861) in Trafalgar Square originally sat alongside Nelson, General Sir Charles Napier (who suppressed Chartist agitation in northern England before conquering Sindh in present-day Pakistan), George IV and General Gordon of Khartoum (now relocated).[40] Havelock arrived in India a year after William Lewin, also served in the First Anglo-Burmese War, and in 1857 was second in command at the Siege of Lucknow, soon after which he died of dysentery. Havelock left the Anglican Church and became a Baptist in 1829. In the same year he married Hannah Marshman, the daughter of Joshua Marshman of Serampore, and was baptised there by John Mack. Havelock was regarded as a notorious Bible-basher who distributed Bibles to soldiers, and held temperance and prayer meetings among the troops. His followers were known as 'Havelock's Saints'.[41]

Havelock had become intimate with the Serampore missionaries soon after his arrival in India in 1823. John Clark Marshman, son of Joshua Marshman and Havelock's brother-in-law, wrote a hagiographical biography, first published in 1860.[42] Graham Dawson has revealed Marshman's intent as constructing a minimalist, vindicating, hero-worshipping biography, on the back of a wave of public sentiment after Havelock's death at Lucknow in 1857. Marshman's text is reverent and sensationalist, devoid of critical distance and unable to do more than appropriate Havelock to model very particular versions of the imperial adventurer and soldier hero. Any rounded sense of Havelock's domestic experience is manipulated and subsumed to the master motif of adventure, which, as Dawson contends, leads 'the narrative into an engagement with the profound contradictions between public and private spheres that have structured British masculinities since the early nineteenth century'.[43]

In very many respects, Lewin and Havelock had much in common. Both arrived in India within a year of each other, both served in Burma (where Havelock too contracted a debilitating illness), both were troubled by a lack of financial security, both had eight or more children (three of whom died), and both were profoundly influenced by their religious beliefs, having had religious epiphanies on their initial voyage to India. Where in Marshman's carefully constructed public rendition there is little of the detailed intimacies of Havelock's domestic life, the narrative importance of which is shackled to his career search for promotion and financial security, the meanings of fatherhood, domestic affection, separation and anxiety are much more explicit in Lewin's private, unfiltered correspondence. Dawson rightly identifies in Marshman's work a number of narrative tensions which can be 'interpreted in terms of the contradictions (between "public" and "private" masculine identities) produced by the gendered separation of spheres, of which the mid-Victorian, middle-class career-soldier affords perhaps the most extreme instance'.[44] Lewin's letters too betray such tensions and anxieties (about health, career, financial security), but he also is able to express the more personal implications of family life: 'There are, of course, great anxieties and troubles connected with a family, but I make no doubt that domestic life contains the chief *remains* of happiness that have survived the Fall, if not the only'.[45]

While the Queen's Regulations for the army in 1859 had stipulated that the individual soldier was 'at full liberty to attend the worship of Almighty God according to the forms prescribed by his own religion when military duty does not interfere', soldiers could only officially return their religion as Anglican, Presbyterian or Catholic, and any whiff of Methodism – as William Lewin had noted in the 1820s – was frowned upon.[46] Christian principles could transcend narrow sectarian boundaries. Havelock had demonstrated this in part through transferring his allegiance to the Baptist faith, but he also most clearly expressed it at a meeting of the Evangelical Alliance in Bombay, where Christians, whatever their denomination, could meet in a spirit of Christian brotherhood: 'They laid aside, for a moment, at the threshold, the canons, the articles, and the formularies of their section of Christianity, but carried along with them, up to the table at which he was speaking, the very essence and quintessence of their religion'.[47]

Havelock had been studying Persian and Hindustani with a view to securing an appointment as interpreter in H.M.'s 16th Foot. On 28 February 1834, he and his wife Hannah and family set off for Cherrapunji for the benefit of their health, in company with Mrs D.

Marshman and Rachel, Hannah's sister. Rachel was married to the Danish physician-botanist Dr Joachim Otto Voigt, the medical officer at Serampore and later temporary director of the Botanic Garden at Calcutta. Havelock proceeded to Calcutta to sit an examination at the Fort William College, while the others went on to Cherrapunji. Henry Havelock had been to school with William Lewin's brother-in-law George Grote, and 'knew him intimately',[48] so there is a distinct possibility that as the Serampore visitors recuperated in the milder climes of the Khasi Hills, they may have made contact with the Lewins, whose daughter Emma was born at Cherrapunji in April.[49] But in his own absence, Havelock's third and infant son Ettrick died at Cherrapunji on 12 June, in the same month that his father took up a new post at Cawnpore, where he received news of his son's death.[50]

That the family experiences of Henry Havelock and William Lewin intersected for a brief moment at a remote hill station in north-east India in the 1830s may be inconsequential. But in tracing their crossed paths at Cherrapunji – and beginning to individualise the characterisation of the place as a military cantonment – the variable vectors of imperialism and Christian influence can start to be teased out. The Welsh missionary project can be understood therefore not only in the context of the earlier activities and influence of the Serampore evangelists in and around the Khasi Hills, but also with reference to the particular exigencies and practices of localised military and political power and authority, which may not have always been necessarily unsympathetic.

Contemplating a name to call his second son, Henry Havelock discarded his wife's suggestion of 'Lionel': 'that signifies "little lion", and there have been lions and tigers enough, and too many, of my race already. I wish the next generation to be lambs'.[51] At times the attitudes of these British soldiers can seem to contradict and oppose stark orthodoxies of brute martial power, and certainly anticipate the flowering of Christian militarism later in the century. But just as soldiers were not devoid of an evangelising instinct, the coming of the missionaries did not signal the zero point of Christian evangelical influence, which was already being modelled at Cherrapunji before the Joneses arrived.

William Lewin may not have been the only soldier who had seen action in the First Anglo-Burmese War of the mid-1820s to have sought Cherrapunji's recuperative air. But the relationship of this isolated outpost to the political consequences of that belligerence on the north-east frontier went further than coincidence; indeed it was the political aftermath of the Burmese campaign to which Cherrapunji owed its very existence as a military and civil station. The sickly Lewin had been

5 Anonymous, 'The Sanatarium at Chirra Poonjee'. 1832.

granted his first leave to proceed to Cherrapunji in August 1832. In the same year, an unknown artist made a sketch of the 'Sanatarium at Chirra Poonjee'.[52] It is a landscape strangely absent of people, but coded with imperial design. The picture focuses on the two central barracks of the sanatarium, elevated on a slight rise on the plateau and nestled protectively against a mountainous backdrop. Juxtaposed in the near foreground is a rider on a white horse to the left, and a group of standing stones to the right. These *mawbynna* are the only hint at native presence, though the watercolour could just as easily depict a panoramic scene in the Scottish highlands or the Welsh mountains as in the Khasi Hills. The indigenous inhabitants are relegated to the margins – of space, culture and history. In stylish blue tail-coat, light-coloured pantaloons and top hat, the rider to the left – a civil and gentlemanly rather than military figure – beats the symbolic bounds of the painting, authorising it as respectable, circumscribed, safe and restorative. The open plain in the foreground is amenable for social as well as military display, and the European barracks, fences, outbuildings and enclosures inscribe the terrain as a familiar and defensible space. This section has explained why it was necessary to see the place in this way, as a foothold secured on a distant mountaintop, far above the plains of Bengal. As a pathway through the imperial network, the track that winds its way to the right of the picture stretches back to Linsday, Scott and Gibson, before it leads on to the visitors from Wales.

Notes

1 Kabbani, *Europe's Myths of Orient*, p. 6.
2 Douglas M. Peers, 'Colonial knowledge and the military in India, 1780–1860', *The Journal of Commonwealth and Imperial History*, 33:2 (2005), 157–80.
3 Yule, 'Notes on the Kasia Hills', 616.
4 T. Lewin to W. Lewin, 14 June 1833, Lewin (ed.), *The Lewin Letters*, volume 1, p. 300.
5 David Cannadine, *The Decline and Fall of the British Aristocracy* (New Haven, CT, 1990), p. 264; Harold E. Raugh Jr, *The Victorians at War 1815–1914: An Encyclopedia of British Military History* (Santa Barbara, Denver, Oxford, 2004), p. 21.
6 IOR L/MIC/10/25 p. 377; Z/O/1/8 No. 2595; F.W. Stubbs, *List of Officers Who Have Served in the Regiment of the Bengal Artillery* (Bath, 1892), p. 21; V.C.P. Hodson, *List of the Officers of the Bengal Army, 1758–1834, Alphabetically Arranged and Annotated with Biographical and Genealogical Notices*, part 3 (London, 1946), p. 47; Holmes & Co., *The Bengal Obituary*, p. 369; IOR N/1/18/f.71.
7 Thomas (Master in Equity, Calcutta) and Frederick Mortimer (in Civil Service in Madras, in India until about 1847; married granddaughter of Clapham Sect member, Thomas Babington).
8 Raugh Jr, *The Victorians at War*, p. 69.
9 War Office Statistical Reports, quoted in Thomas Campbell Robertson, *Political Incidents of the First Burmese War* (London, 1853), p. 235.
10 *Ibid.*, pp. 254–5.
11 *Ibid.*, p. 258.
12 John M. MacKenzie, 'Introduction: popular imperialism and the military' in John M. MacKenzie (ed.), *Popular Imperialism and the Military 1850–1950* (Manchester and New York, 1992), p. 3.
13 See for example Hilary Carey (ed.), 'Introduction' in Hilary Carey (ed.), *Empires of Religion* (Basingstoke and New York, 2008), pp. 1–2.
14 Stephen Neill, *A History of Christianity in India, 1707–1858* (Cambridge, 2002). p. 177.
15 M. Lewin to W. Lewin, 7 March 1826, in Lewin (ed.), *The Lewin Letters*, volume 1, pp. 208–9.
16 M. Lewin to J. Lewin, 17 December 1833, *ibid.*, p. 311.
17 M. Lewin to W. Lewin, 17 May 1826, *ibid.*, pp. 211–12.
18 F. von Koch to J. Lewin, 22 February 1833, *ibid.*, p. 299.
19 F. von Koch to W. and J. Lewin, 15 August 1836 and 15 October 1836, *ibid.*, p. 346.
20 M. Lewin to W. Lewin, 3 September 1826, *ibid.*, p. 214.
21 M. Lewin to J. Lewin, 29 November 1833, *ibid.*, pp. 309–10.
22 M. Lewin to J. Lewin, 3 September 1834, *ibid.*, p. 321.
23 H. Grote to F. von Koch, 27 January 1843, Lewin (ed.), *The Lewin Letters*, volume 2, p. 23.
24 Maud Diver, *The Englishman in India* (London, 1909), p. 18 in Richard Holmes, *Sahib: The British Soldier in India 1750–1914* (London, 2006), p. 485.
25 Elizabeth Buettner, *Empire Families: Britons and Late Imperial India* (Oxford and New York, 2004), p. 1.
26 John Tosh, 'From Keighley to St-Denis: separation and intimacy in Victorian bourgeois marriage', *History Workshop Journal*, 40 (1995), 204, cited in Buettner, *Empire Families*, p. 130.
27 Buettner, *Empire Families*, p. 136.
28 M. Lewin to J. Lewin, 29 November 1833, Lewin (ed.), *The Lewin Letters*, volume 1, p. 310.
29 F. von Koch to W. and J. Lewin, 15 August 1836 and 15 October 1836, *ibid.*, p. 345.
30 T. Lewin to W. Lewin, 14 June 1833, *ibid.*, p. 300.
31 *Ibid.*
32 Trev Lynn Broughton and Helen Rogers, 'Introduction: the empire of the father'

in Trev Lynn Broughton and Helen Rogers (eds), *Gender and Fatherhood in the Nineteenth Century* (Houndmills and New York, 2007), p. 18.

33 W. Lewin to G.H. Lewin, 12 November 1829, Lewin (ed.), *The Lewin Letters*, volume 1, p. 241.

34 W. Lewin to G.H. Lewin, 15 July 1842, Lewin (ed.), *The Lewin Letters*, volume 2, p. 15.

35 MacKenzie, 'Introduction', p. 1.

36 Raugh Jr, *The Victorians at War*, p. 21.

37 Olive Anderson, 'The growth of Christian militarism in mid-Victorian Britain', *The English Historical Review*, 86:338 (1971), 46.

38 Anderson, 'The growth of Christian militarism', 49.

39 MacKenzie, 'Introduction', pp. 4–5.

40 On the hero myths of Henry Havelock, David Livingstone, Charles Gordon and T.E. Lawrence, see John M. MacKenzie, 'Heroic myths of empire' in John M. MacKenzie (ed.), *Popular Imperialism and the Military, 1850–1950* (Manchester and New York, 1992), pp. 109–38.

41 James Lunt, 'Havelock, Sir Henry (1795–1857)', *Oxford Dictionary of National Biography*, Oxford University Press, September 2004; online edn, May 2006, www.oxforddnb.com/view/article/12626 (accessed 9 June 2008); Holmes, *Sahib*, pp. 459–60; see Graham Dawson, *Soldier Heroes: British Adventure, Empire, and the Imagining of Masculinities* (London and New York, 1994); Anderson, 'The growth of Christian militarism', 49–50.

42 Marshman, *Memoirs*.

43 Dawson, *Soldier Heroes*, pp. 127–8.

44 *Ibid.*, p. 135.

45 W. Lewin to G.H. Lewin, 15 July 1842, Lewin (ed.), *The Lewin Letters*, volume 2, p. 15.

46 Anderson, 'The growth of Christian militarism', p. 56.

47 Quoted in Marshman, *Memoirs*, p. 34.

48 Marshman, *Memoirs*, p. 42.

49 IOR N/1/38/f272.

50 Marshman, *Memoirs*, pp. 43–4; Notes from Periodical Accounts of the Serampore Mission, New Series, volume 1, from January 1827 to December 1833 in CMA 27159; Bengal Directory and Annual Register, 1835, p. 563.

51 Marshman, *Memoirs*, p. 38.

52 Anon, 'The Sanatorium, Chirra Punji 1832', IOR WD492. The BL catalogue notes that the sketch was in the same album as Sir Charles D'Oyly's drawings, which include sketches in Dacca and Bihar (c.1827), and river scenes on the Ganges (c.1829). D'Oyly was stationed at Patna on the Ganges from 1821 to 1832. He was an amateur artist and studied under George Chinnery. In 1832 he visited Cape Town, and it is possible that before he took his leave, he visited Cherrapunji.

PART III

The work on the hills

CHAPTER EIGHT

The banner of the cross

At last, on the night of 22 June 1841, Thomas and Ann Jones reached Cherrapunji. John Roberts in Liverpool and the Jones's family and brethren in Wales waited anxiously for news, but Thomas's first letter of 28 July recounting their arrival did not reach Liverpool until mid-October, with extracts published in the November *Y Drysorfa*. 'At last I have the pleasure of writing to you from this place', he informed Roberts, 'where I hope and expect to be instrumental in raising up the banner of the cross'. Lieutenant Lewin had received advanced warning of the missionary's arrival, and just as he had assisted Jacob Tomlin and his wife during their visit in 1837, so too he appeared eager to accommodate the Joneses. Jane Lewin was pregnant with their fifth child Octavius, and the William Lewin who greeted the Joneses at the top of their climb up the mountain was a diseased soldier whose life was 'a perpetual agony'. At one level worlds apart, as professed Christians the paternalistic sympathies of an English soldier and a Welsh missionary, both rooted in a discourse of missionary philanthropy and both looking for subjects to reform, easily overlapped.[1]

The Joneses were relieved to take one downstairs room in Lewin's house. The conditions in the first months after their arrival were trying. Lewin 'has behaved towards us with respect and kindness', but the house was small and Lewin's family large. Relieved from the stifling heat of the plains, the climate of the hills immediately presented other difficulties. The house was damp, and the Joneses spent most of their time trying to keep their already damaged possessions from being completely ruined: 'by the time one trunk has been opened and dried out', Jones complained, 'others will have become mouldy; and if they are not opened immediately, and placed by the fire, their contents will have rotted. Since the rains began even the clothes that we are wearing have begun to rot'.[2] On 6 August Jones secured one of two houses that were on sale on the military station, and on 6 September moved into the first mission house at Cherrapunji; he grandly reported to Roberts that on this red-letter day, after so much wandering, they had 'taken possession of the "Welsh Missionary Society" Mission House in India, on the other side of the Ganges'.[3]

Divine destiny and territorial acquisition in Asia

In the midst of the First Anglo-Chinese War (1839–42), as Britain was pressing China to permit the free trade of opium and other goods, the prospect also beckoned of the closed shop of China being opened up to foreign missionaries. After centuries of Chinese antipathy towards religious heterodoxy as a threat to social and political stability, the propagation of Christianity in China seemed a real possibility as the British put enormous political and military pressure on the Qing Dynasty.[4] British forces had captured Hong Kong in August 1839, and as Jones sat in his bungalow at the close of 1841, barely 300 miles from the Chinese border, he enthused at the prospect of further Welsh missionaries streaming into the Chinese kingdom whose 'door seems to have been blown open by British cannons'.[5]

Whether providential or merely opportunistic, the mechanism of empire had brought Asia within the evangelical grasp. Jones's version of British imperialism in the north was thus of a benign and essentially reluctant expansionist, never actively seeking territory by conquest, but almost inadvertently amassing kingdoms from the ocean to the Himalayas within a hundred miles of China, and east to Cochin China (Indochina). Assam, Arakan, Chittagong, Tenasserim – even west across the Indus River to Afghanistan; such spoils of the First Anglo-Burmese War (1824–26) and the Anglo-Afghan Wars (1839–42) had happened for Jones 'as if without opposition'. The apparent former cruelty and violence of these old regimes was now mitigated by their protection under British influence; nominally sovereign, the thrones of the princely states 'have been safeguarded from usurpers and their subjects protected from oppression and plunder; which has never happened before since these kingdoms were first established'. For Jones, in the tradition of Carey, the primary rationale of imperial expansion was to open up new worlds to the Christian message, linking divine destiny with territorial acquisition:

> it is certain that the British government is being used by God to hold the rod above these unruly and bloodthirsty kings and princes to keep them still, so that nobody dares unsheath his sword; and while the government teaches them to rule their subjects rightly, improves their trade and labour and brings about other improvements to their country, the Christians of Britain are supposed to teach them in the way of life and in

that religion which is the basis of all true happiness and comfort in this world and in the world to come.[6]

That the Khasi Hills were a byway off the missionary highway was brought home to Jones in a letter from Roberts the following year. In June 1842, Roberts and John Davies, Fronheulog, attended the anniversary celebrations of the LMS, in company with none other than Robert Moffat himself ('the African lion', in Britain on furlough). The precocity of the breakaway Welshmen as neophyte missionaries might not have been far from the minds of those assembled, though the Welsh contingent would have been proud to advertise the advancement of their mission to date. The Reverend John Edmonds, however, an LMS missionary who had worked in Chinsurah in Bengal the 1820s, would remind them of their insignificance: 'Mr Davies told me just now that Mr Edmonds had never heard that there was such a place as Cassia!! What an insignificant place you have got to, – not to be known even by name to a missionary just arrived from India!!'[7] Fear of failure and not wanting to be seen as churlish renegades were clear and present incentives for the Welsh to persevere with their initial choice. Jones also appealed ultimately to the perceived providentialism of the Khasi Hills as the appropriate place for the Welsh, drawn to their attention so fortuitously by Jacob Tomlin: 'can you withdraw from the missionary field that is so obviously prepared for the Gospel, and brought to your attention by circumstances which occurred, since I cannot say *accidentally*, I must say almost *miraculously*'.

Roberts saw to it that Jones's long letter of December 1841 was published almost in its entirety in *Y Drysorfa*. As a justification of the choice of mission station, it was the perfect manifesto to shore up home support. More than that, it closed with an impassioned call to arms to the Christians of Britain to rise to their duty and bring the vastness of Asia under the influence of their belief. Jones's language was swept up in a rising swell of biblical allusions and rhetorical exhortations, peppered with italic emphases, and well suited to be read aloud to congregations across the country as if the preacher himself were standing there before them. Jones pulled no punches, targetting what he saw as the indolent churches with their fireside daydreamers and adventurers, fractured with internecine quarrels and poaching each others' members while millions of pagans perished without a saviour. In the severity of his harsh critique of those who would not answer the call to mission, lies an insight into the psychology of his own experience as a man who was reconciled not to see his own family again:

how long will they be satisfied with such poor excuses as these, 'I do not care to leave my mother, or my sister, or some other relative;' or 'I cannot

> learn the language, – I am afraid of the sea;' or, what I heard one or two people saying 'I do not think I should *like* to live with black people etc.'! I had better *keep silent* on these matters, because words cannot express how unworthy are such excuses, and yet they have been made by some of our gifted young preachers! They should be very ashamed, and if there is anything like shame in heaven, they will be certainly be eternally ashamed of themselves. And as for those who use their childish attachment to their relatives as an excuse – perhaps the Lord in his righteous dissatisfaction will take these relations away through death and leave them to grieve their loss under the scourge of their guilty consciences.

Jones's excoriation of his apathetic coreligionists was tempered by news that his friend the Reverend James Williams, with whom he and William Lewis had studied at Bala College, was to be sent as a missionary to Brittany. Brittany was by the nineteenth century a devout Catholic stronghold, and the Celtic revival from the late eighteenth century anticipated growing interest among the Welsh for their Celtic relations. The need for 'the evangelisation of the Celtic races' had been proposed at a meeting of various ministers in Newport in early 1821, at which interest was also signalled to missionise the 'sons of Madoc' in America. The legend clearly persisted at this time that a Welsh prince had reached America in the twelfth century, well before Columbus's landfall in 1492, and that his descendants through intermarriage with indigenous peoples had formed tribes of Welsh Indians. Spasmodic efforts had been made in the 1820s and 1830s to establish a Welsh mission in Brittany, but after the formal breakaway from the LMS and the establishment of the WFMS, Brittany offered a natural sphere of operation. Williams and his wife arrived in St Malo on 17 August 1842, and later settled at Quimper, where he worked until ill health forced his retirement in 1869.[8]

As for Jones with the Khasis, for Williams the capacity of the Bretons for redemption was not dependent on their race; the peculiarities of their barbaric and superstitious rituals were seen to be similarly Satan-inspired.[9] The Welshmen's brand of religion was one that prioritised the gospel; all other 'nonsense'[10] that seduced these 'poor, miserable creatures'[11] was merely distraction from the doctrine of *sola scriptura* – the authority of the church as vested in scripture alone. For Jones, Christianity was not only the obvious path to salvation for fallen pagans, but the means of teaching them 'to think and to reason'.[12]

Bringing the book: language learning and translation

A small boy came up to Thomas Jones soon after his arrival, and seeing his library of books, asked for one so he could learn English. Jones replied that he did not have such a book to give him, which puzzled the boy, who thought the Padre Sahib should be able to spare at least one. 'He could not comprehend', wrote Jones, 'that I had to come here first to learn their language, and then make books for them'.[13] The predominant narrative of both new and old histories of the Khasi mission is the pre-eminence of Jones as founding missionary and bringer of the book: the prime architect of the Christianisation of the hill tribes, the *de novo* 'father' of Khasi literature in his role as the man who put the Khasi language into written form using Welsh orthography.

When Jones disappointed the small boy, and then embarked on a process of regularising Khasi language and grammar in written form, in one way he established himself as gatekeeper of Khasi culture and thought. Such a claim linked easily with a popular Khasi legend, and drew Jones into Khasi ontologies through a story circulated by mission historians as well as later anthropologists and Khasi scholars. According to Khasi lore, the great God had entrusted a Khasi man and a foreigner each with a sacred book containing his holy law. Returning to their respective homelands, they came to a great river. The foreigner wrapped the book in his long hair and carried it across the flood on his head. The Khasi was short, and though taking the book between his teeth was unable to protect his precious cargo from the swirling waters, and the book was lost.[14]

In the first weeks after his arrival, with the station relentlessly gripped in the embrace of monsoon cloud, Jones took his first steps in a complicated daily ritual. He soon enjoined two Khasi men – U Doowan Rai and U Juncha – to teach him the rudiments of their language. The trio faced off in a curious spectacle of posture, motion and utterance, their bodies moving to communicate particular meanings as in turn the everyday objects of the material world were enacted in physical display. As a prelude to the main act, Jones would recite English words, to which in reply they would give their corresponding word. But as the men's rudimentary knowledge of English grammar and vocabulary was exhausted, the verbal exchange of statement and refrain took on a more gestural mode. Pointing to the sky, Jones could glean the Khasi word *ka bneng*, or to a goat grazing nearby, *ka blang*. Miming a cat and a bird to the bemusement of other onlookers elicited *ka maow* and *ka sim*. The charade would become more and more puzzling as the players riddled with more complex actions and concepts. Khasi words could also be much more specific than their English equivalents. The word for 'wash' was different depending on whether one was talking about the face (*bata*), hands (*tet*), head (*sleh*), body (*sum*), clothes (*sait*) or a vessel (*kling*).[15] Sometimes, after manoeuvring himself for a quarter of an hour or more, Jones would have to give up in frustration and progress to another word.

On the basis of this theatrical interchange, Jones was progressively able to compile an alphabetical list of Khasi words, as well as longer sentences with literal translations. If many of the words were hard won from their enigmatical performances, their textual rendering could be no less obstinate a task. Jones grappled with the problem of pronunciation, as he struggled to determine not only the nature of individual Khasi phonemes, but also how to render such unfamiliar sounds in familiar textual symbols. As Jones strained with all his faculties to deduce the subtleties of the spoken tongue, U Doowan Rai and U Juncha would move nearer to him and repeat words closer and closer to his ear, underneath the accompanying din of rain's incessant tattoo. Adding to the complexity of the task was the fact that at times the two Khasi men would need to consult each other as to the pronunciation of a particular word, and if themselves uncertain as to an agreed version, or would open up a discussion with the bystanders as to how a word should be pronounced. To Jones's frustration, this seemingly haphazard and vexatious procedure could merely throw up an even greater variety of possible versions, so that 'I am left in the end to guess which one is correct'.

Jones described his two interlocutors as youths or young men: U Juncha was twenty-five or thirty years old, from the *Ding-doh* tribe; U Doowan Rai, from Leihiam, was about twenty.[16] It is likely, however, that they were somewhat older. Both had been students of Alexander Lish a few years earlier, hence their basic knowledge of English. Moreover, the U Dewan Rai who had assisted Lish in his school was noted as the same who had been converted by Krishna Chandra Pal in 1813. If he had been a young teenager at this time, then in 1841 he would have been around forty years old, or ten years older than Jones. But Jones in the end admitted he was guessing at their ages: 'when asked they always reply "We Khasians never know how old we are". Nevertheless they believe that they will live to 100 years old before they die of old age. Consequently the same word is used in their language to signify age and generation, namely *carta*'.[17] The missionary's knowledge of Khasi vocabulary was quickly progressing to more complex concepts.

The heroic version of Thomas Jones the missionary as cultural saviour belies the lineage of debts, relationships and negotiations in which indigenous peoples played an active role in shaping cultural and spiritual outcomes, however silent the Khasi voices are in the archive. Jones built upon the legacy of the Serampore missionaries and their cultural interactions with the Khasis: U Juncha and U Doowan Rai most likely honed their skills at charade at the foot of Alexander Lish. The idea of the missionary 'reducing' native languages from oral to literary form smacks of linguistic colonialism. The orality of Khasi, with its untamed fluidity of meaning and pronunciation, might demand tempering and containment by the missionary, in order to impose structures of moral as well as cultural hegemony. Yet as Jane Samson has noted in her revision of 'translation-as-violence' in the case of missionary renderings of Pacific languages, translation in fact involved a process of 'mutual conversion'. The missionary was required to gain a sophisticated understanding of the traditions of the people he proselytised if he was to achieve any degree of linguistic sophistication in their tongue. Citing Vicente Rafael, Samson asserts the need for more complex readings of the interactions that take place in the process of missionary translation: 'translation and conversion produce the vernacular as that which simultaneously institutes *and* subverts colonial rule'.[18]

Many missionary and other published accounts tend to skip over the role of indigenous informants in the process of translation. Jones himself was overt about the role played by U Juncha and U Doowan Rai, whose service he had engaged at the rate of six rupees a month: 'they are teaching me'.[19] Written Khasi was co-produced by U Juncha, U Doowan Rai and Jones, as well as by the onlookers of their odd display. Jones's motives are transparent; the Khasi men partook of the exchange for their own reasons, but for them Jones was the artless innocent. When U Doowan Rai had enough facility in English to enter into correspondence himself with John Roberts, the mission secretary thanked him for teaching Khasi to Jones: 'I think that if you would continue to take pains, you would very soon become a good writer, and be able to write as good as many english [*sic*] boys who think themselves beautiful penmen'.[20]

Jones was not simply putting Khasi vocabulary into writing in a straightforward act of transliteration; he was reconciling different sets of beliefs into a single phraseology, inserting his own prejudices and preconceptions into the form of written Khasi. 'I am obliged', he noted, 'to devise so many new words and phrases, and to use others to signify concepts which they have never before been used to signify and to review the whole sphere of divine truth, and decide upon and organise, as far as possible, the most suitable vocabulary and the best way of setting out the truths of the Gospel'.[21] 'Mastering' the language involved fixing it in a grammar and a dictionary. With regional speech patterns prevailing across the hills ('no more than the difference which exists between the various counties of England and Wales'), Jones settled on the Cherra dialect as the 'middle road that suits them all'.[22] Fixing the Cherra dialect as the *lingua franca* was contentious in those communities within whose bounds other dialects prevailed, but established it as a vehicle for the later mobilisation of collective cultural and political identity among the Khasis as a group.

With no knowledge of Bengali script, Jones employed the Roman alphabet when recording Khasi words. This was in most respects simply a pragmatic decision. He soon learned, however, that there were actually very few people in the region who could write in the Bengali script, and that those who could had little desire to do so: 'The Khasians generally avoid the Bengali script with a superstitious dread, and they fervently believe that if they try to write letters, they will immediately be struck down with blindness, or a deadly disease. In several places people have told me that so and so tried to write and that they were struck blind!'[23]

In October 1841 he informed Roberts of his decision to use Roman characters to render the Khasi language in print, and to utilise the Welsh alphabet's character set in doing so. Even here, some qualification was required as to precise pronunciation: the *ch* in the name of Jones's informant U Juncha was pronounced neither as in English nor in Welsh, 'but as an plosive *c* (or *k*) – something between the Welsh *c* and *ch*'.[24] In Jones's view, Khasi vowel sounds had general equivalence to the Welsh vowels (a, e, i, o, u, w, y), aside from *u* (pronounced like English 'ee'), to which he assigned the sound as in the English word *tube*. In his first four months on the hills, Jones estimated that he had devoted only one month's attention to the task of learning Khasi, and claimed that by the time Roberts received his November 1841 report, and despite the fact that he had 'been reckoned to be remarkable for my stupidity in learning languages', he would have learned enough to begin preaching in Khasi.[25] Roberts was indeed surprised at the missionary's success in acquiring a working knowledge of such 'a strange & uncultivated tongue' with such speed: 'what! friend Tom mastered the language in so short a time? is it possible?'[26]

As became common practice over the course of their correspondence, Roberts selectively translated and edited Jones's letters for publication in *Y Drysorfa*, and from the outset he was keen to reserve from public consumption any views that might be seen as contentious or inimical to the good reputation of the venture. After all, part of the purpose of publishing the missionary's accounts was to confirm the validity of the society's course of action in separating from the LMS, as well as to drum up financial support for the mission in the form of collections from the congregations in Liverpool and across Wales.

While the originals of most of Jones's letters do not survive, it is clear from Roberts's personal correspondence to Jones that the secretary was perturbed by implicit and explicit criticism that Jones had made of his missionary predecessors, including Alexander Lish. The warm welcome initially given to 'Padree Sahib' Jones by some of the Khasis, their eagerness to attend his school and even their apparent 'appetite for divine matters', soon gave way to disappointment. Jones reported that parents would send their boys to his school to learn English only in the hope that they might secure government jobs, and that girls would similarly court his wife's attentions in the hope of receiving gifts: 'once they realised that I had neither the means nor the inclination to waste my possessions, they began to withdraw, one by one, with a new realisation, that not all Padrees are as generous as my predecessor; and in this respect he has certainly had a harmful effect'.[27]

While his disassociation from Lish's missionary techniques was reported in the columns of *Y Drysorfa*, his specific critique of other missionaries was not. Jones's painstaking and interactive process of translation quickly revealed to him the inconsistencies in the Serampore translations, which he soon discarded in favour of those produced through his own methodology; 'it is strange', he wrote, 'how good and educated men have been satisfied with some superficial knowledge in foreign languages. I am sorry to say that in my opinion, of that which has been written in this language, not one word in fifty is correct'.[28] Roberts was particularly taken aback by Jones's criticisms of Carey's Khasi translation of parts of the New Testament, as well as by other remarks about Jacob Tomlin, and excised them from the published version of the letters. Jones's imputation was that the Serampore Baptists were more concerned with the speed with which they could claim they had started preaching, and the quantity rather than quality of their translations.

While some of the Khasis who had spent a little time with the missionary could now converse in basic English, Jones was adamant about the need to teach the Khasis to read and write their own language first before attempting to learn English.[29] While Lish had made some tentative steps towards codifying Khasi words in Roman characters – a specimen of Khasi vocabulary was published in this form in 1838[30] – his broad approach of printing books with English text juxtaposed with Khasi (in Bengali characters) had been palpably unsuccessful: 'after years of enormous labour and expense there is not one Khasian who can read a page of the books which he used nor understand a paragraph of the simplest expressions in the English language'. In Jones's view, knowledge of Khasi grammar was prerequisite for Khasis to then tackle the peculiarities of English grammar.

Lish's *Dr Watt's First Catechism for Children, Translated into Khasee for the Use of the Churra Mission Schools* had been printed at Serampore in 1836.[31] Isaac Watts, Independent minister and hymnist, had published his catechisms in 1730, and they were widely disseminated into the nineteenth century for the religious instruction of children. The twenty-four questions and answers were designed for a child of three or four years of age, instilling basic Christian precepts of creation, the sacredness of the Bible as God's word, a Christian's duty towards God, Jesus Christ as saviour, the nature of sin and the possibility of redemption.[32] The catechism was interactive in style, simple to remember, easy to digest, laying out religious precepts in a graduated format. Such a tool suited missionary work well; to the paternalistic evangelist, the Khasi was like a child, artless and naive. Following Watts's principles, the child was to be instructed partly by reason but partly also by the authority of the parent. The role of the religious instructor was also to 'teach children how to draw their religion out of the Bible . . . by shewing them how to distinguish the most useful parts of scripture from the rest'. The Bible, after all, was a vast compendium of church history and doctrine, some of its precepts antiquated and others of its doctrines and duties so 'promiscuously scattered abroad in this large volume of the scriptures' that the ignorant needed some direction in order to make sense of them.[33]

Jones was completely unprepared for the appetite of the Khasi people to learn English. He had brought no specific teaching books with him, and wrote to some of his Calcutta contacts in the Calcutta Christian Tract and Book Society for copies of suitable books for English beginners. By August 1841, the mission's agent John Wallis Alexander had dispatched from Calcutta as a gift to the school on his own account, twenty copies each of the schoolbooks published by the Book Society, of which he was a member. Jones also asked Roberts to send from Liverpool copies of some English schoolbooks, Religious Tract Society hymn books,[34] the Welsh catechisms *Rhodd Mam* (Mother's Gift) and *Rhodd Tad* (Father's Gift), Testaments, the Confession of Faith, as well as the Constitutional Deed of the Calvinistic Methodists. In anticipation of being able to have his own books printed, he wrote out a few in Khasi, including an almanac for the use of local traders and porters to help them keep their accounts and recognise the days of the month.[35]

The missionary would also have been mindful of Watts's other proscription, that learning by rote did not equate to religious understanding: 'Wisdom and goodness does not consist in such fatigues of the brain, and such a treasure of unknown words'.[36] Jones ultimately considered the format of Watts's English catechism excessively verbose. He chose instead to translate John Parry's Welsh children's catechism *Rhodd Mam*, first published in 1811 and one of the most well-known books in Wales in the nineteenth century, preferring the variety of its religious content and considering that the brevity of its questions and answers made it easier to remember.

In 1842 Jones made a translation of an English catechism available in Calcutta ('It starts as follows, "I sin, he sins, you sin, all sin" which translated reads, "Nga pobp, Oo pobp, Phi pobp, Baroh pobp"'), and his translation of *Rhodd Mam* was printed in Calcutta in the same year.[37] During a delay of over seven months through 1842, as Jones waited for his first two books to roll off the press in Calcutta, he was forced to spend much of his time writing out books by hand for his students.[38] By the end of 1842, John Roberts was fully convinced about Thomas Jones's decision to translate Khasi using Roman characters. Alexander Duff regarded it as 'one of Satan's errors' that variations in scripts were perpetuated; 'in circumstances such as yours', he advised Jones, 'when the natives had no script of their own, trying to use curly, ugly, expensive and imperfect script such the Bengali script, rather than the Roman alphabet, which is so clear and elegant, and cheaper than the others, in my opinion deliberately raises a fresh barrier against the entry of the Truth into the country'.[39] Here Duff rehearsed some of the arguments that had been put in a long-standing debate about the application of the Roman alphabet to the languages of India. Duff had sided with Charles Edward Trevelyan in a dispute ignited at the end of 1833 by the proposed publication of an English/Urdu dictionary using Roman characters.[40] In his support of using Roman letters as the medium for expressing Indian languages, Trevelyan cited the perceived neatness (and cheapness) of English when printed, and claimed that an assimilation of English and Indian languages in a common character would lead to 'mutual good understanding between the two races'.[41] This latter claim was disputed by such opponents as Professor Thomas Jarrett, who argued that even though, for example, Welsh and English were written in the same character, there was little reason to think that an Englishman could relate many Welsh words to English ones.[42]

In the opposing camp were also arrayed the oriental scholars James Prinsep and John Tytler, who argued that any exclusive use of English would only prevent the development of native literature.[43] Trevelyan regarded Indian characters as being intrinsically 'barbarous'. This association between the subjective aesthetics of written symbols and civilisation had also been expressed by Duff in his letter to Jones. From his vantage point in Liverpool, Roberts described Bengali characters as being 'of so peculiar a construction, and difficult to understand'; Duff was less equivocal about breaking the nexus between 'ugly' text and savagery: 'No! Our aim is always and should always be to facilitate and not to hinder the spread of correct knowledge of all kinds; and one way to do that is to support everywhere the use of the Roman script, instead of the native alphabets, which are connected, and interwoven, and as it were steeped in all things idolatrous'.[44]

Welsh pedagogical traditions

Thomas Jones went to the Khasi Hills with the express aim of educating the Khasis: 'I have come here with the aim of teaching'. Unprepared on his arrival for the appetite and impatience of many Khasis to learn English – whatever their motives for this might be ('we cannot expect them to have anything in mind but temporal gain', although 'they all know that I am a religious teacher as well as other things') – in the first months he had to turn eager students from his door as he had no printed teaching materials.[45] The extent to which Jones had any formal pedagogical training is also pertinent to any understanding of his methods and influence in the early years of the mission. As Stuart Piggin has detailed, the training received by British Protestant missionaries in India in the first half of the nineteenth century was a product of individual society policy as well as the broad state of theological education in Britain through the period.[46] While there was no typical pathway for a missionary candidate, and a multiplicity of formal and informal institutions offered training to the novice, many missionaries were educated at the Baptists' Bristol Academy (where Joshua Marshman enrolled in 1795), the LMS's Gosport Missionary Seminary (from 1800), or the Church Missionary Institution at Islington (opened 1825). While Piggin portrays the Scottish and Irish Presbyterians as the best educated missionaries to India in the first half of the nineteenth century (the former under the particular influence of Thomas Chalmers), he characterises the training of Welsh candidates as decidedly inferior, even with the opening of Bala College in 1837 at which the six missionaries prior to 1859 were trained – Thomas Jones, William Lewis, Owen Richards, Daniel Jones, Robert Parry (arrived 1856) and Thomas Jones II (arrived 1857). A seventh, William Pryse, who came to the Khasi Hills in 1849, was trained at Trefeca College.[47]

Aside from the low regard of Welsh missionary candidates held by the LMS, opinions of the Welsh were elsewhere unflattering. The educational system at the Bristol Academy in the early decades of the nineteenth century was, according to Piggin, compromised by the 'the large percentage of Welsh students who had to be taught English'.[48] Like many missionaries to India from other denominations, the Welsh also had perfunctory training in medicine, teaching and Eastern languages.[49] But the bilingualism of those such as Thomas Jones might yet be reckoned a metalinguistic advantage in learning a third language, Khasi.[50] If the Welsh, as Piggin characterises them, were less educated than their English, Scottish and Irish peers, perhaps they also therefore avoided the 'erudite inflexibility' he attributes to the more conservatively trained missionaries of the early decades of the nineteenth century.[51] Bala College was a theological college for the Welsh Calvinistic Methodist Connexion, not specifically a missionary training institute, but under the tutelage of Lewis Edwards and David Charles, Jones was educated in the tradition of Thomas Charles and had access to his library there. It is unclear to what extent its first students were exposed to the particular precepts of missionary practice, though it is clear that Jones subscribed to many of the axioms established by Scottish Presbyterian David Bogue at Gosport: the importance of education, the danger of sectarianism, the need to learn the local language, the training of indigenous preachers, and the general quality of martyrdom demanded of a missionary.

The Welsh Sunday school tradition in which they had been raised was a more certain model for their pedagogy. Thomas Jones may have been taken out of formal schooling at an early age,[52] but like many of his compatriots he came under the influence of an important educational institution in the form of the Sunday school. As Snell has argued, the *Ysgolion Sabathol* wielded an even more significant influence in Wales than it did in England, with extremely high levels of attendance (in 1846 around a quarter of the population of north-east Wales). Thomas Jones's father Edward had run a Sunday school at Brithdir, and his neighbour John Jones conducted a school in the Pied House farm – the involvement of ordinary people in the organisation of the schools was one of its distinctive features. In a country where long distances and inhospitable terrain could separate parish churches, house meetings served the scattered rural populations as practical alternatives to chapel worship.

As well as being the centre of religious education, the Welsh Sunday schools also played a significant role in Welsh language maintenance, in teaching reading and writing, as well as inculcating the tenets and virtues of social discipline, such as abstinence, good order and personal hygiene.[53] An emphasis on scriptural knowledge was key to Calvinistic Methodist teaching; those women who recited large tracts of the Bible while walking miles to chapel or Sunday school were maintaining Welshness as well as Calvinism. Through the institution of the Welsh Sunday school, a largely illiterate people learned to read the Bible, but also importantly to *read*. The memorising of set verses and the scriptural recitations at morning service involved committing to memory vocabulary and word and sentence patterns that could then form the basis of more advanced language learning.

The importance of education for the Welsh was stressed by generations of their leaders and preachers. John Elias, who had died around the time in June 1841 that the Joneses were *en route* to Cherrapunji, had decades before asserted the crucial role of education for worldly and spiritual well-being: 'I think if I have to make a choice', Elias wrote to his son, 'whether to have all India, or Sir William Jones's learning, I should prefer the latter'.[54] It would be as absurd a proposition, Griffith Jones had argued in 1740, to teach Welsh people in English as it would be to teach English people in French.[55] Thomas Charles himself had strongly advocated the teaching of the Welsh in their native tongue, and the Scots and Irish in their native Gaelic: 'Welsh words convey ideas to their infant minds as soon as they can read them, which is not the case when they are taught to read a language they do not understand'.[56] The orality of the Welsh system transferred very effectively to teaching a people whose culture and identity were based entirely on memory and oral recitation. The Welsh missionaries brought with them, therefore, a particular set of familiar and culturally specific ideologies and strategies that linked education and evangelism.

Through 1843 Thomas Jones set about translating the first half of a revised catechism, arranged with full scriptural proofs 'according to the most recent revision by the Revd D. Charles'; this was printed by the middle of 1844.[57] One advantage of the catechism as a teaching aid lay in the fact that it not only impressed fundamental Christian precepts on the minds of its readers, but in its supporting scriptural proofs or examples, led its readers to acquire a good stock of scriptures.[58] At the back of all their minds was the burning question – when would the brethren at home see the first tangible fruits of the mission? In lieu of news of converts, Jones's Khasi texts provided tangible and measurable proof for the mission's friends and sponsors that the foundation was being laid for their ultimate goal, that of conversion. In December 1842, Jones posted to Roberts a copy of the *Rhodd Mam* translation, as well as some of the schoolbooks, and Roberts was delighted to be able to publish extracts of the newly printed Khasi catechism in the November 1844 *Y Drysorfa*.

According to a later source, Jones also published a Khasi primer in Calcutta in 1846 under the title *Ca Citap nyngcong ban hicai pile ci ctin Cassi*.[59] Jones's translation of the Gospel of St Matthew – *Ka Gospel Jong u Mathi* – was published in Calcutta by the Calcutta Auxiliary Bible Society in 1846. In early 1847 he noted his desire to print a new edition of the children's catechism, and translations of *Rhodd Tad* and the Confessions of Faith. By this point hundreds of short tracts had also been printed for the use of Khasis in the village schools.[60]

Patrons and allies

If the missionaries sensed the importance of courting the favour of indigenous elites, their relationship with British authority in the region was more circumscribed. The invalided Lieutenant Lewin was a useful patron and ally, but the nature of any interaction with higher lines of authority was yet to be determined. There is no evidence that the Welsh mission, having chosen the Khasi Hills as their sphere of operation, had made any contact whatsoever with British authorities there before they sent Jones off in 1841. A few days after his arrival, Thomas Jones, accompanied by Lewin, went to visit the officials on the British station. 'As a result', he wrote to Roberts, 'we are to consider one another as friends from now on. But I cannot expect more from them than common civility, because they are not very well-disposed towards missionary activities'. Jones made particular mention, however, of Frederick Lister, who as 'the most senior authority in national and military affairs' had a reputation of being a kind and benevolent officer, and who had personally offered his services in financial matters should Jones require them.[61]

The missionary's desire to be among his pagan flock was also motivated by a wish to distance himself from the 'wicked' Europeans on the cantonment, and while Lewin was a friend and supporter and Lister at least counted as some kind of ally, of the other Europeans, 'There is not one of them . . . whom I would wish to be nearer to me than my opponents'.[62] The Muslim and Hindu *sepoys* of the Indian army stationed at Cherrapunji, however, were a *bona fide* object of proselytism. Jones ensured that parts of the scriptures in Bengali and Hindustani were distributed around the station to Brahmin priests and others 'as much in need of the word of life and of the Saviour who is proclaimed in it as I or the Khasians'.[63] In early 1844 William Lewis also noted that a few of the Europeans on the station were attending Wednesday prayer meetings.[64]

As Jones began to travel further afield from Cherrapunji, he would later confront the effects of previous native encounters with Europeans. In the early months of 1842 Jones made a ten-day journey through the hills, to villages where he reasonably assumed no Europeans had ever penetrated, though the bell-wether of their aggression had clearly been a source of great fear and anxiety: 'And since the Europeans have caused such destruction wherever they have been, burning villages and persecuting the inhabitants like so many sheep, my appearance in their villages caused enormous tumult and fear in the minds of the people; and upon my first visit I failed to gain their trust and remove their fears'.[65] In September 1842, Jones again toured the region, on the first night reaching Nongkynrih where he preached, before pushing eastward to Jaintia territory. On this trip he was accompanied in the informal role as missionary's accomplice by Lieutenant Lewin, whose by now lengthy acculturation in India had led him to turn Christian rather than to 'go native'. Their other companion was the twenty-two-year-old

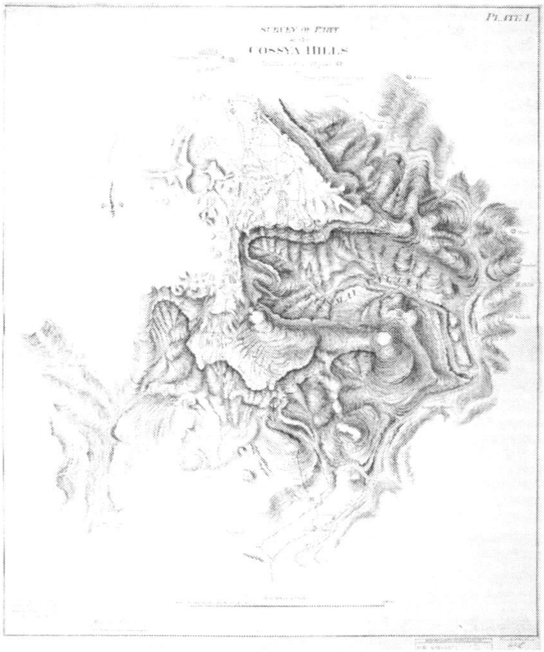

6 Henry Yule, 'Survey of part of the Cossya Hills', 1843.

Lieutenant Henry Yule of the Bengal Engineers, who after his short stint at the Aden observatory had recently been assigned to report on the means of transporting Khasi coal to the plains.[66]

Yule had studied under Henry Parr Hamilton, later dean of Salisbury, and James Challis, who had been ordained 1830 and became Plumian professor of astronomy and experimental philosophy at Cambridge. Later accounts of Yule's character infer a deep-seated instinct for the humane and an abhorrence of tyranny, only matched by his anger at authors who didn't provide indexes to their works.[67] Whatever the case, Yule clearly took a shine to Jones, and Jones found a soulmate in the Scottish Presbyterian. Jones wrote excitedly to Roberts in October 1842 of the young officer's undertaking to underwrite the support of twelve Khasi boys in his school, to be specifically trained as teachers. Yule had already been supporting the education of four boys and two men, and on his departure for England in 1843 to marry his cousin, he pledged a further 600 rupees to support his scholars: 'Don't you think that this is a princely gift? I was afraid that his departure would mean a loss; but it would appear that he is increasing his contributions rather than reducing them!'[68]

Expansion of the Welsh mission

Jones's abundant vision for the spread of the Welsh missionary cause was laid out in his first report from the hills in July 1841. From his beachhead at Cherrapunji, Jones imagined a steady flow of Welsh missionaries sent in pairs to Jaintiapur, Silchar in the Cachar district, Manipur, the Hajongs and Garos, Sylhet, and Comilla in plains Tipperah. Native evangelists and teachers, once raised up, would then carry on the work of these founding European missionaries. In the meantime, he asked that three missionaries be sent without delay, two for Cherrapunji and one for a new station inland.

He was soon cheered by the news that two young preachers trained at Bala by Lewis Edwards – William Lewis (twenty-seven years) and Owen Richards (twenty-eight years) – had recently offered their services as missionaries. This was a time for optimism in the Calvinistic Methodist cause; efforts were being finalised to unify the north and south Wales associations,[69] and a seminary was established at Trefeca in 1842 under David Charles. Edwards had written to Jones that three of the brethren in Bala were prepared for missionary work, and Jones was already acquainted with Richards, for whom he had a great regard. Owen Richards's medical training would also be a boon for the mission, quite apart from the fact that he was from Calvinistic Methodist royalty. Richards had married Maria Charles, the granddaughter of the great Thomas Charles, Bala, and was also the brother-in-law of Lewis Edwards. Perhaps there was some family loyalty in Edwards's view that Richards was 'decidedly one of the best scholars they ever had at Bala';[70] the brethren had also been rocked by the death of Maria in February 1836, a few days after giving birth to a son, Owen Charles Richards.

Richards had obtained permission to preach by the end of 1841, and while both had been approved as missionary candidates by the Bangor Association, Lewis felt he needed another six months' preparation before embarking on a missionary career. William Lewis was born in Manchester, but his parents were both from Montgomeryshire. His father James was a machinist from Carno, and his mother Jane Swancott was a farmer's daughter from Llanllugan in the parish of Llanwyddelan. William himself worked for a time in a textile warehouse, and later was an apprentice engineer.[71] Originally hoping to go to China as an LMS missionary, Lewis went to Bala in 1839 where he was accepted as a missionary candidate.

William Lewis's wife Mary Roberts had been influenced in the mission cause by her Baptist mother Catherine. Her father was an excise officer, and her mother had at one time been a member of the church of Dr Ryland, one of the founders of the BMS. Mary Lewis dated her desire for missionary work from this period, when at the age of around ten years old her mother would read to her the exploits of Carey, Marshman and Ward. The Roberts family had lived for a time in Llanidloes, where they were acquainted with the Welsh missionary Evan Evans after his return there in 1826 after ten years work in South Africa.[72] It was here too that Mary received her first religious impressions. Mary's family had also lived for a period in the 1830s at Berriew, where she may well have been acquainted with Thomas Jones and his family. Later, at Llanfair Caereinion, Mary was baptised by the Reverend John Elias. It was here too that she witnessed the 1840 Association that formed the WFMS, and where Thomas Jones stayed at her family's home for some days during the event.

Lewis and Richards were both ordained in Liverpool at Whitsun, 16 May 1842, and William and Mary were married the following day. The Lewises, together with Owen Richards and his six-year-old son Owen Charles, sailed for India on 16 July 1842, and in October Jones joyfully received news of their departure: 'the fields are not only white and ready for the harvest, but are almost spoiling for want of labourers'.[73] Roberts had secured their passage on the *Malabar*, and regarded it as an auspicious fact that this was the same ship that had in 1821 taken Congregationalist missionary the Reverend David Griffiths to Madagascar for the LMS, where he later translated the Bible into Malagasy.[74]

Where Thomas Jones had not received specific instructions on his departure, Lewis and Richards had more direct advice from the WFMS committee. On their arrival in Calcutta, they were directed to make the acquaintance of the various missionaries there, and in particular Alexander Duff and the Reverend J. Macdonald at the Church of Scotland mission. Once in Cherrapunji, they were urged to remain there until they had become proficient in Khasi. They should furthermore exercise financial economy (expecting an annual salary of £150), as well as 'unanimity and cooperation in all matters pertaining to the Mission'.[75] The party reached Calcutta on 24 November 1842, set off for the Khasi Hills on 10 December, and were greeted by Ann Jones at the Mission House at Cherrapunji towards the evening of 2 January 1843. Richards lodged with the Joneses, while the Lewises rented a small dwelling further away on the edge of the jungle from John Bird Shadwell, assistant in the Political Agent's office at Cherrapunji.[76] By August, Jones was again calling for more support by way of another three missionaries, experienced men who should have at least two years' probationary experience.[77] Despite repeated calls for support, it was not until February 1846 that the next missionary arrived, in the form of Daniel Jones with his wife Ann.

7 Henry Yule, 'My house in Kasea Hills 1841–2'.

Thomas Jones's first house was located in the military compound, at some distance from the native village further up the plateau. While some curious Khasis would come to the house, it was too far distant from the native villages at Cherra and Mawsmai to glean many regular attendees. By mid-1842 Jones had built two schoolhouses, the first at Mawsmai and the second at Mawmluh, with the hope of teaching a hundred children in each.[78] A missionary's ability to interpose into local cultures and economies was premised on success in garnering patronage within local political hierarchies. As Elbourne notes, the success of missionaries and chiefs alike lay in their ability to accumulate people and goods, and to foster diplomatic access.[79] For Jones this included financial arrangements with the *Syiem* of Cherrapunji, as well as taking high status pupils into his classroom, including four heirs to the kingdom of Cherrapunji (Bor Sing, Bor Manic, Ram Manic and Sing Manic), and the nephew of the former *Syiem* (U Bir). Only weeks after his arrival in the hills, the clean and well-dressed sons of rich villagers were queuing up for tuition. In April 1842, the *Syiem* of Nongkhlaw also asked Jones if he would take in his nephew when the school at Mawmluh was established.[80] Yet the fervour with which the Khasi elite may have embraced him, and the expectations they placed on him, might be double-edged. His own motives and practices became precariously imbricated in the machinations of Khasi polity and social relations, and caught between the often competing, nepotistic and unpredictable alliances of the local British and Anglo-Indian military, political, commercial agents and interests. As elsewhere in other mission fields, such a complex set of indebtedness would slowly unsettle the confidence felt by his own masters in Liverpool in his motives, actions and decision-making processes.

Jones had trained a local native teacher, U Jom, who initially taught children in his own house at Cherra. A small and out-of-the way building served for a time as a temporary schoolhouse. The delay in building a more permanent schoolhouse at Cherra was apparently due to the reluctance of the *Syiem* to allow land to be annexed in his village for the purpose, a concession he had also previously denied to Alexander Lish. After some delay, Jones won his trust, and the *Syiem* agreed to send men to clear a site of Jones's choosing. Jones's account attributes the change of heart on the part of the *Syiem* to his own negotiating skills, and the sight of his newly printed books. But knowing 'that the old man is poor (although he is a Rajah)', Jones also offered a financial incentive.[81]

There may also have been an incipient generational change from the old to the new regimes. Bor Sing, a nephew and second heir of the incumbent *Syiem*, was a former scholar of Lish, and in deputising for his uncle he had taken a leading role in inviting the missionaries to set up their station at the native village.[82] The characteristics of the old man's supremacy were, however, more opaque to Jones; while his rule appeared to extend to around twenty-five villages encompassing about 10,000 people, he exhibited little obvious authority, and was poorer than many of his subjects: 'As far as I know him, he appears to be quite a sulky man, very nervous of all change, and fond of showing off his authority . . . but he is the Rajah'.[83] Bor Sing, in contrast, made more of an impression on Jones, who described him as exemplifying the desired qualities of the receptive student and potential convert: quiet, humble, innocent, friendly, thoughtful, perceptive. Outshining any of Lish's other former students, 'he appears to be very well disposed to the truths of the gospel, as if they affected him deeply'.

In spatial terms, their concrete positioning now inside the native village was a critical step for the missionaries in their goal of cultural insinuation. They now had more opportunity of being embedded in the everyday favour of the Khasis, as well as distancing themselves from the British military cantonment. The site chosen for the new stone building, which served as schoolhouse and chapel, was considered providential by Jones – 'close to the marketplace, near the main thoroughfare and in the middle of the most populous area',[84] while for Lewis it was a critical means of 'removing the prejudice of many people against us'.[85] By mid-1845 a chapel had been built at Mawsmai, and another soon constructed in the heart of the village at Cherra.

Notes

1 Alison Twells, 'Missionary "fathers" and wayward "sons" in the South Pacific, 1797–1825' in Trev Lynn Broughton and Helen Rogers (eds), *Gender and Fatherhood in the Nineteenth Century* (Houndmills and New York, 2007), p. 153.
2 Jones to Roberts, 28 July 1841, *Y Drysorfa*, November 1841.
3 Jones to Roberts, 8 October 1841, *Y Drysorfa*, January 1842.
4 Paul A. Cohen, *China and Christianity: The Missionary Movement and the Growth of Chinese Antiforeignism 1860–1879* (Cambridge, MA, 1963), pp. 20–34.
5 Jones to Roberts, 6 December 1841, *Y Drysorfa*, April 1842.
6 *Ibid.*
7 Roberts to Jones, 29 June 1842, CMA 28720.
8 Morris, *The History*, pp. 244–82.
9 Williams to Roberts, 25 August 1842 in *Y Drysorfa*, October 1842.
10 Catherine Williams, cited by Williams to Roberts, 25 August 1842 in *Y Drysorfa*, October 1842.
11 James Williams, 1844, cited in Morris, *The History*, p. 258.
12 Jones to Roberts, 6 December 1841, *Y Drysorfa*, April 1842.
13 Jones to Roberts, 28 July 1841, *Y Drysorfa*, November 1841.
14 See Rafy, *Folk-tales*, pp. 137–9. One of the earliest written versions of this story occurs in 'W', 'Historical fragments', *Calcutta Christian Observer*, March 1852, 128–9.
15 William Robinson, 'Notes on the languages spoken by the various tribes inhabiting the valley of Asam and its mountain confines', *Journal of the Asiatic Society*, 27 (1849), 336.
16 Jones to Roberts, [January] 1842, *Y Drysorfa*, July 1842.
17 *Ibid.*
18 Vicente Rafael, *Contracting Colonialism: Translation and Christian Conversion in Tagalog Society under Early Spanish Rule* (Durham, 1988), p. xv, in Samson, 'Translation teams', p. 97.
19 Jones to Roberts, 28 July 1841, *Y Drysorfa*, November 1841.
20 Roberts to Dewan Roi, 30 April 1842, CMA 28720.
21 Jones to Roberts, 7 April 1842, *Y Drysorfa*, July 1842.
22 *Ibid.*
23 Jones to Roberts, n.d. (received December 1842), *Y Drysorfa*, January 1843.
24 Jones to Roberts, 9 February 1843, *Y Drysorfa*, May 1843.
25 Jones to Roberts, 8 November 1841, *Y Drysorfa*, March 1842.
26 Roberts to Jones, 29 January 1841, CMA 28720.
27 Jones to Roberts, 8 November 1841, *Y Drysorfa*, March 1842.
28 Jones to Roberts, 28 July 1841, *Y Drysorfa*, November 1841
29 The following discussion is based on Jones to Roberts, 8 September 1842, *Y Drysorfa*, December 1842.
30 Lish, 'A brief account of the Khasees', 143.
31 Reference in R.W. Pryse, *An Introduction to the Khasia Language: Comprising a Grammar, Selections for Reading, and a Vocabulary* (Calcutta, 1855), p. 121.
32 George Burder, *The Works of the Reverend and Learned Isaac Watts, D.D.*, volume 3 (London, 1810), pp. 231–2.
33 *Ibid.*, pp. 205–6.
34 Most likely sent was the Religious Tract Society's *The Cottage Hymn Book* (London, 1838). According to Pryse, Jones published a translation of 'Through all

the dangers of the night' from this hymn book in 1845 (Pryse, *An Introduction to the Khasia Language*, p. 116).

35 Jones to Roberts, 28 July 1841, *Y Drysorfa*, November 1841.

36 Watts, Isaac, 'A discourse on the way of instruction by catechisms, and of the best method of composing them' in George Burder, *The Works of the Reverend and Learned Issac Watts, D.D.*, volume 3 (London, 1810), p. 208.

37 The title page of *Rhodd Mam* was *Ka jingai ka kumi ia la ki koon; lane ka jingkuli nungking ia ki kun kunna ba la shim na ka ktin oo Bleih.*

38 Jones to Roberts, 8 September 1842, *Y Drysorfa*, December 1842.

39 Duff to Jones, n.d. [1842], cited in *Y Drysorfa*, January 1843.

40 Monier Williams (ed.), *Original Papers Illustrating the History of the Application of the Roman Alphabet to the Languages of India* (London, 1859).

41 'Mr. C.E. Trevelyan's first minute in support of Mr. Thompson's dictionary and of the application of the Roman alphabet to Hindústání' (Calcutta, 1834) in Williams (ed.), *Original Papers*, pp. 3–30.

42 Second letter of Professor Thomas Jarrett to the Editor of *The Times*, in Williams (ed.), *Original Papers*, pp. 252–3.

43 Mr James Prinsep's Second Minute, 2 January 1834, in Williams (ed.), *Original Papers*, p. 35.

44 Duff to Jones, [1842], cited in *Y Drysorfa*, January 1843.

45 Jones to Roberts, 28 July 1841, *Y Drysorfa*, November 1841.

46 Piggin, *Making Evangelical Missionaries*, p. 156.

47 *Ibid.*, pp. 227–8.

48 *Ibid.*, p. 172.

49 *Ibid.*, pp. 238–43.

50 L3 speakers have better insights into how language works. See for example M. Clyne, C. Rossi Hunt and T. Isaakidis, 'Learning a community language as a third language', *International Journal of Multilingualism*, 1 (2004), 33–52. As Thomas Charles had argued when supporting education in Welsh, 'Previous instruction in their native tongue helps them to learn English *much sooner*', Williams, *Welsh Calvinistic Methodism*, p. 194.

51 Piggin, *Making Evangelical Missionaries*, p. 248.

52 LMS, Candidate papers.

53 K.D.M. Snell, 'The Sunday-School movement in England and Wales: child labour, denominational control and working-class culture', *Past & Present*, 164:1 (1999), 128–9, 162. See also Griffith, *Nationality in the Sunday School Movement: A Comparative Study of the Sunday School Movement in England and Wales* (Bangor, 1925).

54 Elias, 14 August 1819, in Edward Morgan (ed.), *John Elias: Life, Letters and Essays* (1844 and 1847: revised edition in one volume, Edinburgh, 1973) in R.M. Jones and Gwyn Davies, *The Christian Heritage of Welsh Education* (Bryntirion, Bridgend, 1986), p. 39.

55 Griffith Jones, *Welsh Piety* (1740) in Jones and Davies, *The Christian Heritage of Welsh Education*, p. 50.

56 Charles to Christopher Anderson, 4 January 1811, in Jenkins, *The Life of the Rev. Thomas Charles* in Jones and Davies, *The Christian Heritage of Welsh Education*, p. 64.

57 The first part of the catechism was printed, according to Roberts (*Y Drysorfa*, November 1844), as *Ca jing cylli ca Gospel. Ca ba don ha ca ni'amblei ci christ'an ca ba la shim na ca cti'n u blei bad ba la pynneh da ca cti'n jong u ba la shim na ca beibil.* Jones then commenced translation of the remainder of the catechism. Pryse (*An Introduction to the Khasia Language*, p. 121) notes publication in Calcutta in 1845 of Jones's translation of the catechism as *Ka jing kylli ka Gospel, ka ba don ha ka niamblei ki Christan, ka ba la shim na ka ktin u Blei bad ba la pynneh da ka ktin jong u, ba la shim na ka Beibil.*

58 Richards to Roberts, [May] 1843, *Y Drysorfa*, September 1843.

59 Pryse, *An Introduction to the Khasia Language*, p. 121.

60 Jones to Roberts, 28 February 1847, *Y Drysorfa*, June 1847.
61 Jones to Roberts, 28 July 1841, *Y Drysorfa*, November 1841.
62 *Ibid.*
63 Jones to Roberts, 3 August 1843, *Y Drysorfa*, December 1843
64 Lewis to Roberts, 6 March 1844, *Y Drysorfa*, June 1844.
65 Jones to Roberts, 7 April 1842, *Y Drysorfa*, August 1842.
66 Jones to Roberts, 10 November 1842, *Y Drysorfa*, February 1843; Jones to Roberts, 12 April 1843, *Y Drysorfa*, July 1843; IOR L/MIL/10/32, 347.
67 C. Markham, 'The Royal Geographical Society', *RGS*, 461 in Driver, 'Yule, Sir Henry'.
68 Jones to Roberts, 9 October 1842, *Y Drysorfa*, January 1843; Jones to Roberts, 29 May 1843, *Y Drysorfa*, September 1843.
69 Morris, *The History*, pp. 45–7.
70 Roberts to Jones, 25 November 1841, CMA 28720.
71 Morris, *The History*, p. 312; Mary Lewis, 'A brief narrative of the early life of William Lewis', n.d. [c.1890], CMA 27222.
72 Rees (ed.), *Vehicles of Grace & Hope*, pp. 118–19. Rees also notes Thomas Jones stayed with the Roberts family at Llanidloes during the Llanfair Caereinion Association in 1840.
73 Jones to Roberts, 9 October 1842, *Y Drysorfa*, January 1843.
74 John Roberts, 19 July 1842, *Y Drysorfa*, August 1842.
75 11 July 1842, CMA 27221.
76 Jones to Roberts, 9 February 1843, *Y Drysorfa*, May 1843; Mary Lewis, 'A brief narrative', CMA 27222.
77 Jones to Roberts, 3 August 1843, *Y Drysorfa*, December 1843
78 Jones to Roberts, 8 September 1842, *Y Drysorfa*, December 1842.
79 Elizabeth Elbourne, 'Mother's milk: gender, power and anxiety on a South African mission station, 1839–1840' in Patricia Grimshaw and Andrew May (eds), *Missionaries, Indigenous Peoples and Cultural Exchange* (Brighton, 2010), p. 19.
80 Jones to Roberts, 7 April 1842, *Y Drysorfa*, July 1842.
81 Jones to Roberts, 8 September 1842, *Y Drysorfa*, December 1842.
82 Jones to Roberts, 8 December 1842, *Y Drysorfa*, March 1843; Jones to Roberts, 9 December 1844, *Y Drysorfa*, March 1845.
83 Jones to Roberts, 7 April 1842, *Y Drysorfa*, August 1842.
84 Jones to Roberts, 9 December 1844, *Y Drysorfa*, March 1845.
85 Lewis to Roberts, 6 March 1844, *Y Drysorfa*, June 1844.

CHAPTER NINE

Cultural transactions: the letter and the gift

In 1843, the boys at the schools spent much of their time copying out the catechisms as well as committing them to memory for oral recitation. Roberts requested that a copy of the catechism be made by boys under William Lewis's instruction and sent to him as evidence of their progress. Lewis gave the task of writing out chapters to five boys aged between eight and sixteen: U Sor, U Ragen, U Turang and U Amor (all from Mawsmai), and U Jom, a teacher from the school at Cherrapunji. For most of them, this was the first time they had written on paper. Perhaps in their timidity, they repeatedly asked Lewis to mend their pens, but when the task was finished Lewis observed that the rest of his students were themselves 'trying their hand at writing with every piece of paper they can get hold of, whatever colour it is'. Lewis was impressed at the boys' powers of observation – they noticed the slight differences between the script they were working from and the one Jones had sent to the printer. He also reported on the character of each boy in turn (U Sor 'modest and humble'; U Rugen 'courageous' and 'amiable'), but as a whole their refractory nature and resistance to his authority perturbed him, and he construed their 'wild ways' and 'uncontrolled habits' as intrinsic qualities of their base savagery:

> I have often observed them, while studying their lessons, suddenly becoming excited, like a warhorse approaching the battlefield, or a greyhound nearing the hunting ground, when they hear a shout from the top of a nearby mountain; indeed, their entire nature appears to be in a state of excitement, so that at any moment you might expect to see them all rushing out of school, as if their hearts were leaping in the expectation of enjoying the mountain breezes, feeling that the restrictions I had placed upon them at the school were very different from the freedom they enjoyed previously.[1]

When the catechism came back from the printer later in 1843, Lewis extolled the benefits of 'placing these important truths for free in the hands of our readers'. Overjoyed at the fact that some of his scholars had already memorised all of the nine chapters, Lewis took religious inspiration in the precision of their memorising ('The verses are recited so correctly sometimes, that I can only feel that to some extent they understand the mindset of the holy writers'). From the perspective of the Khasi boys, it is much more difficult to determine their feelings and their motivations. Perhaps in shouting out very loudly the verses they had memorised, they were subverting Lewis's attempts at authority ('so far all my attempts to get them to change their ways and to read silently have been in vain').[2]

On his tours through the hills, Thomas Jones encountered many villages where the inhabitants had not set eyes on a European since the British had taken possession of the region in the 1820s. His visits 'caused enormous tumult and fear in the minds of the people',[3] apprehensive as they were of the persecution that many villages had experienced at the hands of other colonial agents. It may well be that the overlapping desires of the Khasis for restitution of their book, and the evangelical Christian emphasis on the almost 'magical potency' of the Bible, explained the appetite of both parties for 'the extraordinary tool' of literacy.[4] But for the Khasis, the tool of literacy could be less a device for enlightenment, and more the pragmatic means to enhance their ability to trade. In the immediate absence of the gift of the book, however, Jones was in a more tenuous bargaining position. His oral grasp of Khasi and the site in the village gave him a toehold in the hills; further alliances were necessary with those high-ranking Khasi elites who had already experienced some tutelage under Lish. The question of gift-giving was strategically essential to establish allies as well as possible converts. The processes of reading and writing had further meanings, not just for the Khasis themselves, but also for negotiating the relationship between centre and periphery. While John Roberts in Liverpool brokered the supply of gifts and supplies, the paper correspondence between the mission secretary and his field agents was itself a material and symbolic transaction of personal and professional power and authority.

Moral and worldly economies: the transvaluation of objects

Jones had been critical of Lish's material generosity, but he soon learned that gift-giving was essential to missionary success. The missionaries periodically wrote to Roberts for schoolroom supplies in the form of paper, copybooks, writing slates, pencils, a pair of globes or a set of maps. But equally needed in the first months were requisitions of calico, cotton and buttons to distribute among the 'poor children', who otherwise would be admitted naked to school. In July 1842, Roberts advertised for 'a few gifts to give the Khasians in order to gain their trust and their attention to his message when he travels amongst them'. Jones wrote that 'before we can get them to listen to our message of mercy', he was 'in great need of suitable gifts in order to gain acceptance by the chieftains and inhabitants of the villages'.[5] The call was heeded, and in December 1842 Jones expressed his 'heartiest thanks' for a quantity of plaid or patterned woollen cloth that had been sent from Wales. A sufficient length to make a frock coat was given to Bor Sing, Jones's most promising scholar, and also significantly the Cherrapunji *Syiem's* nephew and one of his heirs. The remainder of the plaid was divided between his other scholars, Bor and Ram Manic, Sing Manic and U Bir.

Missionary and Khasi understandings of the gift of clothing and the concept of nakedness did not of course accord. Where Jones was eager to clothe the nakedness of the perceived savage as a prerequisite for his programme of religious indoctrination, his eagerness to distribute material gifts among the Khasis betrayed other anxieties. With little else to give, clothes were an obvious bargaining tool. Yet they were not given altruistically, or just to clothe nakedness – their exchange performed a further symbolic role in attempting to establish a relationship and an obligation to reciprocate, either through the general patronage of the Khasi elites, or through direct attendance at the mission school.

Gifts from Wales were not just raw or industrially manufactured materials; in November 1843, John Roberts could not help peeking at a bundle of items – destined for the Khasi girls under the care of Ann Jones – which had been sent from a group of female friends at Denbigh in north Wales. The beauty and practicality of the handiwork exemplified for Roberts the feminine attributes of charity, industry, skill and thrift. This gendered production of labour was particularly rooted in the local domestic activism of the Welsh Nonconformist tradition. At Bala 'knitting nights', an economically pivotal cottage industry could also be a fundraising occasion as well as a forum for the exchange of religious views: by 'contributions and subscriptions and the sale of woollens, they gathered enough to build a chapel – though it took a mountain of socks to build a Bethel'.[6] The church projected the maternal role of the women of Denbigh not only to the nation but overseas towards the Khasi girls whom they would never meet. The work of the ladies at Denbigh – making frocks, shirts, aprons and tippets for Khasi children – inspired friends of the cause in Bala to establish a similar circle. By early 1844, two-dozen women, including Maria Charles, met fortnightly in the College library at Bala, sewing trousers and pinafores while Mrs Davies read uplifting passages.[7]

In the moral economy of Protestantism, charitable giving was the 'purchase price of salvation'; to give was to enact Christ's sacrifice and to be rewarded in the afterlife.[8] The notion of missionary martyrdom was at the heart of Jones's work on the hills ('to which I have consecrated my life'). His 'dear friends' who had 'donated so generously' with their gifts, as he himself had done bodily, 'will certainly receive their reward'.[9] The ladies of Denbigh sent gifts (and Jones received them) with the inherent expectation of spiritual reward. In the space between how gifts were given and how they were received by the Khasis, however, lies a transvaluation of the meaning of the objects. As Nicholas Thomas notes, 'different parties to various stages of a transaction may have quite different conceptions of the things at issue in exchange'.[10] Implicit in Jones's requisition for gifts was a devaluation of Khasi moral and worldly economies. It was apparent to Jones that the Khasi *Syiems* put great value on sartorial elegance, at excessive cost, though this was evidence to the missionary of vanity and wastefulness. Privileged Khasis traditionally dressed in an outer garment of dark cloth about ten feet in length, a headdress of silk, and were adorned with silver, gold and other precious stones. Any gift of clothing, to be deemed acceptable, would need to be 'in the brightest and most splendid colours' or else 'the chieftains will scarcely be grateful for them'. But Jones judged that the uncivilised native had no regard for proper systems of value: 'They know and think little of the quality of the cloth; and it must always be borne in mind that they have less regard here for what you might consider to be valuable than for poorer materials in bright and lasting colours'. By this logic, the gifting of inferior materials could be explained away. Ann Jones advised Thomas that cheap cottons in smart colours, of the sort used to make curtains in Wales, would be perfectly acceptable to the Khasis.[11]

From the Khasi perspective, exchange relations with Europeans, as with plains people, were not novel. In many respects too, the missionary depended more on the Khasi (for commodities, food and access to land) than the other way round. In accepting the missionary's gifts, the headmen were actively manipulating the introduction of new material goods as part of their own tactics of control and modernisation, and the politics of gift-giving assumed different meanings in terms of their own obligations and socio-economic ties. The Welsh may have been donating remnants and castoffs to sue for attention; the *Syiems*, rather than demonstrating 'naive hunger' for exchange objects, could appropriate them for their own purposes, ones which were not necessarily apparent to the missionary.[12] As Murray has cautioned, such interweaving of different motivations should not invalidate the core inequality of the power relationship,[13] but it can still be instructive in determining the vectors of obligation and relationship as well as the agency of the Khasis. Relationships are maintained between people, reminds Karen Sykes, 'by remembering their obligations to give to another'.[14]

Gift-giving enabled Jones and Roberts to make an imaginative leap in convincing themselves of the possibilities as well as the legitimacy of their evangelising mission. The young prince Bor Manic 'looks very well in the plaid', and to Jones the other four 'are very nice lads, such as are not often seen in England or Wales'.[15] Here Jones saw the refashioning of Khasi dress as a primary stage in transforming their moral status. Five thousand miles away, John Roberts, delving through the package of clothes from the ladies of Denbigh, found with some surprise 'a garment made from a gown which was once worn by Mrs. Charles the wife of the late, renowned Thomas Charles of Bala!'[16] In his mind's eye, in a fantasy of transference, Roberts saw the authenticity of the Calvinistic Methodist cause reified in a relic destined to be worn by a simple Khasi girl.

The abilities of the miller's son are credited by many later writers as being fundamental to the mythologising of Jones as a pioneer; this Jones was as much interested in the material as the spiritual welfare of the Khasis. From the time of his first letter from Cherrapunji, Jones requested from Roberts a steady stream of tools and materials. Jones asked for nails, latches, rings, ropes, hooks and screws; Roberts sent a steady stream of saws, spades and sickles, bundles of wire and slates, by the end of January 1842 already dispatching two dozen packages of various articles for furniture making, building and agricultural purposes. Jones concluded that improved techniques were labour-saving and more efficient of resources. Requesting a two-handled saw and a pit-saw for his own use, he also intended to teach the craft of sawing to the Khasis: 'Their method is very laborious and wasteful. They go to the forest and fell a tree, and they start to hew it into a plank, and however big the tree is they only get one plank out of it. This waste has caused a shortage of trees in some popular areas'.[17] Jones regarded his own interventions in traditional agricultural and manufacturing practices as a clear way of ameliorating the social condition of the Khasis: 'the best way to reform the temporal condition of the people is to improve their ironworks because it appears that this is the main craft by which they try to make their living'.[18]

In October 1842 Jones asked Roberts to send appropriate materials for the construction of a forge and furnace, 'in order to teach the people a better way of smelting iron, and preparing it for market'. While himself not familiar enough with the tools used in a smithy to be able to specify them individually, Jones requested help from the brethren at home in donating the necessary items. In whetting their appetite for new technology, Jones was also establishing a contract with the Khasis: 'I have promised to show some of these tools to some of the people who call themselves blacksmiths in this country; and in such a country as this all promises should be fulfilled as soon as possible'.[19] Roberts advertised a call for materials in *Y Drysorfa*, privately exclaiming to Jones on the attempt 'in setting you up as a *Smith*!'[20] While translation was the foundation stone of his work in the hills, Jones much preferred preaching and teaching.[21] Between November 1843 and May 1844, in the dry period between monsoons, Jones spent more time building than preaching. One of the factors that contributed to the decline of the Indian iron industry in the nineteenth century was the shortage of fuel due to the excessive amount of timber required to make charcoal.[22] With the exorbitant cost of obtaining lime, and with a growing scarcity of the wood used to burn it, Jones taught the Khasis to use coal in the burning process and so reduced the cost of the lime by two thirds. 'I could have made a profit from my practical knowledge in this matter', he informed Roberts, 'but I deemed it to be more in keeping with the character of a Missionary to let the Khasians have the advantage, and I did so. If they make use of the improvement for the benefit of their own houses, this will be sufficient reward for me'.[23]

The theological colleges in Britain produced 'workmen who need not be ashamed' (2 Timothy 2:15),[24] replete with their 'spiritual equipment'. As well as a Bala graduate, however, Jones had been carpenter, wheelwright and miller. Such practical skills may not have been the *sine qua non* of the missionary candidate, but it is evident that it was Jones's facility in the workshop as much as in the classroom that enabled him to attract Khasi interest. Only a few months after his arrival in the hills, Jones was boasting that bands of up to fifty Khasis would travel great distances 'to see the man who can do and teach the Kassians everything'.[25] The report of his abilities spread quickly through the hills: astonished at hearing him speak to them in their own language, they would stand before him in stunned amazement, 'staring at me as though they had never seen a man before'. 'What is behind this', reported Jones, 'I do not know, because I am certain that I did not say such a thing to anyone'. Suspicious at his abilities, 'when they see that I have succeeded, they break out into shouts of joy and laughter, which usually ends with some of them saying that I am like God, that I can do everything'.[26]

However unorchestrated was the admiration from Jones's perspective, the appearance of out-of-the-ordinary abilities – mediated by novel material culture – took some hold on the Khasi view of Jones and enabled him to gather people to him, perhaps first in awe, then ambivalence or hostility: 'Once in a while one will come to me with great joy, saying that he wishes to stay with me to learn to do everything that I can do; but as soon as he realises that he cannot learn without working, he walks away quietly'. The view of Jones as practical pioneer also needs to be qualified in the light of the previous decade and a half of British presence in the hills. David Scott had introduced new agricultural products and techniques, and Charles Fenwick had supervised Assamese prisoners on public works projects at the sanatarium in a range of trades including blacksmithing, carpentry and lime-burning. Some of the items sent from Wales to the missionaries were already available in India, if at higher cost, and Khasi/European interactions occurred despite the spatial separation of the cantonment from the native villages. Jones's interventions were as opportunistic as they were practical: 'I assume that it stems from the fact that the Europeans who live here are extremely ignorant about the common matters of this life, and that the Kassians have seen me doing various tasks, or showing them how to do them, which in India would require several different craftsmen to accomplish; and that I have taught them to do other things of which they were previously ignorant'. Jones had intention as well as opportunity, and saw the benefits to his proselytising mission in being the man who could tell the Khasis on what day of the year their moon would change.[27]

Power relationships and epistolary practice

Letters were important lifelines in maintaining professional and personal relationships. Jones requested gifts for the *Syiems*, but his letters were themselves part of a relationship with Roberts based on mutual exchange, in which the letter as gift 'is concerned with maintaining a relationship rather than repairing absence'.[28] A letter sent presumed a letter written in response; the letter writer was also a letter reader, and as Stanley has argued, the letter itself stood in for its writer in a powerfully metonymic fashion.[29]

The exchange of letters between Jones and Roberts reinforced the physical separation between the two men. As a conversation between the mission secretary and his man in the field, it can be read as a regular summary of missionary experience, producing a narrative and apparently seamless version of their ongoing views and experiences. But their epistolary communication needs to be read not just as their version of *what happened*, but with an awareness of the ways in which its textuality constructed a space where the correspondents presented particular and mutable versions of their roles and identities. If letters

8 Thomas Jones I.

have such a rhetorical aspect, they might be read as 'a theatre for the construction and performance of self in which the distance of time, space and the absence of face-to-face encounter enables rather than disables communication'.[30] Reading the letters in this way is also to be attuned to the emotional cadences of separation and intimacy, imagination and practice, control and expectation.

'Not a single day passes', wrote Roberts to Jones in September 1841, 'without our thinking of you'. The bonds of attachment were both public and domestic. Jones was the religious emissary of the Welsh Calvinistic Methodists, and in this professional relationship, Roberts the secretary stood for the authority and interest of the mission board, as well as of the church as a broader body. But at a more deeply personal level, Thomas and Ann Jones inhabited the intimate interior space of John and Lizzie Roberts's house, where their pictures were stuck up on the parlour wall.[31]

Only two years apart in age, Jones and Roberts were friends, colleagues and partners in an enterprise on which they had staked their reputations and to which they had dedicated their lives. Neither could perform his role without the other: for Roberts, there could be no mission without a missionary; for Jones, Roberts was not only a material lifeline, but also voiced the missionary through the broader circulation of the letters, and through his role and authority as secretary. Roberts was to remain secretary to the mission, without pay, for twenty-six years, and edited *Y Drysorfa* from 1846 to 1852.[32] 'I may, & I trust I shall', wrote Roberts to Jones in February 1843, 'have the pleasure of seeing *you* before I die, but I must rest satisfied with the imaginative ideas I am able to form of your adopted country from the description which you may give me occasionally in your letters'.[33] The two men were never to meet again.

For Roberts, Jones was not only emissary and friend, but missionary hero. His picture on the parlour wall at 19 Mount Street in Liverpool sat next to that of Robert Morrison, and Roberts in his letters consistently constructed Jones as a linguistic and evangelical pioneer in the mould of such luminaries as the Scottish missionaries Morrison and Moffat. If Jones's portrait was a daily *aide memoire* to the general missionary cause, the arrival of a letter from Jones was a more explicit moment of emotional connection between the two men. The letter was a bodily trace of the sender – 'their characteristic phrases or mistakes, their hand having folded the paper and sealed the envelope'[34] – and a powerful signifier of his presence. It moved Roberts accordingly. These were precious words to be read and reread; they were also a conversation to be experienced privately, before becoming more public property.

Their letters mutually reinforced an intimate personal connection, as the men invited each other to empathetically enter a shared emotional space. 'My dear and amiable friend', reported Jones in his first letter from the hills: 'You can well believe that sentiments which are much easier to imagine than to describe arose within me, when I found myself, and my dear companion, after crossing great oceans, and travelling along lakes and rivers, and exposed to thousands of dangers, at last safely arrived at our journey's end . . . Thankfulness rose up as it were irrepressibly in my heart, despite its wickedness'.[35] Any suggestive excess of feeling was properly circumscribed in religious rather than worldly terms. When Jones learned that Owen Richards was to be sent out to join him, he 'had great difficulty in restraining myself from behaving as my dear old sisters do sometimes in Wales when there is an outpouring of blessings from heaven'.[36] The physicality of his response was appropriately contained (he only *felt* like jumping), formalised (there might not be anything wrong with jumping – the 'jumpers' were descendant of religious practices dating from the 1762 revival in Llangeitho), but also gendered (men do not show excessive emotion in public).

If Roberts was short on information about what was happening in the Khasi Hills, he could mentally fill in the gaps: 'Neither of your two last letters say any thing about your Schools, but I suppose that you & Mrs Jones have daily a host of little tawny creatures about you learning A.B. &c'.[37] An idea of India was constructed through the gaps as well as the details in the correspondence. In the distance between himself and Jones, Roberts's appetite was clearly for information, but also importantly for narrativising Jones as missionary hero. After the new missionaries Lewis and Richards were dispatched from Liverpool, they inhabited a liminal space in the imagination for Roberts – between their departure in July 1842, their arrival in Cherrapunji in January 1843, and news of their arrival finally reaching Roberts by mail by March 1843. In a letter to Jones on 27 February 1843, Roberts lyrically emploted the meeting, visually assembling the scene and dialogue of the encounter, double-voicing the emotional responses of the participants.

> I have thought a great deal about you since; and often have I fancied to myself the affecting scene (as doubtless it must have been) of your meeting. I have seen you take your stand on the summit of a rock that overhangs the plain through which the [Burampooter] winds its way, now taking a look through the spying-glass, & gazing most eagerly to catch a glimpse of a Dingey with Europeans in it, & then turning the leaves of a Book muttering rather disappointedly, – 'Where can they be? why don't they come,' and again lifting the glass to your eye, & at length crying out in ecstasies "Yonder they are, – the Lord be praised!" I have watched your

> hurried footsteps to the waterside, & seen the pearl-drops chasing each other down your sunburnt cheek, whilst landing your friends ashore, & bidding them welcome to Bryniau Cassia. – But what pictures the fancy even of one who is no artist can chalk out! Be mine a correct one or not I feel pretty certain that the meeting, whenever it took place, was *a scene* well fitted to form a beautiful frontispiece to your to-be-published 'Labors &c, &c, in Cassia.'[38]

Roberts also significantly placed himself as an observer in the scene. This desire to be present was at one level an admission of helplessness in the face of inseparable distance. 'I often & often again wish it was in my power to fly to Cassia', wrote Maria Charles from Bala to her son Owen Richards in August 1843 in anguished terms: 'hope keeps me alive, and nothing is impossible'.[39] For Roberts, however, his insertion into the imaginary narrative served a further purpose. This preacher and mission founder, by day a clerk in a shipping company, who had written accounts of the exploits of his Liverpool contemporary Josiah Hughes as a missionary in Malacca, saw in Jones the personification and fulfilment of his own vocational desires.[40] The inability to be present – and the absence of any 'official' version of the scene – also offered Roberts the possibility of multiple replays. Writing to William Lewis on 3 March 1843, Roberts further imagined the meeting of the missionaries:

> I have often followed you, in imagination, step by step, and I have watched your anxious countenance as it brightened more & more the nearer you approached the end of your journey, and have sympathised with you in all those feelings with which your bosom has heaved on viewing the various scenes alluded to in your letter. And what a scene there must have been at Pondwar when dear brother Jones first shook you by the hand, and again when you all sat together at the table of the Lord![41]

In the scene of his meeting with Jones, Roberts described Lewis's 'anxious countenance', and elsewhere constructed a reading of Lewis as a worried and overly serious character. In December 1842, Roberts sent lithographs of Lewis and Richards. 'Our little friend Lewis', he wrote to Jones, 'is made not *quite* so stern-looking as when he was taken at the Mount gardens; but I confess I could not help laughing heartily when I first saw the proof engraving, & asked "Well what has Richards done to offend his brother that he should thus turn his back upon him, & look so serious?"'[42] Roberts's teasing tone, his slight condescension towards Lewis and his manifest idolising of Jones, would be tested by subsequent events, as his personal and official relationship to Jones came into conflict.

In the compact between writer and addressee, the letter was at once 'a response to previous letters and a cause for new ones'.[43] Yet from the moment he arrived in India, Jones subverted this assumption of reciprocity. It was quite clear that for both Roberts and Jones, the absence of receiving mail was destabilising to their sense of self and their emotional well-being. On 29 September 1841, Roberts had not received word from Jones in the previous two monthly mails, and chiding Jones for his lack of correspondence, urged him to write every mail.[44] Jones was not to receive this letter until early December but in the meantime had in fact already written to Roberts on 28 July and 6 August, though both letters would not be received by Roberts until 14 October.

Jones too fretted about the absence of letters from home, but in his first letter of 28 July 1841 he was already renegotiating the basis of exchange. 'I was very disappointed', he chided, 'not to have received more letters from you and other friends. I entreat you to write at least once a month, and I hope that I am not forgotten by my other kind friends. I cannot promise to reply to every letter, because this would be too much of a drain on my time and my pocket'. In the physical separation from his friend, Jones was refashioning his persona in the relationship newly enabled by the epistolary framework.[45] There may have been a tension here, as Miller observes, between the denial and inward focus expected of a missionary, and the almost narcissistic act of self-representation in a missionary's letters.[46] In disengaging from expected norms of reciprocity, Jones was asserting his own importance and recalibrating the power relationship between the two men, both as friends and as agents of the mission. Effectively out of reach, Jones was aware that his stance might be construed as hubris, and despite his apparent defiance of the writer–addressee relationship, was quick to qualify his actions as being in no way signalling either a lack of deference to his mentors or a sign of excessive pride: 'Do not think that I, in any way, in making the previous remarks, am wishing to teach you or the Association, or that I suppose myself in India to be something other than I was in Wales'.[47] While promising to report to Roberts as circumstances permitted, Jones sent a clear message to his other friends that while they should write to him, they should not expect any regular correspondence in return: 'it would be very foolish, not to say sinful, for me to be sent all the way to India, to spend my life writing to my friends at home'.[48]

In the flow of information, therefore, John Roberts played a crucial role, and the correspondence was intimate and everyday, as well as part of an official genre.[49] As a personal friend, he stabilised Jones's sense of self. As mission secretary, he relayed Jones's correspondence not only to the mission board but also to a broader constituency of readers. Jones's digests for Roberts survive as the only evidence of his correspondence, though he may at times have written to others. Roberts was also determined to be the gateway for any exchange, advising readers of *Y Drysorfa* that it 'would also be better for all letters written to the Missionary to be sent to the same address, to No 19, Mount Street, Liverpool'.[50]

There were more political reasons why Roberts wished to control the flow of information and to stage-manage public perceptions of the mission's progress. As David Gerber notes, what is 'hidden or held back' is of as much significance as what is said in historical personal correspondence.[51] With little expectation of quick conversions, it was essential that mission propaganda reflect its progress and potential in as positive a light as possible, particularly if the church's ongoing fund-raising efforts were to be successful. Jones's early criticism of the linguistic abilities and methods of Carey, Lish and Tomlin was deemed by Roberts to be too delicate for broader circulation ('I shall of course keep this piece of information out of the sight of the public'). In the same letter of January 1842, Roberts expressed his surprise that the costs of living in the hills were greater than anticipated: 'Perhaps however I had better say nothing about this yet, lest it should prejudice the minds of some of our friends against the mission'.[52] Hard as it was for Roberts to convince his brethren 'that they need to spend more money on a preacher in India than one in Wales',[53] he was required to act as go-between in balancing the economic realities as reported by his trusted friend in the field, and the stringencies of church finances. Privately, in a letter to Tomlin, he double-checked Jones's version of the inflated accounts (as well as his use of Roman characters in writing Khasi) – 'had we known we might never have sent him there'.[54] Publicly, Roberts reported the names of congregations who had made significant annual contributions to the mission – in 1841, Coed-Llai and Mostyn in Flintshire, and Salem in Denbighshire – as a means of encouraging healthy competition.

Jones addressed his letters to Roberts personally, yet he was also well aware that they performed more public functions. At times he wrote specifically with that broader audience in mind. Letter writing was an individual and mostly private act, but letter reading could be a more social, communal and collaborative practice.[55] Letters may have been 'writing's historical substitution for oral exchange',[56] but in mid-nineteenth-century Wales, as Bill Jones has suggested, they circulated in a transitional historical space between oral and written cultures: 'Letters encouraged the perseverance of orality by being read publicly whilst at the same time they clearly contributed, and were shaped by, emerging literacy'.[57]

Roberts read letters from the missionaries to his committee, excising certain parts along the way. Jones wrote what were in a sense open letters, and he knew they would be commonly read aloud; he was alert to the elevated position he occupied in relation to the community at home, and the didactic power of his words when addressed to that constituency.[58] At their most powerful rhetorical level, some of Jones's letters are most like scripts for sermons, constructed in the full knowledge that his sentiments would be channelled by an interlocutor. Copies of Jones's first letter of 11 May 1841 from Calcutta – one of only two letters not to be published in *Y Drysorfa* – were circulated throughout Wales. Most often in Liverpool, it was Roberts himself who voiced the missionary – in October 1841 he read portions of two letters to a crammed chapel and gallery at Rose Place, and in early 1843 reported reading extracts at a meeting of the Total Abstinence Society. Elsewhere, Roberts encouraged the public performance of the letters as a means of spiritual elevation as well as fundraising.

The form and nature of letter-writing had consequences for the ways in which individuals understood their roles, negotiated interpersonal relations and were able to respond in times of crisis. The epistolary network threaded them to the social protocols of home, but its slippages in time and space also required them to depend on themselves, and perhaps gave them the chance to act true to nature, for better or for worse. The vagaries of postal services and their transforming technologies 'helped change people's experience of time and impacted on their understandings of and feelings about physical separation and sense of distance'.[59] The organisation of postage was a complex but necessary dimension in shaping missionary experience and practice.[60] Letters sent from Jones to Roberts took an average of around ten weeks to arrive, then another three or four weeks until they were published in *Y Drysorfa*. In other words, news from the missionary front was already over three months old by the time it was publicly circulated. In 1841, Henry Yule, Jones's friend at Cherrapunji, penned a short ditty illustrating the mixed feelings of anticipation, dependence, despair and jubilation felt by the British residents of the station in regard to the monthly mail service.[61]

> Those odious Mails, those odious Mails,
> That come by Falmouth or Marseilles!
> How oft to us they nought impart
> Save hope deferred and sickened heart.
> No post to-day? Well, banish sorrow
> 'Twill but more surely come to-morrow.
> . . .
> Perhaps they've sent (the best will err) a
> Post bag to China, 'stead of Cherra.

If a post-bag for Cherrapunji could be accidentally diverted to China, what effect on a historical reading of events does the shape of the surviving archive actually have? Stanley posits the notion of the 'epistolarium' as 'a radical force in bringing together, indeed more strongly in *creating*, what never was',[62] as well as for ways of reading individual letters that were not conceived of by their authors as being necessarily part of a totality of collated correspondence. In the correspondence between Roberts and Jones, how can we better understand the context of how the letters were written, sent, read, edited, translated, published and archived? And what can such an analysis reveal about the particular concerns of the missionary and the mission over time?

Between 1841 and 1846, Jones wrote twenty-five letters to Roberts, and all save three were published in *Y Drysorfa*. As time passed, Jones's correspondence tailed off, while that of his co-workers Lewis and Richards picked up. Jones had made clear from the outset that he saw his role in the Khasi Hills as being a good missionary ahead of being a regular correspondent. Despite the structured office practices of the Mission Society, and its subsequent construction as a formal archive, for reasons that will become clear not one of Jones's original letters exists in his handwriting in his slim file now located in the CMA archives at the National Library of Wales.

As a dialogue between Jones and Roberts, the letters of the former might be seen to be official reports, the latter to be commentaries on these reports. An extant letterbook of the general secretary includes eighteen letters from Roberts to Jones up to March 1843 – thereafter, this side of the correspondence is silent until 1847, an absence that determines our reading of Jones's subsequent letters. Jones's letters hold further ambiguities for the historian, not only insofar as the originals do not survive, but also through the ways in which they were filtered by Roberts for selective publication in *Y Drysorfa*, as well as in the process of translation from Welsh to English for the purposes of this study. In Stanley's terms, Jones's letters exist as 'a kind of palimpsest: the original letters are there, but in shadowy half-erased form and having an ambiguous relationship with their transcribed and printed versions'.[63]

Roberts forwarded to John Parry extracts of letters he received from Lewis, Richards and Jones. Parry, the author of the *Rhodd Mam* catechism, edited *Y Drysorfa* from 1831 until his death in 1846. Of some importance here is the fact that Roberts translated *English* letters into *Welsh* for publication in the Welsh-language newsletter. The language issue becomes bound up not only in questions of access and audience, but in the socio-political context of the Liverpool Welsh themselves. When Roberts read portions of Jones's letters to the Rose

Place assembly in October 1841, he 'translated as well as I could'.[64] While all of Roberts's letters to Jones are in English (though some of his letters to other correspondents are in Welsh), his inclination to translate the missionary's letters into Welsh for publication and circulation must at least partly have been motivated by the exigencies of an urban Welsh-speaking community in Liverpool at a particular moment of its formation. As E. Wyn James has detailed, Liverpool was the economic and cultural magnet of north Wales, and the Liverpool-born Roberts was part of a middle-class ethnic minority whose sense of self, in the face of pressure to assimilate, was mediated primarily through its sense of Welshness.[65] In this context, Roberts was making a very deliberate statement about Welsh identity in his overt efforts to communicate and write in Welsh rather than English. 'Some of our friends', he wrote to Thomas Jones in October 1841, 'say you ought to write in *Welsh*: & doubtless your letters would tell with greater effect if written by yourself, than when translated by me. Think of this, & do as you like'.[66] While Jones most likely spoke Welsh to his countrymen, he was clearly literate in both languages. That Thomas Jones ignored this request perhaps says less about any overt desire on his part to be appropriated as a Welsh cultural champion, and more about Roberts's own motivations.

With the English originals of Thomas Jones's letters now lost, and their echo only accessible to the historian in Welsh translation (and that of only selected parts rather than the letters in their entirety), the epistolarium entails a complex set of transmutations, elisions and back-translations. For the contemporary translator of these flowery and bombastic texts, the letters in *Y Drysorfa* pose multilayered problems of linguistic analysis and textual interpretation. The highly developed literary tradition of nineteenth-century Welsh had its roots in both the bardic tradition as well as in the Christian Bible, and Jones's writing is peppered with biblical allusions and quotations, as well as structured with Welsh rhetorical devices. Individual words – such as *merch*, *bachgen* and *mab* – themselves pose problems of interpretation. Throughout Wales, *merch* (plural *merched*) can mean daughter, girl or woman, so is not always an indication of the more specific age of an individual. In the same way, *bachgen* (plural *bechgyn*) can mean boy, but can also refer to men. *Mab* (plural *meibion*) can refer to sons, but also young men or even men generally. In specific cultural terms, where Khasi girls tended to marry young, a girl of fourteen or fifteen could be designated a woman. It is also clear, as previously mentioned, that the missionaries had some trouble estimating the ages of Khasis – Tirahsing is referred to as an old man in one letter, though forty years old in another.[67]

The letter sent, the letter received and the letter unsent all carried very specific meanings and entailed particular consequences for the correspondents. In a very real way, the letters opened by Roberts from Jones were a powerful sign of religious belief, in themselves taken as providential symbols of God's faith in the missionary project. When the first letter from Jones was published in *Y Drysorfa*, Roberts was almost at a loss to describe its spiritual impact: 'Were I not afraid of taking up too much space in Y Drysorfa at one time, I would relate to you the effects which the letter had upon my thoughts . . . I feel very sure that the reading of it will cause many of your readers, like myself, to "thank God, and take comfort"'.[68]

A letter received could also confirm the missionary's ongoing survival in the face of rumours to the contrary. 'You will see', observed Roberts in the columns of *Y Drysorfa*, 'that Mr Jones's letter is dated more than a month after the one mentioned in the last issue . . . consequently your readers will presumably have no trouble comprehending that the story which recently spread so swiftly throughout the country is incorrect, that our brother was cruelly murdered while pursuing his missionary activities'.[69] Yet paradox, observes Stanley, 'is at the heart of epistolary matters: the "real" message of letters is not quite what is written'.[70] A letter unsent could also affirm the absence of unanimity on the mission front: ominously, a letter that Roberts asked that Jones and Lewis send jointly in 1843 as 'ocular demonstration' of their unanimity, was never penned.

Notes

1 Lewis to Roberts, 6 March 1844, *Y Drysorfa*, June 1844.
2 Lewis to Roberts, 3 August 1844, *Y Drysorfa*, November 1844.
3 Jones to Roberts, 7 April 1842, *Y Drysorfa*, 1842.
4 Annalisa Oboe, 'Of books and the book: the evangelical mission in South African literature' in Gerhard Stilz (ed.), *Colonies, Missions, Cultures in the English-speaking World: General and Comparative Studies* (Tübingen, 2001), p. 235.
5 Jones to Roberts, 7 April 1842, *Y Drysorfa*, August 1842.
6 Anthony Jones, *Welsh Chapels* (Stroud, 1996), p. 12.
7 Maria Charles to Owen Richards, 29 January 1844, NLW Thomas Charles Edwards (1)/4708.
8 Jonathan Parry, 'The gift, the Indian gift, and the "Indian gift"', *Man*, 21 (1986), 468 quoted in Mark Osteen, 'Introduction' in Mark Osteen (ed.), *The Question of the Gift: Essays Across Disciplines* (London and New York, 2002), p. 12.
9 Jones to Roberts, 8 December 1842, *Y Drysorfa*, March 1843.
10 Nicholas Thomas, 'The cultural dynamics of peripheral exchange' in Caroline Humphrey and Stephen Hugh-Jones (eds), *Barter, Exchange and Value: An Anthropological Approach* (Cambridge, 1992), p. 38.
11 Jones to Roberts, 7 April 1842, *Y Drysorfa*, August 1842.
12 Thomas, 'The cultural dynamics of peripheral exchange', pp. 23, 38.
13 David Murray, *Indian Giving: Economies of Power in Indian-White Relations* (Amherst, MA, 2000), p. 12.

14 Karen Sykes, *Arguing with Anthropology: An Introduction to Critical Theories of the Gift* (London and New York, 2005), p. 59.
15 Jones to Roberts, 8 December 1842, *Y Drysorfa*, March 1843
16 John Roberts, 20 January 1844, *Y Drysorfa*, February 1844.
17 Jones to Roberts, 28 July 1841, *Y Drysorfa*, November 1841.
18 Jones to Roberts, 7 April 1842, *Y Drysorfa*, August 1842.
19 Jones to Roberts, 9 October 1842, *Y Drysorfa*, January 1843.
20 Roberts to Jones, 29 December 1842, CMA 28720.
21 Jones to Roberts, May1844, *Y Drysorfa*, September 1844.
22 H.C. Bhardwaj, 'Development of iron and steel technology in India during 18th and 19th centuries', *Indian Journal of History of Science*, 17:2 (1982), 232.
23 Jones to Roberts, May 1844, *Y Drysorfa*, September 1844.
24 Piggin, *Making Evangelical Missionaries*, p. 245.
25 Jones to Roberts, 8 November 1841, *Y Drysorfa*, March 1842.
26 Jones to Roberts, 8 November 1841, *Y Drysorfa*, March 1842.
27 Jones to Roberts, 28 July 1841, *Y Drysorfa*, November 1841.
28 Sarah Poustie, 'Re-theorising letters and "letterness"', Olive Schreiner Letters project, Working Papers on Letters, Letterness & Epistolary Networks, Number 1, University of Edinburgh, 2010, www.oliveschreinerletters.ed.ac.uk/PoustieWPLetterness.pdf (accessed 1 December 2010), p. 15.
29 Stanley, 'The epistolarium', 212.
30 *Ibid.*, 208; See also Margaretta Jolly and Liz Stanley, 'Letters as/not a genre', *Life Writing*, 2:2 (2005), 93; Poustie, 'Re-theorising letters and "letterness"', p. 4.
31 Roberts to Jones, 29 September 1841, CMA 28720.
32 E. Wyn James, 'John Roberts ("Minimus"; 1808–80): not the least among Liverpool Welsh Methodists', Paper delivered to the AHRC Research Network: 'Language, Religion and Print Culture in the Welsh Diaspora', Bangor University, 18 September 2007.
33 Roberts to Jones, 4 February 1843, CMA 28720.
34 Stanley, 'The epistolarium', 209.
35 Jones to Roberts, 28 July 1841, *Y Drysorfa*, November 1841.
36 Jones to Roberts, 8 October 1841, *Y Drysorfa*, March 1842.
37 Roberts to Jones, 29 January 1842, CMA 28720.
38 Roberts to Jones, 27 February 1843, CMA 28720.
39 Charles to Richards, 29 August 1843, NLW Thomas Charles Edwards (1)/4107.
40 Roberts later wrote to Lewis that he 'regretted that I did not go out as a missionary myself'. Roberts to Lewis, 17 January 1852, CMA 27222.
41 Roberts to Lewis, 30 March 1843, CMA 27221.
42 Roberts to Jones, 20 December 1842, CMA 28720.
43 Susan M. Fitzmaurice, *The Familiar Letter in Early Modern English* (Amsterdam and Philadelphia, 2002), p. 2.
44 Roberts to Jones, 29 September 1841, CMA 28720.
45 Jolly and Stanley, 'Letters as/not a genre', 93.
46 R.A. Miller, 'The missionary narrative as coercive interrogation: seduction, confession and self-presentation in women's "letters home"', *Women's History Review*, 15:5 (2006), 752.
47 Jones to Roberts, 28 July 1841, *Y Drysorfa*, November 1841.
48 Jones to Roberts, 8 October 1841, *Y Drysorfa*, March 1842. The reference is to Proverbs 13:12.
49 David Barton and Nigel Hall, 'Introduction' in David Barton and Nigel Hall (eds), *Letter Writing as a Social Practice* (Amsterdam and Philadelphia, 2000), pp. 2–3.
50 *Y Drysorfa*, November 1841.
51 David A. Gerber, 'Acts of deceiving and withholding in immigrant letters: personal identity and self-presentation in personal correspondence', *Journal of Social History*, 39:2 (2005), 315.
52 Roberts to Jones, 29 January 1842, CMA 28720.
53 Roberts to Jones, 31 May 1842, CMA 28720.

54 Roberts to Tomlin, 26 March 1842, CMA 28720.
55 Poustie, 'Re-theorising letters and "letterness"', p. 12; Barton and Hall, 'Introduction', p. 4; Jolly and Stanley, 'Letters as/not a genre', 95; Bill Jones, 'Writing back: Welsh emigrants and their correspondence in the nineteenth century', *North American Journal of Welsh Studies*, 5:1 (2005), 29–30.
56 Jolly and Stanley, 'Letters as/not a genre', 97.
57 Jones, 'Writing back', 30.
58 Stanley, 'The epistolarium', 207.
59 *Ibid.*, 216.
60 See also Jones, 'Writing back', 40.
61 H. Yule [Anonymous], *Fragments of Unprofessional Papers Gathered from an Engineer's Portfolio after Twenty-three Years of Service* (Calcutta, 1862), p. 31.
62 Jolly and Stanley, 'Letters as/not a genre', 108.
63 Stanley, 'The epistolarium', 222.
64 Roberts to Jones, 28 October 1841, CMA 28720.
65 James, 'John Roberts ("Minimus"; 1808–80)'.
66 Roberts to Jones, 28 October 1841, CMA 28720.
67 Compare Lewis to Roberts, 31 July 1847, *Y Drysorfa*, November 1847, with Lewis to Roberts, 13 January 1847, *Y Drysorfa*, April 1847. With particular thanks to Sylvia Prys Jones for these observations.
68 Roberts, 16 October 1841, *Y Drysorfa*, November 1841.
69 Roberts, 21 November 1842, *Y Drysorfa*, December 1842.
70 Stanley, 'The epistolarium', 214.

CHAPTER TEN

Intimacy and transgression

After months of anguished waiting, Maria Charles finally received the good news of her son and grandson's safe arrival in India. Though the boy had been ill on the voyage, the pair was now safely ensconced with the Joneses at Cherrapunji. The engravings of the missionaries were selling well in Bala, and four-dozen of Owen Richards had been sold by the end of February 1843.[1] Owen Charles Richards turned seven on 28 January, and on 10 February Ann Jones gave birth to a baby daughter Ann Jane. Though she did not know Thomas Jones's wife personally, Maria felt reassured that Ann's maternal presence on the mission station would be beneficial to her grandson: 'I feel very partial to her, thinking she will be very kind to O.C.'.[2]

Nineteenth-century racial theory as well as evangelical Christian doctrine set the image of the strait-laced Christian as diametrically opposed to the sexualised savage; here was a fundamental moral justification of missionary intervention into indigenous cultures. By examining sexual improprieties on the mission station, as well as representations of the role and status of missionary wives, the stereotype of Christian propriety can be tested against the lived experiences of the Welsh missionaries. If the missionary couple and family was a central axis of missionisation, then the Welsh mission was a textbook study of disequilibrium. While the work of the mission in Christianising and educating the Khasi people proceeded steadily through the 1840s, it is perhaps anomalous that men and women associated with this daily task often failed demonstrably in the mission's formative years to model moral conformity to the ideal Christian family. If sexual mores were the boundary between European righteousness and native depravity (or as Ann Stoler puts it, if sexuality was an important feature in discerning the 'the moral parameters of European nations'),[3] what happened when these boundaries were breached? To consider the missionary body less as a generic imperial elite and more as a dynamic and transforming system, is to reveal subtle, conflicting and even contradictory attitudes to empire and religion. The repercussions of scandal in the Welsh mission had personal ramifications for Thomas Jones, and political ones for British authority in the hills.

Scandal and censure: the Owen Richards affair

In worrying about the welfare of her widowed son and motherless grandchild, Maria Charles was depending on a set of behaviours of the missionary men and women at Cherrapunji that were governed by normative paradigms of gender propriety and domesticity. A series of explosive scandals would test these assumptions. Early in 1843, Lieutenant Lewin's large household at Cherrapunji had increased by the sum of his two orphaned nieces, Lucy Marsh, aged nineteen, and her elder sister Mary Ann, both of whom had been under the care of their elder brother Hippisley Marsh of the Bengal Army. In January 1844, Lewis Edwards received a letter from his brother-in-law Owen Richards detailing a charge that had been levelled against him of inappropriate attentions paid to Lucy. The facts of the case may never be known. They were not agreed on by participants at the time, and are revealed at times only second or third hand in the extant accounts. What the case does reveal, however, is a range of underlying stresses and tensions which challenge the image of the mission being produced through John Roberts's carefully edited extracts in *Y Drysorfa*. The case also points to a more private network of correspondence and opinion, and the role of scandal and gossip in reflecting and transforming imperial relationships.

As a medical missionary, Richards not only ministered to the Khasis, but from an early period after his arrival in January 1843, also attended Europeans on the station. Around the end of September, it appears that Thomas Jones forwarded to John Roberts a charge against Richards that had been made by William Lewin. Richards knew nothing of this until early November, when he quickly wrote to John Roberts and Lewis Edwards to defend his honour.[4] In Richards's version of events, he noted that he had often been asked to prescribe for Lewin's family, including Lucy Marsh, 'who often complained of some slight nervous symptoms'. On one such visit, 'she declared herself attached to me'. Richards claimed that he had not encouraged her affections and had dissuaded her on the grounds that a missionary's life was one of difficulty and privation. Despite his protestations, Lucy professed her attachment and told her uncle that she wished to be married to Richards. Lewin wrote to Hippisley Marsh, who offered no objection to the union. Richards continued, however, to declare his position, that 'for certain reasons I did not chose to divulge, I did not feel at liberty to marry', and it was agreed that any intercourse between the pair should cease as a matter of propriety. The matter did not end there. According to Richards, Lucy 'persisted in throwing herself in my way by meeting me & overtaking me on the road, writing notes &c'. On 7 September, Lewin and Richards had heated words, and by the October mail Lewin's account of the matter was forwarded by Jones and William Lewis to Liverpool. According to Richards, Jones and Lewis refused to detail what specific charges they had in fact laid against him. As further evidence of his case, Richards cited part of a note that Lucy had written to him on 28 September, in which she had resiled from her actions: 'The agonies of mind I have suffered & still continue to suffer are beyond discription [*sic*], night after night have I lain awake reproaching myself most bitterly for my conduct throwing myself in your way & tempting you to continue intercourse, against my God have I most grievously sinned'.[5]

Lewin's version of the case differed little in chronology, but much in motive and intent.[6] After Richards's arrival at Cherrapunji, Lewin took him to be polite, obliging and friendly, though his interest in Lucy 'excited some degree of suspicion' in the mind of his wife. Lewin was 'put off my guard' by confidential information (that could only have been supplied by Jones or Lewis) that Richards was committed to a life of celibacy, having resisted certain opinions prior to his departure that he should embark on his missionary career as a married man. Lucy suddenly announced to her uncle that Richards had declared his attachment to her, which she had accepted. Lewin was perturbed that as Lucy was under age, the pair had engaged in private and unchaperoned intercourse unbeknown to the girl's family, and wrote to Richards expressing his concern at his unchristian and ungentlemanly behaviour. After a heated meeting and with Richards refusing to write to Lucy's brother and guardian, Lewin took it upon himself to contact Hippisley. In the meantime, Lucy and Owen's liaison continued clandestinely.

In Lewin's opinion, his niece was not suited either by education or religious proclivity to contemplate being a missionary's wife. Hippisley was more sanguine. In his view, should Lucy wish to persist in the engagement, and should Richards prove himself to be 'an estimable, upright, and valuable man', then he would not withhold his consent to their marriage: 'he had rather that she should marry a man of solid character, serious piety, and amiable qualities, though in a grade of life somewhat below hers, than run the risk of wrecking her domestic happiness for life by some ill-advised union with an equivocal character, in her own rank of society'. Richards continued to deny interest in any liaison with Lucy, but asserted 'that if Miss M came casually in his way, he could not help showing her civility'. Throughout his version of events – which he 'considered to be a very moderate statement of the case' – Lewin variously appealed to Richards's sense of Christian duty, self-command, prudence, propriety, rectitude and generosity. In the light of Richards's 'complete haughtiness', Lewin 'left him in utter disgust, satisfied that my neice [*sic*] was in imminent danger of being ruined for life under the snares of such a man', and took steps to remove her from Cherrapunji.

As his letters of defence hit the shores of Liverpool in January 1844, they sent a shockwave through the home community. By early April 1844, Richards received word that he was being recalled from India. Writing again to Lewis Edwards on 2 April, Richards declared his innocence: 'I had no wish to carry on any intercourse with her. I never proposed to her. I never employed any means to gain her affections'. Richards reserved most scorn for Thomas Jones and William Lewis, who had been acquainted with the particulars of the affair right from the start, and to whom he had consistently advanced the innocence of his designs on Lucy Marsh. Richards advanced a dysfunctional view of his fellow missionaries, in which competitive, vindictive and manipulative motives had underscored their relationships from an early period:

> Mr Lewis seldom came near at the time. Mr Jones & he could scarcely speak to each other. I was given to understand from Mr Jones that either Mr or Mrs Lewis had been making insinuations to the Lewins that I was of bad character before leaving home. Mr Jones would never mention Mr Lewis without endeavouring to lead me to speak ill of him. Mr Lewis would never mention Mr Jones without indulging in the same propensity. As I joined with neither, each supposed me a greater friend of the other than of himself, & thus became obnoxious to the designs of both.[7]

Excised from a copy of the letter in the archives, though present in the original, is also a clue to the nature of the engagement he made before he left for India: 'how distressed I feel that I have occasioned any grief to Miss Davies. I fear she is very ill. It is a great relief to my mind that she has made you acquainted with our engagement'. Jane Davies, the wife of Bala draper Robert Davies (brother of John Davies, Fronheulog), had been recently widowed prior to Richards's departure for India, and it is possible that the widow and the widower had made some kind of compact that at least tentatively bound each to the other. In any event, the two were married in 1844 soon after Richards returned to Wales.

With Richards recalled to Wales, the matter did not rest there, to the chagrin of the mission authorities. Meetings had been convened in Liverpool in March 1845 to deliver a verdict on the merits of the case. In Richards's view, the committee was a kangaroo court, and he refused to attend in person. In mid-April he circulated to the press an extensive 'statement of facts relating to the Welsh Missionary Society', in which he publicly defended his character and innocence.[8] More particularly, he was critical of the whole process of his indictment: that he had been denied natural justice, that the committee had been stacked with his opponents, that he had not been allowed any appeal, and that he had never been given a copy of the charges. A key point of contention was the letter of 3 August 1843 from Thomas Jones to John Roberts. Excerpts of this had been printed in *Y Drysorfa* in December 1843, in which Jones commented on the need for more missionaries to be sent out. 'It is not necessary', Jones wrote, 'for them all to make some great show of learning and much less to be able to boast in their family connections'. Richards presumed that this 'malicious insinuation' was directed at himself, and that it had been provoked by an unnamed circumstance that had occurred a few days before Jones wrote the 3 August letter, an event 'which was calculated to excite feelings of jealousy'. In the reluctance of the secretary to produce the original copy of Jones's letter, and in its selective quoting, Richards charged his accusers with manipulating the truth and suppressing information that would be to his advantage: 'That letter would, I firmly believe, afford some clue to the secret springs of the diabolical Khassia conspiracy'.

Richards's statement also condemned Jones's role in secretly sending home allegations against him, while for months 'I lived in the same house, & at the same table with Jones; but had no idea of the villainy to which he had been a party'. While Jones and Lewis had it seemed barely spoken to each other since Lewis's arrival, in their joint accusation of Richards, 'they acted the part of Herod & Pilate'. Richards did not reproduce Jones's descriptions of Lucy Marsh 'out of delicacy', but quoted from a letter Lewis had written to a compatriot, in which he described Lucy Marsh as 'a canaanitish woman, a young girl yet in her teens, who is as ignorant as she is destitute of religion'. William Lewis also excoriated Lewis Edwards's role as Richards's mentor:

> what will Mr E think of the man whom he has extolled to the very heavens, in letters to individuals, & that to the injury of those in whom it is his duty to take an equal & lively interest in? I think it would have been as well for Mr E to have been a little more modest concerning Mr R, who is a relation to him, & not to have observed such studied silence concerning those who had been with him in school, & never gave him any trouble, but have loved him like themselves.[9]

Richards felt betrayed by the man with whom he had shared his voyage to India, and suggested that Lewis's jealousy had been further fuelled by 'the success which I met with among the natives'. As far as Jones was concerned, 'the case of the individual who boasts of having *tricked the London Missionary Society*', Richards contended, '& of having been instigated to do so in Liverpool, is very different. I have a right to complain that the Secretary did not inform me of that manoeuvre: I should then have been able to anticipate what art would be employed in the event of joining him'.[10]

Richards had also mustered support from a range of quarters in the Khasi Hills, and he reproduced testimonials from some of the mission's key friends and supporters. Political Agent Frederick Lister upheld Richards to be a zealous missionary and doctor. It was largely due to Richards's medical work that he had removed 'the Cassya prejudice of not taking medicine, of which, before he came among them, they entertained great dread, from superstitious motives'. An address in Richards's favour from local Khasi chiefs and respectable inhabitants was forwarded in English translation by magistrate Harry Inglis, who also sent his own character reference. 'You must not be backward', Inglis counselled, 'in producing all the evidence within your reach to clear yourself, although your "Kind friends", perhaps may suffer from it. I know you naturally shudder to expose one, although you suffer by it yourself'.[11]

There is some indication in the correspondence reproduced by Richards that Thomas Jones had attempted to undermine the *bona fides* of Henry Inglis, and therefore by implication of the Khasi address that he had translated: 'it was most ungrateful on the part of Mr Jones: for when complaints were preferred, Mr Inglis, did, I believe, on each occasion, all he could to screen him from disgrace'. What these 'complaints' against Jones were, remain a mystery. But in order to confirm the weight of his testimonials, Richards asked Jacob Tomlin for an opinion, which he readily gave: '*Very few* missionaries have endeared themselves so much to the natives by kindness & consideration as Mr Richards has done, especially in so short a time'. Richards also provided a detailed account of his expenditure and income to counter 'slanderous insinuations that had been made on this head'.

Circulation of Richards's statement spurred the mission board into action, and a final printed statement was circulated in Welsh on 30 April 1845, in which board chairman Henry Rees and mission secretary John Roberts refuted his claims, defended their investigation as being compatible with Christian integrity and brotherhood, and reiterated the determination of the March committee in Liverpool to terminate the missionary's relationship with the society.[12] Morris's history determines that the directors were 'fully justified by the evidence presented at the time, and indisputably confirmed by subsequent events', and both he and D. Ben Rees briefly posit the scandal in a progressive narrative frame wherein it was a test to the missionary cause, which was subsequently overcome.[13] But what might a closer look at the circumstances of Richards's purported sexual indiscretion, and the gossip and scandal that circulated about it, reveal about the power structures of the society within which it occurred? At its core, the case revolves around an individual's transgressions, if not overtly sexual, then certainly overstepping the carefully prescribed bounds of intimacy and appropriate courtship behaviours. Censure of Richards's behaviour, at the very least, was confirmation if it were needed of the norms of sexual morality, which were to apply just as well in Cherrapunji as in Cardiganshire. But as Gamson has noted, sex scandals at their heart are also 'institutional morality tales', intrinsically connected to the institutional frameworks within which they occur and are subsequently represented.[14]

When Thomas Jones originally received news that Owen Richards was to be sent out as a missionary, he seemed genuinely exalted: 'I have never been so overjoyed, as when I read the name of Dr Richards amongst them . . . I have a great regard for him, since I first knew him'.[15] The first evidence of tension between Jones and Richards lies in the letter of 3 August, in which Jones obliquely criticised Richard's family connections, and which Roberts was prepared to have circulated publicly in *Y Drysorfa*. What could possibly have happened to alter Jones's opinion of Richards in the space of seven months?

Late May saw the monsoon wrapping Cherrapunji in its constraining arms. 'We are all healthy', wrote Jones, 'but confined to the house at present by the rains, and we shall be for some months yet'.[16] By their own admission, the missionaries had very little to do with the other Europeans at Cherrapunji. In mid-1843, the missionary circle comprised the childless William and Mary Lewis; Owen Richards, widower, and his young son Owen Charles; Thomas Jones, his often sickly wife Ann, and their baby daughter; the invalid William Lewin, his pregnant wife and their five living children, their eldest Jane turning sixteen years old. The Lewins were their closest friends, having hosted Ann and Thomas on their arrival. Richards lived with the Joneses, with the Lewis's house three or four hundred yards distant. Into this intimate and relatively closed social world, through the incessant and confining monsoon season, stepped nineteen-year-old Lucy Marsh, and it is not hard to speculate that her presence created sexual tension in the group. Owen Richards became the focus of such a possibility, but there are claims that Thomas Jones himself may have had some kind of intimacy with Lucy. Ann Jones, the wife of missionary Daniel Jones who arrived at Cherrapunji in February 1846, writing to Mary Lewis in 1847, remarked that 'Few of the friends know of Miss March [sic], and he'.[17] William Lewis was later also to assert that 'only two or three months after he had consigned the remains of his late wife to the silent tomb, he commenced a most imprudent intercourse' with Lucy Marsh, and that his intentions of marrying her were thwarted at the last minute by some of her relatives: 'Mr Jones' conduct therein, was verbally but severely animadverted upon, both by the European community here [Cherrapunji] and at other stations'.[18]

Jealousy over the attentions of a young woman may go some way towards explaining the developing friction on the mission station. From William Lewin's perspective, his avuncular responsibilities to take Lucy under his care would have been accepted without question, but certainly placed additional strain on a man whose illness and existing family responsibilities made life already onerous. Fiercely protective of Lucy's reputation (and therefore marriage prospects), he also constructed her as culpable (in hiding her relationship with Richards from him) and inferior (lacking education and religious sensibility), objectifying her worth in terms of familiar gendered ideologies. William Lewis's dismissal of Lucy as a 'canaanitish woman' – a lustful and immoral temptress – characterised her as sexual object, and implied that she was not worthy to be a missionary's wife. Lewis also implied that she rather than Richards was intrinsically to blame for any immoralities that may have occurred. In Lewin's text, Richards ultimately becomes a sexual predator from whose rapacious clutches his niece needs to be immediately removed. In the space between these two constructions, Lewin found room to contemplate Richards as a viable marriage partner for Lucy, as he encouraged Richards to follow through with an honourable settlement. Lucy's guardian and brother Captain Hippisley Marsh, though conscious of her potential drop in status in marrying somewhat below her class, also had a clear interest in marrying her off. In an unsigned and undated scrap in the Richards file, one of his defenders wrote: 'I am sure if you saw all the letters sent here and there you could but see a plot had been laid to saddle Mr Lewin's illegitimate relation on him'.[19]

Lewin's financial insecurity had long been a source of personal concern and discussion among his family members elsewhere. While an unmarried niece or sister could be a financial liability, particularly at a remote station in India where marriage prospects were highly constrained, Lucy Marsh had significantly just become an asset to a potential suitor. William Lewin's father and Lucy's grandfather Thomas Lewin died on 15 June 1843, news of which would have reached Cherrapunji by August. Among other beneficiaries in his will, he bequeathed £5000 to William, and £2000 each to the Marsh girls and to Hippisley.[20] Lewin's alliances were with his military colleagues (he engaged station medical officer Dr James Davenport as a witness against Richards), as well as with Jones himself, and the home authorities were loath to risk losing his patronage. As gossip turned into full-blown scandal back in Liverpool and Wales, John Roberts was also more likely to protect the idol he had created of his friend Thomas Jones, the pioneer missionary, than the reputation of the new missionary Richards, however well connected he may have been. Richards's relationship with Lewis Edwards, and the appearance of favouritism, was clearly a point of vulnerability for a mission under stress, desperately trying to attract both financial support as well as new missionary candidates. Richards's reputation was in a sense sacrificed to the exigencies of realpolitik, and his family connections made him more rather than less vulnerable to gossip.

Gossip thrived as the details of the case were relatively unclear, becoming scandalous when it entered the public domain. In manipulating a private correspondence with John Roberts about Owen Richards, Thomas Jones was attempting to consolidate his intimacy with John Roberts and his position as a key player in the mission in the face of newly arrived colleagues. Gossip operated here as 'a confidence, a sign of trust and closeness', and constructed an insider and an outsider group.[21] It is clear too – in analysing the individual, social and political pressures on the key players Lewin, Lewis, Richards, Jones and Roberts – that gossip has more potency in contexts of structural tension, of competing obligations and of social stress in terms of material and symbolic resources.[22] The Richards affair had the effect of galvanising power interests in Wales; at Cherrapunji the missionaries were left without a fellow labourer, and a valuable medical man at that. But the scandal had also drawn to the surface a set of complex political alliances. Magistrate Inglis and Political Agent Lister had revealed themselves to be friends and supporters of the mission generally, and of Richards particularly, but at the same time to be detractors of Thomas Jones.

The removal of Richards was a way of controlling aberrant moral behaviour, but the very existence of scandal in the Khasi Hills mission served to compromise the ways in which the missionaries could confidently model the normative moral order that was at the heart of their evangelising project. In other colonial contexts, such scandals could be terminal. Aboriginal Protector Charles Sievwright was dismissed from public office in the Port Phillip District after a private sexual scandal undermined his ability to model gendered norms of respectable domestic behaviour. Where Lester and Dussart have directly linked the demise of the Aboriginal Protectorate in the late 1840s to Sievwright's dismissal, the endless scandals among the Welsh missionaries did not have a similar long-term impact. The home mission authorities had far too much invested in their breakaway enterprise to have it fall over at an early hurdle, and the Welsh missionaries were less troubling to the colonial authorities in India than Aboriginal protectors in New South Wales whose attempts to bring settlers to account for frontier violence were an annoying distraction to colonial policy makers. It was therefore not the hypocrisies of public versus private behaviours *per se* that led to unavoidable personal and profession downfall, but the specific political contexts in which they occurred.[23]

Back in the Khasi Hills, construction of the sexual depravity of their indigenous subjects may well have been a means of rationalising colonial supremacy. If, as Erlank argues, 'sexual mores were a principal way in which colonial societies attempted to distinguish themselves from indigenous ones',[24] then with Richards recalled in disgrace, and Lewis and Jones apparently not on speaking terms, the extent to which the mission was able to discharge its brief was under critical pressure.

Missionary wives

If transgressions of appropriate gender codes were at the heart of the mission's troubles through 1843 and early 1844, John Roberts sought to reassert equilibrium by appealing to the moral role of the missionary wives. On 28 February 1844, Roberts wrote a stern letter to Mary Lewis, chiding her for any 'unpleasantness' that had existed between Richards and the Lewises, and recommending a rapprochement in their relationship: 'a great deal depends in this matter, upon the females connected with the mission; for if they do not cultivate the most cordial good will towards each other, but allow some petty jealousies or coolness to exist between them, it will be impossible for the husbands long to continue to work in unison'.[25]

In an era before women were formally accepted as missionary candidates in their own right, it often seems that the missionary wife has been characterised either as exceptional missionary heroine or simple domestic helpmeet. Such stereotyping could lead to a misreading of the interplay between mission and home society expectations on the one hand, and women's agency on the other. Jeffrey Cox has suggested that while both European and Indian women are often absent from missionary histories, in reality 'missionary' usually meant a married couple. Narratives of the heroic individual male missionary occlude the significance of women, who were not necessarily subordinate to men either by action (performing key roles in mission enterprises) or numerically (for example, by the end of the nineteenth century, 60 per cent of the missionaries in the Punjab were female). As Cox has shown, 'a solid majority of all missionaries in the late nineteenth century were female', and in the gap between literary and historical portrayals and what missionaries were actually doing, might be found a variety of ways in which gender roles were being improvised according to the local settings within which they operated.[26]

Ann Jones and Mary Lewis played similar yet at times contradictory roles as missionary wives and as missionaries themselves. The absence of any documentary evidence at all in Ann Jones's own voice, coupled with the realities of her constant sickness, make analysis of her role in the mission elusive. At the valedictory meeting in Rose Place Chapel in 1840, the Reverend John Hughes, Pontrobert, publicly addressed first the missionary, and then his wife: 'And as for his wife, – if she receives assistance to learn the language, she can accomplish a great deal. She can support him mentally; she can be up when he is down, etc.'. The Reverend John Parry, Chester, was then called upon to address the audience:

> Then the speaker turned his gaze upon the gallery, where the Missionary's wife was sitting, and said, I can almost hear his wife saying, I am not a missionary, what is there for me to do? "Go ye also, and teach – teach the women and children of Kassiah as much as you can; teach by your example; teach by being of every assistance to your husband. I truly think that you have a bit of the Missionary Spirit in you, otherwise you would not have married such a man who had decided to leave his country and friends."[27]

While Ann Jones's subordinate position was reflected in the seating arrangements (she in the gallery, he on stage), she was publicly accorded status as both companion and co-labourer. Indeed there was an expectation that she would indeed be more than just a helpmeet, and an acknowledgement that she was perhaps animated by a similar religious spirit, the zeal of the true missionary.

While the missionaries were at sea, John Roberts was still contemplating the role of the missionary wife. On 2 December 1840 he wrote to John Wilson, and mentioned that he had given Ann Jones a copy of Wilson's memoir of his late wife.[28] Margaret Wilson was dead within five years of her arrival in India, but far from disappearing from view, her missionary labour was celebrated by her husband in print in 1840. This eulogy to her sacrifice, self-denial and industry, though selectively edited and framed by a grieving husband, stood as an exemplar of the missionary wife not simply as adjunct 'homemaker and friend', but as a co-labourer of independent thought, spirituality, responsibility and action.

Ann Jones, on reading the *Memoir*, may well have aspired to follow in Margaret's footsteps, but must also have feared sharing her fate and the fate of other missionary women before her. Ann had been unwell for most of their voyage, and had lost a baby soon after her arrival in Calcutta. By the time she reached Cherrapunji, she had only marginally recovered, and updates on the state of health were regularly published in *Y Drysorfa*. Through 1842, there were periods, particularly in the wet season, when Jones struggled on his own to cope with his wife's infirmity in the claustrophobic atmosphere of the monsoon: 'my wife has been very ill, and there was no one here to look after her but myself. I have for some time now been confined to the house on account of the rains'.[29] Ann Jones gave birth to a daughter Ann Jane on 10 February 1843, a child who this time was to outlive her.

On 12 August 1845, Ann Jones gave birth to a son. She died of wasting and fever on 22 August after terrible suffering. She had in fact rarely been well 'for a whole day at a time' since she had first arrived in India. The possibilities for the personal happiness let alone the domestic success of the Joneses as models for the natives of the Christian family were clearly frustrated by these circumstances. Jones was devastated. His despair magnified the oppressive isolation of his situation. Left alone 'in this sorry wilderness . . . in the midst of these ungodly natives', he felt a deep personal loss, as well as the loss of the mother of his two small children, though the baby boy was himself to die soon afterwards. Ann's death was for Thomas a release as well as a torture: 'for the last six weeks of her life her agonies were truly dreadful'. Broken by constant sickness, Ann had long since withdrawn herself from the public affairs of the mission: 'You could summarise her religion in three words – her Bible, her room and her God . . . I feel a great loss of her prayers for me'.[30]

For Jones the death of his wife also elicited a more ambiguous commentary, one constructed very much for public consumption:

> you may well imagine that I found it very interesting, and yet terrifying, to listen to her conversations and her words of advice from the brink of eternity! I am not so foolish as to think that my wife had no faults or blemishes; but I can venture to say that there has never been a woman so honest, simple, unostentatious, faithful and devoted to her husband and her Saviour. She so detested all forms of ostentation, pomp and affectation, and she saw so much of it around her, that she was never eager to mix much with other people.[31]

In the light of the animosities between Thomas Jones and the Lewises, it is possible to read his eulogy as being less about his wife and more as an avowal of his own views concerning his co-missionaries. It also appears that in her febrile state, Ann Jones suffered such delirium that she would not permit anyone else in her room but William Lewis – it was he who attended her sickbed rather than Thomas Jones, and he who was the only one with her when she died. Mary Lewis later recalled that 'she would not have any one near her but Mr Lewis, and she used to call him, the little man with the soft hand'.[32]

Lewis's account, which was published alongside Jones's, constructed Ann's death in terms of her role to the end as dedicated mother and model Christian: 'she asked to see her little boy', wrote Lewis, 'and when he was brought in she made a great effort to look at him; but the hand of the "King of Terrors" was upon her . . . A few moments before she died I asked her if she was contented? and she replied "Yes" and her spirit departed without a struggle'. Lewis also took the opportunity of constructing a symbolic reconciliation between the two women: 'I shall never forget how affectionately she squeezed my wife's hand, when she came in quietly to see her'. Ann was buried on a small hill near the mission house; 'there I hope', wrote Jones, 'that my own body will be laid to rest when I depart from it'.

Ann died at half past two in the afternoon. By five o'clock, a large number of Khasis had gathered at the station, and the missionaries took the opportunity to address them in the schoolhouse. William Lewin prayed in English, before some of the Khasi scholars carried the coffin to its burial place, followed by the missionaries, a few of the Europeans from the station, and the school children two-by-two. 'Well, my friend', reflected Lewis to Roberts, 'this is something new and foreign in the history of our little Mission. The Lord seems to be making us at home here, for now we have a place to bury our dead!'[33] A description in 1845 of the burial ground in a generic missionary station in the *Calcutta Review* (edited by Alexander Duff) could have been written for Ann Jones. Where 'almost every European grave in India is the record of an untimely death', for the missionary family the toll was even more exacting, as 'One after another of their slender band is removed; now an infant, now a mother; perhaps the patriarch of the enterprize . . . Each is laid in the quiet enclosure on which his eyes had daily rested; and of the survivors, each reckons on being sooner or later buried there too'.[34]

The mission was an intense emotional landscape, the site of desire, separation and loss, for men as well as women. Ideas and practices of masculinity and fatherhood were also crucial to the evangelical theology of the period in which the language of God-as-father provided a template for authority and obligation within the family.[35] The advice of the Reverend John Hughes, Pontrobert, to Thomas Jones on his departure was embedded with this paternal idea of God: 'There is a great necessity for a missionary to show much affection to those amongst whom he labours; to be friendly and cheerful and yet to keep his distance'.[36] Children were born and children died with regular monotony through the early decades of the British military station and the Welsh mission at Cherrapunji. Such mortality affected men's identities as fathers, as breadwinners and as moral leaders who saw their roles as being to educate, protect and discipline.[37] Many of them were young men embarking on married life at the same time as a new career, and had been set loose from an intensely hierarchical world in Wales where the old lions of their religion still very much held sway. Both Thomas Jones and William Lewis had married just months before sailing to India. After losing their respective wives, Owen Richards and Thomas Jones were also forced to renegotiate their domestic circumstances in a milieu that restricted their social circle, but also freed them to some extent from the social pressures and expectations of home. As Strange notes, 'the death of a wife and mother was thought to precipitate the disintegration of domestic economy and the splintering of the nuclear unit'.[38] Ideas of masculinity, femininity and fatherhood were reworked as the conditions of family life were subjected in the Khasi Hills to isolation as well as a sense of freedom, and confirmed or tested by native contact.

The public role of Ann Jones and Mary Lewis as missionary wives was seen as properly restricted to efforts in female education. 'Will you allow me to suggest here', advised John Roberts to Mary Lewis, 'the propriety of confining your labors to those things which no one can doubt will prove useful to the Cassee girls'.[39] Where Ann Jones had been hampered by the frailties of the body in living up to the invocations of the mission board and the model furnished by Margaret Wilson, Mary Lewis quickly picked up the mantle. Women's work on missions is often seen as being relegated to the private margins and separated from the public narratives of conversion.[40] This is in part, of course, a function of the under-representation of women's letters in mission archives, but it is clear that Mary Lewis, as a missionary in her own right, played a key role in the core business of the mission and in its establishment narratives.

In anticipating her own role in the Bombay mission, Margaret Wilson's self-perceived deficiencies as a woman were countermanded by her faith: 'Though weak in myself, I go forth under the banners of Him who is mighty as the king of his Church'.[41] In her diary of the voyage out to India in July 1842, Mary Lewis similarly articulated the multiple tropes of a paternalistic god, the missionary as his instrument and, self-deprecatingly ('I know there is nothing in one suitable for this great office'), the missionary wife as helpmeet: 'it is my sincere wish to do all things to promote the happiness and comforts of one whom I trust will be a shining light in the dark regions of India'.[42] Mary Lewis's correspondence on the subject of her female school, and in particular about Ka Nabon, the first Khasi woman to be baptised, was also published in *Y Drysorfa*. Six of the first thirteen converts were female, and the Lewises maintained the importance of female conversion to the broader success of their mission. There is an argument that Mary herself maintained the spirit of the mission through the years when her husband became despondent about its progress. She played a key role in the publication of the Khasi New Testament, and translated Bunyan's *Pilgrim's Progress* into Khasi.[43]

An injudicious marriage

The Welsh missionaries had initiated a programme of native education for the Khasis, but Cherrapunji also offered its salubrious location as the setting for an educational institution for the children of Europeans. Aside from Lieutenant Lewin, those other Europeans at the station who attended Ann Jones's funeral in August 1843 may have included Emily Brownlow and her sister Susan Cattell. Emily Mary Halford had arrived in India in 1829, and married Charles Brownlow at St John's in Calcutta the following year. Charles had worked as a clerk and then assistant with Thacker & Co., and later moved to Assam on a business venture, where he died in May 1839 aged thirty-nine.[44] Emily Brownlow's sister Susan Elizabeth Cattell had also recently been widowed after her husband George Cattell, a clerk in the EIC, had died in August 1838.[45]

Emily and Susan issued a prospectus for a new select preparatory school at Cherrapunji, under the patronage of the Governor-General Lord Auckland and his sisters, the Misses Eden, for twenty children up to the age of twelve, to commence on 1 December 1841. If Emily Eden had pictured the Duke of Devonshire's plant collector John Gibson among the savages of Cherrapunji a few years earlier, how much more adventurous were the exploits of two English widows imagined to be in establishing an outpost of civilisation in such a remote location? They had no real formal training as educators, but with eleven surviving children under the age of thirteen between them, their *bona fides* were advertised as 'the general management and instruction of Children'. At thirty rupees a month, with every child 'to be provided with knife, silver fork and spoon, bed linen, towels', Mrs Brownlow's school offered a cheap alternative for invalid officers on the station and other Company officials in Sylhet and the lower provinces who could not afford to have their children educated in Europe.

William Lewin may well have been one of Emily Brownlow's target clients. With a large family to support, he could not afford to send his ten-year-old son Edward even to one of the cheaper English grammar schools, which as the nineteenth century progressed would become the 'nurseries of British national identity for those born overseas'.[46]

In mid-1842 Lewin's children were educated at home in the bungalow at Cherrapunji: 'My occupations in life are compounded of my own studies and the education of my bairns'.[47] Susan Cattell's eldest daughter Emma Jane turned eleven in December 1841, and was most likely a starting pupil in her mother's school. Where Lewin struggled to realise the importance of giving his children a 'socially acceptable education',[48] Mrs Brownlow and Mrs Cattell, as 'very intelligent, discreet young women', could provide stopgap tuition for the children of parents in straitened circumstances.[49] In 1846 the two were still located at Cherrapunji in a list of donors for the orphan institution.[50]

In late August 1845, a week or so after the death of his wife, Thomas Jones went to Calcutta on the advice of his doctor to recover his broken spirit. Jones was also recuperating from the effects of an accident in March when on an expedition with some Khasis to gather herbs for making medicinal tinctures, he had been thrown from a mule and suffered serious injury. Indeed in the months before Ann's death, both she and Thomas had been confined to bed under the care of the Lewises. Mary Lewis had ministered fomentations or hot packs to Thomas's broken ribs, though 'He was never well after this'.[51] In Calcutta, Jones renewed his friendship with other Calcutta-based missionaries and Christian friends, and worked on having the catechism printed and superintending publication of his translation of Matthew's gospel. With Owen Richards recalled in disgrace, the mission board dispatched their fourth missionary couple, Daniel and Ann Jones. Thomas Jones met them in Calcutta and accompanied the new missionaries to Cherrapunji, which they reached on 23 February 1846.

Barely a week after he returned to the hills, Thomas Jones was again suffering from his injuries, and after the onset of the monsoon he repaired to the more comfortable climate of Sylhet. His correspondence with John Roberts had dropped away since his accident and Ann's death, and Roberts was to receive only two letters from him in 1846. Roberts printed excerpts of a letter of 28 March in the July *Y Drysorfa*, anxious to allay rumours that had been circulating in Wales that Jones had asked to be recalled and that the society was to be abolished. The aftermath of the Richards affair was preying on the minds of the mission's supporters as well as its critics. When Lewis's information of Jones's relapse reached Liverpool in November, Roberts was deeply worried: 'I had expected to receive a letter from him by the Mail which has just arrived'.[52] Daniel and Ann Jones stayed with the Lewises at Nongsawlia, and while Thomas was absent in Calcutta and Sylhet, it is unclear who was looking after his three-year-old daughter Ann Jane. What is certain, however, is that while the Lewises were absent for a week at Mawphlang, and without their knowledge, Thomas Jones and

9 Pencil sketch of the mission station at Cherrapunji based on a sketch by the Reverend Daniel Jones.

Emma Cattell were married at Cherrapunji on 16 September 1846 by Anthony Garstin, the chaplain of Sylhet.

Apart from his dealings with Lewin, Lister and Inglis, Thomas Jones rarely mentioned any of the other Europeans at Cherrapunji in his letters, but he would have been well enough acquainted with Mrs Brownlow and Mrs Cattell and their Cherrapunji school, and would certainly have known Mrs Cattell's daughter. Their marriage entry records Emma's age as 'fifteen and three quarters', as if to edge it to something more respectable.[53] Where her sister Emily had five sons, Susan had five daughters to partner. For the mission body at home, however, a Calcutta-born English teenager was utterly antithetical to their image of the role and qualities of the true missionary wife. Here was another seismic scandal waiting to shake the home brethren and to prise open some of the fissures exposed by the Richards affair. Jones's 'injudicious' marriage further distanced him from his fellow missionaries in the Khasi Hills as well as many of his key supporters at home.[54] As Jones well knew – and as Lewis was to later affirm – had Jones entered into such an 'imprudent marriage' in Wales, he would have been expelled not only from the ministry but from church membership altogether.[55] The propriety of marriage was tightly circumscribed among the Welsh Calvinistic Methodists, as with other Nonconformist denominations in Britain.[56] But in India, Jones was out of reach, and from their perspective thumbing his nose at the authority of the Welsh church. In the normal course of events, the Liverpool committee would have got wind of Thomas Jones's marriage by the end of 1846, but over time the official correspondence has been selectively filleted to the extent that any reference to the matter resumes only in August 1847. But it was Thomas Jones's second letter of 1846 – dated 9 December, received by Roberts in February 1847, and reprinted in the March *Y Drysorfa* – that contained other devastating news.

Dissolution

Jones's bold claims for the healthy situation of the Khasi Hills were shattered when with a heavy heart he put pen to paper to convey to John Roberts the news of another crippling blow. Jones had long pointed to the need for other villages to hear the Christian message, and recounted the effect of his preaching at villages such as Nongkrem, where the inhabitants had 'promised earnestly to reject their false gods and their sacrifices and to worship from now on the only true God'.[57] On 5 November 1846 a party comprising Thomas and Daniel Jones, their wives (Emma and Ann), Lieutenant Lewin and his daughter (probably his eldest Jane, now aged eighteen), and Dr George Smyth Mann (Assistant Surgeon to the SLI), set out on a week-long journey to Jowai to select the site for a new mission station in the interior. On their return, Daniel Jones and his wife seemed unwell, and moved into Thomas Jones's former house on the military station. The pair was soon taken with fever, and for over a week Mary and William Lewis, with help from some Khasi women, took turns to come from Nongsawlia to tend them, 'their faces being like fire'. Daniel died on 2 December, aged thirty-three. About an hour before he died, his wife Ann, still feverish, gave birth prematurely to a baby girl, who also succumbed to the illness. When Ann recovered her senses, Daniel and her baby had already been buried in the same coffin in the missionary burial ground. When she was well enough to be moved, the Lewises sewed blankets around her bed and had her carried to their house by some Khasis. Two days after Daniel's death, 'that godly gentleman' Lieutenant Lewin, also died of the same malady.

For the Calvinistic Methodists at home, these travails might easily have been terminal. 'Well, friends', wrote Roberts, 'what shall we then say to these things? [Romans 8:31]. It is better to remain silent, because the Lord did this'. Their God's hand in the setbacks of the Khasi mission might well appear 'dark and mysterious', and some critics of the mission were clearly fixed on Daniel Jones's death as a sign of judgement. But in defending the ongoing viability of the mission, Roberts drew on the fundamental tenet 'Of God's Providence in the Preservation and Government of the World', as expressed in Article 7 of the Calvinistic Methodists' Confessions of Faith that had been adopted in 1823: the wisdom, righteousness and ubiquity of God's providence that 'makes all things work together for good to them that love God'. 'But, even if we have thick clouds between us and his Throne', contested Roberts, 'it is perfectly clear there; and we know for certain that he intended this "for good", like all else that happens to his cause'.[58] In January 1847, when she regained her strength, Ann Jones secured a return passage with the Methodist Captain Hughes on the *Cordelia*, the same ship in which she and her late husband had reached Calcutta a year before. Jane Lewin had already lost her young baby Alfred in April 1846, and after William's death, she left Cherrapunji for good.

What the Lewises had not expected to find on their return from seeing Ann Jones off in Calcutta was the mission station at Nongsawlia in turmoil. Sylhet judge Henry Stainforth had established a farm at Pomreng – for breeding horses and trade in cinnamon, honey and rubber – and installed Thomas Jones as his manager. Jones was to leave Cherrapunji for good, taking with him not only the livestock that Stainforth had purchased and sent on from Sylhet, but also all the Khasi boys from the school. The Pomreng farm did not prosper. According to Mary Lewis's later account, the horses broke their legs falling on the rocks, and tigers took the other stock. Thomas Jones then turned to the lime trade as a means of making money, an enterprise that was to put him in further conflict with Harry Inglis.

Just over a month after Daniel Jones's widow Ann had returned to Britain in mid-June 1847, she wrote to Mary Lewis fresh in the sorrow of her husband's death. Her letter, and another the following month, point to gaps in the surviving official correspondence, but also to the distinct rift that had clearly existed between Mary Lewis and Thomas Jones. Visiting William Lewis's brother in Manchester, Ann dissuaded the Manchester friends from sending any gifts to Thomas and his new wife. Wherever she went, friends of the mission were anxious for her views on Emma Cattell, and she didn't hold back: 'I told Mr Roberts my opinion of him, and her just as plain as I would to you and Mr L'. After her return, Ann Jones had learned of a private letter that was read before the mission board in which Thomas Jones extolled the virtues of his new wife.

> Mr T Jones wrote I may call it a most deceitful & glaring character of his wife . . . I heard from a friend when his letter was read before the Board, that they almost all exclaimed, that such high qualifications were to [*sic*] much to be true. And with his flow of language in the commencement of his letter he quite spoiled all. He said that providence had so highly favoured him in providing him such a partner. He said also that she would be the glory of our mission, and a great many more glaring untruths beside which are not worth naming. I do not know how the man can be so presumptuous towards his faithful brethren. Many have been making great enquiries from me. Some ask if she is a Cassee woman.[59]

The exulted language in which Jones couched his descriptions of Emma had many asking Ann Jones 'if the late Mrs Jones and he lived agreeable together'. Ann Jones's oblique reference in her second letter to an affair between Thomas Jones and Lucy Marsh seem to answer this question in the negative.

John Roberts had become increasingly grieved about Thomas Jones's behaviour, and had now sent instructions to him that all correspondence be countersigned by William Lewis, who was deemed to now be in charge of the mission. Just as the Richards affair had threatened the reputation and viability of the mission, now Jones's behaviour had many home supporters on the verge of withdrawing support. In October Lewis received instructions from a distressed Roberts that Jones was 'to abstain from all interference in the business of the Mission until he hears from me again'. The committee of the WFMS had decided to cease remunerating Jones for his mounting expense claims, and was of the view that 'we should be justified in dismissing him at once from the Society's employ'. The North Wales Board resolved at the Bangor Association in early September to call for the dismissal of Jones, and their decision only needed to be ratified by the next south Wales committee meeting: 'Oh, what a distressing affair it is!', wrote Roberts to Lewis. 'I cannot trust myself to write, or even to think much about it; and were it not for the consoling thought that the work is the Lord's . . . I would at once throw up all connection with the work, and set down quietly to watch for the utter ruination of our little Mission'.[60]

On 6 November 1847, Roberts wrote to Jones 'with feelings of the most poignant distress' to convey the news of Jones's official dismissal as an agent of the mission society, and requesting that any property belonging to the mission be handed over to William Lewis. 'As regards myself', Roberts concluded, 'I am heartbroken on your account'. Not only had the mission authorities taken a dim view of Jones's marriage, his commercial affairs, and even of his servants reportedly desecrating the Sabbath at the Pomreng farm, but they were scandalised at any lack of apparent contrition.[61]

Recovering from a bout of influenza, John Roberts worked late on the evening of 23 December 1847, and it was not until around 2 a.m. on the morning of Christmas Eve that he had drafted three letters, one to William Lewis, enclosed in which were unsealed letters for Thomas Jones and Harry Inglis. Jones had been standing resolute, refusing to hand over the deed of the mission buildings, and other property, furniture, books and articles belonging to the society. He was also demanding expenses of £1529.6.0, as well as £200 to enable him to return to Wales in the event that he could not secure a living in India:

> I had a chance of getting something a few months ago, but as you objected to my receiving the offered assistance, I gave it up to please you, and as soon as I had done that you turn me out, without a house or shelter, or the means of moving any where, and a heavy debt remaining upon me, & withal a broken down constitution, & broken in your service. But you must not think I am going to be disposed of so easily. There is no court of law by which you can ever recover any thing belonging to the Society, for I am under the jurisdiction of no earthly court.

Jones felt betrayed by Roberts, whom he accused of having 'grossly misrepresented' the charges against him. But Roberts chided his threatening tone, and replied with a resolve of his own: 'if you persist in refusing compliance with our request', he warned Jones, 'we shall most certainly – however unpleasant it may be, resort to the most stringent measures that may be requisite to obtain our rights. Notwithstanding all you have said about not being under the jurisdiction of any earthly court, we happen to know that justice can be obtained even in India'. Roberts regretted that out of friendship for Jones and a hope that he would change his ways, he had concealed his knowledge of Jones's conduct from the mission committee: 'Whether I shall continue to keep these matters from my brethren will depend upon yourself'.[62]

John Roberts's threat to Jones was not an empty one; should the recalcitrant agent fail to hand over the mission's property, he should be made aware of the instructions to Inglis contained in the other letter he had penned. If this had no effect, Lewis was instructed to deliver the letter addressed to local magistrate Harry Inglis, 'to solicit your assistance, as the magistrate of the station towards the protection of the Society's property in Mr Jones' hands'.

Notes

1 Charles to O. Richards, 22 February 1843, NLW Thomas Charles Edwards (1)/4705.
2 Charles to O. Richards, 26 April 1843, NLW Thomas Charles Edwards (1)/4706.
3 Ann Laura Stoler, *Race and the Education of Desire: Foucault's History of Sexuality and the Colonial Order of Things* (Durham, 1995), p. 7.

4 Richards to Edwards, 2 November 1843, NLW Thomas Charles Edwards 4712.
5 *Ibid.*
6 'Facts of the case between Mr R & Miss M copied from the original document', [William Lewin], n.d., NLW CMA 27221.
7 Richards to Lewis Edwards, 2 April 1844, NLW Thomas Charles Edwards 4712.
8 Richards, 'A statement of facts relating to the Welsh Missionary Society', [copy], 10 April 1845, CMA 27224.
9 *Ibid.*
10 *Ibid.*
11 *Ibid.*
12 Printed statement in NLW CMA Thomas Charles Edwards 4716.
13 Morris, *The History*, p. 94; Rees (ed.), *Vehicles of Grace & Hope*, p. 187.
14 Joshua Gamson, 'Normal sins: sex scandal narratives as institutional morality tales', *Social Problems*, 48:2 (2001), 188.
15 Jones to Roberts, 8 October 1841, *Y Drysorfa*, January 1842.
16 Jones to Roberts, 29 May 1843, *Y Drysorfa*, September 1843.
17 Ann Jones to Mary Lewis, 4 August 1847, CMA 27221.
18 Lewis to Hill, 15 November 1848, CMA 27221.
19 In NLW CMA Thomas Charles Edwards 4715.
20 Lewin (ed.), *The Lewin Letters*, volume 1, pp. 367–9; H. Grote to F. von Koch, 17 June 1843, Lewin (ed.), *The Lewin Letters*, volume 2, pp. 25–6.
21 Sally Engle Merry, 'Rethinking gossip and scandal' in Daniel B. Klein (ed.), *Reputation: Studies in the Voluntary Elicitation of Good Conduct* (Michigan, 1997), p. 52.
22 *Ibid.*, pp. 53–4.
23 Alan Lester and Fae Dussart, 'Masculinity, "race", and family in the colonies: protecting Aborigines in the early nineteenth century', *Gender, Place and Culture*, 16:1 (2009), 63–75.
24 Natasha Erlank, 'Sexual misconduct and church power on Scottish mission stations in Xhosaland, South Africa, in the 1840s', *Gender & History*, 15:1 (2003), 79.
25 Roberts to M. Lewis, 28 February 1844, CMA 27222.
26 Cox, *Imperial Fault Lines*, p. 5.
27 Supplement to *Y Drysorfa*, 15 December 1840.
28 Roberts to Wilson, 2 December 1840, CMA 28720.
29 Jones to Roberts, 8 September 1842, *Y Drysorfa*, December 1842.
30 Jones to Roberts, [n.d.], *Y Drysorfa*, December 1845.
31 *Ibid.*
32 Mary Lewis, 'A brief narrative', CMA 27222.
33 Lewis to Roberts, [n.d.], *Y Drysorfa*, December 1845.
34 [Lady Lawrence], 'English women in Hindustan', *Calcutta Review*, 4:7 (1845), Calcutta, 1848, p. 99.
35 Broughton and Rogers, 'Introduction'.
36 *Y Drysorfa*, Supplement, 15 December 1840.
37 Broughton and Rogers, 'Introduction', p. 4.
38 Julie-Marie Strange, '"Speechless with grief"': bereavement and the working-class father, c.1880–1914' in Trev Lynn Broughton and Helen Rogers (eds), *Gender and Fatherhood in the Nineteenth Century* (Houndmills and New York, 2007), p. 146.
39 Roberts to M. Lewis, 28 February 1844, CMA 27222.
40 Patricia Grimshaw and Peter Sherlock, 'Women and cultural exchanges' in Norman Etherington (ed.), *Missions and Empire* (Oxford, 2005), p. 175.
41 Wilson, *A Memoir*, 94.
42 Mrs William Lewis, 5 July 1842, Diary of her voyage from Liverpool to Calcutta, CMA 27223.
43 Rees (ed.), *Vehicles of Grace & Hope*, p. 119.
44 *Englishman*, 1 April 1840, in *Friend of India*, 2 April 1840, 213. See also *Friend of India*, 9 September 1841, 566.

45 George Cattell and Charles Brownlow had most likely come out as friends to India around 1820, together with Robert Halford.
46 Buettner, *Empire Families*, p. 154.
47 W. Lewin to G.H. Lewin, 15 July 1842, Lewin (ed.), *The Lewin Letters*, volume 2, p. 15.
48 Buettner, *Empire Families*, p. 167.
49 *Friend of India*, 1 December 1842, 768, 2 February 1843, 80.
50 *Friend of India*, 20 August 1846, 535.
51 Lewis, 'A brief narrative', CMA 27222.
52 Roberts to Lewis, 4 November 1846, CMA 27221.
53 IOR N/1/70/55. The legal marriageable age for girls in England and Wales was twelve, with parental consent.
54 Morris, *The History*, p. 106 uses the word 'injudicious'.
55 Lewis to Micaiah Hill, 15 November 1848, CMA 27221.
56 Kenneth D. Brown, *A Social History of the Nonconformist Ministry in England and Wales 1800–1930* (Oxford, 1988), pp. 173–4.
57 Jones to Roberts, 21 April 1843, *Y Drysorfa*, July 1843.
58 *Y Drysorfa*, March 1847.
59 Ann Jones to Mary Lewis, 21 July 1847, CMA 27221.
60 Roberts to Lewis, 23 September 1847, CMA 27221.
61 Roberts to Jones, 6 November 1847, CMA 27220.
62 Roberts to Jones, 23 December 1847, CMA 27220.

PART IV

The borderlands of law and belief

CHAPTER ELEVEN

The pen and the sabre

In mid-January 1848, Thomas Jones opened the letter from John Roberts informing him of his dismissal as a representative of the WFMS. He could not have been surprised. Roberts had also put in motion auxiliary steps to reel in his rogue agent, and the Christmas letter to William Lewis, with its enclosures to Harry Inglis, would have arrived in Cherrapunji the following month. Lewis had expressed some caution about 'the undesirableness of appealing to the world on matters connected to the Kingdom of Christ', but Roberts was more sanguine about calling on the assistance of the civil authorities in India. Though yet wary of the role that Inglis might play as a party not naturally in full sympathy with the objects of the mission and who might attempt to turn the matter to his personal advantage, Roberts was resolute, determined to take that risk in engaging Inglis to do his bidding.

Lewis had no hesitation in handing over the instructions to Inglis, who at an official level at least excused himself from being involved in what he considered the private affairs of the missionary society.[1] To take this at face value, however, would be to underestimate the extent to which Jones represented a threat to British authority in the hills. It would also underestimate the complex ways in which the Political Agency wielded control over its frontier subjects, Khasi and European. For the WFMS, Jones was now *persona non grata*. For Inglis, Jones represented a threat to his family's private commercial interests. From the point of view of the government, Jones as renegade challenged the effective rule of law. The extent to which these concerns became intertwined, and the implications of this for the authority of the Political Agency in the north-east, had serious ramifications for mission and government alike. Tarnished as a renegade, Jones's ideologies of mission also underwent explicit transformation. What slippages might have existed between the centralised authority and proscriptions of religion, trade and political power, and their everyday actualities and local enactment?

A thousand oranges: the Inglis ascendancy

In November 1841 on a tour of the 'south-eastern frontiers of our wonderful empire', the Right Reverend Daniel Wilson, Bishop of Calcutta, embarked on a 'wild kind of journey' from Chhatak in Sylhet, first in a covered boat, then on the back of an elephant, and finally borne up the scarp on a *tonjon*. At Cherrapunji, George Inglis presented him with the extraordinary gift of a thousand oranges. If the Khasi Hills were the orange bowl of Bengal, the apparent simplicity of the tribute belied the piquant mix of commercial and political power that it symbolised.[2] Over the half a century or so after Scottish-born George Inglis arrived in Sylhet as a twenty year old in 1794, few British residents or visitors to the region would not have come under his family's influence, or been a guest at the Inglis house elevated on its picturesque rise by the Surma River. Dacca judge Henry Walters had breakfasted with the 'respectable lime merchant' at Chhatak in 1828,[3] and the Inglises had facilitated John Gibson's collecting trip in mid-1836. But if oranges were the tangible fruits of the Inglis domain, theirs was an empire built on *chunam*.

The late eighteenth-century British collectors in the Sylhet district – Lindsay and Thackeray – had made their fortunes out of the lime trade. The Company's commercial ascendancy in the region had been assured after the British victory over the Nawab of Bengal at Plassey in 1757. Successive treaties from 1760, including the 1765 grant of *Diwani* under which Sylhet came under Company control, enabled it to wrest control of the lime trade from the Bengal Nawabs. As the lime quarries in the southern foothills of the Khasi range fuelled the development of Calcutta's rapidly expanding building infrastructure, private British merchants soon entered the trade. In 1790 regulations were passed allowing Europeans obtaining a *parwana* from the collector of Sylhet to reside and trade in the Sylhet district. George Inglis teamed up with Henry Thomas Raitt and formed a joint company whose combined capital soon had it securing lucrative government contracts and establishing an effectual trade monopoly. Despite modification of the regulations in 1799 that prohibited trade north-west of the Surma River, lack of enforcement saw the Khasi lime trade flourish. Raitt Inglis & Co. leased quarries at Langrin in the west Khasi Hills from local chiefs at negligible rents, and profited from the mark up on their products. The company gradually expanded its depot at Chhatak, and after Raitt's death, George Inglis became sole proprietor in 1819.[4]

While the ascendancy of the Inglis commercial empire in the Khasi

Hills drove the transition from barter to a cash economy, opened up improved routes for transporting products and fostered the growth of market centres, it also crystallised power struggles between different hills elites.[5] By the early 1820s, challenges to the Inglis monopoly came from the Nongstoin Khasis, neighbours of the Langrin state, who together with *talookdars* of the Laur Hills in Sylhet, one of the three principalities of Jaintia, had attempted to break the Inglis cartel by various measures including intimidation of the labourers at the Inglis quarries. The complex relationships of dependence and exploitation between the Inglis company and local Khasi elites, and the sub-regional political alliances formed to counter them, threatened instability on the north-east frontier. The boundary dispute between Nongstoin and Langrin was soon overtaken, however, by the political contingencies of the Anglo-Burmese conflict after 1824, which saw David Scott's policy of direct intervention through agreements with the rulers of Cachar and Jaintia, and arrangements with the chiefs of Cherrapunji and Khyrim to allow construction of the road connecting Assam with Sylhet. The surreptitious but steady engrossment of the Khasi economy by British commercial interests, and the growing political need to bring any refractory Khasi states under British influence, turned economic blockade into a new and important weapon in the imperialist arsenal.

At his family compound at Chhatak, George Inglis took a local Sylhet girl Bebee Begum (alias Bebee Mary Ann Inglis) as his wife. George and his 'affectionate female friend' had six children between 1798 and 1814,[6] and it was their second son Henry – ubiquitously known as Harry Saheb – who was to join his father in the family business. At the outbreak of the Anglo-Khasi war in 1829, volunteer Harry Inglis played a crucial double role. As an intermediary with Khasi language skills, he sued for their submission with the various intractable chiefs with whom his company had established longstanding relationships. But in so doing, he could also ensure that Inglis & Co. benefited from the terms of such one-sided agreements; when the chiefs of Shella and other tracts in the southern part of the hills surrendered in 1829, they also gave up rights to the British to quarry their lime.

On 10 January 1832, Harry Inglis married Sophia Lister at St John's Cathedral in Calcutta.[7] Her father Lieutenant Frederick George Lister was commander of the SLI, which had been raised in 1824, moved its headquarters to Cherrapunji in 1826, and became one of three units responsible for the military security of the north-east.[8] That his father-in-law was his commanding officer did not appear to be an impediment to his career as a local lieutenant, but government regulations prohibiting its military staff from engaging in commercial enterprises forced Inglis to reluctantly resign his commission in September 1834. When

Inglis licked salt from the sabre of U Tirot Sing in January 1833, he not only sealed a pact that snared the Nongkhlaw *Syiem*, but also his own personal fortunes. At the end of his term in early 1834, outgoing Government Agent T.C. Robertson had no doubts about the crucial role that Lister and Inglis had played in establishing British supremacy in the hills over the period of the Anglo-Khasi war and quelling the martial actions of the 16,000 strong force of Khasi warriors.[9] 'I feel myself bound to name Capt Lister and local Lieut Inglis', Robertson wrote to the government, 'as those to whom I consider myself mainly indebted for being able to make this charge over to my successor in a more tranquil state than it was in when two years ago it came into my hands'.[10]

The interweaving of economic and political power was now complete. The running end of British political control was spliced with the brute everyday exigencies of dominant commercial power to strap the Khasi states over the ensuing decade and a half in an ever-tightening knot of nepotistic enforcement. The efficiency of the Political Agency ultimately strained to breaking point at this troubling nexus of authority; the relationship between Harry Saheb and Padre Jones was to be a critical mechanism in its rupture.

Lister's instructions were somewhat discretionary; the government advised him to intervene in community disputes only in 'cases which had a direct tendency to endanger the Peace of our own Provinces, or the permanency of our arrangements in the Hills'.[11] He was instructed not to be over zealous in bringing to book each and every offence that came under his notice, and to cede a calculated degree of independence to local village chiefs. 'The powers with which you are now vested', he was instructed, 'are certainly somewhat vague, but it can scarcely be otherwise in the case of a country situated and circumstanced as the Cossyah High-lands are'. Inglis was appointed Assistant, with authority to try cases and mete out punishments of up to one year's imprisonment. The government regarded his 'long habits of close and intimate intercourse with the Cossyah Chiefs as eminently fitting him for the above situation'. Inglis was required to relinquish his commercial speculations in lime, but despite the standing rules of the public service precluding its agents from engaging in mercantile speculations, he was allowed as a particular favour to retain his expanding interests in the orange trade.[12] Despite Lister's assurance to the government that his son-in-law would not 'directly or indirectly enter into any trade',[13] Harry's political position directly enabled him to serve his father's commercial interests. In lieu of fines imposed in 1829 by David Scott as punishment for their disobedience to British authority, the Shella chiefs traded a portion of their debt by granting a fifteen-year lease on their orange groves to Inglis.

Lister and Inglis also played a key role in suppressing an 1835 uprising in Jaintia, the largest state in the Khasi confederacy. Inglis used his intimate knowledge of the Jaintia finances, gained through his commercial dealings, to break the *Syiem's* trust and convince Robertson to extract more tribute as part of the British annexation of the Jaintia Hills.[14] The establishment of the Political Agency's civil administration under Lister and Inglis marked the effective transferral of sovereign power from the Khasi *Syiems* to the British, with on the one hand political suasion insofar as British interests were concerned, and on the other the local powers of a magistrate. Petty cases could be dealt with by the traditional Khasi judiciary across the smaller Khasi states such as Khyrim, Nongstoin, Langrin and Nongspung, while serious cases were to be directed to the Sudder Court in Calcutta (the chief court of appeal from the district courts). Any cases concerning British subjects, or any appeals against the disposal of justice in the Khasi states, were directed to the court at Cherrapunji headed by the Political Agent.[15]

The Cherra Court: the borderlands of the rule of law

In March 1848, Thomas Jones moved from Pomreng with his wife and mother-in-law, and built a house at Mawkrih in Mylliem country near Shillong.[16] By September, Lister had forwarded to government a petition from Hajar Singh, the *Syiem* of Mylliem, together with various petitions from a number of his subjects, alleging that Jones had built upon the Shillong land without permission, had oppressed the local *ryots*, and destroyed crops and fir plantations. Jones had been subject to a *moochulka* to the value of 500 rupees not to commit further offences.[17] The dispute escalated a war of words between Jones and Inglis. In his defence, Jones claimed that the whole case had been concocted by Inglis 'for the mere purpose of annoying me'. Jones admitted that he and Mrs Cattell had done 'some trifling damage' to two small areas of cultivation, for which they had already engaged to compensate the *Syiem*. The charges of levying a toll and setting dogs on people, however, were in his view 'absurd and gratuitous'.[18] Jones claimed that Inglis had coached the witnesses and had manipulated the biddable *Syiem* Hajar Singh, 'a mere boy and a tool of Mr Inglis to whom my presence in the interior is not very agreeable, as many of the respectable families in his territory were talking of coming to live close to me, so that I might succour them against Hajar Sing's violence when extorting money from them for what he calls "the company"'.[19] Jones also claimed to have previously entered into an agreement with the *Syiem* for his occupation of the land:

> I am a humble missionary and have been instructing these people for more than 7 years. My object in settling out in the interior, was to set up something like a Moravian Establishment where I could teach these poor people, not only the pure doctrines of the Gospel but also the productive arts and cultivation. And it is not likely that I would do any thing to offend the people whom it is my chief solicitude to please and to collect around me.

Lister and Inglis countered Jones with allegations of their own as to the 'conduct and character of the missionary'.[20] Unlike his 'mild and conciliatory' brethren Lewis and Richards, Jones was accused by Lister of being overbearing in manner, while 'the highly offensive language he habitually used when addressing the people on the subject of their religious superstitions gave much disgust'. Lister reminded the government that Jones had been dismissed from the WFMS, and Harry Inglis underscored his own unblemished record of service: 'my character', he fulminated, 'is slandered by a man an *ex* member of the Welsh Mission, expelled and discharged by his society for disgraceful and improper conduct as is well know to all the community here and discarded even from the society of his colleague the Revd Mr Lewis, and who is at this present moment living entirely on his wits'.[21]

The war of words had become slanderous and brutal. Whatever the merits of either side of the case, in submitting his defence to government Thomas Jones demanded adjudication by an independent person or committee unconnected with the functionaries of the Cherrapunji court. Jones directed a torrent of correspondence to the government alleging the many ways in which Inglis bribed and manipulated his Khasi contacts and perverted the course of justice. The Bengal government had challenged Jones and his Khasi co-complainants to put up or shut up – in other words, to make their allegations against Inglis under oath before the Cherra Court. According to Jones's account, while Lister had at first agreed to take evidence from the Khasis after swearing them in under their traditional solemn oath, on advice from Inglis he simply allowed them to make a 'vague affirmation'. Jones's Khasi witnesses clammed up. The accused Inglis sat on the bench with his father-in-law, who addressed Jones's witnesses 'in a most threatening and angry manner violently striking his fist against the table and with his lips quivering with rage more than once seemed as if he was going to strike me'.[22]

Inhabitants of Cherrapunji and other villages also petitioned Inglis directly with complaints as to his forcible deprivation of their orange plantations,[23] while *Syiem* Sing Manick accused Inglis of bribery and himself admitted to taking payments to obtain favourable decisions.[24] Sing Manick was the chief of the Khyrim territory, a 300 square mile area that contained a dependent population of 116 villages of around 4500 thousand houses, with a total population of approximately 20,000. The *Syiem* had never signed a treaty with the British, and while his dependants were under his own authority, any cases that involved issues of concern to the British government were referred to the Cherra Court.[25]

Now that he was no longer operating under the aegis of the WFMS, Thomas Jones was becoming more individually exposed through the conflict with Inglis. The rumbling controversies in the hills might threaten his missionary purpose, and Jones entered into correspondence with the Calcutta press to explain his actions and shore up support for his operations. In late October 1848 the *Bengal Hurkaru* noted in its editorial that while it was curious that this pioneer of education and language translation had separated from his mission society, he had laboured under greater obstacles than his successors, and his designs for an independent mission and 'industrial establishment' were laudable. Any rumours that may have been circulating in the capital about his morals or motives were minimised with reference to his ethnicity: 'Mr Jones is a Welshman, and probably possesses and displays the warm temper of his race; but, from all we have heard, this is about the worst that his most watchful enemy could say of him'.[26]

His defenders at the *Hurkaru* were matched at the offices of the *Calcutta Christian Advocate*. Here Jones was the epitome of the selfless missionary hero: 'He plunges into the jungle with his wife and children where their lives may at any time be the forfeit of their temerity. Without any prospect or promise of food and raiment, he casts himself upon Divine Providence. He asks for money, not for himself and family: but for the carrying out of his designs of mercy'. Yet there was a caution to Jones that he must ensure that there was 'no moral stain upon his principles, his conduct, and his prudence, otherwise he would scarcely hope that his seclusion from European society in the hills would prevent enquiry into the reasons of his present isolated position'. The paper was more circumspect about Jones's intemperate and in its view unsubstantiated critique of the '*horrid oppression extortion and cruelty*' of government officials. It also counselled him not to believe 'as gospel' the word of 'depraved' and 'semi-barbarous' tribes who may be motivated by a simple desire to evade paying government taxes.[27]

The editor of a third paper, the *Calcutta Christian Observer*, had no wish to buy into the 'painful controversy', but simply laid before its readership the objects of the new scheme.[28] Jones's Pomreng experiment was an attempt to establish a new Christian settlement along explicitly Moravian principles. Jones had become increasingly frustrated with his dependence on voluntary subscriptions from Wales; the Cherrapunji missionaries had struggled for years to evangelise a circumforaneous people who lived in scattered settlements. At Pomreng, Jones wished to isolate the Khasis from their friends and families, and to feed and clothe them as an inducement to attend: 'Not one of the better classes who do not take pay from us have ever stayed long enough to learn any thing of value to them'. Pomreng also had the advantage of being out of reach of the worst effects of the monsoon, though he was contemplating a further move to the east or Jaintia Hills side of the Um Ngot valley.[29] For the moment he had ten boys, eight men and four women, splitting their time between classes and practical labour. One couple had been baptised, and the man conducted services in Jones's absence. Counting Henry Stainforth's employees, there would be around fifty Khasis at Sunday services. Apart from the business relationship with Stainforth, the 772 rupees raised towards the Pomreng experiment were funded primarily through regular donations from Henry Yule and Sylhet civil and sessions judge Fulwar Skipwith,[30] from Jones's mother-in-law Susan Cattell, and from other employees of the Bengal Civil Service. Jones's letter was effectively a call for further subscriptions to fund building works, tools and other supplies for his venture.

The conduct and character of a missionary: Lewis's riposte

The instability of events since 1845, and in particular the fall from the mule which made living at Cherrapunji increasingly difficult during the wet season, were further motivations for a different approach to mission work. Jones had surveyed the Jaintia Hills for a suitable site on the fateful expedition in late 1846 after which Daniel Jones and William Lewin had perished. Jones's vision for a self-supporting Christian settlement of a hundred people emerged from a long-held belief in the Moravian model of Christian settlements, which he claimed had also been suggested to him by John Roberts. In this view, the learning of trades and crafts outweighed theological education, and religious freedom was more explicitly fundamental to the mission model than any overt ties to the colonial state under which they operated.[31]

Jones's appeals to the Calcutta press may have galvanised some of his friends and supporters there, but they also inspired William Lewis to fire off a salvo of his own. In a long letter address to the *Christian Advocate* editor Micaiah Hill (founder of the LMS mission at Berhampore), Lewis wrote that he 'would gladly and forever efface from my memory' the conduct of Jones, but that the recent press articles had moved him to defend the interests of the WFMS. Lewis drew Hill's attention to the cases of missionaries Sylvester Bareiro at Barisal, and the Scot John

Campbell at Calcutta, both of whom were dismissed from the BMS and the LMS respectively, without the true cause being made public. Bareiro was in fact removed 'on a charge of immorality',[32] while Campbell was 'discovered *in flagrante* during his wife's sick leave in Scotland'.[33] In making such covert connections between Jones's behaviour and that of these missionaries, Lewis was suggesting that Jones's indiscretions transcended the mere 'injudicious' marriage with the youthful Emma Cattell. The 'perniciousness & intractability' of Jones's attitude to his mission superiors, Lewis argued, justified his divulging the detailed circumstances of their intimate disagreements and providing Hill with copies of correspondence between John Roberts, Jones and others.

Lewis's letter chronicled the history of disagreement between Jones and his mission superiors over the course of the previous two years, including his imprudent intentions towards Lucy Marsh ('only two or three months after he had consigned the remains of his late wife to the silent tomb'), his marriage to Emma Cattell ('he was more fit to be her parent than her husband'), his alleged desecration of the Sabbath, and his speculative commercial ventures undertaken without the sanction of his superiors. Where Jones's new model of communal mission was a more costly one than that prosecuted at the Cherrapunji mission station, Lewis attributed the 'lamentable change' that came over Jones after his marriage 'to his vain ambition in wishing to conform to Indian etiquette, which was so congenial likewise, to the views & feelings of his young wife, in company with her many relatives here'. Lewis concluded the litany of misdemeanours with a report of the case brought against Jones by the *Syiem* at Shillong. Here too Jones was accused of seeking commercial gain by scouring the hills to secure leases on coal and lime quarries by bribing locals with liquor that he himself distilled at the mission house.

Lewis's artful missive was calculated to counteract any public support for the rogue missionary that may have been growing in the Calcutta Christian establishment. Presented as a catalogue of self-evident facts ('upon the truth of which you may implicitly rely'), the letter was in fact a carefully constructed character assassination raised on technical truths embellished with innuendo and allegation. Lewis's self-professed restraint and regret at having to write to Hill was offset by the length of his denunciation (over 5500 words, including more than twenty exclamation marks), despite his having to 'omit abundance of matter'. As a narrativised chronology of Jones's failings and misdeeds, the letter appealed to claims of universalised moral rectitude, yet Lewis encouraged Hill to be his surreptitious interlocutor. While seemingly confidential ('I beg that you will regard this as a *private* communication to you'), Lewis explicitly encouraged Hill to 'use your customary discretion in making known its contents, to any of our dear Brethren & Christian fellow laborers, in the great mission field of India'.

Lewis's due deference to Hill as 'one of the Patriarchs of Indian Missionaries' reflected the struggle for authority of the continuing Welsh mission in the light of Thomas Jones's renegade actions. This battle for authority was a contest over the hearts and minds of the Calcutta establishment, a carefully constructed web of patronage, validation and sympathy that dated from the earliest days of the Welsh missionary effort. Like Thomas Jones, William Lewis, Owen Richards and Daniel Jones before him, the latest envoy the Reverend William Pryse and his wife were drawn into the Calcutta missionary network as soon as they arrived in late January 1849. They drank tea with Alexander Duff at the house of the superintendent of the Baptist Mission Press, and later took part in a conference at the house of the Reverend David Ewart. The conference drew together over thirty missionaries from Denmark, Switzerland, America, Scotland and England who were working in Bengal and beyond, including Mr Morgan of the Baptists 'to represent dear little Wales with me'.[34] Pryse's somewhat self-deprecatory characterisation of the Welsh is eloquent of the tenuous though determined part that they played in the much larger drama of evangelism in northern India, and therefore of how critical were the sponsorship and benefaction of their more numerous and illustrious brethren.

Even were there no other charges against Thomas Jones save his irregular marriage to Emma Cattell, argued Lewis, his moral character was utterly impugned. His fall from grace was irrevocable and consequential; sin plucked on sin, each minor fall amplified the next in a crescendo of corruptibility. In the eyes of his colleagues, at the very heart of his corruption lay indiscipline, imprudence, the disrespectful tone of his correspondence, and his ultimate defiance of his colleagues and the secretary's attempts to rein him in. Lewis and Jones perhaps individually embodied the theological, institutional and ethnic tensions and particularities of their denomination. Here, Janus-faced, lay the contradiction at the heart of Welsh provincial Nonconformity: on one aspect, conscience-driven even to the point of great individual cost; on the other, mired in the exceptional, autocratic and totalising nature of a church authority with nationalist overtones.[35]

Jones's personal sinfulness thus extended by association, according to Lewis, to the Khasis he had decoyed from the Cherrapunji mission and who had then followed him to Pomreng. In Lewis's view, the Pomreng experiment marked the total repudiation of ecclesiastical obedience: 'they are now establishing the lamentable features of a deadly apostacy! [*sic*]' The nature of the loyalty established between

Jones and the Khasis who followed him, as well as those who stayed at Cherrapunji, is difficult to determine. When the widowed Ann Jones remembered her Khasi charges in correspondence with Mary Lewis, she gave a sense of the personal divisions that had rent the mission station: 'I do not blame Ca Tuber for not asking after me, as that only reflects the bad example of Mr T. Jones, and Emma. I pity the poor natives who are under their pretended instructions'.[36]

Lewis contested the veracity of Jones's commitment to a Moravian model, and was dismissive of the money-grubbing civil servant with whom Jones had teamed up. Lewis did not mention Henry Stainforth by name in his letter to Hill, referring to him simply as someone 'far from being a Christian, being sceptical as to his views'. The reflex antipathy felt by Lewis and the home brethren to any whiff of commercial venture perhaps occluded any understandings of the motivations Stainforth may have had in setting Jones up at Pomreng. The judge's evangelical pedigree, while no guarantee of his personal motivations in India, gives some cause to reconsider the nature of Lewis's attack on the Pomreng venture.

Henry Stainforth was born at Clapham, London, in 1805, and arrived as a writer in India in 1824. After various posts he was appointed officiating civil and sessions judge at Sylhet in 1837.[37] In 1826 he had married Isabella Fraser, and they had at least ten children by the mid-1840s. Stainforth's Clapham connections were not incidental. Henry's mother Maria Baring was the daughter of Sir Francis Baring, an EIC director and chairman. Henry's two brothers Frederick and Francis also saw Indian service, and Frederick married into a family not only noted for its devotion to the Company, but also in the very engine-room of evangelical reform in the late eighteenth and early nineteenth centuries. In 1832, Frederick Stainforth married Eliza Thornton, granddaughter of John Thornton, noted evangelical and friend of Henry Venn. Eliza's great uncle Henry Thornton was one of the founders of the Clapham Sect and the Church Missionary Society (CMS) (1799), first president of the British and Foreign Bible Society (1804), and friend of William Wilberforce (his second cousin). John Thornton, Eliza's brother, married the daughter of Bishop Heber of Calcutta. To further cement the Clapham link, in 1814 Henry Stainforth's sister Harriet had married Church of England abolitionist the Reverend Dr William Dealtry, rector of Clapham and another promoter of the CMS. Far from being the rogue and scamming official on a remote frontier – a characterisation that was mobilised to suit the Welsh mission's disownment of Thomas Jones – Henry Stainforth was another key vector in the complex and unpredictable mathematics of empire. In Stainforth, Jones found an ideologically sympathetic and financially more affluent associate; in Jones, Stainforth could reconcile small-scale commercial advantage with the everyday enactment of evangelical ideology.

The Dunbar Inquiry: rights, obedience and political insubordination

The public and private parry and thrust played out by Jones and Lewis in the Calcutta press in October 1848 was in many ways academic, sealing the complete breakdown in relationships between the WFMS and its progenitive agent. More serious and instrumental proceedings were about to unfold. In November 1848 the government ordered Scottish-born John Dunbar, the Commissioner of Dacca, to proceed to Cherrapunji to investigate the charges against Harry Inglis, who was suspended from duty on full pay pending the outcome of the inquiry. Dunbar was provided with all the petitions, letters and other paperwork relevant to the case; in a letter to his father-in-law, Inglis was keen to get on file one final accusation against the 'malicious and vindictive' character of Thomas Jones, that the missionary had violently beaten one of his domestics, an accusation that had originated in correspondence from a mission member back in Wales, who could only have been Owen Richards.[38]

Dunbar's findings were the consummate act of political compromise and diplomacy. Inglis was acquitted on all charges, but the report censured the fact of his having powers as a magistrate (together with his father-in-law) over people over whom at the same time he exercised (together with his father) a trade monopoly of their lime and orange groves. Pencilled marginalia in the Political Department records back in London are less circumspect than any official documentation: 'Is it to be believed that exercising a monopoly for 15 years against the interests of many cultivators & with political and [magistracy] power in his hands, that there should not have been an abuse of these powers?'[39] Thomas Jones's disputed right to settle at Shillong was approved under Act IV of 1837 which allowed British subjects to hold property in Company lands, as it was held that the Mylliem territory was under the jurisdiction of the Company for the purposes of the act. In light of the compromised position in which Inglis found himself, Dunbar recommended he be transferred to another appointment. Inglis resumed his post in April 1849, but was given six months from 1 December 1849 to draw his official duties to a close.[40]

Dunbar's investigation did not quell the unrest in the north-east. From the Jaintia Hills came further complaints about Inglis's methods. In February and March 1849, villagers of Nartiang complained that the Political Agent had sent a party of *sepoys* to detain thirty or forty of their headmen and spiritual guides, and had prevented others in the Jaintia Hills from giving evidence against Harry Inglis.[41] A decade and a half before, Inglis had licked salt from U Tirot Sing's sabre as a gesture of honour. As Thomas Jones now acted as scribe for the Khasi complainants, they touched the pen he wrote with as their own sign of trust. Local systems of authority had disintegrated; according to custom, the *doloi* or local Khasi village headman was elected by the villagers, and enjoyed certain privileges such as the collection of particular duties and access to special paddy crops. While in usual circumstances a good *doloi* could be re-elected and a bad one deposed, the current despotic *doloi* had under Inglis's influence held the position for nearly six years. Twenty-eight Khasis travelled a day and a half from Nartiang to Thomas Jones's house at Shillong to touch his pen. The March document was written at Pomreng, a day's journey from their village, and fifty-one villagers put their hands on Jones's pen to attest to 'this outrage on our civil and religious rights'. Jones was aware that it was his word against the word of Inglis, whose interpreters he also accused of being in his pay. Jones made a clear distinction between the actions and motivations of Inglis and his father-in-law, the latter whom he regarded as an honourable man blinded by his family connection. The government in Calcutta still took no action.

Towards the end of April 1849, an entourage of around thirty men from the village of Jowai left for Sylhet with a band of music, with the purpose of bringing back with them in triumph the ex-Rajah of Jaintiapur, who was to be reinstated to his hill possessions. This act of political insubordination openly defied the direct orders of Oosing Duly, the headman of Jowai. Rumours were abroad that the people of the Jaintia Hills were no longer required to obey the orders of the EIC emanating from the Cherrapunji Court, and that from henceforth any matters would be adjudicated by the *Syiem* Sing Manick and Thomas Jones. Defendants later interrogated by Assistant Political Agent Inglis revealed Thomas Jones's hand in the affair. U Het, Jones's personal servant of two years, along with a number of other sworn witnesses, deposed that the order to publicly proclaim that the Company had no further authority in the hills had come directly from his trusted master Thomas Jones in Sylhet.[42]

In late 1848, three petitions had been presented to Inglis at the Cherrapunji Court from *ryots* in the Jaintia Hills. Oohet Dulloy and Sajur Patter of Maskut and Ookat Cassiah of Mukhla accused a number of the *ryots* of the Khyrim *Syiem* Sing Manick with forcibly plundering their paddy crops. Proof of the crimes was adduced at a preliminary inquiry, and warrants issued to *sepoys* for the arrest of fifteen men. By then the suspects had gone to ground under the protection of the

Syiem, and in defiance of Lister's authority, despite five official letters demanding that the men be delivered to the court. On 1 June 1849, a frustrated Lister wrote to the Governor of Bengal with an update on the case. Lister noted that letters sent to him from Sing Manick containing counter claims of the destruction by order of Harry Saheb of the crops of eighty of his own *ryots*, letters countersigned by Thomas Jones as his *mooktear*, were not only 'subterfuge' but indicated that Jones 'is doing all in his power to incite the people to insurrection'. To suppress any possibility of disturbance in the hill territories, Lister recommended an economic blockade of the bazaars in Sing Manick's territory.

Lister argued to the government that if there was any truth in the counter claim of the *Syiem* of Khyrim, he should have laid it before Commissioner Dunbar's inquiry; Sing Manick maintained in December 1848, however, that he had advised his *ryots* not to complain about the damage to their crops until his own claims of bribery against Harry Inglis had gone before the court: 'The Officer who will try this case is Defendant in the case I have instituted and if he has the trying of the case how will he do so impartially?' At the end of April 1849, Sing Manick complained to Lister that while Dunbar had investigated the bribery claims against Inglis, he had not extended the terms of his inquiry to a range of other complaints against him. Having lost confidence in the independence of the Cherrapunji Court, the *Syiem* had bypassed its authority and sent a *durkhast* drawn up by Thomas Jones directly to the government in Calcutta to have it adjudicate in the dispute over the destruction of the crops.

The Political Agency read the crisis of authority between the lines of correspondence that were criss-crossing the territory. Lister was suspicious of Manick Rajah's oppositional attitude, and read Thomas Jones's hand in the *Syiem's* intransigency. Curious that the letters he was receiving from the Jaintia Hills were in fact sent by the Sylhet *dâk*, and observing subtle breaches of formal epistolary protocol (omission of the usual forms of address: 'in letters received from you formerly, each began with "Your obedient" followed with your name and title & Country'), Lister demanded that in future all correspondence should be structured in the appropriate form, and not improperly devised by a third party.

The government's response to the issues contained in Lister's letter of 1 June was unequivocal. Deputy Governor Sir John Hunter Littler upheld the findings of the Dunbar inquiry and saw no need for any further investigations. Sing Manick was to be informed that his contumacy and improper style of communication was viewed by the government with extreme displeasure, and that should he not show 'voluntary obedience' to British authority, that any 'coercive measures' deemed necessary by Lieutenant-Colonel Lister (without the need for further reference to government) would be fully justified. By July the Political Agency had taken possession of Khyrim country. Sing Manick was arrested and fined 1500 rupees before being allowed to return to his people.[43] While imprisoned in a small hut near Inglis's house, the *Syiem* had made accusations against Henry Stainforth, discrediting the judge and Thomas Jones. 'If ever the rajah becomes a free agent', claimed Stainforth, 'I am confident that he will admit that he was compelled to present the petition and that its particulars are false'.[44]

Littler also noted that he was in receipt of the petition from Thomas Jones, and hoped 'that Mr Jones will see the wisdom of ceasing to excite any of the wild people of the Cossiah Hills into opposition to your authority; if, as there is too much reason to believe, he has entered upon such a course'.[45] Littler considered that the 'paramount political considerations' of possible insurrection in the Khasi Hills demanded a decisive action against Thomas Jones. He 'reluctantly' gave Lister an order to resurrect provisions of the *Charter Act*, which might be used to constrain entry into India by British subjects, and to ascertain whether Jones had a licence to reside 'in our more newly acquired possessions'. The *Government of India Act 1833* had restricted the Company's trade privileges, and also opened India up to the ingress of Europeans, a change in policy that had materially assisted the access of missionaries to Company territories. Under Section 81 of the Act, a licence was not required for residence at 'any port or place having a Custom-house', but was technically required for residence in the interior. There is no evidence to suggest that Thomas Jones had either sought or been granted such a licence when he arrived in India, suggesting that the law was a discretionary instrument when it came to residency requirements. If Jones had been granted a licence, Littler recommended to Lister the possibility of its recall.[46]

Thomas Jones's manifesto: coercion, oppression and native rights

On 25 May the *sirdars* of Sohbar, a village just south of Cherrapunji, petitioned against the corruption and nepotism of the Cherrapunji Court. Their attempts to take their complaints to Calcutta had been thwarted: 'on account of the violent and unlawful acts of Col. Lister and Mr Inglis we have not been able to go further than Sylhet; they have seized and carried away those intending to come down with us and we were threatened by Mr Inglis people that we would be killed on the way if we attempted to go down so we dare not go ourselves'.[47] The central government remained resolute in support of its local officials, regretting that villagers had 'allowed themselves to be so misled as to set themselves up in opposition to the constituted authorities'.

On the same day that Littler sent orders to Lister, he also directed a letter to Thomas Jones. On 31 May Jones had sent from Sylhet a lengthy petition to the government of India.[48] It was a manifesto of sorts, a declaration of principles from a British subject living in the Khasi Hills in which Jones formed his own narrative of his history in the hills over the previous eight years, and weighed the gravity of the position he had taken against the government against his own methods, motivations and above all his moral principles. To his Welsh missionary brethren he was *persona non grata*, to the Calcutta officials a renegade, to the Political Agency an agitator who threatened the edifice of political and commercial interests they had spent decades building. Jones's intermediate status between church and state, which had for so long allowed him to prosper his cause as a mediator of native affairs, now left him vulnerable.

His eight years in the hills 'mixing freely with the natives' and able to speak their local dialects had given him the opportunity to observe at close quarters the extent of corruption and oppression visited on 'the poor comparatively innocent Kassias' by the venality of 'Mr Inglis and his underlings under an official cloak'. Jones argued the case that Khasi complaints of corruption had become so widespread and vociferous, and were established as corroborated facts, that he could not fail to hear the clamour against coercion and repression: 'as no other European knew what I did, I felt it to be my duty to bring their grievances to the notice of Govt'. Jones was fully sensible of the risk of pitting himself against the legally constituted authorities, and the difficulty in proving any of his accusations 'against a man of such vast resources, wealth & power as Mr Inglis – wielding as he has always done, through his father-in-law the supreme authority on the Hills'. When any allegations were raised or inquired into, Khasi witnesses were simply bribed or intimidated, while 'the other Europeans at Chirra would either think and believe in the same way as their commanding officer and the Head of Society at the Station, or else keep neutral when the time came for speaking out'.

In deciding to advocate for the 'poor Mountaineers' who had come to him with their complaints, Jones identified with the cause of 'thousands of oppressed Kassias whose welfare is inseparable from mine', and assumed personal responsibility as their spokesman (on behalf of 'me and my people'):

> I am only one to be inconvenienced but if I shall thereby be prevented from taking an active part in the cause of these people there will be some 200,000 comparatively innocent & upright people helplessly consigned

> to the most remorseless oppression. Any damages Mr Inglis could get from me would be only as the dust of the balance compared with what he will lose if the Kassias get justice.

As their self-appointed champion, Jones was also a reluctant and anxious one ('I hesitated a long time'), fearful of the consequences to his own safety, distracted from his missionary operations and financially distressed. Jones's petition was not a general ideological plea for native rights under colonialism, but a critique of the specific application of the general rule of law. As such it appealed to a broad discourse of truth, personal duty, moral courage and obligation. As a broad truth claim, he had expected the trust and reliance of government in reviewing the merits of the case:

> I feel as firmly convinced of their truth as I do of my own existence and it would be a far less violation to my mind and senses to doubt the existence of the Council and Govt of India than to doubt the truth and reality of the complaints of the Kassias: so firmly am I convinced that were it possible I would not hesitate to risk my eternal destiny upon it. With so much irrefragable evidence before me I felt that if I kept silent I would be a partaker of the sins of their oppressors and totally unworthy of the name of a benefactor of the suffering Kassias as well as inconsistent with my professions as a Missionary of the Gospel.

In the eyes of the Calcutta authorities, however, an overt attack on local authority was a threat to their supreme authority in India.

Inglis had been acquitted by the Dunbar inquiry, and though he was later to relinquish his post as Assistant Political Agent, his return to interim office occasioned anxiety on the part of his opponents for the retribution the Cherrapunji Court might visit on its detractors. Lister had already imprisoned a number of Jones's allies, and others feared that they would share a similar fate when Inglis returned to Cherrapunji. Together with a number of Khasis who intended to accompany him in taking their case directly to officials in Calcutta, Jones sought refuge in Sylhet under the protection of the magistrate. Other potential allies were harried: 'two of my most important witnesses were carried away and the rest all fled to the jungles, many of whom I hear have since been arrested, and it is impossible for me to get evidence to defend the case'. There was little doubt in his own mind and in that of the government that Jones was a man on the run. With warrants issued for the arrest of any of Jones's supporters, *sepoys* and police *peons* scoured the hills, and Inglis's men were stationed at Sylhet and on the river route to intercept any deputation to Calcutta. Jones was cornered; incapable of effectively communicating with the hills, he was also unable to get witnesses to Calcutta to defend Inglis's actions against him. Jones had feigned travelling to Cherrapunji but had slipped out of the hills down a by-path. Trapped in Sylhet, Jones concluded his petition with an appeal to the government to appoint a new and impartial court to whom the Khasis could take their cases.

Deputy Governor Littler's response was swift and unambiguous.[49] He again upheld the findings of the Dunbar inquiry, restated the government's confidence in its two long-serving and loyal officers, and informed Jones that he would issue no such orders for an alternative local authority. The word of a renegade could not undermine the government's belief in its own authority let alone its own existence. Jones had insinuated in his petition that the government was protecting the Cherrapunji Court, 'more specially as they presume on the friendship which is supposed to exist between the present Deputy Governor and Mr Inglis'. The exact nature of this relationship is difficult to determine; the sixty-six-year-old Littler had only recently taken up the position as Deputy Governor in March 1849, but it is clear that Littler, Inglis and Lister had been acquainted for at least a decade. Between 1838 and 1841, Littler had been commanding officer of artillery and other regiments headquartered at Sylhet, at the same time that Lister commanded the SLI at Cherrapunji. Two of Littler's children had been born at Sylhet in 1838 and 1841; John Mount Stewart Littler was baptised at Cherrapunji on 12 November 1841 by John Henry Pratt, domestic chaplain to Daniel Wilson, on the same visit during which George Inglis had presented his gift of a thousand oranges to the Lord Bishop of Calcutta.[50]

On 14 June Thomas Jones sent a further petition to the government of Bengal, repeating much of the substance of his previous complaints against the nepotism of the Cherrapunji Court and incompatibility of the lime and orange interests of Harry and George Inglis with the dispensation of justice across the hills.[51] The 'state of the Kassias', Jones wrote, 'is quite an anomaly for the nineteenth century their hardships and grievances are so many and of so serious a character that few will believe that such oppression can exist in any country under British rule and influence'. The 10,000 Khasis who had some connection with the Inglis trade monopoly were completely compromised in their ability to secure justice: superstitiously fearful of the Company and in the thrall of its agents; ignorant of the workings of a British legal system conducted in an unfamiliar form and an unknown language; and having succumbed in part to the deleterious influence of European and plainspeople so that they 'are more like demons incarnate than men'. For Jones the situation was 'monstrously absurd, so scandalous to the British name, that I cannot believe that Government can have properly understood the case'. The challenge to government was to consider who was civilised, and who was savage: 'Barbarians as the Kassias may be considered they have never been sufficiently barbarous to tolerate such a thing among themselves'.

For Jones, the connection and equilibrium between familial self-interest and objective arbitration had been 'destroyed by the catastrophe of Eden'; hence the development of a legal system 'to arbitrate between contending interests and to prevent the powerful from crushing and oppressing the weak'. Still the government in Bengal gave no orders. More threatening for Jones, not only did the government deny his petitions, but Littler also offered him a stern and ominous caution:

> The Deputy Governor has seen reason to believe that you have entered upon a course of exciting a part of the wild people of the Hills to set themselves in opposition to the Govt, of which Col Lister is the Representative and Agent. Such a course of conduct may have results so serious to the misguided people, who are practised upon, that whatever may be necessary to check it must certainly be done. I am directed to take this opportunity of warning you, that the Agent will be supported by Govt in any lawful measures that may become necessary in order to check this course. If such measures shall involve consequences serious to you after this warning, you will only have your own misconduct to blame.

Civilised and savage: an endgame

Jones had already complained in his petition of the heavy handed way that the Cherrapunji Court was pursuing warrants for himself and his followers. At some point after the charges had been levelled against him at Mawkrih near Shillong, Jones had moved his family back to the property at Pomreng. Four weeks after Lister had received the effective imprimatur from government to use whatever force deemed necessary to counter the obdurate Jones, a group of *sepoys* from the Cherrapunji Court came to Pomreng looking for Jones.

In a petition to the government dated 30 July 1849, Emma Jones gave her version of events. A *burkendaz* and half a dozen *sepoys* had gone to Pomreng on orders from Lister to deliver a letter to Emma's husband on the matter of whether he had a licence to reside in the hills, and to bring him to Nongkrem. The contingent surrounded the house, and finding Emma holed up inside with her mother Mrs Cattell, and sisters Ellen (fourteen), Emily (twelve) and Maria (ten), they smashed down the door and forcibly entered. Thomas Jones was not at the house ('as Mr Jones' health was not very good and as a mauling by the Chirra Police and Sepoys was not likely to improve it'), but the *sepoys* were not convinced. The women were terrified, Jones's servant U Het was brutally beaten, and although the intruders had no warrant from Lister, every door in the house was broken in the search for the missionary. Emma claimed that the men had told her that it was 'Colonel Saheb Bahadoor's hurcaru to break open every door in the house'.[52] As his men trashed the house, the *burkendaz* teased the frightened family: 'where can they go to complain?'

In addressing the higher authorities, Emma Jones stood by the claims of her beleaguered husband about the injustices meted out to the Khasis over the previous decade. 'If we had been thus barbarously attacked by cannibals and savages', she argued, 'we would not have been surprised & we would not have troubled Government about the matter, but when we are thus outraged by the Government Servants we have a right to expect protection'.[53] Lister later denied having given such orders. In lieu of capturing Jones, Emma's brother Eugene Brownlow Cattell along with the rest of the Khasi servants were arrested and taken to Nongkrem. On 18 August, the government ordered an inquiry into the complaints. Lister took evidence in the case against himself and his representatives at his own house, and sent his report to government on 1 October. While finding the statements of various parties 'conflicting and unsatisfactory on many points' and concluding that that the evidence of Mrs Cattell and her daughters 'cannot be implicitly relied on',[54] the Cherrapunji Court did find that the *burkendaz* had exceeded his orders, and he was later sentenced to six months imprisonment and dismissed from government service.

Three days after Lister's posse had terrorised his family, Thomas Jones sent the Political Agent a response to the letter they had over-enthusiastically delivered to his wife on the matter of his licence to reside in the Khasi Hills:

> I have never had any license to live in any part of the world excepting the implied one from my creator by his having caused me to exist upon the Earth, and the devil has been trying to deprive me of that for the last twelve months.
>
> I have no authority for having been in this particular part of the Earth excepting the command of my Lord to teach all nations, and this nation being without a Teacher I considered it my duty to obey, and my occupation is serving him, in that capacity.[55]

The next day he wrote again to Lister with a request that Sing Manick be treated considerately 'notwithstanding he complained against your son in law'. Jones also informed Lister that he was necessarily avoiding the police under fear for his own physical safety ('as it would be but a poor satisfaction to me after being maltreated and beaten to be told that the man exceeded his orders'), but that he would 'not conceal myself from you or any other Gentleman and I shall never shrink from the consequence of any of my acts'.[56]

It is unclear what happened to Jones through August and early September. He was still on the run and pursued by *sepoys* from the Cherra Court, and according to a later recollection of Mary Lewis, contracted jungle fever and made his way to the house of the Reverend William Robinson, a Baptist missionary and the Inspector of Government Schools in Assam who lived at Dacca.[57] Robinson had commiserated with William Lewis the previous year on Jones's 'defection',[58] but it is clear that he and Jones had been well known to each other and shared an interest and expertise in native languages. Robinson's article on the languages of Assam and the adjacent hill territories, published in the *Journal of the Asiatic Society* in March 1849, was explicitly indebted to Jones for the Khasi vocabulary it contained.[59] Jones sufficiently recovered his strength at Dacca to then make his way to Calcutta.

Where William Lewis's letter to Micaiah Hill had painted Jones as a worldly and corrupted man lurching from one egregious error to another and sapped of moral stamina, Jones's own accounts of his activities during 1848 and 1849 assert an explicit and 'conscious separation' from the WFMS whose methods he saw as insufficient. His aim to educate the Khasis in a self-supporting community in the interior became bound up in a desire to ameliorate their economic and social condition, which put him at odds with the man whose corruption and oppression he attempted to document. Under protection in the territory of *Syiem* Sing Manick, he also found one of the few local rulers willing and able to resist the complex net of British commercial and political hegemony: 'he is the only chief on the Hills who has sufficient moral courage to withstand the evil machinations of the Cherra court'. Jones paid the price for exposing colonialism's guilty conscience, whereby the morality of the church and the rule of British law were proven to be historically elusive concepts and far from absolute truths.

The surviving correspondence between Roberts and Jones ends with the Christmas letter of 1847, and Roberts's subsequent letters to Lewis, if they mentioned Jones at all, were preoccupied with recouping the money and property owed to the society. New missionary William Pryse wrote to John Roberts on 18 September with an update on the progress of the mission, and the report was published in the January 1850 edition of *Y Drysorfa*. If they had not already learned from rumour, the brethren in Wales read the one brief sentence at the end of Pryse's report about an occurrence on 16 September in the Calcutta house of the Reverend Ewart of the Free Church of Scotland: the Reverend Thomas Jones was dead.

Notes

1 H. Inglis, memo, March 1848, IOR P/143/30, 23 August 1848, No. 62.
2 W. Crawford Bromehead, *A Short Account of the Lives of the Bishops of Calcutta* (Calcutta, 1876); John N. Norton, *Life of Bishop Wilson of Calcutta* (New York, 1862), pp. 286, 287.
3 Walters, 'Journey across the Pandua Hills', 499.
4 Rita Dorothy Dkhar, 'The Inglis and Company and the lime trade in the Khasi Hills', PhD thesis, The North Eastern Hill University, Shillong, 1987.
5 *Ibid.*, pp. 303–30.
6 George Inglis will, made 28 January 1843.
7 IOR, N/1/33 f.15. On Sophia's birth certificate in 1813 no mother is listed, and she was possibly also Anglo-India.
8 Ian Heath, *The North-east Frontier 1837–1901* (Oxford, 1999), p. 12.
9 As estimated by Heath, *The North-east Frontier*, p. 18.
10 Robertson to C.E. Trevelyan, 28 February 1834, IOR F/4/1506/59036, No. 38.
11 Extract Political Letter from Fort William, 13 July 1835, F/4/1549/61881.
12 IOR F/4/1555/63494, Extract 7 February 1835, Governor-General to Lister; IOR F/4/1583/64358, Extract Political Letter from Government of India, 15 February 1836.
13 Lister, 21 March 1835, to W.H. Macnaghten, IOR F/4/1583/64358, extract Fort William Political Consultation, 6 April 1835.
14 Dhkar, 'The Inglis and Company', p. 134.
15 Giri, *The Khasis*, pp. 102–7.
16 Rendered as 'Mowkrap' in correspondence, located on the road from 'Moolleem' to 'Moroprem'. 'I have fixed upon going to live near "Shillong" on the road from "Sadew" to "Jewduh" and about half way between the two latter places': Jones to Inglis, March 1848, IOR P/143/30, 23 August 1848, No. 62.
17 Complaints preferred by the Rajah of Moleem and his subjects against Mr Jones, Letters to/from the Court of Directors in the Judicial Department of the Government of Bengal, Volume 31, Nos. 79–81, 10 October 1848, WBSA; Lister to Halliday, 7 September 1848, IOR P/143/24, 10 October 1848, No. 79. The translation of Hajar Singh's petition was vouched for by Lister.
18 Jones to Lister, 12 August 1848, IOR P/143/30, 14 March 1849, No. 62.
19 Jones to Halliday, 21 August 1848, IOR P/143/30, 14 March 1849, No. 57.
20 Lister to Secretary to Government of Bengal, 23 August 1848, IOR P/143/30, 14 March 1849, No. 60.
21 Inglis, 19 August 1848, 23 August 1848, IOR P/143/30, 14 March 1849, No. 62.
22 Jones to Halliday, Secretary to Government of Bengal, 18 October 1848, IOR P/143/30, No. 69.
23 See for example Petition from proprietors of Cherrapunji orange groves, 8 September 1848, IOR P/143/30, 14 March 1849, No. 64; Petition from inhabitants of 12 villages on the Boga Panee, 18 September 1848, IOR P/143/30, 14 March 1849, No. 68; Jones, 18 and 25 October 1848, IOR P/143/30, 12 March 1849, No. 69.
24 Rajah Sing Manick, n.d., IOR P/143/30, 14 March 1849, No. 72.
25 See Lister to Secretary of Government of Bengal, 9 October 1849, IOR P/143/39, 24 October 1849, No. 128.
26 *Bengal Hurkaru*, Weekly Supplement Sheet, 28 October 1848, 483.
27 *Calcutta Christian Advocate*, 28 October 1849.
28 *Calcutta Christian Observer*, November 1848, 515–19.
29 The village of Pomreng no longer exists but was located to the east of Puriang and roughly equidistant between Nongkrem and Nartiang, on the west side of the Um Ngot valley. The location is near the present-day village of Mawber, and is noted on 'Map of part of the Khasi Hills', Plate VII of Thomas Oldham (ed.), *Memoirs of the Geological Survey of India*, volume 1 (Calcutta, 1859).
30 Henry Yule's second marriage in 1877 was to Mary Wilhelmina Skipwith, daughter of Fulwar Skipwith (civil and sessions judge at Sylhet). Writing to Colonel T.H.

Lewin in 1885, Yule recalled 'my good mother-in-law, Mrs Skipwith (who was, like myself, a friend of your Uncle William Lewin at Cherrapoonjee': Lewin (ed.), *The Lewin Letters*, volume 2, p. 355.

31 Colin Podmore, *The Moravian Church in England 1728–1760* (Oxford, 1998); Stephen Neill, *Christian Missions* (Harmondsworth, 1964), p. 237.

32 H. Beveridge, *The District of Bákarganj: Its History and Statistics* (London, 1876), p. 261.

33 Jackson, 'From Krishna Pal to Lal Behari Dey', p. 182.

34 Pryse to Roberts, *Y Drysorfa*, May 1849, July 1849.

35 Brown, *A Social History*, p. 11; Simon Goldsworthy, 'English Nonconformity and the pioneering of the modern newspaper campaign', *Journalism Studies*, 7:3 (2006), 394.

36 A. Jones to M. Lewis, 4 August 1847, CMA 27221.

37 Prinsep, *A General Register*, p. 357.

38 Inglis to Lister, 21 October 1848, IOR P/143/30, 14 March 1849, No. 81.

39 Signed 'H.S.'. IOR E/4/807, Political Department, London, 3 January 1851.

40 Giri, *The Khasis*, pp. 119–21; Commissioner of Dacca, 5 February 1849, IOR P/143/30, 14 March 1849, No. 91.

41 Petitions of inhabitants of Nartiang, 20 February 1849 and 13 March 1849, IOR P/143/31, 11 April 1849, No. 107; 18 April, No. 82. Petition from T. Jones, 4 June 1849, IOR P/143/34, 11 July 1849.

42 Lister to Secretary to Governor of Bengal, 1 June 1849, IOR P/143/34, 11 July 1849. P/143/33, 20 June 1849, No. 30 and enclosures, from which evidence cited in the following paragraphs is drawn.

43 Lister to Secretary of Government of Bengal, 9 October 1849, IOR P/143/39, 24 October, No. 128.

44 H. Stainforth, 4 October 1849, IOR P/143/39, 24 October 1849, No. 121.

45 J.P. Grant to Political Agent, Cossiah Hills, 20 June 1849, IOR P/143/33, No. 126.

46 3 & 4 Wm IV C. 85 Sec 81.

47 Sirdars of Sohbar Poonjee, 25 May 1849, IOR P/143/33, 20 June 1849, No. 127.

48 Petition of T. Jones to Government of India, 31 May 1849, IOR P/143/33, 20 June 1849, No. 135A.

49 J.P. Grant to Jones, 20 June 1849, IOR P/143/33, No. 135B.

50 IOR N/1/60/184.

51 Petition from T. Jones to Government of Bengal, 14 June 1849, IOR P/143/34, 11 July 1849, No. 79.

52 *Bahadoor* was a title commonly appended to the name of European officers. Yule and Burnell's *Hobson-Jobson* (p. 48) noted that 'In Anglo-Indian colloquial parlance the word denotes a haughty or pompous personage, exercising his brief authority with a strong sense of his own importance'.

53 Petition of Emma Jones and other British subjects of the Kassia Hills, Pomreng, 30 July 1849, IOR P/143/39, 24 October 1849, No. 131.

54 Lister to Secretary to Governor of Bengal, 1 October 1849, IOR P/143/39, 24 October 1849, No. 133.

55 Jones to Lister, 26 July 1849, IOR P/143/35, 8 August 1849, No. 59.

56 Jones to Lister, 27 July 1849, IOR P/143/39, 24 October 1849, No. 133A.

57 Lewis, 'A brief narrative', CMA 27222.

58 Robinson to Lewis, 4 September 1848, CMA 27221.

59 Robinson, 'Notes on the languages'.

CHAPTER TWELVE

The refulgent cross and the heathen carnival

The core questions of this book have been to determine something of the nature of British imperialism in the Khasi Hills, and to explore the ways in which the motives and expectations of its various agents were interconnected. As a study of elements of Christian religious belief and practice, the book's final chapters will use Thomas Jones's alienation and demise as the turning point around which the evangelism of the Calvinistic Methodists may be further measured. As an analysis of the micro-politics of British intervention and hegemony in north-east India, the Political Agency can be placed as a transitional period of British sovereignty over an indigenous polity. If the force of empire is more carefully to be measured in its aftershocks, the book will finally track the active fault lines and residual stresses that were the personal legacies and mythologies of this imperial epicentre.

'Something other than I was': religion, control and autonomy

'Poor Thomas Jones! With all his faults – and they were many – we would not speak harshly to him . . . Was he not the Society's first messenger to the heathen?'[1] Morris devotes less than two evasive pages of his history to Thomas Jones's fall. Of most concern was the knowledge that Jones had died in a state of grace with the hope of personal salvation. David Ewart had taken the sick missionary into his Calcutta house, and over a period of some days had nursed his illness and witnessed his passing. In a letter to the mission directors, Ewart narrated Jones's good Christian death. The Scottish minister had questioned Jones as to his wayward actions, his poor judgement and his lack of forbearance, and Jones seemed to hold out the prospect of reconciliation with his brethren. 'I know him to have been a man of God, an earnest and zealous missionary', assured Ewart. 'I have good reason to believe that he died as a Christian minister . . . He several times expressed a desire to live . . . He seemed to think that some things wanted explanation'.[2]

If Jones was reconciled to the will of God, his head did not rest easily on the pillow as he fought the fever that wasted him. Ewart's interrogation of his Christian character, and the home mission's ultimate summation of his erratic and wilful career, did not sit so easily with the image Jones projected of himself and which was revealed through his extant writings. What things did he wish to explain as fever addled his consciousness? If his life flashed before him, he may have regretted some of his intemperate language, but he drew a straight and consistent line from his first stirrings of missionary desire fifteen years earlier to his harrying deathbed. Between the lines of his formulaic 1839 application to the LMS, he had laid out certain precepts of thought and action in answer to their questions for prospective missionary candidates. Unthinking compliance and rank self-interest were never his motivating factors; a practical outlook, self-sacrifice and a certain headstrong mindset were characteristic. Jones was determined to become a missionary 'whether any Society would send me or not', while the aspiration 'of improving my worldly circumstances does not enter into this application, because I have never considered it as such'. Believing himself to be the instrument of his Christian God, he accepted that a qualification of a missionary should be 'readiness to seal his Mission with his blood', and that personally it was 'worth sacrificing everything . . . though I die in the attempt'. The proper duty of a Christian missionary, moreover, was to 'civilise' as well as Christianise his people 'in the best way he can according to circumstances'.

Jones was no armchair evangelist, and had been scathing of those of his brethren who sat comfortably at home while espousing Christian action. His 1839 statement also encapsulated the Christian theological doctrine of justification – God's forgiveness of a sinner – by faith alone. For Jones and his fellow Calvinistic Methodists, human nature was entirely corrupt and condemned, and 'their recovery is to be effected entirely by the agency of the Holy Spirit'. The doctrine of justification was one of the lines in the sand between Protestant and Catholic belief (for the latter, justification can be determined by good works). But skirting the far frontiers of the doctrine of justification were the nether lands of antinomian belief in which faith rather than strict obedience to Christian law was an animating principle. While never explicit in Jones's theology, his physical separation in India from the ritual and institutional fabric of his church enabled a kind of lawlessness that was read by his religious brethren – and by the agents of British sovereignty in the Khasi Hills – as potentially anarchic. Yet his antinomianism, if that's what it was, did not explicitly sanction overt permissiveness or immorality, but rather placed the Holy Spirit as the key reference point of his ethical decision-making. If Jones saw his Christianising role as teaching the gospel, educating the Khasis and converting heathen souls, his civilising role was to be further achieved through agitating for equality within the law, however corrupt he considered implementation of that system of law to be, rather than wholesale rebellion against it. Jones's missionary model had developed from the station at Cherrapunji to the Moravian-inspired commune at Pomreng, but to label his call for justice in the hills as liberation theology would be anachronistic as well as misleading.[3] Furthermore, no explicit connection can be made to the direct influence of the Chartist ideals for social and political reform that had been brewing in Britain before his departure in 1840. Though his radicalism was perhaps as much theological as political, it still posed a major threat to the credibility and authority of both church and state.

In his first letter from India, perhaps already aware of the budding tension between autonomy and control, Jones had assured John Roberts: 'Do not think that I, in any way . . . suppose myself in India to be something other than I was in Wales'.[4] The illness and depression which followed his fall from the mule in March 1845 and his wife's death in August that year were critical factors in crystallising Jones's single-minded attitudes. In November 1845, recuperating in Calcutta but anticipating being restored to full health, he looked forward to being able 'to climb the mountains once more'.[5] In March 1846 he wrote to Roberts of his principal purpose: to complete a translation of the New Testament 'so good that no one who comes after me can ever *improve* it, although they can *change* it', and then to establish a native church, after which 'I am content to die, or to leave the [mission] field; but not before'. While able to continue this work in Sylhet as in Cherrapunji, his attachment to his 'beloved hills' had grown, just as his engagement with Wales had faded, and he had scant desire at all to return to Wales. 'I have little regard', he told Roberts as well as the *Y Drysorfa* readership, 'for those missionaries who are always looking for an excuse to return home, and my desire to see you all progressively diminishes with each passing year, and my affection for this country increases. After all, you and I must go where the cloud and the pillar lead us'.[6]

Continued bouts of illness through 1846 hampered Jones's progress. While his translation of the Gospel of Matthew was published in Calcutta,[7] the rift with his fellow missionaries following his marriage to Emma Cattell in September, and the deaths of Daniel Jones and William Lewin in December, were further blows. The move away from Cherrapunji to the interior, first at Pomreng and then Shillong, also removed him from the immediate purview of the Cherrapunji authorities. Here Jones aligned himself with the sympathetic Khyrim *Syiem* Sing Manick, for whom the missionary became a strategic interlocutor in his battles with the Cherrapunji Court. For Jones, the evolving sense and purpose of his mission had been active and dynamic from the moment of his first arrival in the hills in 1841. The home authorities may have sent their personnel and finances, but their experience of the mission was inevitably bureaucratic and paper bound, their expectations diverging radically over time from their active emissary. 'I have never once entertained the idea of leaving these people', Jones wrote in 1848, 'whatever my supporters at home may do'.[8]

An eclectic empire of belief: the Inglises and religiosity

Lewis and Pryse sold the old mission house back to the Inglis family for 500 rupees in August 1849, and by 1850 Pryse had established a new mission station on the plains at Sylhet, leaving William and Mary Lewis again labouring alone in the hills. Their operations at Cherrapunji, Mawsmai and Mawmluh were augmented in 1851 with a new schoolhouse at Shella, a large village to the south-west of Cherrapunji, where a new church was also constructed in 1853. Schoolhouses were also opened at this time at Nongkroh, Nongwar, Jowai and Sohbar.

It was Harry Inglis who funded Lewis's new Shella schoolhouse, and the 'liberality' of his support did not go unnoticed by John Roberts.[9] The ongoing kindness of the Inglis family towards the Welsh mission may have appeared to contradict the personal enmity between Harry Inglis and Thomas Jones that had festered through the 1840s. The Inglises could be generous to those who did not contradict their authority, and supportive of those who did not undermine the pecuniary advantage they had established in the hills. The conditions under which they were able to thrive were completely consistent with a political economy of empire. Existing native economies were ineluctably drawn into a dependent and exploitative relationship, in which the subjugation of native populations was part of a broader 'civilising' and 'pacifying' process. These practices were consistent with the hierarchies of scientific racism that had their origins in such works of enlightenment science as Linnaeus's *Systema Naturae* (1769) and Kant's *On the Different Races of Man* (1775), whereby the culture of the western European stood at the apex of human social evolution. The everyday dynamics of race were also critical in other ways. Harry Inglis and his wife Sophia were both Eurasian (though not to Khasi mothers). But stitched into the fabric of European identity and power through Captain Lister and George Inglis, they escaped the 'troublesome' tag that had attached, for example, to Charles Fenwick at Cherrapunji in the early years of the 1830s. Harry Inglis's capture of U Tirot Sing in 1829 had immense personal symbolism for a man who wanted there to be no doubt which side of the racial divide his sympathies were on.

Harry Inglis's exploitative labour practices, nepotistic political methods and antipathy towards a Christian missionary were not necessarily inconsistent with his own religious or political values. Inglis was one of empire's entrepreneurs *par excellence*, a tough, uncompromising and astute businessman, a survivor for whom the frontier was not simply a place but a state of mind whose hazy limits could only be determined by trial and error, and at times by overstepping the boundary in order to create it. Harry's financial support of the Welsh mission may on one level have been a reward for William Lewis's loyalty, but the religiosity of the Inglis clan was visible in other ways. Harry's brother John was reputed to have been deeply religious, and had donated land for a church at Sylhet.[10] When Bishop Wilson had passed through Chhatak on his 1841 tour of the north-east, he conducted a service for the Inglis family of seven, during which three were confirmed, all took the Holy Sacrament and there were 'many in tears'.[11] After his death in 1850, the wife of patriarch George, who had wooed the Bishop of Calcutta with oranges, had a memorial window installed to his memory in St John's Church.[12] Sophia Inglis also left money in her will for the Bishop of Calcutta to raise an Inglis Orphanage Asylum Fund for the education and welfare of Christian children in Calcutta.

It is difficult to determine the extent to which particular religious belief was foundational to the daily life of the Inglis family in India over the six decades since George had arrived from Scotland in the 1790s. Whether Christianity was a precious and sacred underpinning, or simply the window dressing of handpicked dogma and ritual for more secular show, the Inglises were less in the business of religious conversion than financial gain. Theirs was an eclectic empire of belief in which the diverse practices of Khasi animism, Christianity, Hinduism and Islam could potentially be accommodated. Whether evidence of calculated expediency or deliberate pluralism, the fact was that the Inglises were responsible for facilitating religious as well as commercial connections across the hills and plains. According to Dkhar, the Rath Jatra or Hindu Festival of Chariots of Lord Jagannatha was celebrated at the Inglis house at Cherrapunji, to which the deity was conveyed from Chhatak on an elephant.[13]

'God is in her belly, and who can pull him out?'

In the decade or so prior to the arrival of the Welsh missionaries, elements of Khasi religion had been superficially described by European visitors to the hills, though they barely advanced on late eighteenth-century characterisations of the tribes of north-east India as heathen savages who practised human sacrifice. In their excursions to the hills, Dacca judge Henry Walters (1828) and the anonymous 'C' (1831, possibly Dacca judge William Cracroft) commented on the Khasi practices of ancestor worship, the erection of monumental memorial stones and the Khasi belief in spirits or minor deities inhabiting places.[14] 'On the subject of religion', opined Alexander Lish, 'very little can be said'. While culturally ignorant in their understanding of Khasi beliefs, the published accounts of Lish (1838) and Henry Yule (1844) noted a number of key practices inherent in Khasi religious observance: the supposed belief in a single supreme God as creator (U Blei or Ka Blei); the belief that minor deities or malevolent spirits inhabiting forests or caves could be appeased by animal sacrifices; and that the prediction of events through observing auguries – particularly by ovomancy (egg divination) or hepatoscopy (inspecting the livers of sacrificed pigs or fowls) – occupied a central role in Khasi religion.[15] Khasi egg divination involved smearing the outer eggshell with red earth before dashing the egg on a wooden board and reading omens from the final placement of shell fragments. Yule also referred obliquely to the Khasi belief in *U Thlen*, a giant and malevolent shape-shifting serpent that can only be appeased through human sacrifice.

'The religion of this people – if so it may be called', noted an anonymous commentator in 1852 with a heavy dose of cultural absolutism, 'is nothing more than a contemptible demon worship; and an occasional wealth-seeking bribe to an imaginary goddess, under the misnomer *sacrifice*'.[16] For the missionaries, the Khasis seemed to lack any institutionalised form of religion, and in Jones's words had 'only some vague belief in a spirit or spirits, to which they offer sacrifices, one could write on most of their altars the words "to the unknown God"'. Jones therefore constructed himself as the authority who could lead them to an understanding of the nature of God ('they place a great emphasis on this, "the man who can tell us about the God, or Gods"').[17] Along with other missionaries and European commentators, he also falsified Khasi religion by refashioning it with Christian concepts (like devils and monotheism) that bore little actual relationship to Khasi structures of belief.[18]

The first generation of Welsh missionaries rarely chronicled Khasi religious beliefs (unlike later generations of religious ethnographers), and where they did it was to construct the Khasis as depraved, superstitious, foolish and naive. In his early letters Thomas Jones wrote for example of the Khasi practice of keeping ancestral bones in a stone; on ceremonial occasions the bones were taken out and washed three times before being replaced along with offerings of food, tobacco and other valuable items.[19] Yet Jones always interpolated his value-laden reading of local rituals and practices. He saw as wasteful their habit of hoarding jewellery and rich garments while living in apparent poverty, only to expend their savings when they or a relative fell ill, by breaking eggs or sacrificing birds, goats or pigs. Jones also noted the Khasi belief that people (called *U Nongshohnoh* by Gurdon) who were in league with *U Thlen* went about cutting off small pieces of hair or clothing from their victims, who would subsequently die unless sacrifices were made to appease the serpent.[20] 'The entire history of their nation throughout the ages', wrote Jones self-servingly, 'is nothing but a repetition of such foolish and regrettable acts. They often perceive and recognize the folly and vanity of their customs, but they add "What shall we do? Thus all our forefathers have done, and thus we have been taught. We have no books as you have, and we cannot read about the God, nor take medicine; if we knew the things that you do, we would do likewise; but until we come to such a place, what can we do other than as we have been taught?"'

Many of the missionaries' letters are reported as dialogue between themselves and their Khasi enquirers or opponents. The verbal exchange implied by Jones, however much it may have voiced actual conversations, was a highly constructed textual strategy. As reportage for home consumption, it theatrically drew his audience into the rhetoric of conventional conversion narratives. Jones's comments on the Khasis displayed the kind of 'double-vision' described by Anna Johnston, whereby missionaries both denigrated and defended their heathen flock, needing to portray them as degraded, but also eminently salvageable.[21] In Jeff Cox's terms, the 'denigration of the other' drew on defamatory synecdoche whereby an individual vice or evil was taken to stand for a whole culture.[22]

Jones saw the work of his early years on the hills as merely preparatory to the business of securing converts, but as the years went on the need for tangible outcomes became more pressing, particularly at those times when scandal rocked the mission. Finally, on Sunday 8 March 1846, nearly five years after Jones had arrived in the Khasi Hills, U Amor and U Rujon became the first Khasis to be baptised. Others followed: in 1847 (U Luh, U Ramjan, U Tirahsing), 1848 (Ka Nabon, the first female to be baptised); and 1849 (Ka Nimon, Ka Berton, Ka Bir, Ka Phuh, U Nimor, U Jarkha). By the time of Thomas Jones's death, there were around ten additional converts. In January 1850, the first Christian wedding was celebrated between U Luh and Ka Phuh. U Luh placed a specially made silver ring on his wife's finger, engraved with the word *synjut* (pledge) and the year 1850.[23]

Over time, as scholars or enquirers were admitted as candidates for baptism, opposition from the families of Khasi Christians grew. To the missionaries, resistance on the part of Khasi Christians to the often-violent opposition of their families was taken as evidence of their steadfastness. What else indeed could it be that signalled true conversion? Literacy and the acquisition of scriptural knowledge were obviously important, though there was some wariness that this could simply be a charade. For Lewis, the measure of authenticity was as profound as it was precarious: 'There was that indescribable "something" of which the late R.D. Williams used to speak so memorably in the society at home – that something which the poor sinner feels, but which he cannot express, when his heart is pricked by the truth'.[24] Jones too drew on his Welsh experience: describing the attitude of his first follower U Juncha in May 1845, Jones noted that he was showing admirable signs of resisting the superstitions of his fathers, refusing to take part in sacrifices and even closing his shop on Sunday. Yet in Jones's view, he was 'not yet entirely what God's grace could make him; – he needs as the old folk used to say "to be broken in"'.[25] Preaching to villagers in the marketplace at Nongkynrih in October 1842 during a trip to the Jaintia Hills with Yule and Lewin, Jones was delighted with the manner in which his audience was moved to high emotion, springing to their feet and placing 'their faces as close as they could to my face, as if they were trying to meet the words as they fell from my lips! They appeared very serious, indeed they were weeping copiously; and they indicated their fervent approval of what I was saying, just as a Welsh congregation would do'.[26]

In the same letter, Jones saw the general uprising of opposition to the gospel as a positive sign, to the extent that 'it is worth the devil's while to take notice of it and persecute it'. Instances of persecution were regularly reported in the pages of *Y Drysorfa*. Converts were beaten by their families, had their clothes stripped and their books or jewellery stolen, and the mission schoolrooms at Nongsawlia and in other villages were set on fire. As converts increasingly took the missionaries' medicine, cut their hair (boys traditionally wore their hair long like the girls), and refused to break eggs or take part in ceremonies to venerate ancestors, family members would blame them for any misfortunes and at times take them away from the mission compound by force. The breaking of eggs was a constant source of augury as to whether or not Khasis should take medicine or attend school. 'Sometimes the egg says that it is wicked to speak to us', wrote Lewis, 'at another time that it is wicked to read our books; and even to stay with us'.[27] To the Khasis, the meddling of the missionaries and their effective interference in traditional customs and systems of authority were profoundly disruptive. The

Christian practice of burial rather than cremation led to violent opposition from families of Khasi Christians who were unable to perform traditional funeral rites. The relatives of Ka Ribon managed to secure a single hair from her head before she was buried as a Christian, and were then able to burn it in her place in their own separate ceremony.[28] When a Khasi died, they were said to be eating *kwai* (betel-nut) in the house of God.[29]

The baptism in 1848 of Ka Nabon was a moment of particular celebration for the Welsh mission, and the subject the following year of a published account of her conversion and persecution.[30] Female conversion was seen to be particularly important in the context of the matrilineal and matrilocal Khasi social system, though there were many barriers to overcome. Mary Lewis later recalled that the Khasis were suspicious of the missionaries' motives and believed they had come to decoy the girls away and make prostitutes of them, in the same way that some of the soldiers had done previously. It was also believed that women would not be able to have children if they learned to read, and that they should not handle the writing quill, a sacred object derived from the fowl, which in Khasi lore was man's intercessor before God.[31] When the seven Khasi ancestral clans were expelled from heaven, the earth was cast in darkness by a huge tree, and it was the cock which sacrificed itself to allow the sun to shine again for the sake of mankind.[32]

By early 1848, the Thomas Jones case had made John Roberts eager for better tidings. 'Make haste', he implored William Lewis, 'and send me further news of this dear young disciple . . . It is highly necessary, at the present moment, to exert all the energies one possesses to keep up what feeling remains for the Mission amongst our friends'.[33] The April 1848 *Y Drysorfa* triumphantly headlined William Lewis's 'Astonishing news from Khasia'.[34] Not only could this fifteen year old girl read, write and sew, as well as speak from the heart on spiritual matters, but she had survived the sustained attempts of her family to remove her from the influence of the missionaries. On one occasion her family captured her and took her back to Mawmluh, threatening to kill her if she returned to the mission. Bor Sing, the young *Syiem* of Cherra, had previously attempted unsuccessfully to negotiate with Ka Nabon's relatives and dissuade them from their attempts to separate her from the mission.[35] Now the Lewises called on Political Agent Frederick Lister to adjudicate, and a Khasi official was sent from the Cherra court in an unusual instance of state intervention. The whole village was in uproar and a massed crowd looked on as the court official asked Ka Nabon whether she wished to stay or to leave. When Ka Nabon indicated that she wished to rejoin the missionaries, her mother responded by untying her own hair and spreading it over her daughter, crying, pulling her hair and ripping out her earrings, and feigning to stab herself. 'God is in her belly', the villagers are reported to have said of Ka Nabon, 'and who can pull him out?'

In the 1840s and 1850s, some Khasi Christians started to distance themselves from traditional customs and practices. Unwilling to attend a family offering when summoned by their parents, boys living on the mission station in 1845 instead sent a turban (*ka jainspong*) to serve the same purpose as their bodily presence.[36] Any simplistic missionary/indigenous dichotomy belies complex and transformative processes of resistance, accommodation, realignment of traditional values and opportunistic appropriation of colonial systems on the part of the Khasis.[37] While a close reading of the emergence of indigenous Christianity in the first decades of the mission is frustrated by the paucity and one-sidedness of the sources – and its trajectory through the latter part of the nineteenth and into the twentieth centuries is beyond the scope of this book – this chapter will pick up on some instances from the 1860s and 1870s that point to the ways in which an understanding of the indigenous appropriation of the Christian message is vital to a full understanding of the missionary encounter.

The mission continues: converts, recruits and controversies

On the plains at Sylhet, William Pryse's house soon attracted a handful of public and secret enquirers after the Christian religion as well as the English language skills he dispensed. Sweating in shirt sleeves, Pryse breathlessly enjoined the crowds who filled the public rooms of his house, scholars from government schools eager to learn English and become translators, for hours on end debating the fundamental truths of Islam, Christianity and Hinduism.[38] The Pryses had gone down to Sylhet in late 1849, and by February the following year William and his wife, together with Ann Jane Jones, had twenty-five regular Bengali scholars. Pryse was also working on a Khasi/English dictionary – Thomas Jones's widow Emma had sent him her husband's writings, including lengthy word lists.[39] Judge Stainforth had also obtained all the Khasi writings of Thomas Jones for Pryse, who collated over 2000 Khasi words for his dictionary and whose *Khasi Grammar* was published in 1855.[40]

Robert Parry and his wife Ann joined the Cherra mission in 1856, and moved to Pryse's station at Sylhet in 1859. Left with four small children after the death of his wife from cholera in 1861, and increasingly marginalised by his brethren for his embrace of unorthodox theologies, Parry resigned from the mission in 1863. Parry had been influenced by the publication of *Essays and Reviews* in 1860, a controversial and in some quarters heretical collection of essays on Christianity by seven liberal Anglican ministers. Published hot on the heels of Darwin's *On the Origin of Species* (1859), the essays championed rational religion and threw down a challenge to traditionalist interpretations of biblical authority.

Pryse had also been joined in 1857 by Thomas Jones II and his wife Gwenllian, who moved to Cherrapunji after Parry relocated to Sylhet in 1859. James Roberts and his wife Grace arrived in 1860, but were recalled soon after due to a confrontation with the other missionaries, and perished when their ship the *Sedgemoor* was lost on its return journey.[41] The crises in authority echoed the travails of the Welsh mission in the early 1840s when Owen Richards had been recalled. The correspondence of the 1860s was similarly marbled with innuendo and accusation; the claims of educated Khasis were also now being interleaved into the conflicted drama of personality and belief. James Roberts's mother-in-law Maria Owen forwarded a letter from the 'poor persecuted Christians of Cherrapoongee' complaining of Thomas Jones II's 'vexing and punishing us' and blamed his 'unchristianlike behaviour' for her daughter's shipwrecked demise.[42] Susan Cattell found such claims astonishing, and blamed the 'Sceptic' Parry for manipulating the Khasis. 'I was astonished', she wrote to Mary Lewis, 'to hear that some of the Christians who were *perverted* by those vile people Mr & Mrs Roberts have lately written to her Mother reiterating the slanders of Mr & Mrs R calling *Mr Jones harsh*! & *cruel*! or something of the sort – it is a strange coincident that that letter was posted at the time Mr P was last here . . . he is a bad man'.[43]

Susan Cattell kept up a correspondence with Mary Lewis, who had left India in December 1860 with her husband William after eighteen years of uninterrupted work in the hills. If the views of Khasi Christians were now entering the critical spaces of evangelical authority to negotiate and contest the meanings of mission, then how potent a message was the figure of U Larsing, a Khasi Christian who accompanied the Lewises when they returned to Britain in May 1861.[44] U Larsing exemplified the non-European evangelist as Christianity's double-agent; as Peggy Brock has noted, such figures have ambiguous insider/outsider relationships to their own communities as well as to their mission brethren.[45]

U Larsing was born in Mawsmai near Cherrapunji in 1838, baptised in 1851, and early noted as a stylish preacher. U Larsing describes in letters home to his countrymen the experience of visiting the fountainhead of the mission. Arriving in London, U Larsing was 'giddy' with the endless bustle of its streets.

10 The Reverend William and Mary Lewis with U Larsing.

> England is a flat country having only a few little Hills here & there, and is filled with large & small towns. But Wales is a mountainous country. It is like your Jynteah country in many parts, and in some parts like our Khasi country. The land of the country is not extremely better than the Jynteah country; but the industry and the perseverance of the people are very great indeed. There is not much of jungle, and there is no part of the country without being cultivated . . . All the Rivers glide smoothly and pleasantly along as if they were silver snakes! But they do not dig the earth away & sink deeply like our rivers in the Khasi country. When I am in Wales, I feel on this account – just as if I were in my own Khasi country. But when I am in England, I feel as if I were in Bengal.[46]

In apprehending new horizons, the meanings U Larsing chose to give to new places were shaped by his previous landscape cognition, as well as by his emotional states of hope, trepidation and expectation. U Larsing replicated the Wales/England, Khasi/Bengali cultural dichotomies, and in mimicry as a colonised subject undermined the assuredness of colonial hegemony in a critique of the vices and extravagances of metropolitan culture.

In travelling to Wales, U Larsing saw himself as 'the fruit which was brought lately from Khasi Hills',[47] and experienced at once a homecoming and an exile. U Larsing and William Lewis toured the country together, speaking until they were hoarse in chapels and to thousands assembled in fields and on hillsides, though to U Larsing he was 'a stone in all those assemblies, not one word penetrating to my heart, because I did not understand Welsh'.[48] In Wales, U Larsing performed under well-established conventions of fascination,[49] both the before and after of conversion narratives: as primitive tribesman, breaking eggs in the manner of Khasi divination practice; as Christian, preaching and singing hymns in Khasi to Welsh tunes. U Larsing validated nearly two decades of mission labour and sacrifice, and the contributions scrounged from chapels across the country to support the Welsh overseas mission, justifying the break made with the LMS in 1840. Furthering his education at Holt Academy near Wrexham, and practising the German concertina, U Larsing suffered continually from colds and headaches. He finally succumbed to the rigours of the cold climate in August 1863, and was buried at Chester. U Larsing may have seen himself as the stone and as the fruit. In some respects he was also Lewis's trophy, an exotic sample sent home in the same way that the missionaries sent beetles or samples of cloth as Khasi curiosities. The ships that left Liverpool bearing Welsh missionaries to and from India traded in ideas, objects and mentalities, but the ways in which Welsh constructions of their imperial periphery were shaped from the periphery itself are still to be further revealed.[50]

William Pryse had returned to Britain on furlough in 1861, but after Parry's defection returned to India in 1863 and thereafter spent more of his time working in the Cachar district. Mission honorary secretary and co-founder John Roberts resigned his position in 1866 after a number of years of ill health and financial difficulties. He moved to Edinburgh to take up the position as secretary of the Sabbath Alliance of Scotland, and the incoming mission secretary the Reverend Josiah Thomas held the position for the next thirty-four years.[51] In March 1866 three more missionary couples arrived in the Khasi Hills in the shape of Daniel and Margaret Sykes, Griffith and Elizabeth Hughes, and Hugh and Elizabeth Roberts. The new missionaries signed a more detailed agreement with the WFMS – confirming their adherence to the Articles of Doctrine as elaborated in the Confession of Faith, to the rules of discipline, and also attesting that if they resigned or were terminated within seven years, that they return all expenses incurred by the society on their account.

Native evangelist Gour Charan Das suspected William Pryse of adultery with his wife, and Hugh Roberts had accused Pryse of drunkenness and breaking the Sabbath. Pryse himself claimed that he 'only has a little in house for medicinal purposes and drinks a pint of beer or porter with my tiffin but not daily – a quantity which I think could make no man drunk',[52] but his increasingly erratic behaviour led to his dismissal from the mission in 1866. He died in Sylhet two years later. Pryse himself consistently denied the allegations brought against him; like most ministers and missionaries of the period, he was not a teetotaller.[53] Through this period John Roberts continued to counsel the new secretary Josiah Thomas on the need for delicate handling of the controversies that still beset the mission. 'Our friends in Wales', cautioned Roberts, 'are – as you must know – so prone to gossip, and so often careless as to how much they add to a story, that incalculable mischief may be done, unless great care be taken'.[54]

After Parry's departure and Pryse's return from furlough in 1863, Thomas Jones II at Cherrapunji and Pryse at Sylhet were the only two Welsh missionaries in the field. During the Jaintia uprising, before rebel *Syiem* U Kiang Ningbah was captured and hanged at Jowai at the end of 1863, Jones had won plaudits from military and government alike for his conciliatory role in reducing the bloodshed and persuading many *Syntengs* to surrender. Thomas Dillon (Political Agent, Manipur) and Brigadier General H.F. Dunsford both praised Jones's character and service, while Colonel Haughten at Mawphlang sought the missionary's strategic advice; 'how changed times are', reflected Susan Cattell to Mary Lewis, 'that Missionaries are this encouraged by the heads of Govt'.[55]

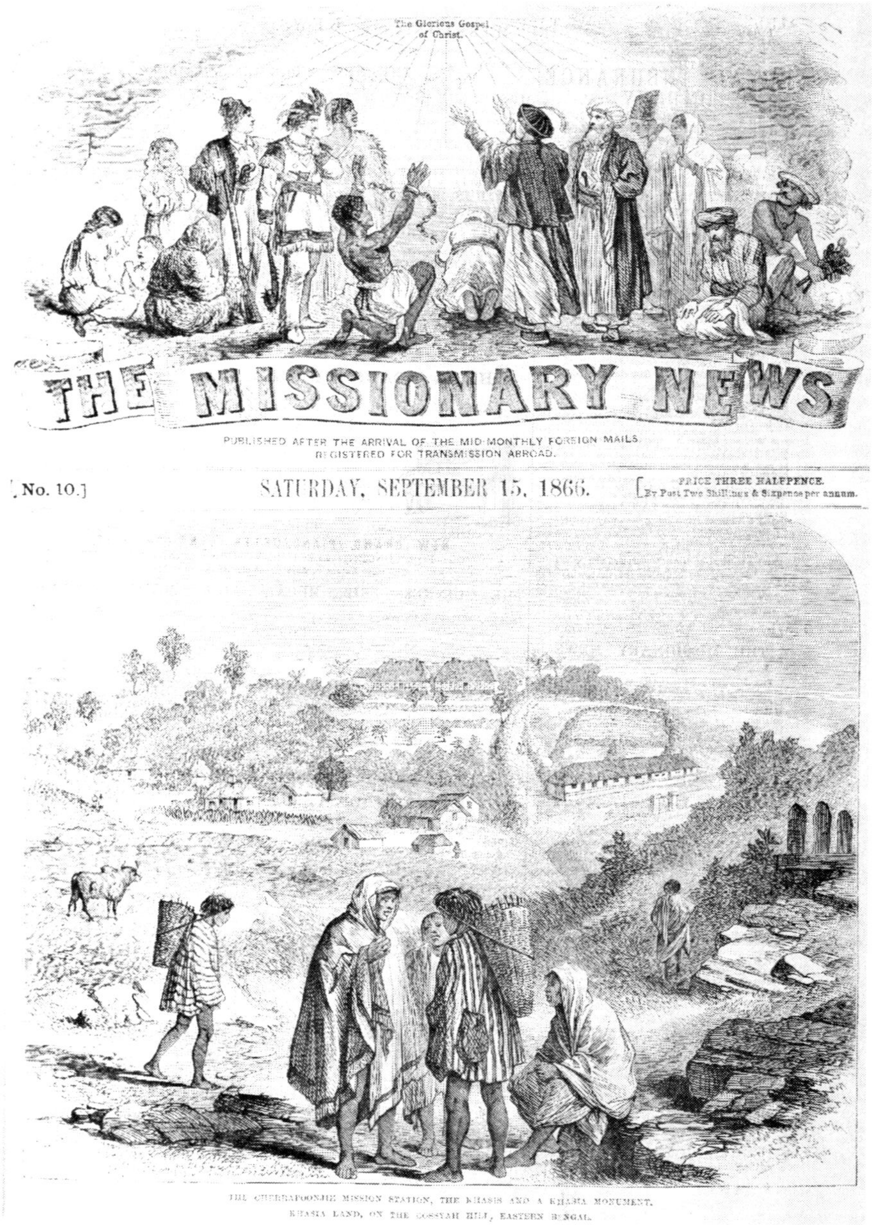
The Glorious Gospel of Christ.

THE MISSIONARY NEWS

PUBLISHED AFTER THE ARRIVAL OF THE MID-MONTHLY FOREIGN MAILS.
REGISTERED FOR TRANSMISSION ABROAD.

[No. 10.] SATURDAY, SEPTEMBER 15, 1866. [PRICE THREE HALFPENCE. By Post Two Shillings & Sixpence per annum.

THE CHERRAPOONJIE MISSION STATION, THE KHASIS AND A KHASIA MONUMENT.
KHASIA LAND, ON THE COSSYAH HILL, EASTERN BENGAL.

11 'The Cherrapoonjie Mission Station, the Khasis and a Khasia monument. Khasia land, on the Cossyah Hill, Eastern Bengal', *The Missionary News*, 1866.

The arrival of the three new missionary couples in March 1866 provided much needed support, but also set personalities at odds, which would lead to the permanent departure of four of the six by 1873 and would ultimately leave the Sylhet station on the plains without a Welsh missionary between 1873 and 1879. Daniel Sykes had set up at Jowai in 1866, and in a short time had baptised a number of converts. He reported to Josiah Thomas in 1868 that the Khasis were making a clear distinction between the missionaries ('Our Sahebs') as opposed to government officials: 'we are their Sahebs, because we are always ready to speak with them, and we are available every hour, they come to us with their troubles, they ask our advice, they apply for medicines'. If the Christian Khasis made their own distinctions between Bible and flag, so did the missionaries themselves. Sykes was in clear conflict with Assistant Commissioner J.B. Shadwell over the issue of the forced labour of Khasi Christians by local chiefs. Sykes was dismayed when the *dolois* of Shangpung village pressed Christians from the missionary community to work as coolies for surveyors or other government works:

> what astonished me not a little was that Mr Shadwell does not recognise any difference between Christians and semi-savages, but says we ought to be charitable to all '*sects*'! I maintain there is a vast difference & that the rights and privileges of Christians under a Christian sovereign no other than our Queen shall be recognised and that something shall be done to prevent them from being made beasts of burden, by a heathen chief, such as these Dolois are.[56]

Sykes saw the issue as being critical to his 'respectability in the eyes of the natives'. The *doloi* manipulated the presence of the missionaries to his own advantage, and according to Sykes 'bamboozled' the Christians at the mission school into supporting his election to office, making promises about supporting the school building, but once in office forbidding children from attending the school and denying them board and lodging in the native village. Sykes was aware that the provision of free medical aid was an important part of wooing the trust of the villagers, but consciously steered away from any intercession in local politics 'as tending to bring the missionary into conflict with the civil power Viz. assisting the people in their little petty litigations – concerning which they are mighty ready to beg for stratagems'.[57]

Mission control: race, space, gender and belief

When Thomas Jones I had refused to hand over the deed of the old mission house, William Lewis had flattered the Cherra *Syiem* with more gifts of cloth to persuade him to execute a new one. The land embodied quite different theologies for the Khasis and for the Christians. For the Nongsawlia headmen, the site was marked to the north-west by the reddish stream Ka Um-sawlia and the sound of the frogs in Ka Um Jakoid, to the north-east by the great precipice, to the south-east by the trench of Ka Siat-u-dei, then running on the south-west side from the rock at Ka Siat-u-dei past the wall of the burning place at Ka Phan-wan-bri and back up to the frog stream. Khasi land embodied their ancestry, their polity and their cosmology. The Nongsawlia land incorporated natural elements inhabited by the spirit beings that perpetuated life. In his correspondence, Lewis regularly referred to *ein Seion fach* – 'our little Zion' – a beachhead 'placed among the thorns and brambles of this moral wilderness'. Nongsawlia was no longer marked by the red stream of Ka Um-sawlia, but was Zion, a mountain near Jerusalem, metonymic of the promised land of the Christian Bible given by God to Abraham and the Israelites and which lay between the Red Sea and the Euphrates.[58]

Intervention into the ritual and spatial worlds of the village was a more clear-cut method of domination and control. In the first instance, native Christians were forbidden from taking part in any of their traditional pastimes – 'dances, festivals, bullfights, wrestlings & archery'. A further prohibition was specifically placed on the practice of 'Tarro-taking', a local Jaintia belief still practised even by native evangelists whereby a person's *taro* could be possessed by another, revealed in the victim speaking in the voice of the possessor.[59] As time went on Sykes seemed more and more disturbed by and intolerant of the 'savage scenes' that surrounded him.[60] 'Thanks be to God', he wrote in 1869, 'I believe the cross stands firm in the Hills and its refulgence is shining forth more & more – yet even while I write the clamorous yells and confused noise of a heathen carnival rends the air'. On this occasion he observed around a thousand naked men attempt over the course of a day to break in half a massive tree trunk in a muddy pool, the winning side being the one who retained the larger portion. The 'crowning sin' of the practice was, in Sykes' view, 'every husband is common property & every woman is common property!! "Tell it not in Gath, publish it not in the streets of Ascalon"'.

If the vision of a thousand naked men had Sykes spouting the Book of Samuel, his assertion of knowledge claims about Jaintia social disorder generally and Jaintia cultural gender practices particularly was characteristic of much white imperial discourse: negative and overtly racist; reflecting his own cultural values and prejudices rather than stemming from any deep understanding of the Jaintias; and underpinning oppressive interventions.[61] Assuming the right to speak for Jaintia women as presumed victims of male oppression, for Sykes the women of Jowai were indeed unwomanly. Working shoulder to shoulder with their male counterparts as coolies and agricultural labourers, knee deep in black mud, 'were it not for their dress we should often be at a loss to distinguish between the sexes those who have had experience in the mining districts of England & Wales will form some idea of what female character is under such circumstances'. In primitivising and unsexing native women, Sykes also constructed them as a resource, albeit a uncompliant one: 'these are our raw material, and it is no easy thing to find access to them, conscious as they are of our intentions A.B.C &c are things from another world in their estimation and well enough for the Sahebs'. Sykes put his trust in Ka Arabon, a Khasi woman sent from Mrs Roberts's training class at Nongsawlia, to model moral improvement for his Jaintia flock, some of whom he soon had reciting Thomas Charles's catechism by heart.

Visual and textual representations of tribal women in the north-east, and across India more generally, reveal much about what Europeans imagined of the savagery of Indian sexualities. While the evidence is circumstantial, the moralities and sexual behaviours of some of the missionaries themselves hardly embodied their religious or social protocols. Male missionaries at times may have sought to take advantage of social, sexual and pecuniary opportunities in the face of frustrations of the body, pocket and soul. The Enlightenment theories of 'barbarism' and 'civilisation' that animated the moral imperatives of the missionary society often depicted indigenous women as semi-enslaved, unwomanly or sexually precocious. A lithograph of two semi-naked Juang women, from a photograph of a supposedly naturalistic scene by Tosco Peppé, was reproduced in Edward Tuite Dalton's 1872 *Descriptive Ethnography of Bengal*. Textual descriptions of various tribal women emphasised alternately their savagery and their sexualisation, reading their assumed moral demeanour against the superiority of a white European racial standard: the 'long glossy hair of intense black, and the exquisitely formed mouth of the Laos Shan girls'; the 'mongrel race' of Singphos and Assamese female slaves; the 'indecorous' naked dances of female Abors; the 'faithful and obedient' Miri women; a 'typical . . . but not a favourable specimen' of a Mishmi woman; a 'beautiful specimen of a Sikkim Lepcha woman' which 'should have had a page to herself'. Dalton characterised the population of Bengal under nine groups, including the hill tribes of the north-east frontier, of which the Khasis were one. In an infantilised and sexualised representation of the Juang women, their nakedness signified primitivity and indecency, and they and the other specimens in Dalton's anthology were supposed the last remnants of their race within a 'salvage paradigm' of photography.[62]

Zahid Chaudhury has given an acute reading of this figure as a 'fantasy of primitive innocence', where the 'positioning of a "primitive" woman's hands on the breast and genital area of another native is not meant to detract, but adds to the cold scientific racial truth invested in the anthropological photograph'.[63] Just as Jane Lydon has drawn out the dynamic relationship between the photographer and the indigenous subject whereby the latter contested the objectification of the camera's eye,[64] so too Chaudhury reads resistance in the Juang girls' demeanour.

There are no images of Khasi women in Dalton's work, though his descriptions hark back to those of the first Europeans to describe the Khasis. Of the natives during his 1837 visit, botanist William Griffith had 'little to say' aside from the fact that they were a stout and strong people, men and women alike, although the latter were 'decidedly ugly . . . they can scarcely be said to form a worthy portion of the gentler sex'.[65] The presence of missionary wives was therefore regarded as being critical to the education of indigenous peoples and in particular the demonstration of gendered ideals. But while the presence of Ann Jones, Mary Lewis or Elizabeth Roberts was calculated for their profit to the mission as evangelical role models exhibiting the virtues of domesticity, it could be little guarantee of moral stability on the mission station.

Contemporary with Dalton's ethnographic portraits is French surgeon and photographer Oscar Mallitte's group portrait of 'Khasi Women' (c.1870s). The image of four Khasi women – captioned with a pencil inscription 'Khasi Christians' – is one of the earliest extant photographic images of Khasis.[66] The nascent photographic genre on the one hand claimed objective and scientific truth. But the image can also be read as a highly constructed and stage-managed rendition of compliance and colonial control, particularly when read against other visual and textual versions of native savagery and licentiousness. The demure appearance of the four women is a far cry from the mud-caked spectres of Sykes's vision or the sexualised Juang girls; while an image of moral compliance and Christianising civilisation, at a distance it is much more difficult to read the manner in which its subjects may also have engaged in its production with their own understandings of active agency and resistance. There are no obvious trappings of Christianity, but this is a forceful image of a matrilineal society, the figure in the left foreground denying the gaze of the camera, the other three connected in the positioning of hands on shoulder and chair. The image is at once exemplary of colonial modes of control and coded with indigenous symbolism and modes of resistance. The image of the Khasi women appeared in an album of photographs of Assam that included views of Khasi coolies, the badminton club at Shillong, tea gardens in

12 Oscar Mallitte, 'Khasi women, native Christians', c.1870s.

Cachar, and the eastern frontier police force, thus inserting the Khasi Christian women into a broader narrative of economic, political and racial authority.

Mallitte's album also contained an image of 'Native village at the entrance to Shillong: Chapel for Kasia Christians'. In 1866, Shillong had usurped Cherrapunji's role as government and military headquarters of the region. Griffith Hughes had opened the missionary station at Shillong in 1871, and its European residents had contributed £90 to the building of the first chapel there.[67] A further and important tactic of missionary control was the differentiation between the native and the Christian village, the latter marked by masonry houses with glass windows, and daily observance of Christian understandings of neatness and cleanliness. Daniel Sykes well understood the power of space in the Jaintia Hills, and despite the friction with Assistant Commissioner Shadwell, he won decisive and critical spatial and symbolic victories. The government sanctioned the protection of the most sacred native sites – but with the *locum tenens* of native religion sacrosanct, the missionaries had free reign to cultivate or build on any other contiguous crown land they requested. The local magistrate therefore secured a new site for a Christian village at Shangpung, and declared to the *durbar* that should the locals be concerned about pollution from the Christians, they could build a wall around their altars. Sykes was triumphant: 'we have gone into the centre of their sacred spots', he declared to Josiah Thomas, 'and erected the chapel amongst their most revered objects'. The chapel and twenty houses in the new Christian village stood as a symbolic victory over the 'jungle demons': 'it will be a constant wonder to all the tribe entering the village', Sykes advised Thomas, 'and a standing evidence of the authority & strength that is on the side of the Christian religion, altho as the heathen often boast, the Queen herself defends their sacred spots, but be that as it may. The Jynteah cannot understand how it is, that our religion gives such courage to the native, and makes so little of their gods'.[68] Four tutelary spirits, including the Musniang (stone pig), guarded the native village at Jowai.[69] Later missionary W.M. Jenkins juxtaposed photographs of the 'heathen village' and 'Christian village' at Jowai to make explicit the visual vocabulary of order and disorder, morality and savagery.[70]

There was evident friction across the various mission stations between the four missionaries in the field in the late 1860s. Sykes complained to the secretary about disputed accounts for the salaries of teachers, and accused Roberts and Hughes of insincerity, hypocrisy, 'a disregard for purity of conduct, and high principle shocking in the character of missionaries'.[71] Roberts and Sykes wrote from Nongsawlia in April 1869 accusing Thomas Jones II of sending home derogatory letters.[72] Sykes's over-zealous and aggressive methods eventually put him at odds with fellow missionaries as well as Christian and non-Christian Khasis, and he was dismissed in 1870.[73] Khasi Christians were caught in the vicious crossfire of interpersonal rivalry and dispute, and were often forced to side with one or other of their champions. Jones had himself set up a rival mission at Nongsawlia, in direct opposition to the one run by Hughes.

Hugh Roberts and Griffith Hughes were on no more friendly terms. Roberts had first worked at Sylhet, then at Cherra from 1867 and Sylhet from 1870, before eventually returning to Wales in 1876.[74] An accomplished linguist, as was his wife Elizabeth, Roberts learned Hindi, Khasi and Bengali and his *A Grammar of the Khasi Language* was published in 1891. But there were growing concerns about Roberts's belligerent treatment of some of the Khasis under his care, as well as his general attitude of haughty racial superiority. Hughes, who had sailed to India with Roberts, was scathing about his attitude to the natives, and found it increasingly difficult to defend the behaviour of his co-worker: 'To

13 Oscar Mallitte, 'Native village at the entrance to Shillong. Chapel for Kassia Christians', c.1870s.

Mr Roberts the Khasias are "beasts" and the Bengalis are "deceivers" . . . When his race-feeling is such one may think that you committed a mistake in sending him among the "Blacks" to preach Jesus Christ who himself was not ashamed to be called a "friend of the Publicans and Sinners"'.[75] A growing generation of educated Khasi Christians were also interpolating their views and concerns into broader discussions about the propriety and morality of missionary behaviour. U Luh, a native evangelist baptised by William Lewis in 1857, and widower of Ka Nabon, wrote from Nongsawlia in 1871 charging Roberts with aggression and hypocrisy. While the Khasi Christians had certain restrictions imposed upon their behaviour, it seemed in their eyes that some of the Sahebs at the mission 'are to be left to do all kinds of things & to have no religious restraint whatever'. U Luh accused Roberts of abusing the wife of U Bad, whose family had already suffered much persecution after their conversion to Christianity. As she washed her child on her Nongsawlia verandah where they had sought refuge, Roberts reportedly 'went up to her and kicked her, saying why did she dirty the place so'. Universal Christian precepts were difficult to sustain when cut with the bitter flavour of racial bigotry. While some of the Khasi women and children at Nongsawlia had baulked from attending a native dance at Cherra, it was also known that Roberts went down to the plains 'to the Mussalman Feast at Sylhet where there is so much drinking dancing and sport'.[76]

The hypocrisies were troubling for the Khasi Christians, who saw less evil in attending a dance than in the physical abuse of one of their number. 'Why should the sin of a Khassia be looked upon & condemned with a punishment', rebuked U Luh, 'while there is no power to condemn a Sahab whatever rules he breaks?' While U Luh did not condemn all the missionaries, he was also perturbed at the inaction and therefore complicity in Roberts's misdeeds of new missionary Thomas Jerman Jones, who had arrived in 1870 to replace Sykes at Jowai.[77] Thomas Jones II had his reservations about Roberts's demand for absolute obedience from his native disciples. When Hughes publicly debated the matter with Roberts and Jerman Jones and queried the morality of beating another person, the missionaries took refuge in Welsh, and Hughes fell silent. The onlookers were left to wonder: 'It seemed as if they said to each other, "if you say so, you will condemn us at once"'.[78]

U Luh accused Thomas Jerman Jones of procuring a dozen bottles of brandy and port, for other than medicinal purposes. Thomas Jones II defended U Luh and protested the decision of Hughes and Roberts to suspend the native evangelist from preaching for six months. In October 1871, Hugh Roberts and Thomas Jerman Jones wrote a joint and official letter to the directors, accusing Thomas Jones II of slandering their reputation and causing division between the missionaries and natives. Jones had clearly lost his temper in railing against what he saw as the oppressions of his fellow missionaries. One Sunday morning he had turned the words of the gospel against them as he preached from James 3:17: 'The words were reversed and applied to us in the most direct and pointed manner, using such terms as "Europeans" "Padries" &c – giving the natives to understand, and hinting more, that there was a great quarrel between us – representing himself as standing up to defend the natives'.[79]

The attitude of individual missionaries also varied considerably on the issue of Khasi customary practices. To some like Sykes, Khasi rituals confirmed their barbarism and hardened what he saw as intrinsic racial dichotomies; to others like Thomas Jones II, to prohibit Khasi Christians from attending bullfights or native dances at the burning place of the Cherra *Syiem*, would simply be a barrier to their remaining in the church. Christianisation in this latter sense could be a transition rather than a rigid event, a process that allowed for some syncretic practices. Thomas Jerman Jones sided with Roberts, citing Rule 4 of the Rules of Discipline for members of the Calvinistic Methodist denomination – 'That they hold no opinion or tenets contrary to the fundamental principles of Christianity' – despite the fact that other rules seemed to be regularly breached, such as those encouraging temperance (Art. 11), and masters being just and kind to their servants (Art. 25).[80]

In early 1873, John Roberts again advised secretary Josiah Thomas from Edinburgh of the need to keep the minutiae of the altercation with Thomas Jones II out of the pages of *Y Drysorfa* and other public forums. His experience in the Scottish church confirmed his belief that his Welsh countrymen were far more prone to the circulation of scandal, 'but I believe that if they were not indulged, they would gradually cease from expecting & demanding all details in connection with cases of this sort'.[81] Thomas Jones II, like his adaptable predecessor and namesake, was rapidly becoming isolated from the strategies and ideologies of his co-workers as well as from the core consensus of church authority.

Notes

1 Morris, *The History*, p. 107.
2 *Ibid.*, pp. 107–8. A part of Ewart's letter is reproduced in Morris, but the original is lost.
3 Jones has been called 'a theologian of liberation' by Nigel Jenkins (*Gwalia in Khasia* (Llandysul, Ceredigion, 1995) p. 11) and 'a liberation theologian much ahead of his times' by Nongbri ('Thomas Jones').
4 Jones to Roberts, 28 July 1841, *Y Drysorfa* November 1841.
5 Jones to Roberts, 18 November 1845, *Y Drysorfa*, February 1846.
6 Jones to Roberts, 28 March 1846, *Y Drysorfa*, July 1846. The cloud and the pillar of fire, as in Exodus 13:21–22.
7 Thomas Jones, *Ka Gospel Jong U Mathi. The Gospel of Matthew in Kassia* (Calcutta, 1846).
8 *Calcutta Christian Observer*, November 1848, 516.
9 Roberts to Lewis, 6 March 1851, CMA 27122.
10 Dkhar, 'The Inglis and Company', p. 122.
11 Norton, *Life of Bishop Wilson*, p. 287.
12 Bromehead, *A Short Account*, p. 166.
13 Dkhar, 'The Inglis and Company', p. 330.
14 'C', 'Excursion to the Chirra Púnjí Hills'; Walters, 'Journey across the Pandua Hills'.
15 Lish, 'A brief account of the Khasees'; Yule, 'Notes on the Kasia Hills'.
16 'W', 'Historical fragments…', *Calcutta Christian Observer*, March 1852, 132.
17 Jones to Roberts, 8 November 1841, *Y Drysorfa*, March 1842.
18 See Christoph von Fürer-Haimendorf, Review of H.O. Mawrie, *The Khasi Milieu* (New Delhi, 1981) in *Religious Studies*, 19 (1983), 126–8.
19 Jones to Roberts, n.d. [1842], *Y Drysorfa*, July 1842.
20 Jones to Roberts, 8 October 1841, *Y Drysorfa*, January 1842.
21 Anna Johnston, *Missionary Writing and Empire, 1800–1860* (Cambridge, 2003), p. 199.
22 Cox, *The British Missionary Enterprise*, p. 118.
23 Lewis to Roberts, 31 January 1850, *Y Drysorfa*, May 1850.

24 *Ibid.*
25 Jones to Roberts, 31 May 1845, *Y Drysorfa*, September 1845.
26 Jones to Roberts, 10 November 1842, *Y Drysorfa*, February 1843.
27 Lewis to Roberts, 10 January 1845, *Y Drysorfa*, May 1845.
28 Morris, *The History*, p. 137.
29 Gurdon, *The Khasis*, p. 84. The red-stained spittle from *kwai* is ubiquitous about the towns, and Yule noted an early popular expression in 'Notes on the Kasia Hills' (p. 620), that only dogs and Bengalis have white teeth.
30 Anonymous, *Ca Nabon: An Account of a Female Convert, in Connexion with the Missionary Society of the Welsh Calvinistic Methodists. With Notices of Other Converts* (London, 1849).
31 Mary Lewis, 'A few reminiscences of our first years of missionary life in India', n.d., CMA 27222; Lewis, 'A brief narrative', CMA 27222.
32 See for example Bareh, *The History and Culture of the Khasi People*, p. 343.
33 Roberts to Lewis, 6 March 1848, CMA 27221.
34 Lewis to Roberts, 12 January 1848, *Y Drysorfa*, April 1848.
35 Mary Lewis to Roberts, 30 October 1847, *Y Drysorfa*, March 1848.
36 Lewis to Roberts, 10 January 1845, *Y Drysorfa*, May 1845.
37 David Cahill, 'Series editor's preface' in Patricia Grimshaw and Andrew May (eds), *Missionaries, Indigenous Peoples and Cultural Exchange* (Brighton, 2010), p. viii.
38 Pryse to Roberts, 29 July 1850, *Y Drysorfa*, November 1850.
39 Pryse to Roberts, 28 March 1850, *Y Drysorfa*, July 1850.
40 Pryse to Roberts, 29 May 1850, *Y Drysorfa*, September 1850.
41 Rees (ed.), *Vehicles of Grace & Hope*, pp. 196–7. See also file in CMA 27231.
42 Maria Owen, 15 May 1863, CMA 27229.
43 Susan Cattell to Mary Lewis, 14 July 1863, CMA 27222.
44 John Hughes Morris, *U Larsing: Evangelist from the Khasi Hills* (Carnarvon, 1912).
45 Peggy Brock, 'New Christians as evangelists' in Norman Etherington (ed.), *Missions and Empire* (Oxford, 2005), pp. 132–52.
46 U Larsing to Kiang Katphoh, n.d. [1861], CMA 27223.
47 U Larsing, 23 April 1862, CMA 27223.
48 U Larsing to Ko Uncle Luh, n.d. [1862], CMA 27223.
49 On the concept of fascination, see Katharine Fullagar, '"Savages that are coming among us": Mai, Bennelong, and British imperial culture', *The Eighteenth Century*, 49:3 (2008), 211–37.
50 For an exception, see Jones, 'Welsh missionary journalism'.
51 James, 'John Roberts' ("Minimus"; 1808–80), pp. 18–19.
52 Pryse, 4 June 1866, CMA 27227.
53 Oswald Williams, 26 February 1906, CMA 27159.
54 Roberts to Thomas, 13 October 1866, CMA 27200.
55 Thomas Dillon to W. Lewis, 9 March 1862, CMA 27221; Cattell to Lewis, 14 July 1863, CMA 27222.
56 Sykes to Thomas, 10 March 1868, CMA 27234.
57 Sykes to Thomas, 15 April 1869, CMA 27234.
58 Roberts to Lewis, 22 March 1849, CMA 27221; Lewis to Roberts, 31 July 1848, *Y Drysorfa*, November 1848; Deed of Mission Lands in Nongsawlia, 30 August 1849, CMA 27098.
59 Amenah Passah, 'Christian missions in the Khasi-Jaintia Hills: health care and impact on the society' in T.B. Subba, Joseph Puthenpurakal, Shaji Joseph Puykunnel, *Christianity and Change in Northeast India* (New Delhi, 2009), note 23, p. 217. See also H.H. Godwin-Austen, 'On the stone monuments of the Khasi Hill Tribes, and on some of the peculiar rites and customs of the people', *The Journal of the Anthropological Institute of Great Britain and Ireland*, 1 (1872), 135–6.
60 Sykes to Thomas, 29 June 1869, CMA 27234.
61 See Patricia Grimshaw and Andrew May, '"Inducements to the strong to be cruel to the weak": authoritative white colonial male voices and the construction of

gender in Koori society' in Norma Grieve and Ailsa Burns (eds), *Australian Women: Contemporary Feminist Thought* (Melbourne, 1994), pp. 92–106.

62 Clare Anderson, *Legible Bodies: Race, Criminality and Colonialism in South Asia* (Oxford, 2004), p. 128.

63 Zahid Chaudhary, 'Phantasmagoric aesthetics: colonial violence and the management of perception', *Cultural Critique*, 59 (2005), 83.

64 Jane Lydon, *Eye Contact: Photographing Indigenous Australians* (Durham, 2005).

65 Griffith, *Journals of Travels in Assam*, chapter 1.

66 Photo 913/(16), India Office Photographs, British Library.

67 Morris, *The History*, p. 177.

68 Sykes to Thomas, 15 April 1869, CMA 27234.

69 I.M. Simon (ed.), *Jaintia Hills District Gazetteer*, c.1997, p. 222.

70 W.M. Jenkins, *Life and Work in Khasia* (Newport, c.1903), facing p. 18.

71 Sykes to Thomas, 13 August 1869, CMA 27234.

72 Roberts and Sykes to Thomas, 2 April 1869, CMA 27234.

73 Rees (ed.), *Vehicles of Grace & Hope*, p. 214.

74 *Ibid.*, p. 194.

75 Hughes to Roberts, 4 May 1870, CMA 27233.

76 U Luh, 31 March 1871, letter translated by William Lewis, CMA 27230.

77 *Ibid.*

78 Thomas Jones, 5 April 1871, CMA 27230.

79 Minutes of Nongsawlia Presbytery, H. Roberts and T. Jerman Jones, 27–31 October 1871, CMA 27230.

80 *The History, Constitution, Rules of Discipline, and Confession of Faith of the Calvinistic Methodists, in Wales, Drawn Up by their Own Associated Ministers* (Chester, 1834), pp. 44–5. See Thomas Jerman Jones to Thomas, 13 November 1871, CMA 27230.

81 Roberts, 9 January 1873, CMA 27229.

CHAPTER THIRTEEN

The country is ours

The geography of the Shillong plateau has set a physical and mental proscenium framing empire's actors, as they shuffle on and off stage in a deceptively cohesive display. The Lewin correspondence and the mission archive are a reminder that the scripting has been partially determined by the fragmentary archival sources that have survived to the present. This chapter weaves together the strands of four final narratives of British people who lived there, who represented some aspect of British hegemony there, and some of whom found it to be their final resting place. In their own fleeting encounters across the stage, between themselves and with their native subjects and informants, they fashioned a range of public meanings of institutional authority and obedience. The missionary Thomas Jones II, the local magistrate Harry Inglis, the civil servant's wife Emma Shadwell, and the soldier F.T. Pollok, projected their constructions of Britishness, Welshness, gender or indigeneity onto the canvas of the Khasi Hills.

The continued crises of authority in the Welsh mission in the 1860s and 1870s came at great personal cost to Thomas Jones II and his family. Unlike the controversies of the 1840s, however, during the schism of the early 1870s Khasi Christians were able to articulate their own views and grievances to the mission authorities in Wales, however immovable the latter may have been. Where U Larsing was taken to Wales as a trophy, the next generation of Khasi Christians could now use the power of the written word and an intimate knowledge of Biblical precepts to counter what they saw as church hypocrisies and to make greater claims for autonomy.

In a political sense too, the government belatedly censured the nepotism and corruption of the Inglis reign in the hills, but in so doing ushered in a new era of paramountcy that simply entrenched British control and interventionism in Khasi affairs. A succession of *sanads* and *parwanas* further ceded customary rights to the British, monopolised land and natural productions, and controlled the appointment of *Syiems*, *sirdars* and other leaders.[1] For mission and for government, Thomas Jones I and II and Harry Inglis had tested the outer limits of authority, which were subsequently institutionalised in a more conservative and hardened middle-ground. With the usual irony of empire, this also produced the conditions under which Khasi resistance to religious and governmental control of the Khasi native states found voice from the latter part of the nineteenth century and into the twentieth, in movements for political and cultural advancement.

Empire on show was a grand public act, sometimes improvised, often scripted carefully in bold words and gestures of power and influence. For many men, women and children of empire, it could sometimes seem that no one was watching the performance. Behind the scenes, removed of its glitter and pretence, it could be a fearful and lonely avocation for neglected missionary children or for the wives of Company bureaucrats. Emma Shadwell's passionate private letters to her daughter from Cherrapunji and Jowai in the 1860s are a third point of departure. Expressive of empire's penalty as well as its recompense, the correspondence to her children sent back to England provides a rare glimpse of one family's intimate and fragile lives on the north-east frontier. Finally, for Colonel Fitzwilliam Thomas Pollok and his hunting party, the petty lives of low Welsh missionaries or lesser civil servants were just part of the scenery.

Rebels and schismatics: Thomas Jones II ostracised

Thomas Jones II had spent eleven continuous years in India before leaving in 1868 for two years furlough in Wales. When he returned to India he left three of his five children in a small boarding school on North Parade, Aberystwyth. From the moment of his return to India in 1870, the home authorities were wary of Jones's uncompromising stance on a number of issues, and they asked him to apologise for the increasingly defiant tone of his correspondence. His services as a missionary of the society were terminated by early 1873, but he resolutely continued superintendence of the government school at Nongsawlia as an independent agent. Of continuing concern to the mission directors was a breakaway group of native Christians who in May 1873 petitioned the Deputy Commissioner of the Khasi and Jaintia Hills on the persecution of boys and teachers at the disaffiliated school by some of the missionaries, as well as the termination of the Sylhet mission. Nine signatories from Nongsawlia Church, together with ten other Khasis from the churches at Nongwar, Nongbah, Nongkroh, Laitkynsew and Shillong, set out a log of complaints accusing the missionaries of being despotic, dishonest, hypocritical, oppressive in their punishment, and unwilling to meet or conciliate.[2]

The group had already corresponded with the home authorities on the issue, and their appeal was not only to natural justice, but to a higher truth of Christian doctrine, citing 2 John 1:4 'I rejoiced greatly that I found of the children walking in truth as we have received a commandment of the father'. The previous week, Josiah Thomas had penned a long and stern letter to U Miri with an appeal to desist from being led astray by their rogue and selfish former agent Thomas Jones II. The secretary forcefully asserted moral and practical authority over the Khasi mission, and contended that any success in the evangelisation of the Khasis was due entirely to the labours, tears, prayers and financial support of the mostly impoverished people of Wales. Part of the debt therefore was ultimate obedience to home authority; 'beware', cautioned Thomas paternalistically, 'lest you may be led away by others who are not so simple-minded as yourselves . . . whatever they may pretend to say to you about your rights and privileges'. Any sense that the Khasi Christians were sufficiently enlightened to assert independence of action was, in the opinion of the directors, highly precipitate.[3]

His health reduced and now impecunious, Jones eventually agreed to seek some kind of rapprochement with the other missionaries through the offices of a mediator. 'I desire to retrace my steps', he wrote to Dr Brown in September 1873, '& to offer the most ample apology for the hard expressions & unsubmissive spirit which they feel I manifested . . . I would not for any thing be a hindrance to the mission whose service has been to me the greatest pleasure during so many of the best years of my life, & whose interests were to me precious as my own life'.[4] Jones's acquiescence came too late, and the four other missionaries from the stations at Cherrapunji, Shella, Shillong and Jowai rejected his appeal as being a misrepresentation of recent events. Hugh Roberts, John Roberts, Griffith Hughes and Thomas Jerman Jones were unequivocal in their resolution to stamp out the schismatics who challenged their authority and who had ceded under the encouragement of Thomas Jones II.[5] Not only did the WFMS directors reaffirm their decision to dismiss him, but they also wrote to the government of Bengal asking that he not be offered any other employment in government service in the Khasi or Jaintia Hills or immediate neighbourhood.[6] Jones's health and that of his wife were 'shattered' from their long years in India. By February 1874 Jones and his family were staying with Ann Jane Brownlow, daughter of Thomas Jones I. Thomas Jones II was reportedly trading in rice for the distressed districts of Bengal then suffering famine conditions.[7] In May the mission directors paid the outstanding balance of his salary to the boarding school in Aberystwyth, where his

14 Thomas Jones II.

15 Gwenllian Jones.

three children were still under care.[8] On 9 July 1874, after some days of diarrhoea and loss of appetite, Thomas Jones II died of cholera and was buried at Sylhet.

Hugh Roberts and John Roberts visited the grieving Gwenllian Jones at Nongsawlia, but found her hardened against the mission she blamed for her husband's demise. Hugh Roberts was palpably relieved that the mission could be seen to bear little responsibility: 'There is something providential', he wrote, 'in the fact that he was taken away by cholera & not from weakness, or debilitatory or secondary causes as Mrs Jones says'.[9] Henry Muspratt, sessions judge of Sylhet, recommended that the mission should pay her passage home, but as the months passed, Gwenllian Jones remained with a small faithful band of women and other schismatics at Nongsawlia, 'a thorn in Mr Roberts' side – leading the few that have separated' and who were looking to ordain U Miri as their minister.[10] With Gwenllian Jones determined to discredit the other missionaries, they countered with their own accusations: that the Joneses had actually been very well off financially, that they were moneylenders to the Khasis, and that her behaviour was erratic. 'If the kind brethren in "Dwyrain Meirionnydd" [East Merionethshire] knew what we know of Mrs Jones & her doings they would not be in such a hurry about helping her'.[11] The Liverpool directors offered to pay her passage home, an offer that she eventually accepted. In early January 1875, Gwenllian Jones left Cherrapunji for Calcutta, and the remaining Welsh missionaries were 'all of us very glad she is gone'.[12]

By April, Mrs Jones and her children were staying with her brother-in-law, a labourer at Bala; whatever putative financial assets she may have had, they could not be realised. Lewis Edwards wrote to the committee on her behalf, asking that it pay £100 owed to Miss Jones's school at Aberystwyth, and for the continuing costs of educating the two eldest boys.[13] By the end of the year, however, she had returned to India with all five of her children. When Thomas Jerman Jones, Griffith Hughes and John Roberts visited her four years later, they found her in a miserable state, 'extremely weak, scarcely able to walk, and weeping all the time'. While her views on past events had not entirely changed, Thomas Jerman Jones felt that mercy should be exercised and that she should again be encouraged to return to Wales (where 'she will not be the same nor act the same as she did the last time she was there'). They were particularly concerned about the children, 'who are allowed to grow like the natives running about barefooted & half-clad'.[14] It is likely that she never returned to Wales; in the 1880s her son Robert was a tea planter at Chittagong, and in his latter years after World War I managed the Fatikchhari Tea Company at Baramasia until his death in 1924. His mother is reputed to have died at a great age at his home, and during her final illness she lapsed back into her native Welsh, which no one around her could understand any more.

After the death of Thomas Jones I in 1849, his widow Emma had gone to live with her mother Susan Cattell at Cherrapunji. With both her parents dead, six-year-old Ann Jane Jones – daughter of the first missionary – was a tangible reminder to the WFMS of the human cost of their enterprise and the failures of themselves and their agents. The Welsh were not keen to have the child sent home, and Emma Jones was loath to give her up to the care of the missionaries whom her late husband despised. The brethren at the Llanrwst Association advised John Roberts that Ann's stepmother might be persuaded to give her up to the possession of the mission for whom she might become a 'serviceable' asset. Eliza Ewart had herself thought of adopting the sickly girl, who a week before Christmas 1849 eventually arrived in Sylhet to be left in the care of Mrs Pryse.[15]

Susan Cattell had originally disapproved of her daughter's marriage to a poor Welsh missionary, and on her mother's recommendation, in November 1850 at Cherrapunji, Emma married into slightly more respectable and well-off local circles in the form of Charles Mackay, a Eurasian widower almost twice her age who was employed in the Bengal Civil Service.[16] Mackay was Principal Sudder Ameen of Furreedpore, the highest rank of native judge in the *mofussil* or district court. Emma and Charles Mackay's two daughters were born at Cherrapunji and Sylhet in 1853 and 1855, but by November 1855 Emma had died, a month short of her twenty-fifth birthday, and was buried at Dacca.[17]

After her daughter's remarriage to Charles Mackay, Susan Cattell had taken her grandson Thomas Cattell-Jones into her household at Cherrapunji. In January 1852, her fifteen-year-old daughter Emily wrote from 'Ing Maw Sora' (the stone house, Sohra) to her grandmother Susannah Halford with a short account of life at the station: the long rides she enjoyed on a pony given to her by judge Skipwith in Sylhet; her older sister Susan taking a sketch of the bungalow; her Aunt Emily Brownlow making social calls on the Rabans; her younger sister collecting butterflies for Mrs Garstin. Emily also wrote with pride of her little nephew Thomas, who 'chatters away incessantly in English he counts up to ten as quick as possible in English, Bangalee and Kassiah . . . He is admired by every one who sees him for his lovely black eyes'.[18] Susan adopted Thomas Cattell-Jones and brought him back to England. He spent his childhood at her home 'Cherrahurst' in Weybridge, and later studied medicine at Guy's Hospital and in Edinburgh. Jean, daughter of Thomas Jones II, married Thomas Cattell-Jones, the son of Thomas Jones I, in 1884.

Matters of history

In the aftermath of the Jones versus Inglis affair of the 1840s, Harry Inglis preferred charges against judge Stainforth for borrowing money from a European in his jurisdiction, contrary to civil service regulations. While an inquiry found that 'nothing has occurred which tends to affect Mr Stainforth's moral character, or his reputation as upright and well-meaning officer', in 1852 he was moved from Sylhet to another district 'as a public mark of disapprobation'.[19] Harry Inglis remained in the hills, but the government in Calcutta was finally convinced by a groundswell of complaint that a further investigation was needed into the workings of the Cherrapunji Court and the administration of the hills more generally.

On 27 September 1853, A.J.M. Mills, officiating judge of the Sudder Court, tabled his report to the government of Bengal on the Khasi and Jaintia Hills. Mills had been deputed to seek evidence as to irregularities in the administration of justice. His characterisation of the native population of around 82,000, across 564 dependent villages, was typically dismissive – a once 'upright simple people' now 'arrogant, deceitful, and untrustworthy' from their 'association with civilization and wealth'.[20] Intercourse with the British since 1826, the Nongkhlaw massacre, 'the general disaffection of the tribes; the consequent warfare; the apprehension of some of the outlaws; the eventual submission of the chieftains; and the entire subjugation of the country' were for Mills 'matters of history that I need not dwell upon'.[21] But if the Khasis were of low moral character, the report contained a litany of complaints against the administration of justice in the territory, and more particularly the contradictory and competing powers ascribed to the Political Agent as magistrate, collector and judge. 'The country is ours', claimed Mills, 'and it is our duty to see that speedy justice, suited to the simple habits of the people, is administered'.[22]

The bulk of the Mills report scrutinised disputes over the previous two years between Gibson, Duncan and Cattell on the one hand, and Harry Inglis on the other, over the right to quarry limestone at Choon Cherra. A deliberate and persistent harassment of his three competitors by Inglis and his associates had seen Eugene Cattell assaulted, and numbers of their servants illegally arrested and imprisoned with hard labour. Cattell and his cousin Halford Brownlow fled the district through Sylhet disguised as Muslim pilgrims. Mills was heavily critical of the actions of Inglis, and of Lieutenant Cave, the new Assistant to the Political Agent and Inglis's stooge, who in his administration of justice had 'identified himself with Mr. Inglis and been guilty of systematic wrong . . . his official superior was his commanding officer, and the father-in-law of Mr. Inglis, Mr. Gibson's rival in the trade'.[23]

Mills's intelligence as to the disputes was heavily dependent on a deposition from W.H.M. Sweetland, Agent of the Sylhet Coal Company, who in a lengthy and impassioned plea for justice, impugned the Cherra Court (Inglis's 'registered office') at which 'the administration of justice has become a nullity, a bye-word, and reproach'.[24] The question of who was savage and who civilised was one that had at times exercised the minds and consciences of empire's beneficiaries; 'an Englishman would be safer', noted Sweetland wryly, 'alongside John Hikio Pah in New Zealand or among the savages of the Fugus, than in the Cherra jurisdiction, the only difference, perhaps, would be that the latter would, after killing, boil and eat you'.[25] While he could not vouch for the veracity of the claims, Sweetland recounted a version of the events of 1849 in which Thomas Jones I had been hounded to his death and had 'from the multiplied persecutions and indignities he had suffered, shortly died of a broken heart'.[26] Sweetland considered that Jones had paid the ultimate price for his pursuit of justice in the hills, at the hands of agents 'whose escape from the consequences of their own delinquencies absolutely depended upon his extinction'.[27] He also knew that the government might be more worried about the ongoing commercial implications of their ignoring the growing infamy of one of its productive jurisdictions. Jones may have argued for justice on the basis of native rights; Sweetland appealed to government on the basis of the security of the investments and enterprise of British mercantile interests who had underwritten a more than twofold increase in imports and exports from India between 1824 and 1849. But their principle was the same. 'I have now', concluded Sweetland, 'in furnishing these details done, as becomes every Briton, my duty to God, my country, and myself. Let the Government of India do theirs'.[28]

Mills was reluctant to revisit the Jones case, and washed the government's hands of any responsibility for his death by having ignored his complaints. Mired as it was in the politics of a previous regime, to all intents and purposes the Dunbar inquiry had proven Jones's charges to be without foundation, however much recollection of the case in the Mills report may have panged consciences in Calcutta. But Governor-General Dalhousie upheld the Mills report, and censured Lieutenant Cave and the 'evil' of the nepotistic relationship that had been allowed to exist in the Political Agency in the north-east.[29] Inglis may have become disassociated from the direct mechanisms of authority through the office of Assistant to the Political Agent, but it is clear that he continued to wield considerable influence in maintaining his monopoly on the lime trade through the rest of the decade. A further inquiry in 1858 censured the actions – or inactions – of Principal Assistant Commissioner of the Khasi and Jaintia Hills, W.K. Hudson, in being complicit in the Inglis monopoly by ignoring complaints made against him. Further charges of molestation were made by Inglis's opponents, who accused him of being a lawless, nefarious and violent oppressor, while Inglis characterised his detractors as a band of reckless and unprincipled adventurers.[30] Hudson resigned in 1860 to work for Inglis & Co., but with Inglis's death and government assertions of its rights to the mineral resources of the hills, the Inglis monopoly was slowly broken.

Harry Inglis died aged fifty-seven on 31 July 1860 at Berkeley Square in London, having suffered from complications of diabetes. Inglis left all his *zemindaries*, *talooks*, factories, houses, lands, leases of lime stone quarries and any other leases, orange gardens, financial deposits, government securities and all other goods and chattels to his 'dearly beloved wife'. An obituary in the *Standard* noted that he had been 'universally esteemed and respected'.[31] Even in death, Harry did not escape the lure of India, and his widow took his body back to the Khasi Hills and installed it on the verandah of her house at Cherrapunji. By this time Sophia was living with Scottish-born Charles Seton Guthrie, a colonel in the Bengal Engineers, whom she married in 1863.

When Thomas Dillon, the newly arrived Political Agent for Manipur and Cachar, wrote to William Lewis in early 1862, he signalled a hopeful shift in the style of political opportunism that had marked the region. Suggesting that he himself would not wield influence in the same manner as his predecessor Major W. McCulloch ('through the medium of his harem'), Dillon also noted the death throes of the Inglis ascendancy. The Inglis clan was now ostracised; Sophia now lived with Colonel Guthrie, but was indignant at having been turned out of society at Cherrapunji. At the Inglis compound at Kut Madan, perched at the southern tip of the plain at Cherrapunji where the flat plateau abruptly gave way to the precipice and where on a clear day the plains of Sylhet were laid out like a shimmering quilt below, Sophia installed Harry's corpse in a glass coffin on the verandah, telling the Khasis 'that he would rise from the dead and avenge himself on any person who wronged her'.[32] Sophia's logic played on the fear the Khasis still felt of Harry's power, even in death. Under Harry's agreements with the Khasis, his leases on the orange groves were good for his lifetime, which in Khasi translated as 'for as long as he remained above the ground'.[33] In 1864 Sophia Guthrie was living at Garden Reach in Calcutta. Two years later her body was found at the Great Northern Hotel at Kings Cross in London.[34] Kut Madan was sold to John Bird Shadwell, the Assistant Commissioner of the Khasi and Jaintia Hills who had acted as court translator through the Thomas Jones affair (and whom Sweetland, in his evidence to the Mills inquiry in 1853, had accused of falsifying evidence).[35]

Such a wilderness: home and away in the hills

The isolation of a far-flung mountainous hill district like the Khasi Hills is revealed in the correspondence between Emma and J.B. Shadwell and four of their children, who in 1862 had been sent to be educated in England in the care of their aunt Martha Brockway. Shadwell was the son of Captain John Augustus Shadwell, H.C. 26th Native Infantry, and an Indian mother,[36] and had married Emma Brockway at Calcutta in 1849. Shadwell's civil service career saw him rise from being a writer in the Political Agent's office in the early 1850s to assuming the role of Assistant Commissioner at Cherrapunji in 1862. The Shadwell children – Emma (b. 1850), St Clair (1852), Flora (1854) and Howard (1856) – were shipped back to Walthamstowe, north-east of London, leaving baby Lily with her mother.

Emma Shadwell's private letters give an indication of the rhythms of social life on the station, and of the particular dynamics of isolation on an Indian frontier. While her husband was occupied by official duties, Emma's life could at times be a mixture of tedium and intense loneliness. In November 1865 she reported that a Lieutenant Gregory had passed through Cherrapunji and Jowai on his way back to North Cachar: 'He & another Lt are the only English persons in that place & when he came in on his way to Cherra he said I was the first lady he had seen since last March so he is more lonely out there than we are here'.[37]

Her separation from her children extended from months to years. Like the Lewins two decades before them, the Shadwells aspired to eventual repatriation to England, but found themselves stranded in the hills with heavily circumscribed social and financial means. 'Dear papa & I would like very much to settle in dear Old England', wrote Emma, but 'it will be some years before we shall be able to do that'.[38] Emma's letters, mostly written to her eldest child Emma, serve multiple purposes. Ostensibly brief and regular accounts of family and social life at Cherrapunji and later Jowai, they operate in a strangely liminal space. The correspondence coded very particular ideologies of gender, domesticity, race and religious belief. While each letter played an important role in maintaining everyday emotional as well as instructional links with the children, it also became the bitter and heartbreaking talisman of separation and distance.

Emma followed her children in her mind's eye on their way home

16 Emma Shadwell to Emma Shadwell, 11 July 1864, detail.

via Chhatak, and thence on the *Shannon* from Calcutta to England. She reported to them the daily goings on at Cherrapunji: the health of their cat and the dogs, the state of the roses and dahlias, the everydayness of the weather, Captain Cordner taking a charcoal sketch of baby Lily, and papa bringing radishes in from the garden for breakfast. Her letters were also constantly filled with the social news of other British families at the station with whom the Shadwells had professional and social ties, or who moved between engagements at Sylhet, Dacca and Assam. For her eldest daughter, the letters narrativised particular precepts of gendered social roles – the protocols and practices of social interchange ('I often have calls but being Gentlemen only I do not have to return them'),[39] the centrality of women's childbearing and childrearing roles, the appropriate functions and limits of gossip. There were frequent reports of other women giving birth and other family milestones: 'Mrs Lane's baby is to be Christened today', Emma wrote in March 1863 – 'her name is to be Lilian Jane she is a good deal like Mrs Lane very fat & big'. Emma's own little daughter Lily was kept alive in the mind's eye of her distant siblings, as she slowly grew into a toddler, 'her little legs are like two rolley pooly [*sic*] puddings', outgrowing her baby's bathing tub.[40] Emma modelled motherly and domestic roles: 'My Emmah my dear sweet darling child', she wrote, 'your dear likeness came yesterday dear papa and I will prize it very much it is very like you my darling you do not appear the least changed only your hair is dressed differently . . . You are looking very well I think you are stouter & I dare say a little taller your frock is very neat & you look very nice'.[41] Passionately maternal towards her absent daughter, her letters are imbued with precepts of piety, decorum and neatness.

The garden at the house they renamed Emma Ville – 'our quiet little corner' – was an important site, not simply as a productive or decorative space, but as a vital outpost of Englishness. Emma was proud of it in her letters, often reporting the appreciative comments of visitors – for Herbert Raban, 'it was more like an English garden than any at Cherra'.[42] From this fragile oasis, Emma Shadwell recounted the regular deaths as well as the births of babies, and the constant and varied threats of tigers, 'rebels' and disease. In March 1863 the Khasi practice of seasonally firing the lush pasture on the plateau got out of control, almost burning their bungalow to the ground. An epidemic of cholera in mid-1863 saw high mortality among the Khasis, and John Bird Shadwell moved many of the prisoners from the Cherra jail to Sohrarim, 'because they were dying off so fast in the jail here'.[43] Endemic to the subcontinent, cholera spread through India in the decade after 1816, and subsequently hit Europe and North America in pandemic waves. While agents of the Welsh mission had over the years succumbed to it (most recently, Robert Parry's wife in 1861), over 5000 people died in Liverpool in 1849, and the fourth great nineteenth-century pandemic killed significant numbers in the decade after 1863. On 15 November 1849, the Reverend J.R. Hughes had noted in his diary that under a proclamation from Queen Victoria, the day had been set aside as a day of prayer and thanksgiving 'to the all merciful Creator for his goodness in removing from our country the dreadfull scourge and visible judgement the cholera'.[44] Neither divine intervention nor the recipes for the prevention of cholera found among missionary papers (concoctions of laudanum, peppermint oil and tincture of coffee) were ultimately much protection.[45] It was not until Russian-born bacteriologist Waldemar Haffkine tested his cholera vaccine on himself and on thousands of Indians from 1893 that a means of prevention was secured. Many Khasis succumbed to the disease at Cherrapunji in 1863, yet the British residents were themselves not immune. Young Lieutenant Saddler came up to the hills – 'after he arrived he had cholera & got a stroke of the sun on his way up, he died from the effect last Sunday week'. 'Truly in the midst of life', cautioned Emma to her children, 'we are in death'.[46]

Emma's letters were particularly imbued with a strong sense of religious devotion, with a definitive belief in the protective power of her God among the threats and temptations of the world, and the comforts of daily prayer and Bible reading: 'give your young heart to God He delights in those who give him their early days'.[47] Her social world included the missionaries, ex-missionaries and their extended families. Susan Cattell was still living in Cherrapunji at this time, and often asked Emma to be remembered to the children, though 'she feared she had quite died from the memory of the little ones'. The young Miss Ann (Annie) Jones, daughter of Thomas Jones I from his first marriage, was also clearly well known to the Shadwells and their children, and seeing her piquantly reminded Emma of her own daughter now back in England.[48] With scriptural comfort from Luke 12:35, Emma Shadwell reported the death of the elderly Mrs Halford, Susan's mother, in August 1863: 'We are none too young to die. May we be also ready with our loins girt & our lamps burning so that at whatever hour the bridegroom comes he may find us watching'.[49]

Susan Cattell and her sister Emily Brownlow also kept up a correspondence with Mary Lewis, now returned to Britain. Perhaps united with Mary Lewis in her antipathy towards Thomas Jones I, the women were clearly on good terms as Susan reported the latest news from the hills.[50] As far as life at Cherrapunji went, Thomas Jones II and his wife Gwenllian had their hands full with their own three children (including four-year-old daughter Jean), as well as two boys of Robert Parry's. The Joneses were also busy looking after distressed *Syntengs* from the Jaintia Hills. Susan reported the death from cholera three months before of her own daughter Emily, aged twenty-seven, leaving husband Henry Halford Brownlow with a one-year-old baby daughter Ellen.

The missionary's daughter Annie Jones, then aged twenty, was like a sister to Emily Brownlow, and 'weighed down with sorrow' was at her side when she died. Susan eulogised her daughter as a faithful, familial and feminine role-model: 'Oh she was such a loving amiable child, wife & mother. Poor Halford has by the Lord's mercy been wonderfully supported. She had led him the two short years of their wedded life, to the Cross, to Jesus & in Him he has found consolation'. Devastated by the death of her 'guardian angel', Annie Jones was to marry Emily's widower Henry Halford Brownlow at Sylhet in March 1865; her step-daughter Ellen later married the Welsh missionary John Pengwern Jones, whose own wife had died of cholera just a week after their arrival in India in late 1887.[51]

Susan Cattell and her sister Emily Brownlow's sons were running tea estates in Cachar in Assam, to the east of the Khasi Hills. Brothers Arthur, Henry Halford and Charles Brownlow all had tea estates within sixteen miles of each other in an industry that was the direct descendant of Wallich, Griffith and McClelland's expedition for the Tea Commission in 1836. Cultivation of *Camellia sinensis* was sporadic through the 1840s, but after the British annexation of North Cachar in 1854 and variations in colonial policy towards fee simple ownership of land, a mad rush saw many British planters enter the industry. After their difficult dealings with Harry Inglis in the early 1850s, Henry Halford Brownlow and his cousin Eugene Brownlow Cattell had sought other prospects on the Australian goldfields, arriving at Melbourne from Calcutta on the *Mooltan* in May 1853. Eugene Cattell moved another two times between India and Australia before settling by the mid-1870s in Cachar, where he died of cholera in 1883. Henry Halford Brownlow and his brothers were quicker to grasp the possibilities of the tea trade, which in 1882 was characterised by Samuel Baildon as the perfect field for any young and adventurous capitalists too impecunious to buy into medicine, not bookish enough for government service, not righteous enough for the church nor clever enough for the law. For these scions of empire, deracinated from their British origins, an Indian career as a tea planter offered more opportunities than Australia or other new world settler societies where access to land and finance was more problematic.[52]

All the Shadwells wanted, however, was to go 'home'. The coming of the steamer service offered the prospect of cheaper passages to England, and Emma fantasised about disembarking at the East India Docks in London. But on the salary of a minor government official, her husband's means were barely sufficient to send the regular remittances to England to support their children (soon joined by Lily) at school in Walthamstowe. J.B. Shadwell wrote only occasionally to his children; for him the certainty that their return to England was a necessary rite of passage tying them to British norms of culture and education ('I hope the sight of the little world you have got into afford [*sic*] you all a good deal of amusement')[53] perhaps masked the emotion he felt at the prospect of an extended separation. His letters to his son St Clair were more likely to note broader events like the famine in Bengal than the intricacies of the Cherra social scene; for his son the news that tigers had killed several men and women in the Jaintia Hills was deemed more useful intelligence for a boy than Mrs Rossenrode's baby cutting teeth.[54]

The exchange of gifts and tokens between the Shadwells and their children was another important strategy in maintaining emotional and familial ties. Flora sent bon bons for baby Lily, edging for her frock, and made slippers for her father; Emma sent her eldest daughter collars, cuffs, shawls, and local Khasi silk for a skirt, while Emma junior forwarded blue salvia seeds for her father's garden. St Clair received a cap from his father made of animal fur. Trivial domestic items were powerful symbolic cargo. 'I am sorry I could not get something else or better to send', bemoaned Emma in 1868; 'this place is such a wilderness that there is very little to be got'.[55] What Emma Shadwell most craved was 'to feel your dear arms around my neck once more';[56] but everyday material objects were surrogate for the intimacy of touch, a child's arm around a father's neck, a mother's kiss on a daughter's cheek. They could demonstrate not only the accomplishments of herself or her children, but acted as domestic *aides memoire* to a family broken apart by distance and circumstance.

No sooner did she receive photographs of her children in the mail, than the wet climate reduced them to moulded scraps. Where other mothers could take their children on the usual social rounds, a few days after Christmas in 1864 Emma Shadwell tucked the paper substitutes of her Emma, St Clair and Howard under her arm as she went visiting: 'you all look so sweet in the Album. I am going in a day or two to take you all over to visit Mrs Cattell, the old lady will be so pleased to see you'.[57]

In the midst of her everyday reports, there are few glimpses into the lives of local Khasi people. As court translator, J.B. Shadwell was a proficient Khasi speaker, and the children back in England had clearly learned enough Khasi for everyday conversation. Ooojon worked in the garden at Emma Ville, and Emma would buy lemons, chillies and sweet potatoes from an old Khasi woman 'because you & my dear boy St Clair always pittied her'.[58] While the household clearly depended on the labour of Khasi servants, Emma seemed circumspect about close contact; her baby Lily 'does not like going to the Natives at all', she told Emma: 'If I had strength enough I would always keep her in my arms'.[59]

The Shadwell's time in the hills also marked the period of transition from Cherrapunji to Shillong as the seat of authority in the north-east. Through the changing of the seasons each year, Emma tracked the changing feel of Cherrapunji, which aside from the 'hardened' residents like herself, emptied out in the colder months. By the mid-1860s the station was coming on. With improved road and rail services on the plains, and a steamer from Chhatak running twice a week, more people came up to the Khasi Hills for picnics and holidays, enlivening the social scene for its long-term British denizens. By 1863 Jowai had become a regular military station, with numbers of European officers and 'Ladies even' residing there. As the last of the Jaintia rebels was captured and paraded through Cherrapunji in mid-December 1863, the

17 'Group of residents of Shillong, Cossyah Hills, Bengal'.

Shillong *Syiem* was disposing of some of his lands to government for a new military and civil station.[60] In the wake of the Jaintia uprising, Emma felt the vulnerability of life at Cherra when the numbers of *sepoys* were reduced in the cold season. In March 1864 J.B. Shadwell was working in Jowai, and building works commenced at Shillong on a *cutcherry* and jail. The Shadwells hoped to remain at the subdivisional station at Cherra, but were moved to Jowai in September 1865, very sorry to leave. They were back in Cherra at the start of 1866 and, thinking they would stay there more permanently, had the roof of Emma Ville rethatched. Back in Jowai by mid-1867, they rented out Emma Ville, and had a new house built of stone and clay mortar at Jowai which was totally destroyed by the most powerful earthquake in living memory in July 1868.[61]

Unafraid to venture: the mastery of the hills

In October 1869, Colonel Fitzwilliam Thomas Pollok of the Madras Army set off from Shillong on a hunting expedition in the company of some military friends. Pollok spent around eight years on road-making and survey duties in Assam and through the Khasi and Jaintia Hills, and his measure of the region was also calculated in the successful bags of stag, gaur (wild ox), leopard and bear that his Khasi beaters flushed out of their jungle or grassland haunts, or the poundage of fish pulled from the rivers and ponds of the mountain region. In one trip, Pollok and three companions hauled out 736lbs of fish in five days. Stalking the park-like plateau, Pollok and his companions would get the Khasis to fire the grassland so they could shoot at their ease the game that fled the inferno. In this exploitative vision of the hills, terrain was less the cultured habitation of humans than a scaled map of which parts would provide an afternoon's good shooting. On this particular trip, the party often followed Khasi foot tracks and inter-village paths rather than their British cart-tracks, and headed first to Nartiang via Pommura. At Nartiang, Pollok encountered 'a Welsh missionary with a cartload of children in the dâk bungalow', and his party was forced to stay in the school-room, 'which, from its appearance, could not have been used for months and months, and was a mass of filth', being used as a pig pen. Pollok's cursory and passing vision of the mission – and of the Welsh parson 'who seemed to have nothing to do but breed children' – was one of squalor and brute animalism; here the Welsh missionary and his family were at once racially inferior to the English observer, and at the same time reduced to the level of the beasts and the heathens among whom they laboured. 'I never saw his wife', Pollok observed, 'but she must have been a most prolific woman, for there were some dozen or more children of all sizes, with intervals of barely nine months between them'.[62] This from a man who had five children of his own, and was to have four more; but Pollok held his fingers to his nose and moved on, bagging some duck and teal in the *bheels* along the way.

The road thence to Jowai reminded Pollok of the Brighton downs, and on their arrival at the *dâk* bungalow the group was supplied with vegetables and other supplies by Assistant Commissioner Shadwell. Pollok had come prepared to fish the river below Jowai that he had seen swarming with fish on a previous visit, and was equipped with strong tackle and an india-rubber boat. Despite the fact that they were well aware that the river was a sacred place to the local Khasis, the soldiers proceeded to try their luck in filling their creels, but to no avail. The Khasis told the party that they had invoked their gods to send the fish away; 'To console ourselves', wrote Pollok, 'we shot a lot of snipe'.[63]

Further on, they rested for the night at Sohkha, and dined lavishly on a meal prepared by their servants of 'soup, fish, roasted wild duck, snipe on toast, bread-and-cheese, and washed down in libations of icy cold Bass' pale ale'.[64] The next day General Blake sketched the river scenery while Pollok trawled the depths with seventy yards of line and snared a thirty pound monster before breakfast. At their journey's end, at Jaintiapore on the plains, his party's mastery of the native world was linked to British martial superiority, as they picked their way among the dismantled cannons and ramparts, the remnant reminders of the Jaintia rebellion earlier in the decade. The landscape of the hills was a wild canvas on which the clear lines of masterful authority and manly power were delineated: 'no one can expect to keep healthy in those Provinces', trumpeted Pollok, 'who indulges in brandy-panee, and spends half the day in sleep, and who is afraid to venture out for fear of sunstroke'.[65]

For Pollok and his military confreres, Jowai was just a pit-stop on their pleasure tour. As J.B. Shadwell waved the voracious hunting party on its forward journey, Emma stood by with her sixth child at her breast. Despite the earnest expectations of the Shadwells that their family would soon be together again in England, there was no joyous reunion. Jowai was Emma's last resting place, and she died there the following year.

Notes

1 Giri, *The Khasis*, chapter 6.
2 Petition of native Christians, 17 May 1873, CMA 23270.
3 J. Thomas to U Miri, 9 May 1873, CMA 27139.
4 T. Jones to Dr Brown, 25 September 1873, CMA 27230.
5 H. Roberts, J. Roberts, G. Hughes and T. Jerman Jones to Dr Brown, 3 October 1873, CMA 27230.
6 [J. Thomas] to Secretary of Government of Bengal, 23 December 1873, CMA 23270. See also Thomas to Dr Brown, 7 January 1874, CMA 27139.
7 H. Roberts, 12 February 1874, CMA 12 February 1874.
8 Thomas, 16 May 1874, CMA 27139.
9 H. Roberts, 15 July 1874, CMA 27230.
10 G. Hughes, 20 September 1874, CMA 27230.
11 Roberts to Thomas, 12 January 1875, CMA 27230.
12 *Ibid.*
13 Edwards to Thomas, 9 April 1875, CMA 27230.
14 T.J. Jones to Thomas, 4 September 1879, CMA 27109.
15 E. Ewart to M. Lewis, 27 November 1849; W. Pryse, 22 December 1849; J. Roberts to W. Lewis, 18 January 1850, CMA 2722.
16 IOR N/1/78/345; also 'Notes given by Millie Cattell to her niece Noelle Hardy', typed copy c. 1975, retyped 1998 by her son Frank Hardy, author's possession.
17 IOR N/1/88/464.
18 E. Cattell to S. Halford, 5 January 1852, author's possession.
19 IOR E/4/814, Bengal Judicial, 4 February 1852, No. 43.
20 A.J.M. Mills, *Report on the Khasi and Jaintia Hills, 1853* (Shillong, 1901), p. 5.
21 *Ibid.*, p. 1.
22 *Ibid.*, p. 11.
23 *Ibid.*, p. 24.
24 *Ibid.*, p. 93.
25 *Ibid.*, p. 82.
26 *Ibid.*, p. 87.
27 *Ibid.*, p. 95.
28 *Ibid.*, p. 98.
29 Minute from the Governor of Bengal, Dalhousie, 16 November 1863, in Mills, *Report*, pp. 113–15.
30 W.J. Allen, *Report on the Administration of the Cossyah and Jynteah Hills* (Calcutta, 1858).

31 *Standard*, 4 August 1860, p. 7.
32 T. Dillon to W. Lewis, 9 March 1862, CMA 27221.
33 F.T. Pollok and W.S. Thom, *Wild Sports of Burma and Assam* (London, 1900), p. 498.
34 E. Shadwell to E. Shadwell, 24 October 1864, Loesch papers.
35 Mills, *Report*, p. 91. Jones had also claimed that the court interpreter 'is known to be in Mr Inglis' confidence and to have received and shared his bribes': Thomas Jones petition, 4 June 1849, IOR P/143/34, 11 July 1849, No. 78.
36 IOR N/1/10 f. 600.
37 E. Shadwell to E. Shadwell, 3 November 1865, Loesch papers.
38 E. Shadwell to E. Shadwell, 8 March 1864, Loesch papers.
39 E. Shadwell to E. Shadwell, 22 April 1863, Loesch papers.
40 E. Shadwell to E. Shadwell, 7 January 1863, Loesch papers.
41 E. Shadwell to E. Shadwell, 9 November 1863, Loesch papers.
42 E. Shadwell to E. Shadwell, 4 September 1863, Loesch papers.
43 E. Shadwell to E. Shadwell, 16 July 1863, Loesch papers.
44 CMA (2)/12825 Diary of J. R. Hughes 1849–50.
45 Cholera Recipe by Dr Trench, Medical Officer, Liverpool, June 1866, CMA 27221.
46 E. Shadwell to E. Shadwell, 22 April 1863, Loesch papers.
47 E. Shadwell to E. Shadwell, 5 January 1863, Loesch papers.
48 E. Shadwell to E. Shadwell, 24 June 1864, Loesch papers.
49 E. Shadwell to E. Shadwell, 20 August 1863, Loesch papers.
50 Susan Elizabeth Cattell to Mary Lewis, 14 July 1863, NLW CMA 27222.
51 Rees (ed.), *Vehicles of Grace & Hope*, pp. 91–2.
52 Samuel Baildon, *The Tea Industry in India. A Review of Finance and Labour, and a Guide for Capitalists and Assistants* (London, 1882), pp. 35–6.
53 J.B. Shadwell to E. Shadwell, 30 December 1862, Loesch papers.
54 J.B. Shadwell to St Clair Shadwell, 3 September 1866, Loesch papers.
55 E. Shadwell to E. Shadwell, 19 October 1868, Loesch papers
56 E. Shadwell to E. Shadwell, 26 September 1864, Loesch papers.
57 E. Shadwell to E. Shadwell, 26 December 1864, Loesch papers.
58 E. Shadwell to E. Shadwell, 5 January 1863, Loesch papers.
59 E. Shadwell to E. Shadwell, 24 September 1863, Loesch papers.
60 E. Shadwell to E. Shadwell, 22 December 1863, Loesch papers.
61 Sykes to Thomas, 10 January 1869, CMA 27234.
62 Pollok and Thom, *Wild Sports*, pp. 501, 494.
63 *Ibid.*, p. 502.
64 *Ibid.*, p. 503.
65 *Ibid.*, p. x.

Conclusion

Anglican clergyman and political economist the Reverend Thomas Robert Malthus was Professor of History and Political Economy at the East India College (Haileybury) from 1805 until his death in 1834. In *An Essay on the Principle of Population* (1798–1826), Malthus saw the future improvement of society turning on the positive or preventive population checks provided by poverty, disease, war, famine, delayed marriage, prostitution and contraception. While Malthus's views on the relationship between sustainable population growth and food supply were highly controversial at the time, his ideas influenced Darwin's evolutionary biology. Darwin's theories of natural selection, first propounded in his *On the Origin of Species* (1859), were much more fully explored in his detailed study of the co-evolution of insects and orchids, published three years later. Darwin had been procuring flowering orchids for some years before, and had written to John Lindley in 1861 that 'Orchids have interested me more than almost anything in my life'.[1] In the 'curious contrivances' of the *Dendrobium* and the *Cattleya*, chestfuls of which the young gardener John Gibson had brought back from the Khasi Hills to England in 1837, Darwin observed the trifling details of structure to be the result of complex evolutionary relationships rather than 'as the result of the direct imposition of the Creator'.[2]

Empire, like nature, was not particularly a work of grand and coherently intentional design. Humanitarianism and inhumanity, cruelty and kindness, opportunism and altruism, expediency and idealism, all lived in the tissue of imperial praxis. This is not to say, of course, that British imperialism was not some species of systematised territorialism founded on core precepts of political, military, cultural, religious and economic policy and implementation. But its coercive power was not always brutally manifest. As Thomas Jones well knew, the *perception* of authority rather than the might of the sword itself was the Company's most powerful weapon: 'the Kassias generally have a sort of mysterious and superstitious fear of the "Company" and of every one whether a Kassia man or a Bengali who holds any authority from the "Company" and were it not for this fear they would soon rid themselves of their oppressors, notwithstanding the horror the simple minded people seem to have of Mr Inglis and all whom they believe to be in his confidence'.[3]

Multiple and at times conflicting views of what this empire did or might look like thrived on the jungle floor. The empire in the north-east might have been constructed through the paperwork that crossed the desks of the government of Bengal in Calcutta, but the outward form of centralised control and authority could be confounded by the mutable adaptations of its inner and more distant structure. The potential form of empire was always up for grabs, and could always be variously enacted. In mycorrhizal interaction, individual agents of empire colonised the roots of their host, habituating dependencies and developing complex symbioses. From Scott's colonisation plans to Lewin's Christian vision and Inglis's stranglehold on orange production – whether driven by raw self-interest or philanthropy, the shape of empire was contested and contingent. Would the possibilities for Jones's communal vision have germinated under David Scott's regime? The relationships that flourished in the hills could be mutualistic – Lister and Inglis derived joint benefit from their official and blood partnership, increasing the strength of each other's survival; they could be commensal – Henry Yule contributed financial benefit to the mission, but himself remained unaffected; or parasitic – Inglis benefited financially at the expense of his Khasi labourers. Empire's organisms could be cryptic, avoiding detection; camouflaged, blending into the scenery; mimicking, acting like others. The practised subjectivities of individual British agents in the hills – the ways in which they actually experienced the world and intervened in it – could defy the simple nomenclature of their titles in the annually published India lists of chaplains, civil servants, soldiers and merchants. 'Life did not take over the globe by combat, but by networking', according to the American biologist Lynn Margulis. 'Life forms multiplied and grew more complex by co-opting others, not just by killing them'.[4] British imperialism was the exemplar of authority through interconnection.

This book has been concerned with places and peoples on the margins of empire, in Wales and in India. It has also tackled the micro-historical question of the role of the marginal individual in determining the limits of freedom within the social and political systems in which they operate. In this respect, therefore, Thomas Jones represents a 'normal exception' whose behaviour challenged and contradicted authority and in so doing clarified 'the characteristics of the dominant group that defined what was considered normal'.[5] Like Lancelot Threlkeld in Australia, Jones also showed 'willingness to mimic the authenticity and authority of either community at different, strategic moments of colonial encounters'.[6]

The underlying impositions of British hegemony as exerted over the Khasis were in their very nature fundamentally inimical to native welfare, rights, identity, self-determination and sovereignty. British power was achieved through promulgation of its language and its bureaucracies, and the Khasis were co-opted into serving British interests rather than their own. As Jones attested, the everyday equilibrium of this subordination was evident in an apparently tenuous yet deceptively strong web of obligate relationships that naturalised British control as the *status quo*. Khasi and British constructed each other as indigene and imperialist; they mutually relied on each other for their own particular and transforming identities, living on and in each other. Of course the unintended consequence of imperialism's disruptive effect was ultimately its transformative influence on Khasi culture and identity, which was shaped by resistance, agency and its own co-option of those mechanisms of British hegemony, including language, that suited its purposes. Khasi and colonialist co-evolved.

If empire was an organic system, it was neither random nor whimsical. Its life forms were determined by the networks of connection and influence, of knowledge and numbers, of who knew whom – by unsurprising self-interest but also by the similarly predictable motives of common humanity. Whether it had evolutionary purpose or not in terms of group cohesion, the point of Christianity as one of the mechanisms of British hegemony was less about what religion meant (ideological, value-laden, relativistic) and more about how it was utilised; for Jones it was a tool of resistance as well as a tool of subordination. Individual human motives and visions lay at the heart of exploitative aggrandisement, and the success of a flourishing empire was also its inherent weakness; over time jungles can become arid and deserts bloom. Over time too the empire thought, fought and wrote back to the metropole. Through this interchange, facilitated over the course of the nineteenth century by increased education and the proliferation of new forms of mass media, new spaces were constructed in which imperialism was resisted and contested, from within and without, and in which empathy and dialogue could determine other more reasonable and humane outcomes.

The point of this study has been to situate the origins of British imperialism in north-east India within a very particular set of interpenetrating historical relationships. More than this, it has been to expose the imperial relationship between Britain and this part of India as a particular network of *personal* contacts and relationships, which, as Laidlaw has established across their familial, military, administrative and scientific dimensions, 'were of both perceived and actual importance to colonial government in the early nineteenth century'.[7] Networks enabled the power and reach of authority and control over native peoples, but in diverse and historically specific contexts they also moderated its impact in different ways.

The scandal in the hills of rain in the 1840s was individual as well as institutional. Knowing this does not remove the indelible stain of British oppression, in which the missionaries played a notable role. The detailed and successive impact of the mission on Khasi society has not been a principal focus of this book. Since the 1970s Khasi scholars and writers have increasingly turned their own attention to assessing the positive and negative impacts of British rule on the development of Khasi society and culture. Nor has this book reached beyond the initial decades of the Welsh mission. It was not intended as a history of the ruthlessness of high imperialism, but to more carefully nuance its antecedents. In this way it reinforces a more recent revisionist literature that postulates the period up to mid-century or thereabouts as more fluid and culturally interconnected. While the book is therefore deliberately not about the latter period, in the final chapter I make quite explicit by way of a brief foray into the 1870s and beyond, that oppressive and racialised attitudes and practices harden. This is characterised for example in ideological debates among the missionaries about cultural tolerance and syncretic practices, as well as newly literate Khasis writing back to the metropole with their grievances.

In terms of primary sources, this study has not ventured further into an archive much of which for foreign scholars is still locked away in Welsh-language sources. My focus on the first decade of missionary work in the Khasi Hills was partly delimited by my access to these sources. The pages of *Y Drysorfa* and other church publications, and the correspondence files of dozens more missionaries, an increasing proportion of whom were women, will provide vital material for many further excursions into the study of race, gender, belief and authority, as well as of the historical relationship between Wales and India more broadly through the late nineteenth and into the twentieth centuries. As Stoler has reminded us – and as this book has attempted to explore – the 'lettered governance' of the archive itself selectively dictates what it is that we can know of the nature of imperial rule.[8]

Removed to Edinburgh after leaving the WFMS in 1866, former secretary John Roberts could identify a propensity of his Welsh compatriots for hearsay and small-town gossip. The passionate and scandal-loving Welshman is perhaps an overly essentialised caricature of the particularity of the Welsh as imperialists. As John Norton had noted of Madras in the early 1850s, small-talk and tittle-tattle were just as easily endemic in any hermetic Anglo-Indian community.[9] As the early chapters of this book have explored, the particular brand of Welsh Nonconformity that had been forged through the eighteenth and early nineteenth centuries did give a distinct institutional and ideological temper to the Welsh as missionaries. Whether the geographical analogy between the Welsh hills and Khasi Hills ever had more than metaphorical meaning, such symbolic links were noted by the Welsh themselves and in their own minds could confirm that their mission was in a sense predestined.

Aled Jones has suggested that the extraordinary historiographical silence in twentieth-century Wales about its mission in India related as much as anything to the views of a modern, secular and most of all nationalist society for whom any notion of complicity in the broader British imperial project was anathema.[10] The rise of post-colonial studies and a growing interest in the Welsh diaspora have now given such studies new cogency. Scholars have also been reformulating the ways in which trajectories of empire have been multilateral; the ways in which the Welsh, Irish and Scots as particular ethnic constituents of the British have had their own distinctive relationships with that empire, with its indigenous peoples, and with translocations of the meanings of their ethnic identities abroad.[11]

In Jenkins's 1995 book on the mission, Harry Inglis as 'fabulously loathsome human being' could also fit the role of the archetypal English bully-boy.[12] That Khasi scholars too began from the 1970s to excavate the Thomas Jones story and to demonise Inglis was not coincidental. In the wake of Indian independence in 1947, a memorial to U Tirot Sing had been erected at Mairang in 1954. The establishment of the state of Meghalaya in 1972 and the consequent desire of the Khasis for sub-regional identity and autonomy, found in the figure of Thomas Jones a compelling mythology that could be mobilised for cultural and political purposes. If Inglis was the nemesis of Jones, so too was he primarily associated with the capture of U Tirot Sing, who was confirmed historiographically through the 1970s and 1980s as the first freedom fighter of the Khasi people. An entry in the 1974 *Dictionary of National Biography* set U Tirot Sing in a national context, as an inspirational exemplar of 'supreme sacrifice and indomitable courage in the struggle against British imperialism'.[13] A statue was erected to U Tirot Sing in Shillong in 1978. The following decade saw him celebrated as an outstanding hero and great Khasi patriot in the Khasi 'War of Liberty', while Inglis's role in his capture was 'the most treacherous and heinous act unparalleled in the annals of warfare'.[14] It was at this period too that a popular motto was attributed to U Tirot Sing – 'Better the death of a free commoner than the life of a chief who is a slave'. Hamlet Bareh contributed a volume on U Tirot Sing to the 'Builders of Modern India' series, placing the local hero (as a Napoleon or Tipu Sultan) in the panoply of national freedom fighters, while other publications were inspired by the sesquicentenary of U Tirot Sing's death in 1984.[15] On a government website, U Tirot Sing takes his place with Jaintia warrior U Kiang Nongbah and Garo fighter Pa Togan Sangma as one of the 'immortal martyrs' of Meghalaya.[16] Bareh noted but dismissed a story that Ka Ksan Syiem, mother of U Tirot Sing, had warned David Scott of the impending massacre at Nongkhlaw and facilitated his escape to Cherrapunji. The origins of this story appear to lie in the missionary John Roberts's *Fourth Khasi Reader*, and it is unclear whether he was embellishing Khasi folklore or simply committing an oral version to print.[17] In Tiplut Nongbri's rendition of the same story, David Scott is constructed as a coward who leaves Bedingfield and Burlton to their gruesome fate. Though giving more credence to the story of U Tirot Sing's mother protecting David Scott, an episode where 'patriotism should have triumphed over emotions', she also takes the opportunity of celebrating the bravery of women freedom fighters such as Ka Phan Nonglait and Ka Phet Syiem in combatting the British.[18] In a predominantly Christian area of India, the same narrative that constructs Scott and Inglis as imperialist oppressors can also accommodate acceptance of the benefits of education and modernisation brought by the missionaries.[19] While the Welsh missionary impact was significant, its 'success' or indeed its novelty, as this book has suggested, needs to be measured against the pre-existing activities of British imperialists, from Robert Lindsay to Carey's Serampore envoys and David Scott. Successive missions by Catholics and American Baptists to other north-eastern Indian states have also had a high rate of success, where the Bible has been translated into local dialects and where caste has not been so much of an impediment among tribal communities.

This is still an uneasy past in which hagiography and iconoclasm co-exist. On the death of David Scott in 1831, William Cracroft wrote to George Swinton suggesting that a memorial be erected over his remains 'to pay a tribute to his memory & services'.[20]

> By his demise the Government has been deprived of a most zealous, able, and intelligent servant, whose loss is deeply lamented, while his name will long be held in grateful remembrance and veneration by the native population, to whom he was justly endeared by his impartial dispensation of justice, his kind and conciliatory manners, and his constant and unwearied endeavours to promote their happiness and welfare.

This inscription on the rarely visited monument in present-day Sohra provides a text for Khasi Christians who scoff or concur in equal measure.

The road from the plains to the hills has been one organising metaphor of this book; from the side of the track the comings and goings of surveyors, administrators, soldiers and collectors have been part of the broader imaginary process of British consolidation of empire. This is part of what Edney has called the 'geographical rhetoric of British India', which overlaid previous diverse geographies, polities and cultures with a more unitary entities.[21] Here too, Edney suggests that Indian nationalists and sub-nationalists have deployed these constructions, which are then assumed to predate colonialism, in more contemporary political struggles and assertions of cultural identity. Those early renditions and orthographical slippages of Cherrapunji (Chirra, Cherrapoongee) were slowly regularised in the period from the 1820s to the 1850s, as the British both constructed and then controlled India through geography. While both Thomas Jones and William Lewis only once refer to Cherrapunji by its Khasi name (rendered respectively as Sauhrah[22] and Sorra[23]), it was not until the twenty-first century that Khasis reclaimed nomenclature and therefore authority when Cherrapunji was rendered officially as Sohra.

In 1991 a quarter of a million people – more than greeted Pope John Paul II at the same venue in 1986 – gathered on a golf course in Shillong to commemorate Thomas Jones. If Scott and Inglis were being figured as villains, Jones had a more heroic though nonetheless ambiguous legacy. The Seng Khasi movement, which had originated in the late nineteenth century as an indigenous cultural response to the oppressions of the missionaries and other colonialists, would recognise in Jones the double-edged sword of cultural liberation and control that western education would bring. The greater the villain Inglis became as U Tirot Sing's oppressor, the more the mythology around Jones's split from the mission and defence of Khasi rights was elaborated in folklore as well as historiography. The latest biographical account of the life of Thomas Jones, written in Khasi by the Reverend S.S. Majaw, celebrates Jones as father of the Khasi alphabet, founder of Khasi literature, pioneer of the Welsh Presbyterian mission, and 'u Lok jong kiba jynjar trah' (a friend of the underdogs).[24]

Around 37 per cent of Meghalayans speak Khasi – a language long proliferated in newspapers, literature, grammars, and which is accepted at doctoral level at North-Eastern Hill University in Shillong – yet the official language of Meghalaya is English. While some may squarely blame the Welsh missionaries for the fact that Khasi is not the official language of Meghalaya,[25] the legacies of colonialism are rarely

18 'Proposed monument to the memory of the late David Scott, Esq. Agent to the Govr Genl Assam', 1832.

so unambiguous. While not the focus of this book, the contemporary political and cultural dynamics of Meghalaya might be an object lesson in Bengali as much as British imperialism. The last Welsh missionaries in the north-east packed their bags in the 1960s, but the legacy of a century and a quarter of evangelisation in the hills has left an indelible mark. Historian Manorama Sharma has also gone so far as to argue that present-day crises of governance in the north-east should be put in the context of the way in which 'traditional' Khasi institutions such as that *Syiem* or *Sardar* (chief) and *durbar* – for which claims to historical legitimacy are made – have in fact been structured post-contact under the influence of British ideas of representative government.[26]

This book started with initials scratched in a Welsh barn at Llifior Mill. If you walk along the 1820s Scott road – extant portions of which are now gaining heritage and tourism value as the 'Scott Trail' – about half an hour's walk from the Mawphlang sacred grove and high above the Mawphlang River coursing through the gorge below, you encounter a second cryptic inscription. Speculation surrounds the identity of a child named Camilla, surname unknown, whose death in 1843 is commemorated on this isolated mountainside gravestone. The headstone inscription includes a quotation from John Milton's 'On the death of an infant dying of a cough' (1626), but the main memorial stone is also set on either side with two smaller unhewn stones in the style of the Khasi ancestral megaliths known as *mawbynna* (memory stones). Because of the syncretism of the funerary ornaments, many in the hills still believe Camilla to have been the illegitimate child of Thomas Jones. There are many mysteries left unanswered in this history, questions that have been unaccounted stowaways in my story, like the strange boy, the son of a poor Welshwoman, who possibly hid on the *Jamaica* before it cast off from Liverpool and who was never heard of again.[27] Each step of the way has been into mystery, for them and for us. On an intimate scale, as storyteller and historian, I have attempted 'to craft their truths, half-truths, and evident lies into stories that reveal the underlying complexities'.[28]

In February 2004 on my first visit to the Khasi Hills I was somewhat startled to find myself holding a series of press conferences for the local television and print media, and my visit as 'U Khun Ksiew Khnai' – the great great grandson of both Thomas Jones I and II – was splashed across the front pages of the local papers.[29] I was quizzed on a range of issues: the comparative status of Khasi Christianity with the rest of India; the health of the church in Wales; my views on the fact that some of the insurgent proponents of subnationalism in north-east India are also Christians. I was most frequently queried, however, on the widespread local belief that after the death in 1845 of his first wife Ann, Thomas

Jones had married a local girl. While the origins of such a belief might be explained by lexical particularities – 'Ka' being the Khasi feminine article, and the name of Jones's second wife Emma Cattell might possibly be misconstrued as 'Ka Tell' – the fact that Thomas Jones had been expelled from the mission in 1847 and supposedly 'gone native', defending local interests in the face of the exploitations of British merchants, might bear witness to the durability of his legend as both a religious and secular figure. He loved us, Catholic priest Father Sylvanus Sngi Lyngdoh tells me. He esteemed us. He was almost one of us, hence the tale that he married a Khasi girl. For many current-day Christians, some of the essences and rites of Khasi religion can be regarded as preparatory for Christianity, and are incorporated into Christian worship. The Catholic 'Don Bosco Centre for Indigenous Cultures' in Shillong expresses the syncretism encouraged by Pope John Paul II ('A faith that does not become culture is a faith that has not been fully accepted, not thoroughly thought, and not faithfully lived') in its various brochures, dioramas and displays. Shaped like a Naga house and completed in 2000, the centre's mission and culture gallery directly equates the seven pillars of Khasi culture with the seven Catholic sacraments. A cock painted on one wall stares towards the figure of Christ on the cross, surrounded by the accoutrements of egg divination and *kwai*.

How can we finally reckon this empire in the clouds? The year 2010 was the bicentenary of Thomas Jones's birth, and the 175th anniversary of the death of U Tirot Sing. The histories of the Khasis and the Welsh are mutually constituted. If, as Jay Winter suggests, history is memory without affect, and memory is history without archives,[30] then this book has been a singular attempt to reconcile a fragmentary archive with the visceral feel of empire's legacies. Its ultimate claims are modest; 'Research', Wallace-Wells reminds us, 'restrains sweeping, absolute claims'.[31] In 1845 the *Calcutta Review* alerted its readers to the fact that despite 'the apathy and ignorance shewn by the lay inhabitants of a cantonment when the Missionaries were mentioned', they might be surprised to find it a refined and complex 'little world in itself'.[32] If it has done nothing else, this contextual study of a small group of Welsh imperialists has projected this invocation into contemporary re-evaluations of British imperialism in India and elsewhere.

Notes

1 Darwin to Lindley, 18 October 1861, www.darwinproject.ac.uk/entry-3289 (accessed 1 March 2012).

2 Charles Darwin, *On the Various Contrivances by which British and Foreign Orchids are Fertilised by Insects, and on the Good Effects of Intercrossing* (London, 1862), p. 2.

3 T. Jones, Petition to the Government of Bengal, 14 June 1849, IOR P/143/34, 11 July 1849, No. 79.
4 Lynn Margulis, *Origins of Sex: Three Billion Years of Genetic Recombination* (New Haven, CN, 1986), p. 27.
5 Muir, 'Introduction', p. xiv; Levi, 'On microhistory', p. 99.
6 Johnston, *Missionary Writing and Empire*, p. 199.
7 Zoë Laidlaw, *Colonial Connections 1815–45: Patronage, the Information Revolution and Colonial Government* (Manchester, 2005), p. 201.
8 Ann Laura Stoler, *Along the Archival Grain: Epistemic Anxieties and Colonial Common Sense* (Princeton, 2009), p. 1.
9 John Bruce Norton, *A Letter to Robert Lowe, Esq., Joint Secretary of the Board of Control, from John Bruce Norton, Esq. on the Condition and Requirements of the Presidency of Madras* (London, 1854), p. 8.
10 Jones, 'Welsh missionary journalism', p. 243.
11 Tadhg Foley and Maureen O'Connor (eds), *Ireland and India: Colonies, Culture and Empire* (Dublin, 2006); J.M. MacKenzie, 'Irish, Scottish, Welsh and English worlds? A four-nation approach to the history of the British empire', *History Compass*, 6:5 (2008), 1244–63; Evans, *Slave Wales: The Welsh and Atlantic Slavery, 1660–1850* (Cardiff, 2010); Barry Crosbie, *Irish Imperial Networks: Migration, Social Communication and Exchange in Nineteenth-century India* (Cambridge, 2012).
12 Jenkins, *Gwalia in Khasia*, p. 231.
13 L.P. Datta, 'Singh, U Tirot' in S.P. Sen (ed.), *Dictionary of National Biography*, volume 4 (Calcutta, 1974), p. 233.
14 J.E. Tariang, *U Tirot Sing: A Collection of his Reign and Struggle Against British Rule 1814–1834* (Shillong, 1982), p. 43.
15 H. Bareh, *U. Tirot Singh* (New Delhi, 1984); H.B. Sohliya, R. Lyngdoh and H. Bareh (eds), *Celebration of 150th Death Anniversary of U Tirot Singh, Syiem of Nongkhlaw. An Illustrious Khasi Hero and Personage* (Shillong, 1984).
16 http://meghalaya.nic.in/culture/martyrs.htm (accessed 12 July 2011).
17 Jeebon Roy (1838–1903), an architect of the Khasi cultural movement that anticipated the formation of the Seng Khasi movement in 1899, is also said to have recorded in one of his pamphlets the version of the story that attributed Scott's escape to the help of Ka Ksan (Sidney Evans to John Hughes Morris, 4 August 1924, CMA 27159).
18 Tiplut Nongbri, 'Sociological impact of the movement: its conformity with the consistent role of the Khasi standards of statesmanship and review of other social changes' in H.B. Sohliya, R. Lyngdoh and H. Bareh (eds), *Celebration of 150th Death Anniversary of U Tirot Singh. An Illustrious Khasi Hero and Personage* (Shillong, 1984), p. 67.
19 *Ibid.*, p. 70.
20 Cracroft to Swinton, 3 September 1831, PWJF 2811/9.
21 Edney, *Mapping an Empire*, p. 15.
22 Jones to Roberts, 8 September 1842, *Y Drysorfa*, December 1842.
23 Lewis to Roberts, 6 March 1844, *Y Drysorfa*, June 1844.
24 S.S. Majaw, *U Thomas Jones: Bad ka Pyrthei Saitsohpen* (Shillong, 2011).
25 M. Ghosh-Schellhorn, 'Flocking to the colonised mission: Welsh encounters of the Khasi kind' in Gerhard Stilz (ed.), *Colonies, Missions, Cultures in the English-speaking World: General and Comparative Studies* (Tübingen, 2001), p. 139.
26 Manorama Sharma, *Critically Assessing Traditions: The Case of Meghalaya*, Crisis States Programme Development Research Centre, LSE, Working Paper No. 52 (London, 2004), p. 18.
27 Roberts to Jones, 28 January 1841, CMA 28720, Letter Book of General Secretary, volume 4.
28 Guido Ruggiero, *Binding Passions: Tales of Magic, Marriage, and Power at the End of the Renaissance* (New York, 1993), p. 19.
29 *Shillong Times, Mawphor, U Nongsaiñ Hima*, 25 February 2004. In Khasi, *khun-u-*

ksiew is child or 'dog', a further generation removed being represented by *khnai* or 'mouse'.

30 Jay Winter, 'The social construction of silence', lecture delivered at the State Library of Victoria, 19 November 2010.

31 Benjamin Wallace-Wells, 'Right man's burden', *Washington Monthly*, June 2004.

32 'English women in Hindustan', *Calcutta Review*, 4 (1845), Calcutta, 1848, 98.

Epilogue

At around a quarter past five in the afternoon of 12 June 1897, the Great Assam earthquake adjusted the topography of a vast epicentral tract around Shillong, laying waste to an area the size of England.[1] For a moment or so there had been a barely sensible shift. For no apparent reason, birds suddenly rose up from trees at Silchar. Dogs barked, seemingly at shadows, and cyclists in Calcutta were forced to dismount. Civil engineer Ralph Strachey riding on Shillong Peak noticed an unusual rustling of leaves, and bamboo and betel trees in Sylhet began to sway north-north-west to south-south-east. Lanterns, bird cages, saddles strung from ceilings, orchids hanging from verandahs, all started to swing. A woman nursing an officer with typhoid in Shillong recited the Lord's Prayer; women in Sylhet cried loud and long – 'horibole, Alla!, ulu, ulu'.

As the earth rocked like a cradle, bridges were toppled, jets of sand and water mixed with semi-petrified wood and peat spurted from crater-like pits, houses sank in the earth to their roofline, and the ground was variously distorted by cracks, fissures, ridges and furrows. Landslips in the deep forest-clad valleys around Cherrapunji, seen from a steamer sailing up from Sylhet, had now stripped the country to bare white sandstone. The geography of the region was irrevocably altered in an instant, like the changing of a theatre set. After the earthquake, the missionaries near Shillong noticed that a much longer stretch of road was visible on the route leading from Mawphlang to Mairang as it rounded distant spurs. The tombs of the missionaries and British officials that sat on the grassy knolls at Cherrapunji were driven into the loose sand and now leaned over at various angles. Near Rambrai in the west Khasi Hills, large *mawbynna* were shot six feet out of the ground. At Chhatak, the obelisk erected in 1850 to George Inglis was strangely contorted. The two lofty gate pillars at the Inglis bungalow at Cherrapunji crumbled to the ground, while the upper part of the massive Scott memorial also cracked and fell.

The great earthquake was also known as the Jubilee Earthquake; just over a week later, on 22 June 1897, Queen Victoria, Empress of India, celebrated her diamond jubilee. Before setting off to parade the central thoroughfares of her capital, the Queen-Empress had pressed the button on a telegraph machine at the entrance of Buckingham Palace, transmitting to her subjects across the entire empire her royal message: FROM MY HEART I THANK MY BELOVED PEOPLE. MAY GOD BLESS THEM. V.R. & I. From Adelaide to Zanzibar, bonfires flamed, a sea of Union Jacks was waved, British Agents hosted dinners, *durbars*, levees and balls, and governors watched monster processions from raised platforms.

But in parts of the Empress of India's empire, the world had turned upside down. Government House in Shillong lay in ruins. In Guwahati, the Deputy Commissioner's cutcherry was destroyed, and carcasses of Gangetic dolphins floated down the Brahmaputra. Almirahs everywhere were overturned, and elephants knocked off their feet. By 19 June the Viceroy Lord Elgin had received a sympathetic telegram from the Queen, and on Jubilee Day presided over the State ceremonial at Simla. Amidst the calamities of famine and earthquake, Elgin suggested to loud cheers that 'greater confidence between rulers and ruled, more forbearance where racial or religious feeling is apt to lead to strife, juster views of the supreme importance of peace and goodwill' would serve as a memorial to the jubilee more fitting and permanent perhaps than the stone that lay in rubble across the hills and plains of north-east India.[2]

William Lewis had noted the occurrence of a terrifying earthquake in the Khasi Hills in July 1845, and remarked that the safety of all at the mission had been guaranteed through their Christian faith 'in the embrace of the everlasting arms'.[3] While he did not detail the 'foolish opinions' of the 'wretched pagans' as to the cause of the tremors, one Khasi belief held that the earth is like a round plate that sits on four stone pillars resting on U Jumai (earthquake) in the form of a frog, whose movements caused the world to tremble.[4] For the Reverend Robert Evans, the hand of his God was clearly behind the 1897 quake. This 'wonderful visitation' saw the conversion of thousands of Khasis for whom such a massive catastrophe 'was needed to force them to realise the presence and sanctity of God'. The destruction of the village of Shella – 'one of the biggest, hardest and most pagan villages in the land' – was in the missionary's eyes God's consequential vengeance on the heathen.[5] Of the 1542 fatalities recorded in 1897, 916 were in the Khasi and Jaintia Hills.

For subsequent generations, the catastrophe of 1897 marked a zero point in the region's history, but it is also an irresistible final metaphor of the collision of cultures and the aftershocks of empire. The son and the daughter of Thomas Jones I and II were back in India by the mid-1880s, Thomas Cattell-Jones working as a medical officer on tea estates in Cachar. Cattell-Jones worked for Haffkine in his development of the cholera vaccine, from which his own family was not immune. In later years Jean recorded on a single sheet of paper the names of her nine children, four of whom had died before the century's turn, and their successive places of birth and death from Golaghat to Shamshernagar, Dum Dum north-west of Calcutta, and finally Sylhet.

The earthquake was a catastrophic event by any measure for a little girl. My grandmother Gwenllian had already lost her ten-year-old brother Thomas the month before the quake, her nine-year-old sister Rachel died the month after, and eight months later her father himself succumbed to cholera after a day's illness, aged forty-seven. The title page of a small pocket diary – one of the very few heirlooms in my possession – confidently announces a post-earthquake year: 'Dr T. Cattell-Jones, Shiek Ghat, Sylhet Sth, 1898. January 1st to . . .' Pencilled notes appear through January, briefly recording patient symptoms, water supply and medicines. But on 12 February another's handwriting takes over: 'Taken with watery purging gripy early in the morning . . . Choleraic attack continued all day, could not get him warm in spite of stimulants & rubbing dreadful cramps & collapse, took everything that was given him but gradually sank & died about 4am Sunday morning my dear good kind gentle patient husband'.

By 1900 the remaining family ended up in Kalimpong near Darjeeling, where Jean Cattell-Jones became first House Mother of Kiernander Cottage at the recently opened St Andrew's Colonial Homes, an orphanage for Eurasian children established by Scottish missionary the Reverend John Anderson Graham. While most children came from the surrounding tea-estates or the slums of Calcutta, three Khasi girls, Droptimon, Hendrimai and Elisibon, unable to speak Hindi, made 'an interesting addition' in 1908. 'There is a great conglomeration of races and languages in the lace hostel at present', Kate Graham remarked. 'A friend here calls it our miniature heaven'.[6]

Thomas Cattell-Jones had never known his own father, and his own surviving children became fatherless before they were teenagers. Three generations of women kept the family stories alive, lived to old age, and passed their version of the imperial experience in India to their children and grandchildren. As a child it seemed to me that my mother was always 'Scottish', and my granny 'Welsh', although I now realise how contingent and contentious these constructions of identity must have been. A family snapshot of my mother taken some time in the 1930s in a suburban Adelaide backyard shows a young girl in Welsh 'national dress': tall black chimney hat over white cap, white blouse, check skirt. Her mother Gwenllian had been sent from Kalimpong to Edinburgh by 1906, to be schooled at a Home House for Missionaries' Children. She trained as a nurse, and after marrying a Scot in 1922, emigrated to Australia in 1928. Her sister Margaret had followed her to Edinburgh where she trained as a teacher, and later went with her to Australia. Their brother Llewellyn was sent to New Zealand to work on a farm, while Glyn trained at the Cawnpore Agricultural College and became a tea planter.

In the late afternoon before dinner, my mother's grandmother Jean would captivate her with stories of India, laced with exotic sounding names like Cherrapunji, Kalimpong and Baramasia. She would talk of the tigers that would prowl around the outside of their compound at night, and would recall how her father and the servants dug great traps for them at the bottom of which a live goat was tethered. Jean had been sent back to a boarding school for young ladies in Aberystwyth. During this time, when she was sixteen, her father Thomas Jones II died of cholera in Sylhet, aged forty-five. The three-month voyage from Calcutta around the Cape of Good Hope was another source of inspiration for a child's imagination, marvelling at the fact that they carried live sheep and chickens on the ship for food. As she pulled my mother's jumper over her head before bath time, her grandmother would sing the songs of the mariners as they worked the sails.

Living in Melbourne as a child, my family made annual pilgrimages back to Adelaide in the Christmas holidays to visit relatives. I remember my grandmother well – she lived with her unmarried sister Margaret Cattell-Jones in nursing home flats, and showered her grandchildren with such a gentle and kindly manner in a lilting accent, a treacle mixture of Scottish, Welsh and Hindi. Granny McLean spent her last years in a nursing home, transported by old age to a netherworld of dementia where monkeys cried from banks of the River Torrens, snatches of old hymns came to her lips, and she would fly angelically over the Himalayas with her long-dead sister Rachel whom she had not seen for ninety years.

My forebears were hardly the coerced captives of Colley's imperial scenarios, but in everyday ways were subject to imperial trauma, 'the sporadic powerlessness of the apparently all-powerful'.[7] In out of the way places, they were akin to the micro-historian's 'little peoples'.[8] A history of British imperialism in north-east India can also contribute to the history of Britain's imperial descendants, who might have experienced power in some ways in colonial settings, but whose livelihoods, socio-economic status and identities had diverse trajectories. My book is not a family history, but it glimpses in afterthought the diverse and fragmented lives of empire's descendants. Most importantly, such histories are more relevant than ever to British and settler-colonial inheritors of empire. For Aled Jones, the history of the Welsh missionaries is inescapably a story about the Welsh themselves. 'Only by telling their story in this way', he demands, 'can the Welsh, finally, bring their missionaries home'.[9] In the Australian context too, Antonia Finnane has regretted the way in which Australians have shied away from the personal connections and implications of broader imperial processes, and 'have been able to distance themselves from events which, however intimately involved with the Australian experience, have taken place elsewhere'.[10]

The predicaments of these descendants of empire were personal, pecuniary, psychological. When Margaret Cattell-Jones applied for a pension in Adelaide in 1961, it was not just her financial interests that were scrutinised: 'The magistrate . . . even questioned her right to call herself a British Subject as she was born in India!! Poor Aunty was terribly upset when she came back . . . She also told him that there was no question of her not being a British subject when she entered Australia 33 years ago!!'[11] Missionary children and grandchildren were dispersed in an imperial diaspora to the settler colonies of Canada, New Zealand or Australia. The privileges of an empire inheritance did not necessarily mitigate the real ways they succumbed to everyday traumas of dislocation, identity crisis and mixed family fortune, as the meanings of empire itself were transformed.

'We lads from the dear old Homes', boasted Llewellyn Cattell-Jones, 'will do our share in this terrible but glorious fight for the freedom of the weaker nations'.[12] Invalided back to New Zealand, he suffered from the trauma of war for the rest of his life, and died there ill and alone. In a cupboard in the Kalimpong office of the Homes I found a letter written jointly by my grandmother and great aunt to Dr Graham in 1937, and through the cracks and fissures of time their voices appear, resentful and indignant that their names were being used on a printed advertisement distributed in Adelaide on the occasion of his visit.

> In adopting this attitude we are guided by our past bitter experience of the behaviour of 99% of so-called Christian people. It is a grand thing to speak of brotherly love and of showing the spirit of Christ – but the practice of these is very rare . . . Our poverty as a family was in very large measure due to the fact that our grandparents on both sides were pioneer missionaries who went out to India in the early days, to face grave hardships and very real dangers, on salaries that were pitiful in comparison with those given to many missionaries today. The life, in fact, was so strenuous and [taxed] the strength of our grandparents to such a degree

> that both our grandfathers died early, unknown [and] unpraised by the world, leaving families to struggle through very difficult circumstances. To us this [is] no matter for shame, but rather one for quiet pride in our family name.[13]

As if trying to keep their feet in an earthquake, unsteadiness and disorientation dogged them across the shape-shifting landscape of empire. Amidst the surge of time, this history has been my attempt to grab on to something, to rescue micro-narratives of 'what is forgotten as well as what is remembered',[14] to steady myself and for a moment find meaning and compassion in a confusing landscape

In the urgent matter of 'how we "new world" settler peoples imagine that we belong to our beloved homelands',[15] the aftermath of empire needs constant renegotiation. Places of collision and reintegration are not just old places, the mission compounds, merchant godowns or military camps of old empire. They are also in a thousand front parlours and doorways, living rooms and memorial sites – wherever descendants of perpetrators and victims come together. History-writing in this context can importantly 'promote a conversation between the Aboriginal and the post-colonial immigrant'.[16]

A further conciliatory dialogue occurs between descendants, not of colonised and coloniser, but of other empire elites and non-elites. Having by chance tracked down over the internet the great-great-granddaughter of Harry Inglis, I found myself late in 2004 standing somewhat nervously on the doorstep of a house in inner Sydney. The offspring of a renegade missionary, I stood on the street while on the other side of the door awaiting my knock was the inheritor of Jenkins's merchant bully-boy. Our histories were not to be calculated as a single event, but as reverberations, after the fact. History is as much as anything about intensity, the way the past makes us feel. Knowing we were not our ancestors, but prepared to honour their memories as well as judge their actions, we embraced before I went inside, sat down at the table, and over a cup of tea began to untangle time in a conversation that has not yet ended.

Notes

1 Its magnitude is now estimated at 8.1 on the Richter Scale. See R. Bilham and P. England, 'Plateau pop-up during the 1897 Assam earthquake', *Nature*, 410 (2001), 806–9; also R.D. Oldham, *Report on the Great Earthquake of 12th June 1897* (Calcutta, 1899), from which the following accounts are variously taken.

2 *The Times*, 23 June 1897, 15.

3 Lewis to Roberts, 31 July 1845, *Y Drysorfa*, November 1845.

4 I.M. Simon, *Khasi and Jaintia Tales and Beliefs* (Gauhati, 1966), pp. 29–30.

5 Robert Evans, *The Great Earthquake of 1897 in the Khasi-Jaintia Hills* (Shillong, 2003), tr. Basil Morris, first published Caernarfon 1903, pp 21, 23, 39.

6 Mrs Graham, 22 September 1908; K. Graham to Roddie, 15 October 1908, NLS Ac. 6039, Box 9.
7 Colley, 'Introduction', p. 211.
8 Muir, 'Introduction', p. x.
9 Jones, 'Welsh missionary journalism', p. 266.
10 Antonia Finnane, *Far from Where? Jewish Journeys from Shanghai to Australia* (Melbourne, 1999), p. 7.
11 G.A. McLean to S. May, 9 March 1961, author's possession.
12 *Saint Andrew's Colonial Homes Magazine*, October 1916, 31.
13 G. McLean and M. E. Cattell-Jones to Dr Graham, 30 May 1937. Dr Graham's Homes Archive, Kalimpong.
14 Joy Damousi, 'The emotions of history' in Stuart Macintyre (ed.), *The Historian's Conscience: Australian Historians on the Ethics of History* (Melbourne, 2004), p. 30.
15 Deborah Bird Rose, 'New world poetics of place: along the Oregon Trail and in the National Museum of Australia' in Annie E. Coombes (ed.), *Rethinking Settler Colonialism. History and Memory in Australia, Canada, Aotearoa New Zealand and South Africa* (Manchester, 2006), p. 228.
16 Dipesh Chakrabarty, 'Reconciliation and its historiography: some preliminary thoughts', *UTS Review*, 7:1 (2001), 13.

BIBLIOGRAPHY

Primary sources

Manuscripts

British Library, London
India Office Records (IOR)
  E: East India Company, General Correspondence
  F: Board of Control Records
  L/MIL/9: Cadet Papers
  N: Returns of Baptisms, Marriages and Burials
  P: Proceedings and Consultations

Devonshire Manuscripts Collection, Chatsworth, Bakewell, Derbyshire
By permission of the Duke of Devonshire and the Chatsworth House Trust
  Indian Correspondence 1835–37
  Paxton Correspondence
  Sixth Duke's Correspondence

Loesch private collection, London
The Shadwell correspondence is in the private collection of Vivienne Loesch, London, and is used with her permission.

National Library of Scotland, Edinburgh
Acc. 6039, Kalimpong Papers.

National Library of Wales, Aberystwyth
Calvinistic Methodist Archive/Archifau Methodistiaid Calfinaidd
CMA 1(F), 5898.
CMA (2)/12825, Diary of J.R. Hughes, 1849–50.
CMA (5)/27066–27472: Foreign Mission Manuscripts.
CMA 27066, Minute Book of Annual Meetings 1840–51, 1854; Missionary Agreements 1840–1919.
CMA 27109.
CMA 27139, Letter Book of the Reverend Josiah Thomas, General Secretary, 1871–75.
CMA 27159, Correspondence (1903–24) and material relating to *The Story of our Foreign Mission* by John Hughes Morris.
CMA 27220, The Reverend Thomas and Anne Jones, 1847–48.
CMA 27221, The Reverend William and Mary Lewis, 1841–90.
CMA 27222, Mary Lewis, 'A brief narrative of the early life of William Lewis', n.d. [c.1890].
CMA 27224, Dr Owen Richards, 1845.

CMA 27227, The Reverend and Mrs William Pryse, 1859–69.
CMA 27228, The Reverend Robert and Ann Parry 1863–90.
CMA 27229–30, The Reverend Thomas and Gwen Jones 1861–74.
CMA 27502, A register of baptisms of Welsh Calvinists in the County of Montgomery 1807–37.
CMA 28720, Letter Book of General Secretary, volume 4, 1840–43.
CMA 28721, Letter Book of General Secretary, volume 5, 1866–80.
Thomas Charles Edwards (1)/4705.
Thomas Charles Edwards (1)/4706.
Thomas Charles Edwards (1)/4708.
Thomas Charles Edwards (1)/4712–4716, Correspondence relating to Owen Richards withdrawal from the mission field 1844–45.
Thomas Charles Edwards (1)/4718–9, Letters to Owen Charles Richards from Mrs Maria Charles.

Nottingham University Archives
PWJF 2739–2877.
Letters and memoranda relating to military and other matters, sent to Lord William Bentinck, Governor-General of India (unless otherwise stated), in Portland Collection.
PWJF 2781 (1829–33): Letters and enclosures from George Swinton.
PWJF 2791 (1830) Correspondence concerned with North East Frontier.
PWJF 2811 (1831) Correspondence with George Swinton.
PWJF 2820 (1831) Correspondence with George Swinton.
PWJF 2840 (1832) Papers concerned with Assam.
PWJF 2851 (1832–33) Miscellaneous, including letters from George Swinton.

School of Oriental and African Studies, University of London
London Missionary Society Papers.
Board Minutes, Box 26, 1838–40.
Board Minutes, Box 27, 1840–41.
Candidates Papers.
FBN LON 4, Box 6 Folder 4 Jacket A: Home Letters 1835.

West Bengal State Archives, Kolkata
Bengal Judicial Proceedings, volumes 31–36, 1848–52.

Newspapers and periodicals

American Baptist Magazine and Missionary Intelligencer
Asiatic Journal and Monthly Register for British India and its Dependencies
The Baptist Magazine for 1844
Bengal Directory and Annual Register
Bengal Hurkaru
Brisbane Courier
Calcutta Christian Advocate
Calcutta Christian Observer

Calcutta Monthly Journal and General Register
Calcutta Review
Canberra Times
Friend of India
Gardener's Magazine
Gentleman's Magazine
Missionary Register
Parbury's Oriental Herald and Colonial Intelligencer
Quarterly Oriental Magazine
Saint Andrew's Colonial Homes Magazine
Shillong Times
Standard
Sydney Morning Herald
The Times
Y Drysorfa
Y Gymraes

Articles, books, pamphlets, reports

Adam, John, *Memoir of John Adam, Late Missionary at Calcutta* (London, 1833).

Aitchison, C.U.I., *A Collection of Treatises, Engagements and Sanads Relating to India and Neighbouring Countries (Revised and Continued up to 1929). Vol. XII: Jammu & Kashmir, Sikkim, Assam & Burma* (Delhi, 1983).

Aldrich, Rev. J., *The Sacred Lyre: A New Collection of Hymns and Tunes, for Social and Family Worship* (Boston, New York and Cincinnati, 1859).

Allen, W.J., *Report on the Administration of the Cossyah and Jynteah Hills* (Calcutta, 1858).

Anonymous, *Ca Nabon: An Account of a Female Convert, in Connexion with the Missionary Society of the Welsh Calvinistic Methodists. With Notices of Other Converts* (London, 1849).

Baildon, Samuel, *The Tea Industry in India. A Review of Finance and Labour, and a Guide for Capitalists and Assistants* (London, 1882).

Belcher, Joseph, *The First Hindoo Convert: A Memoir of Krishna Pal, a Preacher of the Gospel to his Countrymen more than Twenty Years* (Philadelphia, 1852).

Beveridge, H., *The District of Bákarganj: Its History and Statistics* (London, 1876).

Bromehead, W. Crawford, *A Short Account of the Lives of the Bishops of Calcutta* (Calcutta, 1876).

Buchanan, Claudius, 'Ecclesiastical establishment for British India' in *Two Discourses Preached before the University of Cambridge, on Commencement Sunday, July 1, 1810. And a Sermon Preached before the Society for Missions to Africa and the East; at their Tenth Anniversary. June 12, 1810. To which Are Added Christian Researches in Asia* (London, 1811).

Buck, Charles, *A Theological Dictionary* (Philadelphia and Pittsburgh, 1830, first published 1802).

Burder, George, *The Works of the Reverend and Learned Issac Watts, D.D.*, volume 3 (London, 1810).

C., 'Excursion to the Chirra Púnjí Hills', *Gleanings in Science*, 30 (1831), 172–4.

Carey, William, 'Address respecting an agricultural society in India', *Friend of India* (September 1820), 50–9.

Carey, William, *An Enquiry into the Obligations of Christians* (Leicester, 1792).

Cracroft, W., 'Notes relative to the collection of some geological specimens in the Kásia Hills between Assam and Nunklow', *Journal of the Asiatic Society of Bengal*, 3:30 (1834), 293–6.

Cracroft, W., 'On the Cape Fig by Mr Cracroft', read 10 June 1829, *Transactions of the Agricultural and Horticultural Society of India*, 2 (1836), 4–5.

Cracroft, W., 'Rain at Chirra Púnjí, registered by W. Cracroft, Esq.', *Journal of the Asiatic Society of Bengal*, 1:9 (1832), 420, 1:10 (1832), 477.

Cracroft, W., 'Remarks on the progress of *Horticulture* at Cherra-Poonjee, and on a method of grafting the Apple on the Khasiyah Crab tree, by W. Cracroft', read 14 January 1832, *Transactions of the Agricultural and Horticultural Society of India*, 2 (1836), 81–2.

Dalton, E.T., *Descriptive Ethnology of Bengal* (Calcutta, 1872).

Darwin, Charles, *On the Various Contrivances by which British and Foreign Orchids Are Fertilised by Insects, and on the Good Effects of Intercrossing* (London, 1862).

Dickinson, Violet (ed.), *Miss Eden's Letters* (London, 1919).

Eden, Emily, *Letters from India* (London, 1872).

Evans, Robert, *The Great Earthquake of 1897 in the Khasi-Jaintia Hills* (Shillong, 2003), tr. Basil Morris (first published Caernarfon, 1903).

F., 'Some account of the Cásiah Hills', *Gleanings in Science*, 1:9 (1829), 252–5.

Fenwick, C.A., *Essay on the Colonization of Hindostan by East Indians* (Calcutta, 1828).

Firminger, Walter K. (ed.), *The Sylhet District Records*, 4 volumes (Shillong, 1913–19).

Grant, Charles, *Observations on the State of Society among Asiatic Subjects of Great Britain, Particularly with Respect to Morals and on the Means of Improving it; Written Chiefly in the Year 1792* (London, 1813).

Griffith, William, *Journals of Travels in Assam, Burma, Bhootan, Afghanistan and the Neighbouring Countries, 1847, Arranged by John M'Clelland* (Calcutta, 1847).

Griffith, William, 'Report on the caoutchouc tree of Assam made at the request of Captain Jenkins, Agent to the Governor General', *Journal of the Asiatic Society of Bengal*, 7 (1838), 132–42.

Hodson, V.C.P., *List of the Officers of the Bengal Army, 1758–1834, Alphabetically Arranged and Annotated with Biographical and Genealogical Notices*, 4 parts (London, 1927–47).

Holmes & Co., *The Bengal Obituary* (Calcutta, 1848).

Hooker, J. D., *Himalayan Journals or, Notes of a Naturalist in Bengal, the*

Sikkim and Nepal Himalayas, the Khasia Mountains, &c, 2 volumes (Dehra Dun, 1999, first published 1854).

Horsburgh, James, *The Indian Directory*, volume 1, 5th edition (London, 1841).

Hunter, W.W., *A Statistical Account of Assam in Two Volumes* (Delhi, 1975, first published London, 1879).

Jenkins, W.M., *Life and Work in Khasia* (Newport, c.1903).

Jones, Thomas, *Ka Gospel Jong U Mathi. The Gospel of Matthew in Kassia* (Calcutta, 1846).

Lewin, T.H. (ed.), *The Lewin Letters: A Selection from the Correspondence & Diaries of an English Family 1756–1884*, 2 volumes (London, 1909).

Lindsay, Lord Alexander William Crawford (ed.), *Lives of the Lindsays*, volume 3 (London, 1849).

Lish, A.B., 'A brief account of the Khasees', *Calcutta Christian Observer* (March 1838), 129–43.

McLelland, Dr, 'Fossil shells found in the Kasya Hills', *Journal of the Asiatic Society of Bengal*, 4:45 (1835), 520.

Marsh, Charles, 'Substance of the speech of Charles Marsh, Esq. in a committee of the House of Commons, July the 1st, 1813. In support of the amendment, moved by Sir Thomas Sutton, Bart. on the clause in the East-India Bill, "Enacting further facilities to persons to go out to India for religious purposes"', 1813, in *The Pamphleteer: Respectfully Dedicated to Both Houses of Parliament*, 4:2 (London 1813), pp. 495–530.

Marshman, John Clark, *Memoirs of Major-General Sir Henry Havelock, K.C.B.* (London, 1867).

Mills, A.J.M., *Report on the Khasi and Jaintia Hills, 1853* (Shillong, 1901).

Morgan, Edward (ed.), *John Elias: Life, Letters and Essays* (1844 and 1847: revised edition in one volume, Edinburgh, 1973) in R.M. Jones and Gwyn Davies, *The Christian Heritage of Welsh Education* (Bryntirion, Bridgend, 1986).

Morris, John Hughes, *U Larsing: Evangelist from the Khasi Hills* (Carnarvon, 1912).

Norton, John Bruce, *A Letter to Robert Lowe, Esq., Joint Secretary of the Board of Control, from John Bruce Norton, Esq. on the Condition and Requirements of the Presidency of Madras* (London, 1854).

Norton, John N., *Life of Bishop Wilson of Calcutta* (New York, 1862).

Oldham, R.D., *Report on the Great Earthquake of 12th June 1897* (Calcutta, 1899).

Oldham, Thomas (ed.), *Memoirs of the Geological Survey of India*, volume 1 (Calcutta, 1859).

Pemberton, R.B., *The Eastern Frontier of India* (New Delhi, 2005, first published 1835).

Philips, C.H. (ed.), *The Correspondence of Lord William Cavendish Bentinck, Governor-General of India, 1828–1835*, 2 volumes (Oxford and New York, 1977).

Pollok, F.T. and W.S. Thom, *Wild Sports of Burma and Assam* (London, 1900).

Prinsep, H.T., *A General Register of the Hon'ble East India Company's Civil Servants of the Bengal Establishment from 1790 to 1842* (Calcutta, 1844).

Pryse, R.W., *An Introduction to the Khasia Language: Comprising a Grammar, Selections for Reading, and a Vocabulary* (Calcutta, 1855).

Rafy, Mrs, *Folk-tales of the Khasis* (London, 1920).

Report of the Directors to the Forty-fourth General Meeting of the Mission Society, Usually Called the London Missionary Society, On Thursday, May 10th, 1838 (London, 1838).

Robertson, Thomas Campbell, *Political Incidents of the First Burmese War* (London, 1853).

Robinson, William, 'Notes on the languages spoken by the various tribes inhabiting the valley of Asam and its mountain confines', *Journal of the Asiatic Society*, 27 (1849), 183–237, 310–49.

Samuel, E., *The Asiatic Annual Register* (London, 1811).

Stubbs, F.W., *List of Officers Who Have Served in the Regiment of the Bengal Artillery* (Bath, 1892).

The History, Constitution, Rules of Discipline, and Confession of Faith of the Calvinistic Methodists, in Wales, Drawn Up by their Own Associated Ministers (Chester, 1834).

Titmarsh, M.A., *Notes of a Journey from Cornhill to Grand Cairo, by Way of Lisbon, Athens, Constantinople, and Jerusalem, Performed in the Steamers of the Peninsular and Oriental Company* (London, 1846), reprinted in William Makepeace Thackeray, *Burlesques; From Cornhill to Grand Cairo; and Juvenilia* (London, 1911).

Tomlin, J., *Missionary Journals and Letters Written During Eleven Years' Residence and Travels amongst the Chinese, Siamese, Javanese, Khassias, and other Eastern Nations* (London, 1844).

T.R., 'On the manufacture of the Sylhet lime', *Gleanings in Science* (1830), 61–3.

Walters, H., 'Journey across the Pandua Hills, near Sylhet, in Bengal', *Asiatic Researches*, 17 (1832), 499–513.

Ward, William, *Farewell Letters to a Few Friends in Britain and America, on Returning to Bengal in 1821* (Lexington, 1822).

Watson, Archibald (ed.), *Memoir of the Late David Scott, Esq. Agent to the Governor General, on the North-east Frontier of Bengal, and Commissioner of Revenue and Circuit in Assam, &c. &c. &c.* (Calcutta, 1832).

Watson, Lieut.-Col. Thomas C., 'Chirra Punji, and a detail of some of the favourable circumstances which render it an advantageous site for the erection of an iron and steel manufactory on an extensive scale', *Journal of the Asiatic Society of Bengal*, 3:25 (1834), 25–33.

Watts, Isaac, 'A discourse on the way of instruction by catechisms, and of the best method of composing them' in George Burder, *The Works of the Reverend and Learned Issac Watts, D.D.*, volume 3 (London, 1810), pp. 203–28.

W.C., 'Smelting of iron in the Kasya Hills', *Journal of the Asiatic Society of Bengal*, 1:4 (1832), 150–1.

White, A., 'A memoir of the late David Scott, Esq.' in Archibald Watson (ed.), *Memoir of the Late David Scott, Esq. Agent to the Governor General, on the North-east Frontier of Bengal, and Commissioner of Revenue and Circuit in Assam, &c. &c. &c.* (Calcutta, 1832), pp. 15–67.

Wilcox, Richard, 'Register of the thermometer kept at Nungkhlow, during parts of the months of October and November, 1827', *The Quarterly Oriental Magazine, Review, and Register*, 8:15 (July–December 1827), Calcutta, 1828, 15.

Williams, Monier (ed.), *Original Papers Illustrating the History of the Application of the Roman Alphabet to the Languages of India* (London, 1859).

Wilson, Horace Hayman, *Documents Illustrative of the Burmese War; With an Introductory Sketch of the Events of the War, and an Appendix* (Calcutta, 1827).

Wilson, Horace Hayman, *Narrative of the Burmese War, in 1824–26, as Originally Compiled from Official Documents* (London, 1852).

Wilson, John, *A Memoir of Mrs Margaret Wilson, of the Scottish Mission, Bombay; Including Extracts from her Letters and Journals* (Edinburgh, 1840).

Yule, H., 'Notes on the Kasia Hills, and people', *Journal of the Asiatic Society of Bengal*, 13:152 (1844), 612–31.

Yule, H. [Anonymous], *Fragments of Unprofessional Papers Gathered from an Engineer's Portfolio after Twenty-three Years of Service* (Calcutta, 1862).

Yule, Henry and A.C. Burnell, *Hobson-Jobson: The Anglo-Indian Dictionary* (Ware, Hertfordshire, 1996, first published 1886).

Secondary sources

Articles and books

Aaron, Jane, 'Slaughter and salvation: Welsh missionary activity and British imperialism' in Charlotte Williams, Neil Evans, Paul O'Leary (eds), *A Tolerant Nation? Exploring Ethnic Diversity in Wales* (Cardiff, 2003), pp. 35–48.

Ahmed, A.A. and S.K. Borthakur, *Ethnobotanical Wisdom of Khasis (Hynñiew Treps) of Meghalaya* (Dehra Dun, 2005).

Anderson, Clare, *Legible Bodies: Race, Criminality and Colonialism in South Asia* (Oxford, 2004).

Anderson, Olive, 'The growth of Christian militarism in mid-Victorian Britain', *The English Historical Review*, 86:338 (1971), 46–72.

Arnold, David, *The New Cambridge History of India: Science, Technology and Medicine in Colonial India* (Cambridge, 2000).

Arnold, David, 'Plant capitalism and Company science: the Indian career of Nathaniel Wallich', *Modern Asian Studies*, 42:5 (2008), 899–928.

Arnold, David, *The Tropics and the Traveling Gaze: India, Landscape, and Science, 1800–1856* (Seattle, 2006).

Axelby, R., 'Calcutta Botanic Garden and the colonial re-ordering of the Indian environment', *Archives of Natural History*, 35:1 (2008), 150–63.

Bagster, Samuel, *The Bible of Every Land* (London, 1851), Class I.

Bareh, H., *The History and Culture of the Khasi People* (Guwahati, 1985).

Bareh, H., *U. Tirot Singh* (New Delhi, 1984).

Barkataki, M.S., *British Administration in North East India (1826–1874): A Study of their Social Policy* (Delhi, 1985).

Barker, Nicholas, *The Devonshire Collection: Five Centuries of Collecting at Chatsworth* (Alexandria, Virginia, 2003).

Barooah, N.K., *David Scott in North-east India 1802–1831: A Study in British Paternalism* (New Delhi, 1970).

Barton, David and Nigel Hall, 'Introduction' in David Barton and Nigel Hall (eds), *Letter Writing as a Social Practice* (Amsterdam and Philadelphia, 2000), pp. 1–14.

Bebbington, D.W., *Evangelicalism in Modern Britain: A History from the 1730s to the 1980s* (London, 1989).

Bhardwaj, H.C., 'Development of iron and steel technology in India during 18th and 19th centuries', *Indian Journal of History of Science*, 17:2 (1982), 223–33.

Bhattacharjee, Jayanta Bhusan, 'Social and religious reform movements in Meghalaya in nineteenth and twentieth centuries: Khasi and Jaintia Hills' in S.P. Sen (ed.), *Social and Religious Reform Movements in the Nineteenth and Twentieth Centuries* (Calcutta, 1979), pp. 448–83.

Bilham, R. and P. England, 'Plateau pop-up during the 1897 Assam earthquake', *Nature*, 410 (2001), 806–9.

Bradley-Birt, F.B., *'Sylhet' Thackeray* (London, 1911).

Brenton, Edward Pelham, *The Naval History of Great Britain, from the Year MDCCLXXXIII to MDCCCXXXVI*, volume 2 (London, 1837).

Brock, Peggy, 'New Christians as evangelists' in Norman Etherington (ed.), *Missions and Empire* (Oxford, 2005), pp. 132–52.

Brockway, L.H., *Science and Colonial Expansion: The Role of the British Royal Botanic Gardens* (New York, 1979).

Broughton, Trev Lynn and Helen Rogers, 'Introduction: the empire of the father' in Trev Lynn Broughton and Helen Rogers (eds), *Gender and Fatherhood in the Nineteenth Century* (Houndmills and New York, 2007), pp. 1–28.

Brown, Kenneth D., *A Social History of the Nonconformist Ministry in England and Wales 1800–1930* (Oxford, 1988).

Buettner, Elizabeth, *Empire Families: Britons and Late Imperial India* (Oxford and New York, 2004).

Cahill, David, 'Series editor's preface' in Patricia Grimshaw and Andrew May (eds), *Missionaries, Indigenous Peoples and Cultural Exchange* (Brighton, 2010), pp. viii–xi.

Cannadine, David, *The Decline and Fall of the British Aristocracy* (New Haven, CT, 1990).

Carey, Hilary, 'Introduction' in Hilary Carey (ed.), *Empires of Religion* (Basingstoke and New York, 2008), pp. 1–21.

Carey, S. Pearce, *William Carey D.D., Fellow of the Linnaean Society* (London, 1924).
Chakrabarty, Dipesh, 'Reconciliation and its historiography: some preliminary thoughts', *UTS Review*, 7:1 (2001), 6–16.
Chambers, Paul, 'Religious diversity in Wales' in Neil Evans, Charlotte Williams, Paul O'Leary (eds), *A Tolerant Nation? Exploring Ethnic Diversity in Wales* (Cardiff, 2003), pp. 125–38.
Chattopadhyay, Swato, 'Blurring boundaries: the limits of "White Town" in colonial Calcutta', *The Journal of the Society of Architectural Historians*, 59:2 (2000), 154–79.
Chaudhary, Zahid, 'Phantasmagoric aesthetics: colonial violence and the management of perception', *Cultural Critique*, 59 (2005), 63–119.
Chowdhury, Dewan Nurul Anwar Hussain, 'Lindsay, Robert (1754–1836)', Banglapedia: National Encyclopedia of Bangladesh, 2006, www.banglapedia.org/httpdocs/HT/L_0146.htm (accessed 26 May 2009).
Chowdhury, J.N., *The Khasi Canvas: A Cultural and Political History* (Shillong, 1978).
Clendinnen, Inga, *Dancing with Strangers* (Melbourne, 2003).
Clyde, Robert, *From Rebel to Hero: The Image of the Highlander, 1745–1830* (East Linton, 1995).
Clyne, M., C. Rossi Hunt and T. Isaakidis, 'Learning a community language as a third language', *International Journal of Multilingualism*, 1 (2004), 33–52.
Cohen, Paul A., *China and Christianity: The Missionary Movement and the Growth of Chinese Antiforeignism 1860–1879* (Cambridge, MA, 1963).
Colley, Linda, 'Introduction: some difficulties of empire – past, present, and future', *Common Knowledge*, 11:2 (2005), 198–214.
Copland, Ian, 'Christianity as an arm of empire: the ambiguous case of India under the Company, c.1813–1858', *The Historical Journal*, 49:4 (2006), 1025–54.
Cotton, Evan, *East Indiamen: The East India Company's Maritime Service*, ed. Charles Fawcett (London, 1949).
Cox, Jeffrey, *The British Missionary Enterprise since 1700* (New York, 2008).
Cox, Jeffrey, *Imperial Fault Lines: Christianity and Colonial Power in India, 1818–1940* (Stanford, 2002).
Crawford, Lt.-Colonel D.G., *A History of the Indian Medical Service 1600–1913* (London, 1914).
Crosbie, Barry, *Irish Imperial Networks: Migration, Social Communication and Exchange in Nineteenth-century India* (Cambridge, 2012).
Dalley, Jan, *The Black Hole: Money, Myth and Empire* (London, 2006).
Damousi, Joy, 'The emotions of history' in Stuart Macintyre (ed.), *The Historian's Conscience: Australian Historians on the Ethics of History* (Melbourne, 2004), pp. 28–39.
Datta, L.P., 'Singh, U Tirot' in S.P. Sen (ed.), *Dictionary of National Biography* volume 4 (Calcutta, 1974), pp. 231–2.
Davies, John, Nigel Jenkins, Menna Baines and Peredur I. Lynch (eds), *The Welsh Academy Encyclopedia of Wales* (Cardiff, 2008).

Dawson, Graham, *Soldier Heroes: British Adventure, Empire, and the Imagining of Masculinities* (London and New York, 1994).

de Bruyn, P., K. Bain, D. Allardice and S. Joshi, *Frommer's India* (Hoboken, NJ, 2010), 4th edition.

Desmond, Ray, *Dictionary of British & Irish Botanists and Horticulturists* (London, 1994).

Desmond, R., *The European Discovery of the Indian Flora* (Oxford, 1992).

Devonshire, Deborah Vivien Freeman-Mitford Cavendish, *The Garden at Chatsworth* (Sydney, 1999).

Diver, Maud, *The Englishman in India* (London: 1909).

Downs, Frederick Sheldon, *History of Christianity in India: North East India in the Nineteenth and Twentieth Centuries*, volume 5 (Bangalore, 1992).

Driver, Felix, 'Yule, Sir Henry (1820–1889)', *Oxford Dictionary of National Biography*, Oxford University Press, 2004, www.oxforddnb.com/view/article/30291 (accessed 4 February 2010).

Dube, Saurabh, 'Paternalism and freedom: the evangelical encounter in colonial Chattisgarh, central India', *Modern Asian Studies*, 29:1 (1995), 171–201.

Dunch, Ryan, 'Beyond cultural imperialism: cultural theory, Christian missions, and global modernity, *History and Theory*, 41:3 (2002), 301–25.

Dutta, Krishna, *Calcutta: A Cultural and Literary History* (Oxford, 2003).

Dutta, Promatha Nath, *Impact of the West on the Khasis and Jaintias: A Survey of Politics and Social Changes* (New Delhi, 1982).

Edney, M.H., *Mapping an Empire: The Geographical Construction of British India, 1765–1843* (Chicago, 1997).

Elbourne, Elizabeth, 'Mother's milk: gender, power and anxiety on a South African mission station, 1839–1840' in Patricia Grimshaw and Andrew May (eds), *Missionaries, Indigenous Peoples and Cultural Exchange* (Brighton, 2010), pp. 10–23.

Erlank, Natasha, 'Sexual misconduct and church power on Scottish mission stations in Xhosaland, South Africa, in the 1840s', *Gender & History*, 15:1 (2003), 69–84.

Etherington, Norman (ed.), *Missions and Empire* (Oxford, 2005).

Evans, Chris, *Slave Wales: The Welsh and Atlantic Slavery, 1660–1850* (Cardiff, 2010).

Finnane, Antonia, *Far from Where? Jewish Journeys from Shanghai to Australia* (Melbourne, 1999).

Fitzmaurice, Susan M., *The Familiar Letter in Early Modern English* (Amsterdam and Philadelphia, 2002).

Foley, Tadhg and Maureen O'Connor (eds), *Ireland and India: Colonies, Culture and Empire* (Dublin, 2006).

Foster, Richard (ed.), *Liverpool's South Docks. An Archaeological and Historical Survey. Part I Mann Island–Wapping Basin* (Liverpool, n.d.).

Frater, Alexander, *Chasing the Monsoon* (London, 1990).

Fullagar, Katharine, '"Savages that are coming among us": Mai, Bennelong, and British imperial culture', *The Eighteenth Century*, 49:3 (2008), 211–37.

Gamson, Joshua, 'Normal sins: sex scandal narratives as institutional morality tales', *Social Problems*, 48:2 (2001), 185–205.

Gerber, David A., 'Acts of deceiving and withholding in immigrant letters: personal identity and self-presentation in personal correspondence', *Journal of Social History*, 39:2 (2005), 315–30.

Ghosh, S.C., *The Social Condition of the British Community in Bengal, 1757–1800* (Leiden, 1970).

Ghosh-Schellhorn, M., 'Flocking to the colonised mission: Welsh encounters of the Khasi kind' in Gerhard Stilz (ed.), *Colonies, Missions, Cultures in the English-speaking World: General and Comparative Studies* (Tübingen, 2001), pp. 134–43.

Giri, Helen, *The Khasis under British Rule (1824–1947)* (New Delhi, 1990).

Godwin-Austen, H.H., 'On the stone monuments of the Khasi Hill Tribes, and on some of the peculiar rites and customs of the people', *The Journal of the Anthropological Institute of Great Britain and Ireland*, 1 (1872), 122–43.

Goldsworthy, Simon, 'English nonconformity and the pioneering of the modern newspaper campaign', *Journalism Studies*, 7:3 (2006), 387–402.

Griffith, D.M., *Nationality in the Sunday School Movement: a comparative study of the Sunday School Movement in England and Wales* (Bangor, 1925).

Grimshaw, Patricia and Andrew May, '"Inducements to the strong to be cruel to the weak": authoritative white colonial male voices and the construction of gender in Koori society' in Norma Grieve and Ailsa Burns (eds), *Australian Women: Contemporary Feminist Thought* (Melbourne, 1994), pp. 92–106.

Grimshaw, Patricia and Peter Sherlock, 'Women and cultural exchanges' in Norman Etherington (ed.), *Missions and Empire* (Oxford, 2005), pp. 173–93.

Gurdon, P.R.T., *The Khasis* (Delhi, 1975, first published 1907).

Hall, Catherine, *Civilising Subjects: Metropole and Colony in the English Imagination, 1830–1867* (Cambridge, 2002).

Harrison, Mark, '"The tender frame of man": disease, climate, and racial difference in India and the West Indies, 1760–1860', *Bulletin of the History of Medicine*, 70:1 (1996), 68–93.

Hawes, C.J., *Poor Relations: The Making of a Eurasian Community in British India 1773–1833* (Richmond, Surrey, 1996).

Headrick, Daniel R., *The Tentacles of Progress: Technology Transfer in the Age of Imperialism, 1850–1940* (New York and Oxford, 1988).

Headrick, Daniel R., *The Tools of Empire: Technology and European Imperialism in the Nineteenth Century* (New York and Oxford, 1981).

Heath, Ian, *The North-east Frontier 1837–1901* (Oxford, 1999).

Hill, Christopher, *The World Turned Upside Down: Radical Ideas During the English Revolution* (Harmondsworth, 1975).

Holmes, Richard, *Sahib: The British Soldier in India 1750–1914* (London, 2006).

Hughes, Henry, Bryncir, *Hanes Diwygiadau Crefyddol Cymru* (Caernarfon, [1906]).

Hughes, R. Arthur, 'The romance of Rose Place', 1981, pamphlet in National Library of Wales, CMA E43/7.

Hunter, William Wilson, *The Thackerays in India and some Calcutta Graves* (London, 1897).

Hutton, J.H., 'Primitive tribes' in L.S.S. O'Malley (ed.), *Modern India and the West: A Study of the Interaction of their Civilizations* (Oxford, 1941), pp. 415–44.

Jackson, Eleanor, 'From Krishna Pal to Lal Behari Dey: Indian builders of the church in Bengal, 1800–1894' in Dana L. Robert (ed.), *Converting Colonialism: Visions and Realities in Mission History, 1706–1914*, Grand Rapids, MI and Cambridge, UK, 2007), pp. 166–205.

James, E. Wyn, 'Bala and the Bible. Thomas Charles, Ann Griffiths and Mary Jones', www.anngriffiths.cardiff.ac.uk/bible.html (accessed 14 October 2007).

James, E. Wyn, 'John Roberts ("Minimus"; 1808–80): not the least among Liverpool Welsh Methodists', Paper delivered to the AHRC Research Network: 'Language, Religion and Print Culture in the Welsh Diaspora', Bangor University, 18 September 2007.

James, E. Wyn, 'Welsh ballads and American slavery', *The Welsh Journal of Religious History*, 2 (2007), 59–86.

Jenkins, Nigel, *Gwalia in Khasia* (Llandysul, Ceredigion, 1995).

Johnston, Anna, *Missionary Writing and Empire, 1800–1860* (Cambridge, 2003).

Jolly, Margaretta and Liz Stanley, 'Letters as/not a genre', *Life Writing*, 2:2 (2005), 91–118.

Jones, Aled, 'Gardens of Eden: Welsh missionaries in British India' in R.R. Davies and Geraint H. Jenkins (eds), *From Medieval to Modern Wales: Historical Essays in Honour of Kenneth O. Morgan and Ralph A. Griffiths* (Cardiff, 2004), pp. 264–80.

Jones, Aled, 'Welsh missionary journalism in India, 1880–1947' in Julie F. Codell (ed.), *Imperial Co-histories: National Identities and the British and Colonial Press* (Madison, NJ, 2003), pp. 242–72.

Jones, Aled and Bill Jones, 'The Welsh world and the British empire, c.1851–1939: an exploration', *The Journal of Imperial & Commonwealth History*, 31:2 (2003), 57–81.

Jones, Anthony, *Welsh Chapels* (Stroud, 1996).

Jones, Bill, 'Writing back: Welsh emigrants and their correspondence in the nineteenth century', *North American Journal of Welsh Studies*, 5:1 (2005), 23–46.

Jones, R. Merfyn, 'The Liverpool Welsh' in D. Ben Rees (ed.), *The Liverpool Welsh and their Religion: Two Centuries of Welsh Calvinistic Methodism* (Liverpool, 1984).

Joshi, Hargovind, *Meghalaya Past and Present* (New Delhi, 2004).

Kabbani, Rana, *Europe's Myths of Orient: Devise and Rule* (London, 1986).

Kaczynski, Grzegorz, 'Ambiguity of the mission Christianity in the colonial Africa: historical and anthropological essay', *Africana Bulletin*, 44 (1997), 39–62.

Kennedy, Dane, *The Magic Mountains: Hill Stations and the British Raj* (Berkeley, 1996).

Kharakor, Philomena, *Biblical Influence on Pre-Independence Khasi Literature* (New Delhi, 1998).

Knighton, Donald G., 'English-speaking Methodism' in Lionel Madden (ed.), *Methodism in Wales: A Short History of the Wesley Tradition* (Llandudno, 2003).

Kumar, B.B., 'North East India: crisis of perception & credible action', *Dialogue*, 1:2 (1999), www.nenanews.com/ne.htm (accessed 14 July 2011).

Kumar, Deepak, 'The evolution of colonial science in India: natural history and the East India Company' in John M. MacKenzie (ed.), *Imperialism and the Natural World* (Manchester, 1990), pp. 51–66.

Laidlaw, Zoë, *Colonial Connections 1815–45: Patronage, the Information Revolution and Colonial Government* (Manchester, 2005).

Lemmon, Keith, *The Golden Age of Plant Hunters* (London, 1968).

Lester, Alan, 'Imperial circuits and networks: geographies of the British empire', *History Compass*, 4:1 (2006), 124–41.

Lester, Alan and Fae Dussart, 'Masculinity, "race", and family in the colonies: protecting Aborigines in the early nineteenth century', *Gender, Place and Culture*, 16:1 (2009), 63–75.

Levi, Giovanni, 'On microhistory' in Peter Burke (ed.), *New Perspectives on Historical Writing* (Cambridge, 2001), pp. 97–119.

Lewis, Bernard, *Islam and the West* (Oxford, 1993).

Ludden, D., 'The first boundary of Bangladesh on Sylhet's northern frontiers', *Journal of the Asiatic Society of Bangladesh*, 48:1 (2003), 1–54.

Lunt, James, 'Havelock, Sir Henry (1795–1857)', *Oxford Dictionary of National Biography*, Oxford University Press, Sept 2004; online edn, May 2006, www.oxforddnb.com/view/article/12626 (accessed 9 June 2008).

Lydon, Jane, *Eye Contact: Photographing Indigenous Australians* (Durham, 2005).

Lyte, Benedict, '*Amherstia nobilis*: Plants in Peril 28', *Curtis's Botanical Magazine*, 20:3 (2003), 172–6.

MacKenzie, John M., 'Heroic myths of empire' in John M. MacKenzie (ed.), *Popular Imperialism and the Military, 1850–1950* (Manchester and New York, 1992), pp. 109–38.

MacKenzie, John M., 'Introduction: popular imperialism and the military' in John M. MacKenzie (ed.), *Popular Imperialism and the Military 1850–1950* (Manchester and New York, 1992), pp. 1–24.

MacKenzie, J.M., 'Irish, Scottish, Welsh and English worlds? A four-nation approach to the history of the British empire', *History Compass*, 6:5 (2008), 1244–63.

MacLagan, Robert, 'Obituary: Colonel Sir Henry Yule, K.C.S.I., C.B., LL.D., R.E.', *Proceedings of the Royal Geographical Society and Monthly Record of Geography*, 12:2 (1890), 108–13.

Majaw, S.S., *U Thomas Jones: Bad ka Pyrthei Saitsohpen* (Shillong, 2011).

Margulis, Lynn, *Origins of Sex: Three Billion Years of Genetic Recombination* (New Haven, CN, 1986).

Markham, Clements R., *A Memoir on the Indian Surveys* (London, 1878).

Marshall, P.J., *Problems of Empire: Britain and India, 1757–1813*, volume 2 (London and New York, 2000, first published 1968).

Mathur, P.R.G., *The Khasi of Meghalaya (Study in Tribalism and Religion)* (New Delhi, 1979).

McCracken, Donal P., *Gardens of Empire: Botanical Institutions of the Victorian British Empire* (London and Washington, 1997).

McNeil, Kenneth, *Scotland, Britain, Empire: Writing the Highlands, 1760–1860* (Columbus, 2007).

Merry, Sally Engle, 'Rethinking gossip and scandal' in Daniel B. Klein (ed.), *Reputation: Studies in the Voluntary Elicitation of Good Conduct* (Michigan, 1997), pp. 47–74.

Miller, R.A., 'The missionary narrative as coercive interrogation: seduction, confession and self-presentation in women's "letters home"', *Women's History Review*, 15:5 (2006), 751–71.

Moodley, Devadas, 'Velore 1806: the meanings of mutiny' in Jane Hathaway (ed.), *Rebellion, Repression, Reinvention: Mutiny in Comparative Perspective* (Westport, CT, 2001), pp. 87–102.

Morgan, K.O., *Rebirth of a Nation: Wales 1880–1980* (Cardiff and Oxford, 1981).

Morris, Jan and Simon Winchester, *The Stones of Empire: The Buildings of the Raj* (Oxford, 1983).

Morris, John Hughes, *Hanes Cenhadaeth Dramor y Methodistiaid Calfinaidd Cymreig, hyd ddiwedd y flwyddyn 1904* (Caernarfon, 1907).

Morris, John Hughes, *Hanes Methodistiaeth Liverpool* (Liverpool, 1929).

Morris, John Hughes, *The History of the Welsh Calvinistic Methodists' Foreign Mission to the End of the Year 1904* (New Delhi, 1996, first published 1910).

Moussa-Mahmoud, Fatma, 'English travellers and the *Arabian Nights*' in Peter L. Caracciolo (ed.), *The* Arabian Nights *in English Literature: Studies in the Reception of* The Thousand and One Nights *into British Culture* (London, 1988), pp. 95–110.

Muir, Edward, 'Introduction: observing trifles' in Edward Muir and Guido Ruggiero (eds), *Microhistory and the Lost Peoples of Europe* (Baltimore and London, 1991), pp. vii–xxviii.

Murphey, Rhoads, 'The city in the swamp: aspects of the site and early growth of Calcutta', *The Geographical Journal*, 130:2 (1964), 241–56.

Murray, David, *Indian Giving: Economies of Power in Indian-White Relations* (Amherst, MA, 2000).

Nagaraja, K.S., 'Khasi dialects: a typological consideration', *Mon-Khmer Studies*, 23 (1993), 1–10.

Natarajan, N., *The Missionary among the Khasis* (New Delhi, 1977).

Neill, Stephen, *Christian Missions* (Harmondsworth, 1964).

Neill, Stephen, *A History of Christianity in India, 1707–1858* (Cambridge, 2002).

Nongbri, B.L., 'Thomas Jones: a "scandal" to the church – a "hero" to the people', Seminar Paper, John Roberts Theological Seminary, 22 September 1998.

Nongbri, Tiplut, 'Sociological impact of the movement: its conformity with the consistent role of the Khasi standards of statesmanship and review of other social changes' in H.B. Sohliya, R. Lyngdoh and Hamlet Bareh (eds), *Celebration of 150th Death Anniversary of U Tirot Singh. An Illustrious Khasi Hero and Personage* (Shillong, 1984), pp. 63–72.

Oboe, Annalisa, 'Of books and the book: the evangelical mission in South African literature' in Gerhard Stilz (ed.), *Colonies, Missions, Cultures in the English-speaking World: General and Comparative Studies* (Tübingen, 2001), pp. 235–46.

Oddie, Geoffrey A., '"Orientalism" and British Protestant missionary constructions of India in the nineteenth century', *South Asia*, 17:2 (1994), 27–42.

O'Malley, L.S.S., *The Indian Civil Service, 1601–1930* (London, 1965, first published 1931).

Orlean, Susan, *The Orchid Thief* (New York, 1998).

Osteen, Mark, 'Introduction' in Mark Osteen (ed.), *The Question of the Gift: Essays Across Disciplines* (London and New York, 2002), pp. 1–42.

Panckridge, H.R., *A Short History of the Bengal Club* (Calcutta, 1927).

Passah, Amenah, 'Christian missions in the Khasi-Jaintia Hills: health care and impact on the society' in T.B. Subba, Joseph Puthenpurakal, Shaji Joseph Puykunnel, *Christianity and Change in Northeast India* (New Delhi, 2009), pp. 203–18.

Peers, Douglas M., 'Colonial knowledge and the military in India, 1780–1860', *The Journal of Commonwealth and Imperial History*, 33:2 (2005), 157–80.

Pennington, Brian K., *Was Hinduism Invented? Britons, Indians, and the Colonial Construction of Religion* (Oxford, 2005).

Peterson, Derek, 'Colonizing language? Missionaries and Gikuyu dictionaries, 1904 and 1914', *History in Africa*, 24 (1997), 257–72.

Philips, C.H., *The East India Company 1784–1834* (London and New York, 2000, first published Manchester, 1940).

Piggin, Stuart, *Making Evangelical Missionaries 1789–1858. The Social Background, Motives and Training of British Protestant Missionaries to India* (Appleford, 1984).

Podmore, Colin, *The Moravian Church in England 1728–1760* (Oxford, 1998).

Porter, Andrew, '"Cultural imperialism" and Protestant missionary enterprise, 1780–1914', *The Journal of Imperial and Commonwealth History* 25:3 (1994), 367–91.

Porter, Andrew, *Religion Versus Empire? British Protestant Missionaries and Overseas Expansion, 1700–1914* (Manchester, 2004).

Poustie, Sarah, 'Re-theorising letters and "letterness"', Olive Schreiner Letters project, Working Papers on Letters, Letterness & Epistolary Networks, Number 1, University of Edinburgh, 2010, www.oliveschreinerletters.ed.ac.uk/PoustieWPLetterness.pdf (accessed 1 December 2010).

Prior, Katherine, 'Ryan, Sir Edward (1793–1875)', *Oxford Dictionary of National Biography*, Oxford University Press, 2004; online edn, May 2006, www.oxforddnb.com/view/article/24385 (accessed 3 December 2010).

Pryce, David, 'History of the Calvinistic Methodist (Presbyterian) churches in the Montgomeryshire and Salop borders', n.d., typescript.

Rafael, Vicente, *Contracting Colonialism: Translation and Christian Conversion in Tagalog Society under Early Spanish Rule* (Durham, 1988).

Raugh Jr, Harold E., *The Victorians at War 1815–1914: An Encyclopedia of British Military History* (Santa Barbara, Denver, Oxford, 2004).

Rees, Alwyn D., *Life in a Welsh Countryside: A Social Study of Llanfihangel yng Ngwynfa* (Cardiff, 1961, first published 1950).

Rees, D. Ben (ed.), *The Liverpool Welsh and their Religion: Two Centuries of Welsh Calvinistic Methodism* (Liverpool, 1984).

Rees, D. Ben (ed.), *Vehicles of Grace & Hope: Welsh Missionaries in India 1800–1970* (Pasadena, 2002).

Rees, Thomas, *History of Protestant Nonconformity in Wales* (London, 1861).

Reinikka, Merle A., *A History of the Orchid* (Portland, 1995).

Richards, Jeffrey, *Imperialism and Music: Britain, 1876–1953* (Manchester; 2001).

Robert, Dana, 'Introduction' in Dana Robert (ed.), *Converting Colonialism: Visions and Realities in Mission History, 1706–1914* (Grand Rapids, Michigan, 2008), pp. 1–20.

Ropmay, D., *Ka Centenary History Ka Balang Presbyterian* (1940).

Rose, Deborah Bird, 'New World poetics of place: along the Oregon Trail and in the National Museum of Australia' in Annie E. Coombes (ed.), *Rethinking Settler Colonialism. History and Memory in Australia, Canada, Aotearoa New Zealand and South Africa* (Manchester, 2006), pp. 228–44.

Ruggiero, Guido, *Binding Passions: Tales of Magic, Marriage, and Power at the End of the Renaissance* (New York, 1993).

Samson, Jane, 'Translation teams: missionaries, islanders, and the reduction of language in the Pacific' in Patricia Grimshaw and Andrew May (eds), *Missionaries, Indigenous Peoples and Cultural Exchange* (Brighton, 2010), pp. 96–109.

Sen, Soumen, *Social and State Formation in Khasi-Jaintia Hills: A Study of Folklore* (Delhi, 1985).

Seth, Sanjay, 'Which good book? Missionary education and conversion in colonial India', *Semeia* (2001), 113–28.

Sharma, Hanjabam Surmangol, 'A comparison between Khasi and Manipuri word order', *Linguistics of the Tibeto-Burman Area*, 22:1 (1999), 139–48.

Sharma, Manorama, *Critically Assessing Traditions: The Case of Meghalaya*, Crisis States Programme Development Research Centre, LSE, Working Paper No. 52 (London, 2004).

Sidebottom, John K., *The Overland Mail* (London, 1948).

Silverman, Marilyn and P.H. Gulliver, 'Historical anthropology though local-level research' in Don Kalb and Herman Tak (eds), *Critical Junctions: Anthropology and History Beyond the Cultural Turn* (New York, 2005), pp. 152–67.

Simon, I.M. (ed.), *Jaintia Hills District Gazetteer*, c.1997.

Simon, I.M., *Khasi and Jaintia Tales and Beliefs* (Gauhati, 1966).
Simon, I.M., 'On first looking into Paul K. Benedict's Sino-Tibetan linguistics', *Mon-Khmer Studies*, 27 (1997), 155–9.
Sircar, Dineschandra, *Studies in the Geography of Ancient and Medieval India* (Delhi, 1971).
Smith, D.W., 'Berriew in the eighteenth century', *The Montgomeryshire Collections*, 70 (1982).
Smith, George, *The Life of William Carey, D.D. Shoemaker and Missionary. Professor of Sanskrit, Bengali and Marathi in the College of Fort William, Calcutta* (London, 1885).
Snaitang, O.L., *Christianity and Social Change in Northeast India: A Study of the Role of Christianity in Social Change among the Khasi-Jaintia Hill Tribes of Meghalaya* (Shillong and Calcutta, 1993).
Snell, K.D.M., 'The Sunday-School movement in England and Wales: child labour, denominational control and working-class culture', *Past & Present*, 164:1 (1999), 122–68.
Sohliya, H.B., R. Lyngdoh, H. Bareh (eds), *Celebration of 150th Death Anniversary of U Tirot Singh, Syiem of Nongkhlaw. An Illustrious Khasi Hero and Personage* (Shillong, 1984).
Spencer, J.R. and W.L. Thomas, 'The hill stations and summer resorts of the Orient', *Geographical Review*, 38:4 (1948), 637–51.
Stanley, Liz, 'The epistolarium: on theorizing letters and correspondences', *Auto/Biography*, 12 (2004), 201–35.
Sten, H.W., *Khasi Poetry (Origin and Development)* (New Delhi, 1990).
Stewart, Ralph R., 'Missionaries and clergymen as botanists in India and Pakistan', *Taxon* 31:1 (1982), 57–64.
Stoler, Ann Laura, *Along the Archival Grain: Epistemic Anxieties and Colonial Common Sense* (Princeton, 2009).
Stoler, Ann Laura, *Race and the Education of Desire: Foucault's History of Sexuality and the Colonial Order of Things* (Durham, 1995).
Strange, Julie-Marie, '"Speechless with grief": bereavement and the working-class father, c.1880–1914' in Trev Lynn Broughton and Helen Rogers (eds), *Gender and Fatherhood in the Nineteenth Century* (Houndmills and New York, 2007), pp. 138–53.
Streets, Heather, *Martial Races: The Military, Race, and Masculinity in British Imperial Culture, 1857–1914* (Manchester, 2004).
Syiemlieh, David Reid, *British Administration in Meghalaya: Policy and Pattern* (New Delhi, 1989).
Syiemlieh, David Reid, *Survey of Research in History on North-east India 1970–1990* (New Delhi, 2000).
Syiemlieh, David Reid, 'Thomas Jones' "injudicious marriage?"', *Proceedings, North East India History Association, XIV Session* (1995), 240–4.
Sykes, Karen, *Arguing with Anthropology: An Introduction to Critical Theories of the Gift* (London and New York, 2005).
Talukdar, Sharmila Das, *Khasi Cultural Resistance to Colonialism* (Guwahati and Delhi, 2004).

Tariang, J.E., *U Tirot Sing: A Collection of his Reign and Struggle Against British Rule 1814–1834* (Shillong, 1982).

Thomas, Ednyfed, *Bryiau'r Glaw* (Caernarfon, 1988).

Thomas, Nicholas, *Colonialism's Culture: Anthropology, Travel and Government* (Cambridge, 1994).

Thomas, Nicholas, 'The cultural dynamics of peripheral exchange' in Caroline Humphrey and Stephen Hugh-Jones (eds), *Barter, Exchange and Value: An Anthropological Approach* (Cambridge, 1992), pp. 21–41.

Thornton, William Thomas, *Indian Public Works* (London 1875).

Tosh, John, 'From Keighley to St-Denis: separation and intimacy in Victorian bourgeois marriage', *History Workshop Journal*, 40 (1995), 193–206.

Travers, Robert, 'Death and the Nabob: imperialism and commemoration in eighteenth-century India', *Past & Present*, 196:1 (2007), 83–124.

Twells, Alison, 'Missionary "fathers" and wayward "sons" in the South Pacific, 1797–1825' in Trev Lynn Broughton and Helen Rogers (eds), *Gender and Fatherhood in the Nineteenth Century* (Houndmills and New York, 2007), pp. 153–64.

Unnithan-Kumar, Maya, *Identity, Gender and Poverty: New Perspectives on Caste and Tribalism in Rajasthan* (Providence, RI, 1997).

von Fürer-Haimendorf, Christoph, Review of H.O. Mawrie, *The Khasi Milieu* (New Delhi, 1981) in *Religious Studies*, 19 (1983), 126–8.

Wallace-Wells, Benjamin, 'Right man's burden', *Washington Monthly* (June 2004).

Waterfield, Gordon, *Sultans of Aden* (London, 1968).

Weber, Jacques, 'The British conquest of Bengal (1757–84)' in Claude Markovits (ed.), *A History of Modern India 1480–1950* (London, 2002), pp. 231–46.

Whittle, Tyler, *The Plant Hunters* (London, 1970).

Williams, Glyn, *The Desert and the Dream: A Study of Welsh Colonization in Chubut, 1865–1915* (Cardiff, 1975).

Williams, Richard, 'Montgomeryshire worthies', *Collections Historical & Archæological Relating to Montgomeryshire and its Borders*, 16 (1883).

Williams, William, *The Experience Meeting: An Introduction to the Welsh Societies of the Evangelical Awakening*, tr. Mrs Lloyd-Williams (London, 1973).

Williams, William, *Welsh Calvinistic Methodism: A Historical Sketch of the Presbyterian Church of Wales* (Bridgend, 1998, first published London, 1872).

Wolfe, Patrick, 'Land, labor, and difference: elementary structures of race', *The American Historical Review*, 106:3 (2001), 866–905.

Ziter, Edward, *The Orient on the Victorian Stage* (Cambridge, 2003).

Theses

Cunville, Riewah Robert, 'A study of the growth of the Presbyterian Church in the Khasi and Jaintia Hills', MA in Missiology, Fuller Theological Seminary, 1974.

Dkhar, Rita Dorothy, 'The Inglis and Company and the lime trade in the Khasi Hills', PhD thesis, The North Eastern Hill University, Shillong, 1987.

INDEX